inside
new york
2000

Publisher	Matthew Matlack
Editor-in-Chief	Gabriel Fried
Art Director	Jessica Sbarsky
Research Director	Alexandra Socarides

Associate Publisher	Daniel J. Greenstein
Assitant Editor	Audra Epstein
Music Editor	Chris Smith
Editorial Intern	Rachel Moskowitz
Senior Staff Photographer	Camille Varlet
Staff Writers	Julie Bleha
	Victoria Gomelsky
	Rachel Miller
Researchers:	Pamela Bock
	Rebecca Jones
	Greg Lembrich
	Elisabeth Mayer
	Lorelle Saxena
	Alyssa Sheinmel
	Treena Thibodeau

Contributors: Laurence Alexander, Grant Barrett, Chandler Blockage, Monica Brookman, Hui Min Chan, Nelson Eubanks, Edwin Famous, Jonah Fried, Toby Gardner, Vernon Gibbs II, Janet Morris, Andrew Olinow, Dave Parker, Melissa Ramsay, Alexandra Rudnitsky, Jessica Paul

Printed by: Hamilton Printing

Special thanks to:
ACIS, Steve Feuer, Steve Bateman, Rachel Simmons, Lisa Brettell, Barry Matlack, Emily and Al Sbarsky, Rick and Carol Brettell, Bob Reiss, Janel Joaquim, Alan Yoblon, Lisa Bernstein, Ana Lombardo at FPG International, and the staff and administrators at the Center for Career Services.

For sales or advertising information, call 212-854-2804, email sales@insideny.com, or visit http://www.insideny.com. Please contact BookWorld Companies at 1-800-444-2524 or Ingram Book Company, if your bookstore would like to carry Inside New York.

PHOTO CREDITS
Camille Varlet photos: 12, 38, 39, 40, 41, 80, 81, 84, 85, 57, 58, 59, 115, 121
Toby Gardner photos: 46, 50, 74, 82, 86, 87, 88, 118, 123
Laura Kearney photos: 28, 98, 118, 198, 219
Tali Gai photos: 32, 33, 101, 133, 134, 152
Mia Tran photos: 63, 86, 89, 92
Connie Hwong photo: 92
Greg Tambini photo: 228
Chris Smith photos: 224, 225
Courtesy of Matt Winters: 229
Courtesy of the New York Historical Society: 7, 8, 40, 56, 63, 106, 107, 111
Courtesy of Knitting Factory: 227
Courtesy of the Solomon R. Guggenheim Museum: 197
Courtesy of tribeca bodyworks: 45
Courtesy of Alice Austen House: 157
Courtesy of The SoHo Grand: 71, 73
Courtesy of Poets House: 69
Courtesy of the Public Theater: 77, 207
Courtesy of Dave's True Story: 226

city living

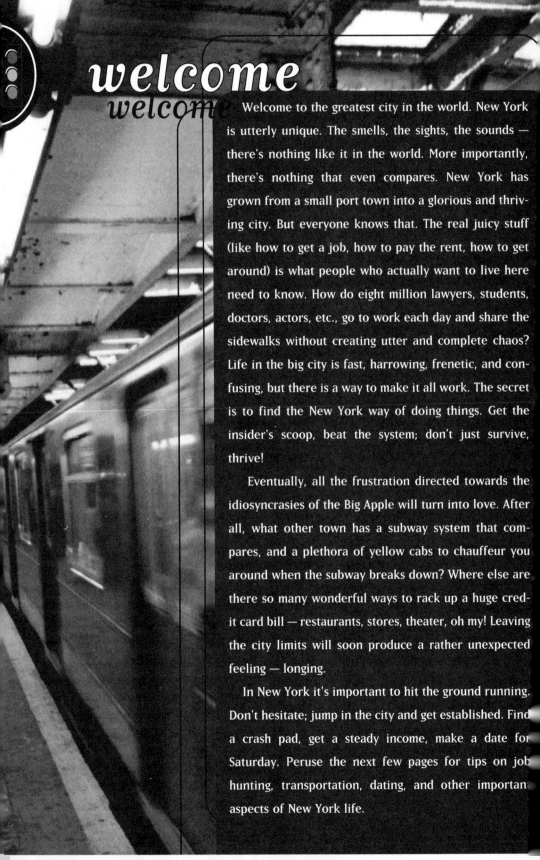

welcome

welcome

Welcome to the greatest city in the world. New York is utterly unique. The smells, the sights, the sounds — there's nothing like it in the world. More importantly, there's nothing that even compares. New York has grown from a small port town into a glorious and thriving city. But everyone knows that. The real juicy stuff (like how to get a job, how to pay the rent, how to get around) is what people who actually want to live here need to know. How do eight million lawyers, students, doctors, actors, etc., go to work each day and share the sidewalks without creating utter and complete chaos? Life in the big city is fast, harrowing, frenetic, and confusing, but there is a way to make it all work. The secret is to find the New York way of doing things. Get the insider's scoop, beat the system; don't just survive, thrive!

Eventually, all the frustration directed towards the idiosyncrasies of the Big Apple will turn into love. After all, what other town has a subway system that compares, and a plethora of yellow cabs to chauffeur you around when the subway breaks down? Where else are there so many wonderful ways to rack up a huge credit card bill — restaurants, stores, theater, oh my! Leaving the city limits will soon produce a rather unexpected feeling — longing.

In New York it's important to hit the ground running. Don't hesitate; jump in the city and get established. Find a crash pad, get a steady income, make a date for Saturday. Peruse the next few pages for tips on job hunting, transportation, dating, and other important aspects of New York life.

i•n•t•e•r•v•i•e•w
with Kenneth Jackson, NYC historian

In your opinion, what events in the 20th Century were the most important in changing New York City?

Kenneth Jackson: My quick answer would be the consolidation of the city in 1898, the passage of the Tenement House Law of 1901 that prohibited the construction of any more "dumbbell tenements," the opening of the IRT subway in 1904, the adoption of comprehensive zoning in 1916, the coming to power of Robert Moses in 1924, the construction of Rockefeller Center in the early 1930s, and the precipitous drop in crime in the 1990s.

In what ways is the city better off than it was a decade ago?

KJ: There is a general feeling that New York is cleaner, safer, and more lively than it was in 1990. Moreover, the economy is stronger, both income and employment are up, there is increased recreational use of the waterways, and colleges and universities are thriving, as evidenced by the near impossibility of gaining admission to Columbia [University] in 1999. There was a widespread perception in the 1960s, 1970s, and 1980s that American cities were dying. Dozens of downtown areas are now experiencing a boom, but New York is clearly leading the urban renaissance in our time.

In what ways is New York worse off than it was in 1990?

KJ: Unfortunately, many challenges remain in Gotham. Infrastructure continues to decline as streets and water pipes age and school buildings and bridges crumble. New York's greatest challenge in the 21st Century will be to restore the public schools to the level of excellence and

respect they enjoyed in the middle of the 20th Century. We also continue to witness too many incidences of racism and sexual violence in the metropolis. New York is the world's greatest experiment in diversity, and it is important to everyone alive that the city continues to demonstrate that it is possible for a wildly disparate population to exist in harmony and peace.

Will individual neighborhoods survive the gentrification trend?

KJ: It is difficult to generalize about New York's more than four hundred distinct neighborhoods. I will say that I am not much concerned about gentrification because demographic change has been almost the single most important characteristic of the city. Moreover, most of American history has witnessed the sequential reuse of residential housing by progressively lower income groups. In other words, the typical process in the United States is for poorer people to move into an area with the passage of a generation or two. The fact that we occasionally see a reverse

Kenneth T. Jackson is a peerless authority on New York City. The Jacques Barzun Professor of History and the Social Sciences at Columbia University, Mr. Jackson is editor of the Columbia History of Urban Life and The Encyclopedia of New York.

process simply means that the city is becoming more desirable. Gentrification in my view is negative when aggressive real estate speculators, who often lack respect for history, start throwing out the very persons who have made an area attractive. But gentrification is positive when individuals restore homes and buildings that were once either vacant or decrepit. In other words, I like to see rehabilitation and investment.

What does New York's resurgence tell us about cities in general?

KJ: For more than a generation, Americans have associated high density living with various pathologies. Conversely, they have regarded the single-family house surrounded by a lot of grass as an ideal setting. Cities thus have represented limited space, heterogeneity, poverty, and crime. However, New York City's recent experience has made us realize that congestion can be beneficial. With a safer and more attractive city, visitors and citizens alike are learning that busy sidewalks, easily accessible shops, dependable public transportation, and world-class cultural offerings can give pleasure and meaning beyond anything that can be experienced in a front yard or on a beach.

What resources of the city are endangered or have recently become extinct?

KJ: After being the most important port and industrial city in the world only a half century ago, New York has lost much of its commercial harbor jobs and most of its factories. The port has been damaged by competition from the south and west and from new methods of containerization. Manufacturing employment in the city exceeded one million; it is now down to about 200,000. Most industries moved first to the suburbs, then to the south, and more recently to the developing world. New York is now in danger of becoming a "precious" city, rather like Paris, Venice, or Charleston, places that are more tourist destinations than real cities. My hope is that New York will continue to be a place where things are made and goods are moved.

What are some of New York's less heralded treasures that people should visit to get a true taste of the city?

KJ. The great thing about New York is that it offers almost endless surprises. But I would recommend that everyone interested in the city visit the real Little Italy in Belmont in The Bronx, the Lower East Side Tenement Museum in Manhattan, the incredible Panorama of New York City (a three-dimensional scale model of all five boroughs) in Queens, the Snug Harbor Cultural Center in Staten Island, and Greenwood Cemetery in Brooklyn. I assume that everyone has already been to Yankee Stadium, as well as Sheepshead Bay, City Island, The New York Botanical Gardens, Battery Park, and [taken a ride on] the Staten Island Ferry. The real star of this place, however, is the city itself, its ordinary neighborhoods and streets, its pace, and its openness to change.

Why should someone visit or move to New York instead of another city?

KJ: In a world that is increasingly multicultural and multiracial, New York offers a vision of where humanity is going. Gotham was heterogeneous centuries before the term had real meaning. Even when New York, then called New Amsterdam, was only a little Dutch trading post with a thousand residents in 1640, eighteen languages were being spoken on its streets. I think living in New York helps make a person comfortable with difference. A tough town that is about achievement, competition, and effort, New York is open to everyone and is a celebration of humanity in all its diversity.

JANUARY & FEBRUARY

Chinese New Year
Celebrate Chinese New Year in Chinatown. Parades, fireworks, and food make it worth the crowds.
❸❻❼❿ to Canal St.

New Year's Day Beach Walk
On Rockaway Beach, Jones Beach, and Sandy Hook; champagne and cookies provided.
(718) 634-6467

Empire State Building Run Up
22nd annual mad dash to the 86th floor, for those who have something to prove.
Every February. Contact New York Roadrunners Club, Inc. for more information (860-4455).

Tisch School of the Arts
Free theater in February from this talented student theater group.
Call for reservations (988-1918). ❶❷❸❹❺❻❼❿ to West 4th St.-Washington Sq.

Black History Month
Black History Month is celebrated throughout the city in the month of February, with readings, concerts, theater events, etc.
Consult The New York Times *and call museums of interest for more specific information.*

International Motorcycle Show New York
Dream machines from around the world sparkle under the fluorescent lights of the Javits Center every year in February.
Call Jacob K. Javits Convention Center for details (216-2000).

MARCH & APRIL

St. Patrick's Day Parade
An annual political event featuring green Guinness, baby-kissing, and gay and lesbian protesters.
March 17th, From 10:30am to 4pm at Fifth Ave. at 44th St., ❸❼❿ *to 42nd St.,* ❼ *to Fifth Ave.*

"Wall to Wall" Marathon Concert
The 24-hour music marathon features a multitude of performers and a different theme each year.

End of March or beginning of April, 11am-11pm. Symphony Space, 2537 Broadway (at 95th St.), 864-5400, ❶❷❸❾ *to 96th St.*

The Annual English Handbell Festival
Features 100 ringers from New York plus guest choirs.
Riverside Church, 490 Riverside Dr. (at 122nd St.), 870-6722, ❶❾ *to 125th St.*

The New York Flower Show
The Garden of Eden comes to New York.
Call the Horticultural Society of New York for details (757-0915).

Artexpo New York
The world's largest trade show in the art business comes to the Javits Center featuring landscapes, posters, sculptures, decorative arts and more.
Call Jacob K. Javits Convention Center for more information (216-2000)

Easter Parade
"On the Avenue, 5th Avenue" the annual exhibit of the good life has become more interesting since it has become a drag-rehearsal for Wigstock.
Easter Sunday. Fifth Ave. (at 49th St., heading up to 59th St.)

Opening Day At Yankee Stadium
A few baseball legends always show up.
Call Ticketmaster or Yankee Stadium for details (718-293-4300). ❸❻❹ *to 161st St.-Yankee Stadium*

Whitney Biennial
Whitney Museum's display of "the most important" American Art. Controversy, every time.
945 Madison Ave. (at 75th St.), 570-3600.

The Cherry Blossom Festival
A great reason to see what's in bloom at the Brooklyn Botanic Gardens.
1000 Washington Ave., (718) 623-7200, ❷❸ *to Eastern Pkwy-Brooklyn Museum*

MAY & JUNE

Memorial Day Concert at the Cathedral of St. John the Divine
The Philharmonic performs at the Cathedral of St. John the Divine on Memorial day at 8pm.

nyc by season

Amsterdam Ave. (at 112th St.), **①⑨** to Cathedral
Parkway (110th St.)

Ukrainian Festival
Sample some of the city's best festival fare
on Seventh Ave.

Fleet Week
On Memorial Day weekend, the city's harbors fill
up with naval vessels while the streets and bars
fill up with sailors. Land ho!

Bike NY: The Great Five Borough Bike Tour
All the boroughs on one bike!
Early May. Call for more details (932-0778).

Martin Luther King Jr. Parade
Celebrate Dr. King in May.
Fifth Ave. from 60th to 86th Sts.

Ninth Avenue International Food Festival
Food galore from around the world, pick what you
eat carefully because there is a staggering amount
to choose from! Also jewelry, music,
and vendors too.
Mid-May. Between 37th and 57th Sts.

Met in the Parks
The Metropolitan Opera gives performances in the
city parks and in New Jersey parks.
Begins in June. Call for schedule (362-6000).

JVC Jazz Festival New York
Well-known performers give free outdoor concerts
in Bryant Park and at venues all over the city.
Begins in June.

The HBO/Bryant Park Film Festival
Films, films, films!
*Sixth Ave. (at 42nd St.). Call for information
(512-5700).*

Puerto Rican Day Parade
Salsa music, dancers, food, and pride in Puerto
Rican culture.
A Sunday in early June. Up Fifth Ave. to 86th St.

Mermaid Parade
Celebrate Coney Island boardwalk's season opening. Enjoy the freaks in all their glory and marvel
at the innovative ways women dress up as mer-
maids, waddling down the boardwalk.
Late June. **⑧⑥⑤** to Stillwell Ave.-Coney Island

AIDS Walk New York
The third Sunday in May, this annual walk raises
money to fight AIDS and for the Gay Men's Health
Crisis, 6.2 miles.
Call for more information (367-1400).

Belmont Stakes
The longest, and final, Triple Crown leg.
Early June. Call for information (718-641-4700).

The Lesbian and Gay Pride March
The annual Gay Pride Parade gets bigger and
better each year.
*Late June. Starts at 52nd St. and Fifth Ave. and
goes down to Waverly Pl.*

Midsummer Nights Swing Dance Festival
Dance the night away under the stars and tango
around the Lincoln Center fountain; also jazz,
zydeco, swing — prices start at $3. Free dance
lessons from 6:30pm.
June thru August. Lincoln Center,
①⑨ to 66th St.-Lincoln Center

JULY & AUGUST

New York Philharmonic Time Warner's Concerts in the Parks
The New York Philharmonic gives concerts in
various city parks.
Call for a schedule (875-5709).

July 4th, Macy's Fireworks on the Hudson
Oooh and aaah at the gala fireworks on display
over New York Harbor. Find a spot in Battery
Park or call on a friend with a downtown view.

Concerts in the MoMA Sculpture Garden
Concerts of classical music among world-
renowned sculpture; free.
*Friday and Saturday nights in July and August,
11 West 53rd St., 708-9400*

Lincoln Center Out Of Doors Festival
Free Music and dances performed, held outdoors.
Call for information (875-5108)

US Open
The drama of championship tennis makes its
way to Queens every year.
Flushing, Queens. Call for information (718-760-6200)

new york ci

Harlem Week
A slew of cultural activities, including concerts, outdoor fairs and educational workshops throughout Harlem.

Dominican Day Parade
The DR celebrates its culture in August.
Sixth Ave. (bet. 39th and 56th Sts.).

Pakistan Independence Day Festival and Parade
Come support South Asian freedom.
Madison Ave. (bet. 41st and 26th Sts.)

SEPTEMBER & OCTOBER

Broadway on Broadway
See the stars of the hottest shows on the Great White Way belt out their signature tunes.
Broadway and Seventh Ave., (bet. 43rd and 48th Sts.), ❶❷❸❹❺❻❼❽❾ to 42nd St.-Times Sq.

The Medieval Festival in Fort Tryon Park
Fort Tryon Park transforms into a New York that never was with falconers, jesters, knights, fair maidens, medieval food, and music.
Each September. Call The Cloisters for information (923-3700). ❶ to 190th St.

West Indian-American Day Carnival and Parade
Crown Heights is lined with food, floats, and shopping.
❷❸ to Eastern Pkwy-Brooklyn Museum

Washington Square Outdoor Festival
Great Art outdoors and all for free! September 6th and 7th, noon-7pm.
❶❷❸❹❺❻❼ to West 4th St.-Washington Sq.

The Downtown Arts Festival
Art education, events and performances at New York galleries and performance spaces. Contemporary art and experimental performances.
Call headquarters (243-5050), or visit www.simonsays.org.

San Gennaro Festival
Little Italy's yearly bash, with or without Vinnie the Chin.
❶❷❸ to Grand St.

Atlantic Avenue Antique Festival
Vast, multicultural street fair in Brooklyn in Sept.
Call for more information (718-875-8993)

New York's Village Halloween Parade
What used to be a carnival of subversion has become a parade of drunken innocents, but it is Halloween, after all, and the goblins turn out in all their fabulous glory.
Begins at Sixth Ave., south of Spring St., goes to 23rd St.

Hispanic Day Parade
An alternative rendering of popular history.
October, Fifth Ave. from 44th to 86th Sts.

Columbus Day Parade
Cheer on Christopher's "discovery" every October.
Fifth Ave from 44th to 86th Sts.

NOVEMBER & DECEMBER

The New York City Marathon
20,000 runners take over the city. Watch them don silver, insulated shawls so they don't die from exhaustion after their trek.
Call for information (423-2240)

Holiday Windows Along Fifth Avenue
New York outdoes itself with whimsy and holiday cheer especially Saks Fifth Ave.
Fifth Ave. in the 50s

George Balanchine's "The Nutcracker"
New York City Ballet and students from the School of American Ballet unite to perform this beloved Christmas classic.
Call the New York State Theater (870-5570).

Macy's Thanksgiving Parade
Beware of a giant Bullwinkle loosing his tether. Wear your mittens and be on guard for pickpockets. Seeing it once is enough.
Thanksgiving Day, Herald Sq., ❶❷❸❹❺❻ to 34th St.

Holiday Lighting Ceremony at the World Financial Center Winter Garden
Over 100 thousand holiday lights lit right after Thanksgiving.
Call for more information (945-0505).

Rockefeller Center Tree Lighting
Gather 'round the city's favorite tree for the ceremonial lighting and celebrity ice-skaters at the ice rink.
❶❷❸❹ to 47th-50th Sts.-Rockefeller Center

Park Avenue Tree Lighting and Carol Sing
Over 45 blocks of trees light up at the flip of a switch at the Brick Presbyterian Church. *First Sunday of December at 6:30pm. Park Ave (at 91st St.), 289-4400,* ❹❻❻ *to 86th St.*

The Chorus Tree
Famous tree sings at the South Street Seaport. *Call for more information (SEA-PORT).*

New Year's Marathon Reading
Held at Paula Cooper Gallery, the reading begins on December 31st and ends when the book is finished. Celebrity writers show up. *534 West 21st St. (bet Tenth and Eleventh Aves.), 255-1105,* ❻❺ *to 23rd St.*

Times Square New Year's Eve Countdown
Dick Clark is ageless, New Yorkers become warm and fuzzy, and the City counts down in delirious unison waiting for that ball to drop. It's epic every year; this winter should be beyond belief. *Times Square,* ❶❷❸❹❷❷❸❼❾ *to 42nd St.-Times Sq.*

YEAR 'ROUND FUN

Films at MoMA
See avant-garde and classic films during MoMA's pay-what-you-wish Friday, starting at 4:30pm. *53rd St. (bet. Fifth and Sixth Aves.), 708-9480,* ❽❶❼❹ *to 47-50Sts.-Rockefeller Center*

Tour Grand Central
Learn about the design and features of one of the nation's most important urban landmarks, Grand Central Station. *Wednesdays at 12:30pm. Meet at information kiosk at the Main Concourse of Grand Central Station (42nd St. at Park Ave.), 935-3960,* ❻❹❺❻❼ *to 42nd St.-Grand Central Station*

Moonlight Ride
Join other bikers for a safe ride through Central Park in the peace and quiet of night. *Last Friday of each month, 10pm. Meet at Columbus Circle entrance to Central Park, 802-8222,* ❹❶❸❻❶❾ *to 59th St.-Columbus Circle*

Normally chaotic, Times Square becomes ➤ *frenzied on New Year's eve!*

Urban Park Rangers
Walk with the Urban Park Rangers in New York City Parks for entomology, ecology, ornithology, and plain old fun. *Saturdays and Sundays at 11am and 2pm. Call for more information (1-800-201-PARK).*

The Historic Orchard Street Shopping Tour
Over 400 stores and boutiques offer merchandise at up to 70 percent off in this historic district, begining with the famous Katz's Deli. *Sundays at 11am, 205 East Houston St. (at Ludlow St.), 226-8742,* ❻ *to Second Ave.*

3,2,1...

When most people think of New Year's Eve in New York City, they conjure up images of a crowded Times Sq., hundreds of thousands of crazy revelers and Dick Clark's countdown as the ball descends the 77-foot flagpole to mark the inception of the new year. After all, it is a tradition that started 95 years ago when the owners of One Times Square began hosting roof-top celebrations on New Year's Eve for friends and business associates. Then, in 1907, *The New York Times* initiated the very first ball-drop on the roof, and each year thereafter, the ball was hoisted onto the rooftop pole and lowered manually by several men to announce the New Year. (The drop wasn't automated until 1995.)

On the other 364 days of the year, the 500-pound, 6-foot-diameter aluminum and rhinestone-studded ball (Saturday Night Fever, eat your heart out!) was locked behind two sets of steel doors in a special room in One Times Square Nowadays, the ritual attracts over 500,000 revelers annually from around the country and more than 300 million TV viewers. For the millennium, New York expects even more people — possibly millions — to swarm the neon-lit

---

Freelance writer Westry Green, contributor of this article, will be at home in Park Slope, Brooklyn on New Year's eve 2000.

square. In a national survey by YP&B/Yankelovich Partners, 46 percent of all Americans want to be in Times Square to welcome the new millennium.

With that much popularity, you better believe that New York has something special to offer for New Year's Eve 2000: "Times Square 2000, The Global Celebration at the Crossroads of the World." For starters, the old ball that we have watched make its way down the pole over and over again was retired last New Year's Eve. Its replacement: an elegant, illuminated crystal ball crafted by Waterford Crystal, just for the millennium. The celebration will begin at 7am EST when the New Year arrives in the South Pacific and every hour on the hour giant screens throughout Times Square will broadcast live the festivities in another part of the world. The cultural broadcasts will include music, pageantry, and special effects in order to give Times Square partiers a chance to feel connected to 24 different cultures across the globe. The broadcasts will continue until New Year has been celebrated in all 24 time zones.

Although the Times Square celebration will be monumental, it's not the only thing going for New Year's Eve in New York. "First Night New York" is an annual city-wide family event that includes music, dancing, art exhibits and even special activities for children at various venues throughout the entire day. The event was started in 1991 as a tribute to the arts and as an effort "to make Midtown cleaner, safer, and more inviting for residents, businesses and visitors alike." Their millennium event promises to be better than anticipated.

If the thought of throngs of people and screaming children seems anything but celebratory, you still have a plethora of adults-only events from which to choose for your New Year's Eve 2000 celebration. A popular choice for 21- to 35-year-olds is to spend the night aboard The Intrepid (a former aircraft carrier and now a sea, air and space museum) for dancing, drinking and noshing until 3am. A midnight balloon drop is the alternative to the Times Square extravaganza (call 1-877-newyears for more information).

If money is no object and you want to spend the Eve in style, the premier restaurant, The Rainbow Room, will host 250 guests for live music and dancing. For $6,000 per couple, celebrate the millennium in the plush society-haunt. For slightly less money ($1,000-$2,500 per person), you can mingle with magician David Copperfield and comedian Joan Rivers at the 22-acre Jacob K. Javits Convention Center of New York. This 12-hour "Celebration 2000: The Party of the Century" will include performances by rockers Sting, Aretha Franklin, Chuck Berry, Tom Jones, Enrique Inglesias and tenor Andrea Bocelli, as well as meals designed by Jean-Georges Vongerichten, chef par excellence and proprietor of Mercer Kitchen, Vong and other hot restaurants.

Celebrating doesn't necessarily need to break the bank. Nearly every restaurant, bar, and club in the city is planning a millennium party with a variety of themes and a range of cover charges — this is the option most popular with native New Yorkers who like to keep things casual but still want to get out and party with their bad selves. Wherever you go, buy your tickets ahead of time — each venue will be packed with people partying like it's 1999. (Whether The Artist f.k.a. Prince meant last New Year's or this one in his hit single has been the subject of many drunken debates!)

Many city-dwellers celebrate in the comfort of their own home with good food, good wine, and good music. Visitors can get the same affect by renting a room in a swank hotel. Millennium Broadway, among others, is offering package deals with views of Times Square and its ball-drop so you can enjoy the festivities indoors.

But whether you watch the ball drop from within the fray or forgo the partiers in exchange for an intimate dinner for two,, the millennial celebration in New York City is sure to be the event of a lifetime.

2000!

For newcomers, possibly the most harrowing aspect of New York is the transportation system. The city's subways seem an underground menace, and the thought of descending into grimy tunnels after dark strikes fear into the hearts of inexperienced travelers. The yellow cab, a New York icon, seems unthreatening on postcards, but the high speeds and the erratic driving style of some cabbies are sure to make newcomers pause before hailing. City buses are pleasant, but who can read the map? New arrivals in New York may opt to walk. While we certainly encourage exercise, we also feel the benefits of the city's transportation system outweigh the problems. With a little practice, all the maps become focused, the subway lines shoot straight as arrows, and cabs suddenly stop on a dime.

New York subways have an undeservedly bad reputation. True, many stations were once unsavory, but the graffiti has since been cleaned up and crime rates have dropped. The subway is the quickest and most efficient way to navigate the city, especially apparent at rush hour, when traffic is stopped dead above ground. While the subway has a few bad points — trains and stations get unbearably hot in the summer and overcrowding can make a subterranean trip unpleasant — keep in mind, that for $1.50, Coney Island, Yankee Stadium, and Kennedy International Airport are all within reach.

Each subway line is assigned a color and a number or letter for identification purposes. These numbers or letters appear on station signs, subway platforms, and the train itself. The conductor usually announces the direction and terminus of the train: In Manhattan, "Bronx-bound" means it's heading uptown; "Brooklyn-bound" means it's heading downtown. Of course, everyone's bound to get lost once or twice; if this happens, don't panic. Ask someone on the train how to get back on course; New Yorkers are nice enough — really! If you're headed downtown

instead of up, or vice versa, get off at a station where you can transfer underground. Don't be afraid to yell over the turnstile to the token-booth clerk. They've heard it all before, and aren't easily bothered. There are maps posted in the interior of the trains — consult them! Remember, the colored lines on the map correspond to the paths of the trains. Under each station name are the numbers or letters of the trains that stop there. Note the important distinction between local and express trains; the latter does not stop at all stations on a line. Listen carefully to the conductor, because sometimes a local train switches tracks and becomes an express, or vice versa, due to construction.

Though subway crime has decreased dramatically, it's still not always comfortable to ride the train alone after 11pm. For those who must, wait in the designated after-hours areas, and stay in view of the token booth. Avoid taking the long underground tunnels to transfer between trains; these can be deserted and potentially dangerous late at night. Stay away from the entrances with no token booths, marked by a red light above ground. A general note on subway safety: keep all valuables hidden, and make sure wallets and money are buried away in a deep pocket.

Buses are slower than the subway, but offer a more scenic trip. They stop every three or four blocks along most avenues, and every block on crosstown trips. Stops are marked either by a glass shelter or a street sign which lists the lines servicing them. Posted schedules at stops are use-

ful when traveling in the evening or on week-ends, when buses run less frequently. All buses are identified by numbers, which are preceded by a letter that denotes the predominant borough of its route: M for Manhattan, Q for Queens, B for Brooklyn, and Bx for the Bronx. Most buses run continuously from 7am to 10pm; after that, service slows. After midnight on weeknights, many lines run as infrequently as once an hour.

To switch bus lines, ask the driver for a trans-fer (or "add-a-ride"), then present it to the driver of the next bus, or simply use a MetroCard (see below), which automatically takes the transfer into account.

The front of the bus is the designated area for disabled and elderly passengers. It's protocol to give up a seat for someone more deserving — a matter of opinion, but usually those with children or heavy packages qualify. Try to use the door in the back of the bus when exiting. Most important, let all the passengers off before boarding the bus; this prevents a traffic jam.

Buses take tokens, MetroCards, or exact change ($1.50), while subways take only tokens and Metro-Cards, both of which may be bought at token booths in subway stations. (They can also be found along with bus and subway maps at various stores and kiosks around the city.)

MetroCard is the most fabulous thing to hap-pen to mass transit since... well, you figure it out. Slide a floppy Pay-Per-Ride card through the sen-sors on turnstiles and bus-fare boxes; do it again in two hours or less, and it's free! That's right, transfer with a MetroCard from a bus to subway, or vice versa, and get a free ride. To get the maxi-mum benefits: plan an errand, take the subway down, come back in two hours or less on the bus, and only pay for one way. The thrill that comes from this process has nothing to do with cheap-ness; it feels like beating system.

When you buy a $15 Pay-Per-Ride card, you get an extra fare; a $30 card gets two, etc. When all the fares are used up, take the card back to the token booth and pay cash to have more added on.

Another option, the Unlimited Ride MetroCard, lets you ride all you want for a set price on sub-ways and non-express buses. As the MTA is found of telling you, "the more you ride the less each ride costs." A 7-Day MetroCard costs $17, while the 30-Day version runs you $63. Do the math to fig-ure out which version is most cost-effective for you. MetroCard also offers The Fun Pass, which, for $4, gives you unlimited access until 3am the next morning. Aimed at tourists, The Fun Pass is also useful for those with an isolated day full of treks around town. While the Pay-Per-Ride and Unlimited Ride MetroCards are available at all subway booths, The Fun Pass can be purchased only at select vendors. To find out where to pick one up, look up *www.metrocard.citysearch.com*

Taxi and Gypsy Cabs are a pricer way to go, though there's less hassle. Head out into the street and wave an arm — a yellow cab will come to a screeching halt. If one drives on by, don't be insulted; it was probably off duty or already taken. (Look at the lights atop the cab: if it has passengers, the lights will be off; if it's empty, the lights in the middle the numbers will be on; if the driver is off duty, the "off duty" lights will be on as well.) Rates for yellow cabs have been steadily climbing over the years and are currently at $2 for the first fifth-mile, then 30¢ for each additional fifth-mile or 20¢ for seventy seconds stopped in traffic. There's an additional 50¢ charge after 8pm. These rates cover all passengers; legally, the driver can carry up to four passengers at a time (though ask nicely for a fifth person and it's usu-ally fine.) Drivers can't refuse service to any desti-nation in the city, whether it's only a few blocks or, conversely, an outer borough. Expect to pay significantly more for destinations outside the city. Fares to Kennedy International and Newark Airports from Manhattan are fixed at $30, with a $5 recommended tip.

Car services and gypsy cabs also provide pri-vate service; in the outer boroughs, they are the only form of taxi consistently available. Although theoretically restricted to telephone orders, these cars — predominantly Lincolns or other large American sedans — often cruise for fares. Always agree on a price before entering the car. While fares are comparable to yellow cab service in the outer boroughs, the cost for a car service in busy districts of Manhattan can be exorbitant. Drivers prey especially on tourists in busy parts of town (e.g. the Theater District) where yellow cabs may be hard to come by.

The renowned Staten Island Ferry connects Manhattan to the only borough not accessible by subway. Not only is this trip free, it affords some spectacular views of Manhattan, Ellis Island, and the Statue of Liberty. Even if Staten Island is not on your itinerary, the round trip is worth it. Call (718) 815-BOAT for more information. Catch the ferry at the Whitehall Ferry Terminal at the foot of Whitehall St below the Financial District.

how to be a
TAXI DRIVER

As we learned in Martin Scorsese's *Taxi Driver*, the Belmore Cafeteria, located on Park Avenue So. until the early 1990s, was the place where cabbies met to jaw about traffic, fares, the Taxi and Limousine Commission, and the union. During the four years I drove a cab, I went to the Belmore a couple of times just to say I'd done it, but as with most closed systems, the camaraderie was more available to career drivers than to college kids like me. More often I went to places with drive through windows, or to Chez Brigitte, on Greenwich Ave., which was nearly as quick and had absolutely dependable filet of sole. Sometimes I'd make a date to meet my boyfriend there for supper, but this wasn't easy to coordinate. He drove, too, for an outfit out of Brooklyn, and we never knew when one of us would get a fare out to an airport and be tied up for hours.

This was twenty years ago, and in those days you either worked for a fleet or you owned your own cab and medallion. I drove for Ann Service, which was on 21st St. and had a small reputation as an arty place (a number of the fleets had characters, I guess; there was a gay garage, too.) On the days I worked I'd show up around 2:30pm and tip the dispatcher, and in the waiting room guys would be sitting around practicing horns, memorizing lines, writing papers, reading Proust. Cabs were assigned in the order they were turned in by the day shift, and those tips to the dispatcher helped ward off the vehicles with loud motors, no a/c, or residual B.O. I usually went out between 3pm and 4pm, and had to have the car back before the morning rush, though I almost never kept it that long. On weeknights I'd knock

Dave King, author of this article, is completing his MFA in Fiction at Columbia University. Editor-in-Chief of Columbia: A Journal of Literature and Art, Mr. King was a New York City cabbie for four years.

off as soon as I'd made a hundred bucks in fares, which was generally between midnight and 1am. On weekends I'd often stay out later, just because it was so easy: the money was right there on the sidewalk, waiting to be picked up, and collecting as much as possible was almost like a game, a version of Supermarket Sweep.

When I dropped off the cab, I paid the figure on my meter to the dispatcher. I kept my tips, of course. I received a paycheck every two weeks. My commission when I started was 41% of my fares, less taxes and union dues. As I built up seniority, my take rose, and at the time I stopped driving, four years later, I was getting around a 46% commission, as I recall. It wasn't bad for a guy with low living expenses; I always had cash in my pockets, usually singles.

As a new cabbie, I got a lot of advice from veteran drivers. The advice tended to revolve around who tipped and who didn't, and most of it was fairly shameful. Women, I was told, were lousy tippers, and not worth stopping for; and the same was said of blacks, who were also likely to take you to neighborhoods where you might not get a fare back — bad risk there. The surprising thing about this kind of profiling was that everybody seemed to do it in equal measure, and to take it as simply a part of the job. Black cabbies warned me away from black passengers, and women cabbies told me never to pick up women. Even among the solid leftists and idealists — and there were many — nobody seemed to feel compromised at all.

But I couldn't work that way. I hated imagining that a small difference in a tip was going to make a difference to my life, and I wasn't raised to judge people by how they looked. It seemed also that the system only worked if all drivers were theoretically available to all passengers and willing to go anywhere. And I loved the idea that each fare was an utterly random encounter; I loved the surrender of volition that occurred each time someone flagged me down, and

I didn't want to mess with it by interfering, even on my own behalf. The result was that I picked up anyone and went to every neighborhood in the city, and I sometimes got into trouble. I was mugged more than any driver I knew, by all sorts of people, and I developed a reflex for hitting the gas quickly if a situation looked ugly. (This was my escape strategy the night my car was suddenly surrounded by a gang of gun-toting preadolescents. Children, among the categories of criminal types, are undoubtedly the most unpredictable.) Occasionally there were offers of gifts — liquor, drugs, sex — along with or instead of with the money for the fare, and once I fell prey to an extraordinarily elaborate swindle and lost all my earnings for the day. So I was a bit of a dope, perhaps, but I enjoyed the process and the typicality of it all, until the crime wave did finally take its toll. When I caught myself sizing up too many fares before I pulled to the curb, I knew it was time to quit.

Toward the end of my time as a driver I began to hear about 'mini-fleets' and 'horse-hiring,' which meant buying twelve hours' use of a medallioned cab. A deal would be struck with an owner — often a driver or former driver — who had two or three vehicles on which he wanted to maximize the

potential, and a flat daily fee would be agreed upon. On most days, the fee proved a better gamble than the percentage the fleets paid their drivers, but the hitch was that horse-hiring was a strict seven-day-a-week deal: the owners wanted to keep their cars perpetually earning, so drivers who took time off had to pay for the set twelve hours, anyway. In my day, no one seemed quite sure if this new system was sanctioned by the union, or even legal, but it was the way all the really ambitious drivers were going.

In the years since, this kind of flat-rate leasing has become the industry norm — a bit surprisingly, since an informal poll of current drivers tells me the job is much harder now than it was when I drove. These days, a huge number of cabbies hire their vehicles for day rates, and though the resulting earnings are higher than what they'd make working for a fleet, the day rate has risen as the practice became legitimized. The hire now averages a hundred bucks a shift, which means a driver will work hours before turning a profit. (Of course, fares have gone up many times since my day!) More stressful, it seems, is the seven-day-a-week commitment, which remains strictly in place. I often meet drivers who claim it's been years since they took any time off.

New York is increasingly a trickier place to drive. The current police administration makes a point of zero tolerance for light speeding and U-turns, which I always treated as elements of my personal flair. All in all, job exhaustion and the repetition of those celebrity seat-belt plugs seem to be the drivers' big complaints today — as opposed to the nuisance riders and bad perfume of my time.

Most drivers survive by imagining the job as an interim thing; even drivers who've been doing it ten years tell me they've got other plans in mind. And of course, the demographic of the typical New York cabbie has changed: Many more drivers are now immigrants, often with upward aspirations. The career drivers, like those who hung around the Belmore in my day, may be a dying breed.

p•a•r•k•i•n•g
no parking

For some New Yorkers, how to feel about Mayor Giuliani's "Quality of Life" campaign depends on whether or not they have to move their car that day. Many Manhattanites find themselves circling, circling, circling — unwilling or unable to pay a $250+ monthly garage cost and not wanting to place their car in the jeopardy of a dark and suspect street, or under a confusing, conflicting, entrapping sign.

Parking citations are a source of millions of dollars in revenue for the city. In Manhat-tan, any parking violation on any main thorough-fare or below 96th St. costs a whopping $55. While the city claims there are no longer any incentive-based parking ticket quotas for Meter Maids, anyone who has ever left a car for two minutes, yellow hazards flashing, in a standing zone, by a fire hydrant, or double parked to quickly run in for a slice of pizza, only to come back to find a fat orange citation under their wiper, may disagree. To call the meter maids overzealous is an understatement. They seem to lurk around corners waiting and watching, no matter where, no matter what time of day or night. And once they start writing up a ticket they never stop. (They claim that's not allowed!)

Let's set the record straight on alternate-side parking etiquette: In New York City, signs indicate which days of the week and which hours are reserved for street cleaning. In most areas of Manhattan, this includes two days a week (usually either Monday and Thursday or Tuesday and Friday) for three hours at a time (either from 8am until 11am of from 11am until 2pm; in certain areas in Manhattan and in much of the outer boroughs, street cleaning may be limited to once a week, or to only 90 minutes.) Days and times are usually posted clearly along a given block. If you park on a stretch of street designated for cleaning, you will get a ticket for

$55, whether or not the cleaning truck has already passed your spot.

While not technically legal, double parking on one-way sidestreets is usually tolerated during cleaning periods. Some neighborhoods are more tolerant than others, though, so check out if residents are double parking during this time period and try to gauge it that way. Be aware that even double parked spaces go quickly in New York; drivers usually sit double parked in their cars for at least fifteen minutes before street cleaning begins in order to secure a spot. Also keep in mind, if you are parked in a good (legal) spot during cleaning, don't count on being able to move your car until the cleaning period expires and others move their double parked vehicles.

If you do get a ticket, there may be some recourse. Confirm that all information written on the ticket has been included by the ticketer and is 100% correct: date and time; address or site-specific details; license plate type and number; car make and body type; registration expiration date (for NY cars) or state of registration; appropriate categorization of offense ("No Parking," "No Standing," "No Stopping"). Note that if the violation is in effect 24 hours a day and/or 7 days a week (i.e. No Standing Anytime) then the ticket doesn't have to indicate the time and date of offense. Otherwise, if there are discrepancies in any of these categories, contest the ticket by mailing it in marked "not guilty," and there's a good chance you won't have to pay a dime.

ferries

If you think that transportation in New York is just the "Honk! Honk!" of rabid roadsters and the "Ding, Dong" of closing subway doors, you're missing out on an alternate mode that's been surfacing recently along Manhattan's watery margins.

Most New Yorkers know of the celebrated Staten Island Ferry. Many, however, aren't aware of numerous other fluvial routes within the city, useful for going to and fro without the bother of bumper to bumper traffic and the stress it creates. In addition to a number of commuter lines from New Jersey — connecting ports like Weehawken, Hoboken, and Port Liberty to the Financial District — one exists in both Queens (Hunters Point) and Brooklyn (Brooklyn Army Terminal). What's more, La Guardia Airport is accessible by ferry from Lower Manhattan, making the trip to the airport simultaneously scenic and speedy.

Water transportation isn't just for the briefcase-toting set, however. Waterways (800-53FERRY), operator of the vast majority of New York City's ferries, runs a variety of services with a recreational bent. From South Street Seaport (Pier 17), that hot spot of tourism, ferries head for both Yankee and Shea Stadia during the baseball season, departing 90 and 110 minutes before game time, respectively. Round-trip tickets cost $10-$12. The ferries make stops en route at East 34th St. and East 90th St., as well as offering services to the games from northern New Jersey and Staten Island. The ferries dock "within a seven minute walk" from each stadium, and leave 30 minutes after games conclude.

Waterways also offers a number of scenic tours within and beyond the city's limits: fifty and ninety minute harbor cruises, as well as day trips to, among other destinations, the Rockefeller Estate, West Point Military Academy, Bear Mountain, and the Upper Hudson Valley. Prices and departures times vary. According to its web page, Waterways' newest options are the fabulous sounding Downtown Disco Cruises, departing thrice nightly on Thursdays in the summer. So take your Dramamine, and get down! And the next time you need to get from point A to point B, consider a smoother (albeit wetter!) trip, leaving gridlock in your wake.

For more information, see the web page for the Port Authority of New York and New Jersey, www.panynj.gov/ferry/ferframe

MTA Metro-North Railroad (532-4900)

Metro-North services Westchester, Putnam, and Duchess counties in New York state, and Fairfield and New Haven counties in Connecticut. Its three major lines (Hudson, Harlem, New Haven) each extend about 70 miles from the City, departing from Grand Central Station (Park Ave. and 42nd St., **S 4 5 6 7**).

Long Island Rail Road (718-217-LIRR)

The LIRR, as it is called, originates at 34th St.-Penn Station (**A C E 1 2 3 9**) and at the Atlantic Ave. subway station (**D Q 2 3 4 5**). It services both Nassau and Suffolk counties.

Port Authority Trans Hudson (800-234-PATH)

The PATH departs from the Manhattan Mall at 33rd St. (**B D F N Q R** to 34th St.), a block east of Penn Station, and is the best buy for transportation out of the city. For a dollar, travelers can ride and transfer among this subway's four lines: 33rd St.-Journal Square and Newark-World Trade Center every day, day and night; and weekdays during the day and evening at 33rd Street-Hoboken and World Trade Center-Hoboken. The lines originating from 33rd also stop at 23rd, 14th, 9th, and Christopher Sts., making transportation cheaper than the MTA subway.

Long-Distance Buses

Out-of-state buses leave from Port Authority at 42nd St. and Eighth Ave.; the station also houses the **A C E** lines and is connected to the 42nd St.-Times Sq. subway stop on the **N R 1 2 3 7 9** lines by an underground tunnel. Heavily-traveled routes, such as those to Boston and Washington, D.C., have regularly-scheduled departures; round-trip tickets go for roughly $50 to each city. Be sure to either buy tickets in advance or show up at least an hour before scheduled departure, or find out the hard way that a ticket in hand does not necessarily guarantee a seat. Many companies, such as Peter Pan Trailways (800-343-9999), do not sell tickets for a specific departure time, just for a particular route, although for Greyhound (800-231-2222) treks to other cities, you are restricted to a specific destination and time of departure after purchasing the ticket. For information on bus transportation to all three airports, the Meadowlands, and Six Flags Great Adventure Park, call Port Authority (564-8484).

to and *from*
THE CITY

Long-Distance Trains

Train travel along the eastern seaboard is cleaner and more pleasurable than the bus, but not necessarily faster: bus travel from New York to Boston clocks in at four and a half hours; the train takes more than five, due to the number of stops in between. The train is also markedly more expensive. Amtrak (800-USA-RAIL) runs regularly-scheduled trains out of Penn Station (34th Street and Broadway, **A C E 1 2 3 9**) to locations all over the country. Reservations are available, but these seats tend to be more expensive, especially on holidays. Prices may depend on whether a route is local, making many stops, or express. They also depend on availability and the class in which you choose to ride. Amtrak also operates an express, the Metroliner, to Washington D.C., running throughout the week; reservations are required.

Airports

There are three main airports accessible from Manhattan: La Guardia Airport (718-533-3400) and Kennedy International Airport (718-244-4444) in Queens, and Newark International Airport (973-961-6000) in New Jersey. All are accessible by cab for a flat fee from Manhattan: $30 plus tolls to Kennedy and Newark, $25 to La Guardia; a $5 minimum tip is recommended. For less money (about $14), you can get to the airports by shuttles — Olympia Trails (908-354-3330) runs a shuttle bus from Port Authority, Grand Central Station, Penn Station, and the World Trade center to Newark for $10 in each direction. If you leave yourself plenty of time, it is possible to reach the Queens airports via public transportation, and for a mere swipe of your MetroCard. The M60 bus hits points in uptown Manhattan (near Columbia University on the West Side) and stops at each La Guardia terminal. Meanwhile, the **A** goes to Howard Beach-JFK Airport, where a shuttle stops every 20-30 minutes and then stops at all terminals. Proposals for express rail links from Midtown Manhattan to Kennedy and La Guardia are also in the works, though with much debate over the possibility of a "two-seat" ride, requiring passengers to change trains mid-route, versus a completely direct "one-seat" ride.

m MEDIA *d* *i* *a*

Newspapers

The New York Amsterdam News
A historic black-owned newspaper, providing an insightful perspective on New York's African-American community.
932-7400

New York Post
New York's tabloids that brashly headline everything lurid. These rags provide a certain hometown pride you can't find anywhere else.
(800) 692-6397

el diario la prensa
New York's award-winning Spanish-language daily dishes out the same coverage as its corresponding English local dailies, but with an eye to Hispanic issues.
807-4600

The New York Times
Excellent coverage of metropolitan and international issues, as well as the goings-on in the Arts. Friday's Weekend section and the Sunday Times are most popular.
556-1234

The Wall Street Journal
A financial paper geared to the business world, with extensive coverage of economic and corporate news; no pictures, only drawn portraits of people in the news.
(800) 568-7625

Manhattan Spirit
What the city would rely on were it stranded about 200 miles to the north. Still, a useful read amidst the hubbub and the hype.
268-8600

New York Press
This weekly contains columns that read like journal entries, and the writing is among the city's best; the Mail never fails to amuse.
941-1130

Resident
Several Residents are published throughout Manhattan, each covering a different neighborhood.
679-1850

Village Voice
The bastion of liberal politics, this free weekly keeps its readers abreast of the machinations of city politicians and provides good coverage of gay and lesbian concerns. Snatch up a copy on street corners Tuesday nights.
475-3300

Magazines

Black Book
Provocative and offbeat, with much attention to the hipper-than-thou downtown subculture. Articles are arranged as if in an address book.
334-1800

Free Time
This monthly gives comprehensive listings for all events in New York that are free or under $5. Available at some newsstands throughout the city or by subscription for $1.25 each.
545-8900

New York Magazine
Check out this glossy for breezy interviews with/or articles about New York celebs. Comes out Mondays for $2.95.
447-4749

The New Yorker
A literary staple featuring fiction and poetry by heavyweights like Munro and Brodsky. Film reviews tend to read more like dissertations on cinema than strings of soundbites.
Available everywhere every Monday for $2.50.
(800) 825-2510

Paper
The shiny bible of the downtown scene, dishing out monthly pronouncements on the latest in fashion, entertainment, and lifestyle. The perfect accessory for every hipster's coffeetable.
226-4405

TimeOut
The most comprehensive listings for entertainment in the city, as well as short articles on different aspects of all things social and cultural in New York.
539-4444

Radio

More interesting and less predictable than commercial radio, the city supports a number of college and public radio stations:

WNYU, 89.1, *New York University* radio, shares its frequency with **WFDU**, *Fairleigh Dickinson University*. NYU's format varies from hard rock to jazz, and their new music show is every weekday afternoon. WFDU leans towards more alternative programming.

WSOU, 89.5, *Seton Hall University*, plays metal, hard core, and punk throughout the day, more than any commercial station.

WKCR, 89.9, *Columbia University*, is the WNYC of college radio, programming jazz, classical, country, world music, and an evening news broadcast.

WFUV, 90.7, is public radio from *Fordham University*. Programming covers various genre, but leans toward college rock.

WFMU, 91.1, *Upsala College*, programs everything from the latest in underground and indie rock to specialty shows like the Hebrew music show.

WNYE, 91.5, programs for *New York public schools* and also broadcasts "Radio France International" late at night and early each weekday morning. On weekends, the station programs a Hellenic broadcast and various talk shows.

WNYC, 93.9, *New York's National Public Radio Station*, programs mostly classical, but runs a number of weekly programs of world music, new age, and other modern instrumental genre. Besides NPR, WNYC also broadcasts "A Prairie Home Companion" and works in conjunction with Symphony Space.

radio
stations

am

Adult Contemporary	WALK 1370
Adult Contemporary	WICC 600
Adult Contemporary	WPAT930
Big Bands/Talk	WLIM 1580
Christian Music	WWDJ 970
Ethnic	WWRV1330
Gospel/Talk	WWRL 1600
Korean Language	WZRC 1480
Music	WNYG 1440
New/Talk	WGBB 1240
News	WBBR 1130
News	WCBS 880
News	WINS 1010
News/Sports/Talk	WEVD 1050
News/Talk	WNYC 820
Nostalgia	WRHD 1570
Oldies	WHLI 1100
Pop Standards	WMTR 1250
Pop Standards	WQEW 1560
Religion	WMCA 570
Spanish Language	WADO 1280
Spanish Language	WKDM 1380
Sports/Talk/Mets	WFAN 660
Talk/News	WABC 770
Talk/News	WOR 710
Talk/Nostalgia	WVOX 1160
Westchester News	WFAS 1230

fm

Adelphi University	WBAU 90.3
Adult Contemporary	WALK 97.5
Adult Contemporary	WBLI 106.1
AdultContemporary	WEBE 107.9
Adult Contemporary	WFAS 103.9
Adult Contemporary	WHFM 95.3
Adult Contemporary	WKJY 98.3
AdultContemporary	WLTW106.7
Adult Contemporary	WPAT 93.1
Adult Rock	WEHM 96.7
Barnard College	WBAR 87.9
Big Band/Nostalgia	WRTN 93.5
C.C.N.Y.	WHCR 90.3
C.W. Post Campus	WCWP 88.1
Classic Rock	WXRK 92.3
Classic Rock	WMXV 105.1
Classical	WNYC 93.9
Classical	WQXR 96.3
Columbia University	WKCR 89.9
Comedy/Rock	WPLR 99.1
Community Services	WNYE 91.5
Contemporary Jazz	WQCD 101.9
Easy Listening	WEZN 99.9
Fordham University	WFUV 90.7
Hofstra University	WRHU 88.7
Jazz	WBGO 88.3
Light Contemporary	WBAZ 101.7
LightContemporary	WHUD 106.7
Light Contemporary	WMJC 94.3
Multi-ethnic	WNWK 105.9
Music/Public	WFDU 89.1
Nassau Comm. Col.	WHPC 90.3
Oldies	WCBS 101.1
Oldies	WKHL 96.7
Oldies	WLNG 92.1
Progressive Rock	WDRE 92.7
Rock	WAXQ 104.3
Rock	WBAB 102.3
Rock	WDHA 105.5
Rock	WNEW 102.7
Rock	WRGX 107.1
Seton Hall Univ.	WSOU 89.5
Stony Brook Univ.	WUSB 90.1
Top 40	WHTZ 100.3
Top 40	WPLJ 95.5
Top 40	WPSC 88.7
Top 40/Urban	WQHT 97.1
Top 40	WRCN 103.5
Urban Contemp.	WBLS 107.5
Urban Contemp.	WRKS 98.7
Varied	WBAI 99.5
Varied	WFMU 91.1

In order to find the cross street of an address, follow these simple steps:

NORTH-SOUTH AVENUES

1. Cancel the last digit of the house number
2. Divide the remaining number by two
3. Add or deduct the key number (list follows)

*On street or address numbers preceded by an asterisk, omit step 2.

For example, take 1100 Broadway:

1. Cancel the last digit so you are left with 110
2. Divide 110 by two, leaving you with 55
3. Subtract 31, the key number for Broadway addresses over 1000. Thus, 1100 Broadway is at 24th Street.

Avenues A, B, C, D	Add 3
First Avenue	Add 3
Second Avenue	Add 3
Third Avenue	Add 10
Fourth Avenue	Add 8
Fifth Avenue	
1-200	Add 13
201-400	Add 16
401-600	Add 18
601-775	Add 20
*776-1286	Subtract 18
Sixth Avenue	Subtract 12
Seventh Avenue	
1-1800	Add 12
1800 + above	Add 20
Eighth Avenue	Add 9
Ninth Avenue	Add 13
Tenth Avenue	Add 13
Eleventh Avenue	Add 15
Amsterdam Avenue	Add 59

Broadway	
1-754	below 8th St.
754-858	Subtract 29
859-958	Subtract 25
1000 + above	Subtract 31
*Central Park West	Add 60
Columbus Avenue	Add 59
Lexington Avenue	Add 22
Madison Avenue	Add 27
Park Avenue	Add 34
Riverside Drive	
*1-567	Add 73
*567 + above	Add 78
West End Avenue	Add 59

EAST-WEST

Addresses for any east-west street begin at the avenue listed below

East Side:

1	Fifth Avenue
101	Park Avenue
201	Third Avenue
301	Second Avenue
401	First Avenue
501	York or Avenue A
601	Avenue B

West Side:

1	Fifth Avenue
101	Sixth Avenue
201	Seventh Avenue
301	Eighth Avenue
401	Ninth Avenue
501	Tenth Avenue
601	Eleventh Avenue

i need a job......now
e·m·p·l·o·y·m·e·n·t

Searching for work in New York City can be overwhelming, because there's so much to choose from. The oddest of odd jobs can be found here — just read *The Village Voice* classified ads. Those with a particular dream job in mind will surely find it offered somewhere in the city — work is always available to the innovative, creative, and persistent. Marshaling all possible resources and use lesser positions as stepping stones, and you will find satisfying, well-paying jobs.

New York is the headquarters for many big-name companies, and post-collegiate professionals flock to the city for a chance at corporate stardom. The market is incredibly competitive for those dreaming of work at Miramax or Morgan Stanley. The best way to land a juicy position is to contact someone directly within the company (Unsolicited résumés usually don't generate much response.)

Those new to New York who find themselves staring at an empty rolodex, there are other methods: Call a potential employer and ask to speak to someone in Human Resources; ask about position openings and offer to send a résumé. Call information (411) for company numbers. Persistence and confidence pay off in New York, so keep calling. If Human Resources can't be reached, search for contact names on the Internet by browsing through home pages.

For those who don't have specific work in mind, several resources exist available to help narrow the search. Turn to *The Voice* or the Sunday edition of *The New York Times*, which boast pages and pages of full- and part-time jobs, as well as listings of employment and temp agencies. (In New York, temp work, while obviously not secure, actually pays much better than many full-time positions.) Classifieds are particularly good for finding work in the restaurant, bar, and club industries.

There are many websites which provide service to everyone and contain job listings sorted by field, duration, and geographic location. However, postings are often outdated and somewhat slim; while searching online may not yield a job, employer profiles and other associated resources are nonetheless helpful. Some popular sites which provide employer profiles, excellent field

breakdowns, résumé registration, and a variety of other helpful resources are: www.monster.com, www.job-hunt.com, www.jobweb.org, www.job-track.com, and www.careerpath.com.

Internships are often the best way to get a foot in the door. Companies in every field need eager beavers, willing to slave away for peanuts. In truth, Interns lucky enough to get a stipend will be working long, exhausting hours, though if you're determined enough to tough it out, you'll will be rewarded with networking opportunities.

Temping is a lucrative livelihood for people who can stomach living on the edge. Sign up with three or four agencies to ensure continuous employment, and make sure to become friendly with an officer at each. Jobs fall somewhere between baby-sitting the phone for $8 per hour to raking in $25 as a copy editor or fact checker for a fashion magazine.

There is other part-time work around the city which provide some extra cash for little stress. Look in the windows of stores and restaurants around your neighborhood; the close proximity will allow you to work longer hours. In fact, most New York restaurants won't give out the better positions unless the applicant has some hard-core city experience. Try bussing or hostessing before waiting tables.

Bust out designer labels for interviews; good looks greatly improve the chance of getting hired. Large department stores like are always hiring — spend the weekends selling perfume and get a great discount on your next purchase. Anyone with a bike can get a lot of exercise while making extra money by making deliveries. Look for help wanted ads in the back of magazines and other New York publications. Bilingual folks can make tons of dough working as part-time translators, tutors, or tour guides, or by teaching English as a Second Language. A little creativity is all it takes to find a part-time employment opportunity. Remember, attach a high value to your time! There's lots of money in this city; employers often don't know the going rate. Don't settle for too little. You'd be surprised at how much you can earn simply by being competent with the internet, a copy machine, or even a hammer and nails.

Everybody and his or her mother wants a piece of the New York real estate pie, and most are willing to pay dearly for it. Labor under no illusions: for most, the perfect (or perfectly located) apartment is probably not out there. There are, however, plenty of places that will suffice, and the real estate market will seem more manageable if approached with an open mind. Here are a few guidelines to assist with the search:

Find a rent bracket. Rents vary in Manhattan according to neighborhood; the more desirable the location, the higher the rent. Decide what's affordable, then concentrate on neighborhoods that have rents in this range. Newspaper ads are arranged by location, so this method saves time.

For the most part, the closer you want to be to the action, the more you have to pay. Expect studio and small one-bedroom apartments in Chelsea, Greenwich Village, and SoHo to begin at $1200/month and climb as high as $2000. The same apartments in Hell's Kitchen or the Lower

East Side — formerly undesirable areas, now claimed by Bohemia — would be slightly less, with a one-bedroom in the range of $1000-$1400. Always popular and posh, the Upper West Side and Gramercy Park are extremely desirable neighborhoods, and rents reflect that, while surprisingly, given its history of opulence, good deals can be found on the Upper East Side: small one-bedrooms may be available for just over $1000.

The trick in New York, it would seem, is to find a neighborhood on the cusp of popularity whose rents still reflect more downtrodden times. Five or ten years ago, no self-respecting hipster would have been caught dead visiting Washington Heights or Astoria, Queens, let alone living in these outskirts; today, folks flock to them to claim some of the best deals in the city. Fifteen years ago, what cool cat would've moved voluntarily to Park Slope, Brooklyn? Now you'd be lucky to find sidewalk space among all the twenty-somethings, never mind low rent!

Of course, real estate brokers are another way to go, albeit not a very pleasant one. They can be pushy, but they'll find you an apartment fast — for a fee. Generally, brokers charge between 12 and 15 percent of the first year's rent for their services. Smaller firms may only charge one month's rent. Finding a broker is most simply done by checking the classifieds: unless otherwise indicated, the phone number attached to apartment listings usually refers to a broker and not to the owner of the apartment. Call the agencies that list appealing apartments and make an appointment to see their other listings.

If an open house is advertised, arrive thirty minutes before the starting time with a check in hand, just in case. Apartments go very quickly, and it pays to be prepared. Be sure to read the lease in its entirety before signing. Be wary of any deviations from the standard lease (which can be obtained from any office supply store). Never make an appointment to see a place without enough money in the bank to cover the first month's rent and a security deposit (usually equivalent to a month's rent). The unhappy truth is that if you're young and without a large income (let alone — gasp! — a student!), even if you have some money in the bank, you're likely to need a

guarantor in the New York metropolitan area, someone with an annual income of 35-50 times the monthly rent, to legally vouch for you. Your guarantor's name will appear on the lease along with your own and he or she would be ultimately responsible for rent or damage to the apartment.

When in doubt, share. Sharing an apartment with a roommate or two significantly cuts costs. Be careful, though: some landlords are picky about the number of people sharing their apartment, and subletting without his or her permission can result in an eviction notice. For those who want to forge ahead, it might be wise to try a roommate-finding service. Roommate Finders (250 West 57th St., Suite 1629, 489-6862), the oldest and largest such service in Manhattan, is the prototype in this case, and charges a $250 up-front processing fee.

Sublets are another way to go. Get a fabulous sublet for the summer (or maybe the whole year) by cruising college neighborhoods around graduation time. Professors and students post listings on walls, street signs, and store fronts in both Greenwich Village and Morningside Heights. A nice perk of subletting or sharing is that the above-mentioned guarantor dilemma is easily bypassed.

For a real deal, though, you're likely to be pushed outside of Manhattan. Brooklyn and Queens have spacious apartments at much lower rents, although by now the ring of neighborhoods closest to Manhattan are as expensive as living in Manhattan itself. Traditional standbys for the young and the penniless — Park Slope, Carroll Gardens, Williamsburg, Fort Greene — and neighborhoods further out, on slower, less convenient subway lines are being explored as alternatives. Neighborhoods like Jackson Heights in Queens and Sunset Park and Bay Ridge in Brooklyn are worth a look at. By being a pioneer now, you may find yourself at a new cultural and social epicenter in three years, by which time your new home will be a chic, enviable locale.

The *Real Estate* section of New York newspapers and magazines contain some

lingo that may seem encrypted to newcomers. Here's some help in

cracking the codes!

· **cozy** — Very, very small

· **EIK** — Eat-in kitchen. Don't be fooled into thinking this means a spacious chef's space. Rather, it could mean room enough for anything from a stool at a counter to a bona fide breakfast nook. (New York kitchens are notoriously cramped!)

· **exposed brick** — Realtors have somehow suckered renters into believing that unfinished red brick walls are a desirable, urban feature. Maybe they do it for you. Knock yourself out.

· **floor-through (often "flrthru")** — An apartment that takes up the entire floor of a building, often a brownstone.

· **garden apartment** — A ground-floor apartment with access to an unspecified amount of outdoor lawn or patio space.

· **No Fee** — Rented directly by an owner, so no broker's fee charged for rental. This means big savings, as much as $1,800 for an apartment renting for $1,000/month.

· **one-month's security** — Standard collateral toward any damage you might inflict on an apartment during your lease, which may or may not be returned in full when you move out, depending on the condition of the rental.

· **Rent Stabilized** — If an apartment is listed as "Rent Stabilized," rent hikes for one-year leases subsequently sign are limited to 2%, as of September, 1998. For complete information regarding issues of rent increase, contact the New York City Rental Guidelines Board at www.nycrgb.com

· **walk-up** — No elevator here, so don't kid yourself about how in shape you are; a 4th floor walk-up will make or break you!

· **wbfp** — Wood burning fireplace.

dogs

Here is a small selection of doggy-oriented services for maintaining a happy pooch:

WALKING
The K-9 Club Inc.
410-3764, covers East 20s-90s and West 50s-90s
Pet Mates
751-5405, covers Houston-96th Sts.
Puddles Pet Service
(888) 760-8349, covers all of Manhattan

GROOMING
A Cut Above Grooming Salon
207 West 75th St. (bet. Amsterdam Ave. and Broadway), 799-8746, Cash Only
New York Dog Spa & Hotel
145 West 18th St. (bet. Sixth and Seventh Aves.), 243-1199, MC, V, AmEx
Pet Superette & Launderette Corp.
187 East 93rd St. (bet. Lexington and Third Aves.), 534-1732, MC, V, AmEx

ANIMAL HOSPITALS
Animal General
558 Columbus Ave. (at 87th St.), 501-9600, MC, V, AmEx
Downtown Veterinary Clinic
148 Ninth Ave. (at 19th St.), 463-8705, MC, V, AmEx
B.Q.E. Pet Supply
253 Wythe Ave., (718) 486-7489, MC, V, AmEx, Diners, D

BOARDING
Canine Country
207 West 75th St. (bet. Amsterdam Ave. and Broadway), 877-7777, MC, V, AmEx, D
Lexington Veterinary Group
133 East 39th St. (bet. Lexington and Third Aves.), 889-7778, MC, V, AmEx, Diners, D
Run Spot Inc.
415 East 91st St. (bet. First and York Aves.), 996-6666, MC, V, AmEx, D

If you've ever seen an otherwise elegant gentleman scooping up the indelicacies of his fluffy Shitzu, you might wonder why anyone bothers owning a dog in New York City. Surprisingly, though, New Yorkers keep canines like they're running kennels!

Dogs need space — a rare commodity here. Apartments are cramped enough without hyperactive pooches. But, according to veteran dogwalker Lowell, "You can house a Great Dane in a studio if you give it enough love." Nevertheless, most New Yorkers opt for small ankle-biters.

Dogs also require time. "They gotta go outside to do their business at least three times a day," says Daron, proud owner of five Pugs. Don't expect to let your loyal friend roam free down Broadway: Unleashed dogs may be subject to $100 fines. However, it's an unwritten rule that dogs can frolic leashless in most city parks before 8:30am and after 9pm.

If you're like many New Yorkers and see your home only in the dark, you'll have to hire a dogwalker. Services start at $12 per dog for a half-hour jaunt. If you give your dogs names like Buffy and Mimi, you may well feel they require doggie daycare, around $50 a day. If you don't have the means, at least take your pooch to a "dog run" in a public park. "It's not just rump-sniffing and roughhousing," observes a local canine psychologist. "Your dog is developing important social skills." (Rump-sniffing and rough-housing aren't important social skills?!?) Don't forget a pooper-scooper — failing to clean up after your dog is not only frowned upon, it carries a $100 fine.

Even rule-abiding owners pay dearly for their four-legged friends. Upscale New Yorkers have been found serving their dogs free-range chopped meats, available at most gourmet supermarkets. If opted for, weekly grooming can cost anywhere from $15 to infinity, depending on how fluffy you want Muffy. Most, though, find it all worth the cost: Owning a dog is rumored to increase your chances of meeting attractive strangers. And if that doesn't work out, you'll still have a devoted lapwarmer and playmate to come home to.

Tale of an Inadvertent, Trend Setting,
URBAN DWELLER

When I was evicted from my East Village apartment in 1995 by a famous comedian who purchased the brownstone for his personal use, the last things on my mind were real estate trends and the forces behind gentrification in New York City. What did I care about urban renewal, its pros and cons? I was too busy indulging in nostalgia. While living on 7th St. near Ave. C, I had delighted in the diversity and vitality of the neighborhood, and was dismayed to learn that I could no longer afford even a studio in Alphabet City.

Before leaving to discover the wonders of Brooklyn, I said goodbye to my favorite over-grown community garden on East 6th St., with its heavy-headed sunflowers and plum tomatoes; and adios to the Puerto Rican kids who raced up and down my block every summer day, playing hide and seek beneath my stoop. The truth was, I had been living in a great space for a steal, and during my five years in the East Village, the gentrification that began earnestly in the '80s had swept clear across Second Ave. to Ave. D, effectively pricing me out.

I had to take this phenomenon called gentrification seriously when I realized it had tailed me to Brooklyn. There in Williamsburg, and more recently in Fort Greene, I found hipsters and investors running amok and putting down roots, albeit with distinct consequences: They were driving up real estate prices and attracting new cafés, lounges, restaurants, and bars. They were bringing in new services and retail, while displacing long-term, low income, and elderly tenants (a consequence which may implicate not renewal, but rather a critical lack of affordable housing anywhere in New York). They were changing the urban landscape.

The change isn't as instantaneous as it seems. "All of a sudden there's a great perception that something happened even though it has been happening all along," says Lynne Sagalyn, an urban planner and director of the MBA real estate program at Columbia University's Business School. "But suddenly it looks different. There comes a point where it hits a critical mass."

Defined by my New Merriam-Webster dictionary as "the immigration of middle class people into a run down or recently renewed city area," gentrification is a relatively recent phenomenon in New York City. As recently as the 1960s, New York City was synonymous with urban decline; in the '70s it was fiscally bankrupt. Any existing gentrification was happening in the suburbs, as people fled urban decay. It was not until what planners call "favorable demographics" and the '80s growth of the service sector that things began to turn around. Sure, there was always the Village (the epicenter of the Beat Generation in the '60s and perhaps the original Bohemia in the city) and SoHo (the artist's refuge of the '70s), but widespread localized renewal is a current phenomenon, fascinating in a city known for the character of its neighborhoods.

So while I have been settled in Brooklyn (in the mid-to-late '90s), other neighborhoods have undergone radical transformations in Manhattan. The fetid Meatpacking District along downtown's west coast became a hyper-trendy club land.

Inadvertent trend setter April Di Como, contributor of this article, currently calls the up-and-coming neighborhood of Crown Heights home.

Chelsea, an out-of the way Hispanic barrio of the '60s, began to buzz with new restaurants and galleries — a sort of high-priced ground zero for NYC lesbian and gay culture. Hell's Kitchen, just north of Chelsea, was renamed "Clinton" by realtors at what seemed a random moment, and residents there shrugged shoulders at higher rents or left. Within the last three years, East Village spur NoLita (North of Little Italy) has replaced its parent district as the nightlife destination of choice.

One factor: Real estate is booming city-wide. Some are calling it the greatest market for property owners — ever! "When most people talk about gentrification, they mean affluence — prices going up," says Kathryn Lilly, owner of Realty on the Greene, located in Fort Greene, where real estate prices have gone up an astounding 25% over each of the last four years. "But prices have gone up mostly because of general market conditions," she continues. "They are up everywhere in the New York metropolitan area, even in the poor slums of East New York and Bushwick."

Still, not all neighborhoods are gentrifying. Modestly inflated real estate all across Gotham may reflect a general trend, but very few people are beating down a path to, say, East New York or Bushwick. Given a strong market, I wondered what makes one neighborhood ripe for renaissance, and another not. What I discovered is that there is no formula (if there were, I'd be rich!), and that each and every gentrifying neighborhood does so for different reasons. There are, however,

some trends associated with rapid urban renewal — factors that improve the likelihood that gentrification will occur.

"Low-cost space is a great incubator," explains Sagalyn. "Artists, students, and small-scale entrepreneurs gravitate to those areas where rent is cheap and where they can experiment with their ideas, where new restaurants and bars, music shops and art galleries don't cost a fortune to start up. What gives rise to trendiness is people doing interesting things. There have got to be people on the streets, pedestrian-based activity — what planners call a '24-hour buzz'."

It's true that the hip usually precede (hard core) gentrification. It seems to begin with those

• ROACHES •

They are unpleasant reminders of the filth and violence that city-dwellers have grown used to. Finding a flurry of the crawly things in your kitchen, bathroom, closet, or bed can break your heart and invite nightmares of alien abduction. You can be the cleanest homemaker in Gotham but this doesn't guarantee a roach-free environment. Taking a few precautions may not eradicate the antennaed menace but it may give you peace of mind:

1. Keep food out of sight and covered.
2. Roaches like water. Keep kitchens and bathrooms as dry as possible. Make sure faucets don't drip.
3. Place baited roach traps beneath refrigerators, ovens, and other electrical appliances that make heat. These innocuous little discs are worth their weight in gold.
4. Roaches like to nibble on the glue that keeps paper bags together. Don't save them.
5. Throw garbage out at least once a day.
6. Use an insecticide in cracks and around baseboards.

If all else fails, stomp on them with a heavy-soled shoe and rest easy knowing that you, with the rest of New York, are fighting the good fight.

who have a lot of vision but very little cash, and a willingness to take a chance on a neighborhood, often without services and safety. "People like to see interesting people, which usually comes from a diversity of uses," Sagalyn continues. "You have to think about the kinds of activities that are attracted to low cost space and the services that follow once they're there." Remember that Madonna lived in the East Village back when cabbies refused to cross Ave. A, and that Spike Lee called Fort Greene home years before anyone had ever heard of "Do the Right Thing."

The physical properties of a neighborhood — the architecture, parks, and views — are critical to renewal. "If you are trying to follow the next big trend, look at the architectural integrity of a neighborhood," says Lilly, referring specifically to brownstone communities. And most gentrifying (or gentrified) neighborhoods contain a park or are situated near one. "Open space and green space are integral to what people call 'hot neighborhoods,'" explains Errol T. Louis, a Brooklyn-based community activist and professor of urban sociology at the Pratt Institute. "History shows the minute you build a Central Park, you get a Central Park West. The minute you develop a waterfront you get an exclusive neighborhood like Breezy Point in Brooklyn. Policymakers often fail to see that preserving natural resources boosts rather than hinders economic development."

Mass transit and convenience are also impor-

tant factors. People often chose neighborhoods for convenience and access to their work and recreational interests. If a neighborhood doesn't have a safe, direct subway line to key locations in Manhattan, chances are it is not going to blossom.

Meanwhile, real estate investors and retailers wait with razor sharp pens in the wings, watching closely the artists and other marginals who set the earliest tones of renewal. Sometimes, as with downtown Brooklyn's MetroTech, they initiate

Other housing alternatives:

If all else fails, snag a room at a YMCA. There are three locations in Manhattan: McBurney YMCA (206 West 24th St., 741-9226), Vanderbilt YMCA (224 East 47th St., 756-9600), and Westside YMCA (5 West 63rd St., 875-4100). All three rent rooms on a daily basis. Rates vary with location, but a single can generally be had for about $50-$70.

For something a little more permanent (but less than, say, a year-long lease), try the de Hirsch Residence at the 92nd Street Y (1395 Lexington Ave., 415-5650). Singles rooms go for about $835 a month, doubles for $690, and there is a two-month minimum stay. The Markle Residence (123 West 13th St., 242-2400) offers single rooms with private baths for about $220 a week (includes 2 meals a day).

the renewal. Often over time, the human diversity that helped make a neighborhood 'marketable' finds itself squeezed out by those who can afford higher rents. And one suddenly overhears Park Slope residents (while sipping café au lait near Prospect Park) complain that if they wanted to live on the Upper West Side they would have stayed there, not fully realizing that they represent what they were trying to escape in the first place. The pros and cons tip the scale this way and that: increased services verses displaced tenants; safer streets versus less conventional residents; and on and on.

And where does that leave me? In Crown Heights, where I thought I was safe from the 'G' word. Alas, a realtor recently told me that the streets near the Brooklyn Children's Museum (including my own) are another spot to watch. Am I trendsetter? Not at all. But I do seem to meet the wave a few minutes before it crests, and then bemoan its tidal consequences. Though I do want my community to have an edge, I also want a bodega that sells *The New York Times*. I would like to think of myself as bohemian, even marginal, but the truth is I'm more like those Park Slopers than I care to admit. I, too, represent gentrification of the most hypocritical kind: I only become irritated when it prices me out.

GAY AND LESBIAN

The bronze plaque outside 53 Christopher St. commemorates the climactic event that launched the gay rights movement in the United States three decades ago. On the night of June 27, 1969, more than 100 men, patrons of a gay bar called the Stonewall Inn, stood their ground in defiance of policemen who raided the establishment as part of an ongoing bullying tactic to subjugate homosexuals. The confrontation was violent and lasted several nights as word and outrage spread through the community, but it was a defining moment for gays lesbians, one that resonates to this day.

Gays and lesbians have always been part of New York City's vivid and eventful history. Though it is easy and understandable from our current perspective to look back at a singular event like the Stonewall uprising and call it the turning point in American gay history, the truth remains that the so-called turning point is part of a much longer curve, veering toward the mainstream and extending back through many generations.

In the early days of the 20th Century, a burgeoning community was establishing itself in the Greenwich Village. Stewart's and Life Cafeterias, now defunct but formerly situated on Sheridan Sq., were well-known gay hangouts, serving essentially as halfway houses where young gays could come out, gathering with others.

The East Village, and the more upscale Greenwich Village, became magnets for artists eager to make their mark. The numerous gay playwrights, actors, painters, sculptors, novelists, poets, photographers, and musicians who flooded into the Village contributed to the area's bohemian flair and intellectual prowess, and made it the city's most famous gay enclaves. Before emigrating to Paris, a young James Baldwin penned *Giovanni's Room* while living in a $100 per month apartment on Horatio St. Playwright Edward Albee, very much a part of the Village gay scene in the late 1950s, walked into the restroom at The Ninth Circle, a now-extinct bar he frequented, and found "Who's Afraid of Virginia Woolf?" scrawled across the mirror; he later used the question as the title for his most famous play. Djuna Barnes, best remembered for her novel *Nightwood*, lived the last reclusive years of her life in a small apartment at Patchin Pl., and some

of the century's most accomplished poets, Allen Ginsberg, Frank O'Hara, and W.H. Auden, lived in the perennially nonconformist East Village.

In recent years, Greenwich Village has remained as much the core of the gay community as it was almost one hundred years ago. Many political organizations have offices in the area, and help organize and publicize local goings-on. Chelsea has also become a predominately gay area, with many young gay professionals calling it home. Every June is Gay History Month, and fun, informative events and celebrations abound. In addition to two popular film festivals, the most anticipated event is, of course, the Gay Pride Parade.

Every year, on the last weekend in June, the march begins with "Dykes on Bikes." The motorcycles are lined up in alternate rows of three and four: the perfect spacing reflects the militaristic discipline of the leather-clad women. Only a few smile to acknowledge the adoration of the crowds lining Fifth Ave. — most are stone-faced, however, intimidating as they are exhilarating. The march culminates in a huge street fair around the now-famous Stonewall Inn, and at night, the top of the Empire State Building lights up lavender and white, a symbol that times really have changed.

Although Manhattan is the "gayest" of New York City's boroughs, and is home to most of the city's exciting clubs (as well as its quaint coffee houses, and its entertaining cabarets), Brooklyn and Queens both have substantial numbers of diverse peoples, who have created their own gay focal points in Park Slope and Jackson Heights.

New York is ultimately one of the greatest cities in the world for fine dining, shopping, museum-and-movie-going, bar-hopping, dancing, sight-seeing, outdoor R&R, and countless other activities enjoyed by gays, lesbians, and heterosexuals alike. However, it is misguided to think of the city as a utopia. "The biggest myth," says 26 year-old gay-rights activist Keith, "is that New York City is a giant gay playground and no one ever gets hurt. Homophobia does exist here, and every new gay resident should be aware of that, if only to spare himself or herself the shock if confronted with a harmless but uncomfortable situation. But in comparison to other American cities, New York seems to have realized that diversity is a tremendous strength and is, in many ways, light-years beyond them in terms of gay-friendliness."

Whatever religious fundamentalists and the conservative press choose to think, homosexuals and organized religion are far from mutually exclusive. The many gay and gay-friendly congregations that march every year in the Gay Pride Parade signal not only their existence, but the desire that many gays and lesbians have for a spiritual community. The following is a modest sampling of these organizations:

Metropolitan Community Church of New York
Founded in the late 1960s by Reverend Troy Perry, the MCC welcomes all individuals and is an interdenominational fellowship.
629-7440

Congregation Beth Simchat Torah
This lesbian and gay synagogue lies in the heart of Greenwich Village, the epicenter of NYC's gay community.
929-9498

West-Park Presbyterian Church
The day after the General Assembly of the Presbyterian Church struck down amendments that would have sanctified same-sex relationships, this progressive church defiantly flew the rainbow flag.
362-4890

Saint Paul the Apostle
This Roman Catholic Parish has a gay and lesbian Catholic Ministry.
265-3495

p•o•l•i•t•i•c•s
politicians

"Don't you see? The rest of the country looks upon New York like we're left-wing Communist Jewish homosexual pornographers? I think of us that way sometimes, and I live here." Although Woody Allen's words in *Annie Hall* may have rung truer in the late '70s, the city's relatively large percentage of open-minded, ultra-liberal residents means that registered Democrats outnumber registered Republicans here by five to one. Manhattan is the most heavily Democratic of the five boroughs, and, together with The Bronx, Brooklyn, and Queens, it has supported Democrats for President by significant margins in every election since World War II. As the most conservative of the boroughs, Staten Island votes Republican with the same consistency that the other boroughs vote Democrat.

As a city, New York is unique in that it contains five counties; nearly everywhere else in the United States cities are within counties and not vice versa. Each borough is its own county: Manhattan — New York County; Brooklyn — King's County; Staten Island — Richmond County; The Bronx — Bronx County; and Queens — Queens County. An 1897 charter established the office of borough president in hopes of preserving borough pride despite consolidation into one city. Each borough president ("beep" for short) serves as a cheerleader, spokesperson, and advocate for his or her own borough. Large, well-funded offices allow borough presidents to hold investigations and commissions, and issue reports and recommendations, but nothing is binding and they possess little real power aside from the fact that the press will quote them regularly. Borough presidents also appoint members of local community boards, neighborhood citizen bodies which deal with zoning issues. Community boards can raise objections to building projects, thereby stopping them permanently or just temporarily. (Call 788-7418 to find the contact information for the nearest community board.) Meetings can range from a real snooze to a royal battle: one meeting in the East Village allegedly had squatters hurling cat feces at board members unsympathetic to their plight.

As mayor since 1994, Rudolph "Rudy" Giuliani is the city's chief elected official. He is responsible for collective bargaining with the city's unionized workers, overseeing the city's budget, making political appointments that run the city's bureaucratic machinery, and serving as a member of many of the city's museums, libraries, and cultural institutions. By appealing to white, ethnic voters living in the outer boroughs, exploiting predecessor David Dinkins' supposed mishandling of racial tensions in Crown Heights, and taking advantage of the paranoia over the city's rising crime rates, Giuliani became the city's first Republican mayor in twenty-eight years, and is

now in his second term. In July, 1999, the City Council, the city's legislative branch, voted to raise the mayor's salary to $195,000 per annum, making Giuliani the highest paid city official in the country. (Council members voted to raise their own salaries as well.)

Second in command is the public advocate, currently Mark Green. Elected by popular vote, the public advocate serves as an ombudsperson dealing with complaints regarding municipal government. Since the mayor and public advocate do not necessarily have to come from the same political party — in this case, the two are politically antithetical — they may have dissenting opinions; this relationship serves as checks-and-balance, resulting in healthy but sometimes grid-locked politicking. When Mark Green dislikes a particular Giuliani administration policy, his staff can investigate and issue a scathing report about the inadequacies of city services.

City Council (and its 51 members), share power with the mayor. The Council votes on everything regulated by city government, including zoning, sanitation, quality-of-life issues, recycling, and setting city-wage taxes. Also, the Council investigates the actions of the executive branch.

Traditionally, the City Council has been monopolized by Democrats. Representation in the Council is roughly proportional to a district or borough's population. In 1990, Brooklyn with 16 Council seats had the largest population at roughly 2.3 million, followed by Queens at 2 million (14 seats), Manhattan (10) at 1.5 million, The Bronx

at 1.2 million (8), and Staten Island (3) at 379,000.

Political involvement in New York City can start with a political club. New York City Democratic political clubs are a holdover from Tammany Hall, New York's legendary Democratic political machine, which controlled city government from the late 19th Century through the early 20th Century. Initially organized by local district leaders who were part of Tammany, the clubs gave the machine its strength by providing constituent services and favors, particularly to immigrant populations. In 1933, Mayor Fiorello H. La Guardia won a three-way race as The Fusion Party candidate who opposed Tammany, and after his three terms the institutions were powerless. Despite their early demise, the clubs still exist today, each covering sets of election districts based on groupings of several city blocks. Particularly thriving are the clubs on the Upper West Side, a traditionally intellectual, liberal neighborhood. They keep Upper West Siders the "most politically active in the city." To find the name and number of a club near you, call the New York County Democratic Committee (687-6540) or the New York County Republican Committee (599-1200).

Of course, the best (and easiest) way to entrench yourself in politics is to vote, but don't be surprised when you're called for jury duty after registering, since the many federal, state, and civil court cases in the city necessitate lots of jurors. For more information about voting in New York City, or to request a registration form, call (800) 367-8683.

new york city's neighborhoods

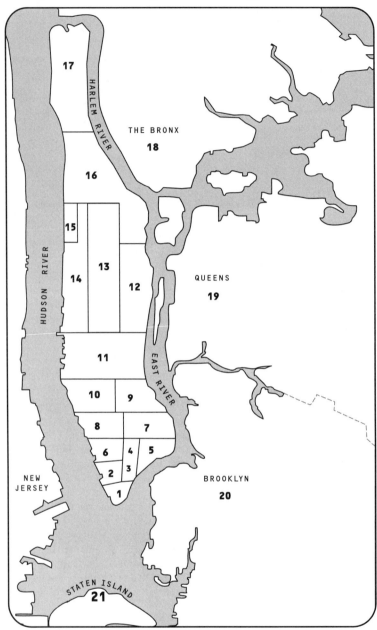

1. Lower Manhattan
2. TriBeCa
3. Chinatown
4. Little Italy
5. Lower East Side
6. SoHo
7. East Village

8. Greenwich Village
9. Gramercy
10. Chelsea
11. Midtown
12. Upper East Side
13. Central Park
14. Upper West Side

15. Morningside Heights
16. Harlem
17. Washington Heights
18. Bronx
19. Queens
20. Brooklyn
21. Staten Island

neighborhoods

lower manhattan

At the center of Lower Manhattan, the Financial District is still the hub of the world's big money transactions, but you don't need a suit and an agenda to appreciate its finer nuances. The district sits below Chambers St., and is covered by a motley assortment of architectural styles: 18th Century Georgian-Federal, 19th Century neoclassical, and modern skyscrapers.

Anyone interested in hurling themselves into murky waters over a deal gone bad will be faced with a plethora of options: the Hudson River? The East River? Or maybe consider pulling a Daryl Hannah and Splash into the Upper Bay of New York Harbor. The Brooklyn Bridge, as well-used by pedestrians and cyclists as it is by motorists, provides awesome views of Manhattan and Brooklyn Heights. The splendor of the bridge's architecture will make you feel that life in the Financial District is, indeed, worth living, however the market is faring.

Activity in Lower Manhattan is not limited to Finances. At the district's eastern edge, trucks from New England make daily 5am deliveries to the Fulton Fish Market, while lawyers and politicians make their daily journeys to the municipal buildings and City Hall, where Mayor Rudy Giuliani holds court. Interestingly, Century 21 and a smattering of discount designer stores make the area their home as well, catering in part to an increasingly large residential community.

Tourists, numbering a billion per year, flood the South Street Seaport, whose mixture of quaint cobblestone streets, sidewalk cafes, and cozy bars, all right on the water, is oddly reminiscent of San Francisco. By twilight, stockbrokers wallow in pints of Guinness in nearby TriBeCa, while other professionals head home to the suburbs and tourists trudge back to their hotels. Even as Lady Liberty lights up the harbor and silence spreads over the deserted streets, the view from atop the Twin Towers reveals that the rest of the city is still on the move; taxis honk their way down Broadway, as, further south, party boats laden with tourists circle the island's southern tip, admiring the panorama of towering buildings. Meanwhile, each round trip of the Staten Island Ferry tugs New York closer towards the next day's dawn.

A scending the steps at the Fulton St. subway station, you are surrounded by high rise buildings and the familiar smell of polluted city air. However, if you wander east a few blocks, your nose will suddenly become infused with a different smell: that of fish! It is then that you realize you've hit **South Street Seaport** — a mecca not only for all you amateur ichthyologists out there, but for entertainment as well!

It's ironic that a place that hosts upscale stores like J.Crew and Banana Republic is set in such a salty setting. As your feet tread upon cobblestone streets (closed to traffic), sailboats are in plain view. More fitting to the scenery than its chi-chi counterparts is a mini street fair in the center of the Seaport. Signs decorate the makeshift tents that house little shops and businesses like Red Rover International, The Koko Co., and African Air Craft. A directory steers you towards public restrooms and telephones, and a delicious smelling food court. If a complex more typical to suburbia isn't coming to mind, it should — the Seaport may be the closest to an outdoor mall that you can get in New York City.

If shopping isn't your thing South Street Seaport still has something for you. There are a number of museums and galleries as well as a variety of special events: a Hawaiian Luau, a human chess game, and shows by performing artists like G. Love and Special Sauce. You can also buy some fresh lemonade for the kiddies at the country style lemonade stand — complete with wooden barrels.

Treat yourself to a little fun in the sun and visit South Street Seaport where, as a welcome sign boasts, "there is always something to do."

H I S T O R Y

Not only does it contain what is known as the world's preeminent financial district, Lower Manhattan is also where New York got its start: It was here that the Dutch established the colony of New Amsterdam in 1624. As a defense against English attacks, the Dutch built a fortification that encompassed the area now known as Wall Street in 1653. Nevertheless, in 1664, Peter Stuyvesant, then governor, surrendered the colony to the English, who renamed it New York in honor of James, Duke of York.

In 1693, the British completed the Battery, at that time a fortress, on the island's southern tip.

By then, the city had reached north to Grand St., had a population of over 10,000, and a burgeoning maritime trade centered around the harbor. Rumor has it, The New York Stock Exchange was conceived in 1792 when twenty-four brokers met under a buttonwood tree on Wall St. and agreed on a standard commission rate.

Castle Clinton was established in 1808 as a defense for New York Harbor. In 1823 it became an entertainment venue that reached its peak in 1850, when Jenny Lind, "The Swedish Nightingale," had her debut. Since then it's been an aquarium and an immigrant processing center; now it's a museum with remnants on display from its chameleon-like past, as well as a ticket booth for the ferries to the Statue of Liberty and Ellis Island.

Even as manufacturing disappeared from the island's southern tier, finance ensured the area's development. Municipal buildings replaced stately colonial mansions and big business ensconced itself in majestic headquarters like the Woolworth Building.

Andrew J. Tobin Plaza

Dominated by a Twin Tower on either side, this five-acre square with a mammoth fountain at its center hosts free concerts and temporary art projects during the summer as well as the permanent work of modern artists.
Between One and Two World Trade Center, ❶❾ *to Cortlandt St.,* ❽❿ *to the World Trade Center* ♿

Battery Park

A gun battery in Colonial times, later an entrance point for millions of immigrants, the park's beautiful river view calms tourists waiting in line for a ferry to Lady Liberty.
South of State St., ❶❾ *to South Ferry* ♿

Battery Park City

Palm trees and remarkable cleanliness seem transplanted from a kinder, gentler city, though the skyscrapers looming in the distance bring back the familiar vertigo; meander alongside the Hudson on this commercial and residential complex's well-maintained esplanade and pretend that the "City Beautiful" movement really did find its way into municipal government.
Bound by Chambers St., West St., Pier A, and the Hudson River, ❶❾ *to Rector St.*

Bowling Green

The oldest extant public park in the city, it once boasted a famous statue of George III which irate Revolutionaries toppled and used for bullets.
Broadway and Battery Place, ❹❺ *to Bowling Green*

The National Museum of the American Indian

The Old Custom House contains this extensive, well-curated museum, one of the few Smithsonian Institutions outside of Washington. The exhibits are fascinating, though the federal architecture and the beautiful rotunda alone merit the trip.

1 Bowling Green (in Battery Park), 668-6624,
Open: F-W 10am-5pm, Th 10am-8pm,
❹❺ *to Bowling Green,* ❶❾ *to South Ferry* ♿

City Hall Park, City Hall

This grassy triangle marks the northern boundary of the district. Washington's army gathered here for a reading of the Declaration of Independence.
Broadway and Chambers St., ❻ *to City Hall* ♿

Statue of Liberty/Ellis Island Foundation

The city's first immigration center, in use from 1892-1932. A single fee covers the ferry ride and admission to both the Statue of Liberty and Ellis Island; visitors can trace an immigrant's path from baggage room to registry room and view the American Immigrant Wall of Honor. "Your tired, your poor, your huddled masses, yearning to breathe free," also applies to the bedraggled tourists laboring up her spiraling steps; the crown offers a spectacular view of the Harbor. Ferries depart from Castle Clinton in Battery Park every 45 minutes during the summer.
Ellis Island, 883-1986, Admission: $3-$7,
❶❾ *to South Ferry* ♿

St. Paul's Chapel

After George Washington was elected president, a magnificent service was held here in his honor. Completed in 1766, this Georgian building is the oldest in continuous use in Manhattan, sponsoring services, lectures, social programs, and free noontime music concerts.
Broadway and Fulton St., 602-0874,
❶Ⓜ❷❷❸❹❺ *to Fulton St.*

South Street Seaport

Within this complex are the Fulton Fish Market, the Fulton Market, Pier 17 shopping, the South St. Seaport Museum, and a life-size ship collection at Pier 16. Gaze at the Brooklyn Bridge from the benches along the water.
Bound by Pearl, Water, John, and Beekman Sts., and the East River, 732-7678,
❶Ⓜ❷❷❸❹❺ *to Fulton St.*

New York Stock Exchange
The world's largest security exchange and the site of some of the greatest disasters in city history. Watch the frenzied activity from a safe distance at the viewing gallery, but please, don't feed the traders.
20 Broad St. (bet. Exchange and Wall Sts.), 656-5168, Open: M-F 9am-4:30pm, ❷❸ to Wall St., ❹❺ to Wall St. ♿

Trinity Church
This 1697 Anglican parish was primped and polished in time for its 300th birthday. Check out the tombstones of Alexander Hamilton and other New York notables resting peacefully in the graveyard. Call for more information about free lunch-time concerts.
79-89 Broadway (at Wall St.), 602-0872, ❹❺ to Wall St. ♿

Federal Reserve Bank of New York
Occupying an entire city block, this edifice holds one-third of the world's gold. Don't get any funny ideas: security cameras watch from every possible angle. Free tours of the vaults are available; make reservations one week in advance.
33 Liberty St. (bet. William and Nassau Sts.), 720-5000, ❷❸ to Wall St., ♿

World Financial Center
The centerpiece of Battery Park City houses American Express, Merrill Lynch, and Dow Jones, among other financial institutions, in its four postmodern towers. The Winter Garden is the focus of the center, with palm trees, sweeping views, and upscale shops and restaurants.
West St. (bet. Liberty and Vesey Sts.), 945-0505, ❹❸❺ to World Trade Center, ❶❾ to Cortlandt St. ♿

The World Trade Center
The 110 stories of aluminum and steel make the Twin Towers the tallest buildings in New York and the second tallest buildings in the country, after Chicago's Sears Tower. A car bomb exploded in a parking garage underneath the towers in 1993, closing them for several weeks. Check out the mall in the lower level, filled with upscale shops.
Area along Church St. and the West Side Highway (bet. Liberty and Vesey Sts.), 435-4170, ❹❸❺ to World Trade Center, ❶❾ to Cortlandt St. ♿

The Alienist, 1994
In this book by Caleb Carr, detectives search for a serial killer, while painting a haunting picture of Lower Manhattan at the turn of the last century.

Wall Street, 1987
This sexy account about the insider ongoings of the stock market in the 1980s is somehow both gaudy and glamourous. Michael Douglas and Charlie Sheen team up in an avaricious scheme to make the dough but, ultimately, can money buy happiness?

Desperately Seeking Susan, 1985
This early Madonna movie uses Battery Park and its native street performers as a backdrop for the mayhem and confusion that ensues when one woman reads the personals too closely.

Fraunces Tavern

Start your morning with some old-world history in this tavern where George Washington is reported to have said farewell to his officers at a reception in 1783. With a healthy assortment of fruit, omelets, and muffins, the breakfast here is considered one of the best buys in New York.
(see Restaurants)

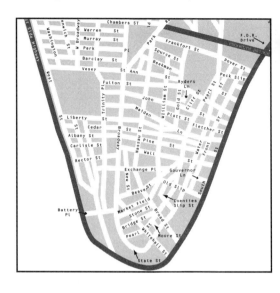

Statue of Liberty/ Ellis Island Foundation

Get some fresh air visiting the Statue of Liberty and Ellis Island. Hop a ferry at Castle Clinton for a large dose of New York history. You'll get to see how beautiful Manhattan looks from the water.
(see Sites & Parks)

[cheap thrills}

Clocktower Gallery

The 13th floor houses an avant-garde sculpture gallery. Continue up the winding stairs for views of Manhattan and an up-close look at the giant clock's inner workings.
346 Broadway (at Leonard St.), 233-1096, Cash Only, Admission (suggested): $4,
ⒶⒸ to Chambers St.

South Street Seaport

Over 100 years ago all goods that were shipped in and out of the city passed through this port. Now you'll find upscale shops, food, and history at this "mall" which begins at Water and Fulton Sts. There's the Fulton Fish Market which sells seafood to most of New York's restaurants, Pier 17 shopping, the South Street Seaport Museum, Pier 16's life-sized ship collection, and 19th Century buildings lining Schermerhorn Row.
(see Sites & Parks)

Bridge Cafe

An unpretentious place to eat some of the seafood this neighborhood is famous for and wind down your day. The intimate setting makes the experience even more of a treat.
(see Restaurants)

Fraunces Tavern Museum

For just a buck or two, you can pretend you're George Washington giving his farewell address to his officers after the Revolution at this Georgian mansion. Or you can just walk around the museum like a normal person.
(see Visual)

Staten Island Ferry

Grab a camera and some friends and be dazzled by NY's skyline along with the gaggle of tourists and commuters that will accompany you aboard.
Staten Island Ferry Terminal, South Ferry, ❶❾ to South Ferry

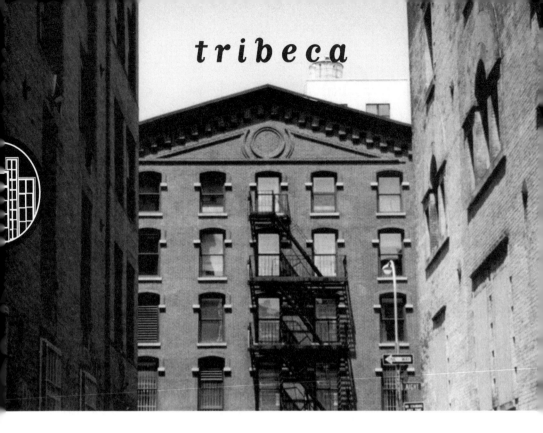

tribeca

After angry editorials, near brawls, community board meetings, and plenty of pouting, the artists who pioneered TriBeCa's minimalist, neo-industrial aesthetic have been forced to accept this neighborhood's latest stage of transition. Having preserved their galleries and performance spaces, the artists have yielded their living spaces to the financiers and other yuppies who can afford the skyrocketing rents.

Just twenty years ago, the Triangle Below Canal slumbered as an industrial wasteland of warehouses, loading docks, and back alleys. The area was ripe for refugees from SoHo, who filtered down and converted the cast-iron buildings into art-friendly living spaces. Slowly, new tenants have inherited the extensive renovations done by these artists who were forced from the neighborhood by the steep rents and the onslaught of expensive shops and high-priced restaurants.

By day, Donna Karan-clad moms push strollers and shop for gardening tools or baby clothes that would swallow most people's daily salary. Washington Market spills over with school kids around 2pm, while at night, Wall Street sends its suits and gold cards up a few blocks to descend upon the clutch of restaurants along Hudson and Franklin Sts. Robert DeNiro, the neighborhood's most famous resident and restaurateur, finances upscale eateries like Tribeca Grill, which, along with Bouley Bakery and Nobu, help define this starlit scene.

TriBeCa, however, is far from an insular, overpriced play-space like some say SoHo has become. The side streets can be foreboding and dimly lit after dark, the swanky restaurants and bistros tucked away into converted storage spaces surrounded by unconverted storage spaces and loading docks. It is nevertheless indisputable that TriBeCa is going the way of SoHo, commercially, and will soon have its very own branches of designer stores like agnès b., Robert Marc, and Marc Jacobs.

Despite TriBeCa's increasing ostentation, the Knitting Factory, a powerful presence on the TriBeCa scene, hosts everyone from Naked City to folk and roots rock to marginalized drama. CityKids, a grassroots organization that promotes youth-to-youth communication, still flourishes. But whether or not the socially conscious and the avant-garde can coexist with the nouveau riche is anybody's guess.

The outside of the building doesn't look like much, but inside, **triBeCa bodyworks** trainers are "preparing people for life."

The gym features a hot trend in physical conditioning, the Pilates Method of Body Conditioning. "Pilates strengthens you equally and symmetrically and helps you excel in everyday activities like skiing, tennis etc.," says bodyworks founder Alycea Ungaro. Pilates separates itself from other types of exercise like aerobics or body building, by working to "define what you already have" and discouraging big muscle development, according to Ungaro. Nonetheless, she quotes Joseph Pilates, who developed the system and said "You will feel better in 10 sessions, look better in 20 sessions, and have a brand new body in 30 sessions." That is, if you are committed to the program.

triBeCa bodyworks boasts eleven qualified trainers who help people use machines whose style (not age) dates back to the 1920s. The 3,000 square foot loft also includes showers and changing rooms, not to mention a rack for shoes — Pilates is done in stocking feet. While bodyworks is 90 percent private training, group classes are also offered five times a week. Recently, it has also opened a physical therapy service which has an office in the back of the building. Once you have mastered the Pilates set-up (which is no easy feat) you can share a trainer with someone else to lower costs. Private lessons are $60 ($65 for the first), while duets are $45 per session, but bodyworks also offers packages which can decrease the price of your workout. Make sure you plan ahead though — reservations for private lessons are usually booked a month in advance!

One main draw to Pilates is that, with few repetitions, "it is not boring like more traditional exercise," says Ungaro. If that isn't enough to entice you, inside triBeCa bodyworks you can see customers exercising on machines with large metal springs and leather straps — sound interesting?

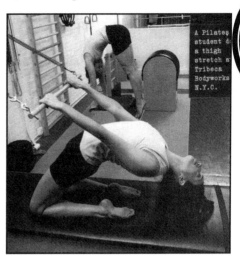

A Pilates student d a thigh stretch a Tribeca Bodyworks N.Y.C.

HISTORY

Named for its geometry, the Triangle below Canal Street was dubbed by real estate developers in the mid-1970s. Its modest beginnings can be traced back to 1813 with Bear Market, which dealt in fruit and produce. By the mid-19th Century, the area was a major point of transfer for the increased shipping and commerce moving through lower Manhattan. Its cast-iron facades and spacious five-and-six story buildings housing stores, factories, and storage facilities helped to make it a thriving light manufacturing zone.

By 1939, Bear Market and the surrounding area were renamed Washington Market, which did more business than all others markets in New York combined. It remained a vital part of the city's produce industry until most companies made an exodus from the city in the early '60s and were quickly replaced by real estate developers. The Washington Market Urban Renewal Project was launched almost immediately and office buildings, institutions such as the Borough of Manhattan Community College, and public parks sprang up in the neighborhood. In the '70s alone, the area's population jumped from 243 residents to more than 5,000, drawn by TriBeCa's new amenities.

Development continued into the '90s, albeit at a slower pace. Construction of Stuyvesant High School, the city's most competitive public secondary school, was completed in 1992. Lofts were quickly converted to residences as they had been 15 years earlier in SoHo; an important distinction was that these lofts were open to non-artists as well as artists. As a result, TriBeCa has become one of the most desirable neighborhoods in New York, with many shops, a booming restaurant scene, and a rich population.

White Street

Typical of TriBeCa's architecture melange: juxtaposed alongside Federal-style buildings are 19th Century cast-iron warehouses. No. 10 is notable for its creative stonework. Nos. 8 & 10 feature shorter stories on the upper levels, a design intended to make the building look taller.

Bet. Church St. and West Broadway, ❶❾ to Franklin St. ♿

New York Mercantile Exchange

Built in 1884, this former poultry and dairy product exchange offers visitors a glimpse of TriBeCa's commercial character, new and old. Note the Romantic architecture and the prominent tower. Converted to offices in 1987.

6 Harrison St. (bet. Hudson and Staple Sts.), 334-2160, ❶❷❸❾ to Chambers St.

Tribeca Film Center

Established by TriBeCa's most famous resident and restaurateur, Robert DeNiro, this space contains screening rooms, production offices, and the New York offices of Miramax Film, TriBeCa Production, and other filmmakers. Downstairs is DeNiro's famous Tribeca Grill.

375 Greenwich St. (bet. Franklin and North Moore Sts.), 941-4000, ❶❾ to Franklin St. ♿

Harrison Street Row

Recalling Federal-Era New York, these restored houses complement the cobbled walkways of TriBeCa's warehouse district.

At Greenwich St., ❶❾ to Franklin St. ♿

Worth St. Theater

Begun as a small-time theater company on its namesake Worth St., it's since grown into bigger digs on Laight St. and remains a testing ground for new productions that larger companies lack the freedom to attempt. A fine place to catch several one-acts that all fit into a grander theme, satisfying the urge for consistency without putting all your eggs in one basket.

13-17 Laight St., 604-4195, Cash Only, ❶❾ to Canal St.

The Screening Room

A place to catch independent and foreign film hits or classics like *Breakfast at Tiffany's* (shown every Sunday). The non-traditional seating makes it feel as comfy as a Blockbuster night, without the Bud Light and the remote. Diners at the restaurant next door get seated first for shows, so with a dinner-and-movie date, you can score a loveseat.

54 Varick St. (at Canal St.), 334-2100, ❶❾ to Canal St. ♿

sites+

Apex Art C.P.

Off the beaten path of art with a fresh perspective, this is one of the best places to find innovative work; appreciating it comes easily also, since the staffers are far less aloof than most of their SoHo counterparts. Shows tend to feature a combination of efforts by a few different artists and include both painting and sculpture.

291 Church Street (bet. Walker and White Sts.), 431-5270, **①⑨** to Franklin St. ♿

TriBeCa Performing Arts Center

Inconspicuously housed in the main building of the Borough of Manhattan Community College, this large venue is easy to miss. That would be a shame since the programming is excellent, offering multicultural music, dance, theater from around the world, and urban youth-themed performances consistent with the diverse student population. The college connection means cheap student-rate tickets.

199 Chambers St. (bet. Greenwich St. and the West Side Highway.), 346-8510, MC, V, AmEx, **①②⑧⑨** to Chambers St. ♿

movies & books

The Proprietor, 1996

The protagonist, French expatriate Adrienne Mark (played by Jeanne Moreau) explores New York City and Paris as she examines the meaning of life and the significance of her memories of her mother, from whom she was forever separated during the Nazi occupation of France.

Leviathan, 1992

While Paul Auster's wonderful novel of literary espionage features many New York neighborhoods, it specifically forecasts TriBeCa's role as an upscale artists' haven when describing glamorous love-interest/photographer Maria's move to a Duane St. loft. Though not the best known of Auster's Gotham-based books, it remains among his most compelling.

parks

a ***saturday***

Bubby's

There's often a wait at this trendy neighborhood brunch standby but since it's Saturday, hang out and do some people-watching. The cheese grits and omelets are worth the wait.

(see Restaurants)

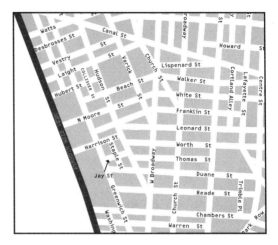

TriBeca Architechture Tour

Stroll off your meal by checking out some of the neighborhood's historic sights. White and Harrison Sts. have an array of federal-style buildings. Pick up a copy of the *TriBeCa Trib* and chill out on the grass at Washington Market Park, the neighborhood's historical epicenter.

❶❾ *to Franklin St.*

[cheap *thrills*]

Harrison Street Row

TriBeCa's all about architecture, so what better (and cheaper) activity than checking out some of the buildings that have helped make the neighborhood so popular and unaffordable.

(see Sites & Parks)

Knitting Factory

After 11pm, there's free music in the tap bar of this New York music scene sensation.

(see Music)

The Screening Room

Dinner and a movie is a classic combo; finding them under the same roof is not. Divine food and comfy little theater, the $30 prefixe includes a three-course meal and movie admission. Sometimes having a Blockbuster night just isn't good enough - this wil do the trick every time.

(see Film & TV)

Knitting Factory

Kick back with a drink and enjoy this multifaceted performance venue, featuring eclectic music, readings, comedy, and theater. Whatever the sphere, shows tend to be hip and entertaining. Check out the music section for an interview with founder Michael Dorf.

(see Music)

TriBeCa Potters

This neighborhood may have become exorbitant, but it still is home to artists and artisans. Watch the artists at work at TriBeCa Potters and browse among the items for sale between 9am and 5:30pm. Call ahead of time on the weekends.

443 Greenwich St., 2nd Floor (bet. Vestry and Desbrosses Sts.), 431-7631, ❶❾ to Canal St.

chinatown

Serried pedestrians, slick fish eyes on blue plastic, the scent of rotten fruit and deep fry — these are just some of the sensations that characterize Chinatown. Here, where Chinese soft-rock drifts down between the laundry lines, crooked alleyways, ancient tea parlors and barber shops still exist in this famous ethnic enclave, below Canal St. and east of Broadway. On Sundays, vendors hawking Chinese-style crullers with hot soy milk, fresh tofu, and bean sprouts congregate under the Manhattan Bridge. The drugstore on Grand St. still weighs out deer antlers and "dragon's eyes" with brass hand scales the way they did in China at the turn of the century, while, on Canal St., dozens of merchants each promise a better deal on imitations designer wristwatches and handbags.

Chinatown is far from the typical residential community. With over one-third of New York's 300,000 Chinese, the community is growing larger by the day. Once confined to the vicinity of Mott St., the neighborhood's burgeoning population has pushed its boundaries past the edges of SoHo and the Financial District. With new arrivals and refugees from Southeast Asia, including Vietnam, Cambodia, Thailand, and Malaysia, the community is in the midst of radical change in its racial composition as well as its geographical size: strips of Vietnamese, Thai, and Indonesian restaurants have joined the rows of Cantonese noodle and tea shops.

The oldest part of Chinatown is centered around Mott and Pell Sts., the area's main tourist drag. But this part of the neighborhood is also slowly changing with shop owners moving to the suburbs and the disappearance of mom and pop stores. In addition, since Hong Kong's repatriation, businessmen are transferring funds from abroad, turning Chinatown into what one woman described as "a little Hong Kong." In all, Chinatown's a neighborhood that calls for close attention as it shifts into the twenty-first century.

Chinatown is a best-kept secret for cooks on a budget. The blocks south of Grand St. on Mott St. and East of Mott St. on Grand St. are lined with greengrocers constantly replenishing mountains of fresh, seasonal produce like baby bok choy and bitter melon, and **fish markets** harboring swelling bins of just-out-of-the-sea fare. The prices vary from vendor to vendor but are always reasonable, especially during peak seasons. A pound of medium-size shrimp goes for $3.50, red snapper for $2.90, and salmon fillets for $4.80. You can also purchase snails, frogs, squid, and lobster without assaulting your wallet.

Kam Man (200 Canal St.), Chinatown's largest grocery store, is another place to find great bargains and wonderfully exotic ingredients. The frozen food section stocks smoked duck and wonton wrappers, while a plexiglass island in the middle of store reveals salted and dried oysters and scallops. Kam Man also sells individual containers of sweet azuki ice cream, fresh seaweed by the bag, quail eggs, and, for less confident cooks, MSG. Downstairs is the table and cookware section, with non-stick rice cookers, porcelain tea pots, and colorful sake sets.

Tea lovers should visit Ten Ren Tea & Ginseng Co, Inc. (75 Mott St.), which carries over 3,000 varieties of green and black tea.

Satisfy your sweet tooth at Fung Wong Bakery, Inc. (32 Mott St.) with almond cookies, lotus seeds cake, black bean buns, moon cakes, and more familiar treats like macaroons, apple turnovers, and sponge cake, or head back up Mott St. to May May Gourmet Chinese Bakery (35 Pell St.), where you can sample an assortment of buns, from custard cream to red bean, as well as vegetable or meat filled pastries. May May also offers a variety of weather-oriented beverages; try the lemon ginger cider in winter and the Ice Coconut Milk in the summer.

H I S T O R Y

The first documented Chinese immigrant came to New York in 1825 and by the 1870s, there were more than 2,000 Chinese within the boundaries of the Bowery and Canal, Worth, Mulberry Sts. — the area which became Chinatown proper.

Migration was not easy for the Chinese. Isolationist leaders forbade them to enter the United States until the early 19th Century, and immigrants were greeted with fear and even hatred when they arrived. Most Chinese settled in California,

working in mining and railroad construction, and were dubbed the "Yellow Menace." After the Chinese Exclusion Act of 1882 — preventing Chinese immigrants from becoming American citizens — many Chinese moved to larger cities and urban Chinatowns began to grow across the country.

Immigrants were limited to a few types of businesses, but soon there were restaurants and shops to attract visitors to the area. The population grew as restrictions and prejudice finally began to wane in the late 1960s. Recent immigrants

continue to arrive, and the neighborhood — now the most populous Chinese community in the Western Hemisphere — has stretched its borders, blurring the boundaries between itself and Little Italy. Eastern SoHo and the Lower East Side now have a significant number of Chinese residents. Despite a current population of around 100,000 and its ongoing contribution to New York City's culture, Chinatown has little representation in city government and, in general, its residents continue to be very wary of city politics.

Chatham Square Library

Four stories of books, including an impressive Chinese Heritage Collection featuring classics, keep Chinatown's avid readers busy. Available resources include free computer workshops, art, poetry, pre-college information sessions, live performances, magazines, popular fiction, videos, and Friday-night Internet training classes.

33 East Broadway (at Catherine St.), 673-6344, ❻ to East Broadway

The Chinatown Manpower Project

A nationally funded intensive bilingual vocational class aimed at teaching recent immigrants English and cooking skills before placing them in jobs in the tri-state area.

70 Mulberry St. (at Bayard St.), 571-1690, ❶❿❻❻❷❻ to Canal St.

Museum of Chinese in the Americas

No Chinatown experience is complete without a visit to this community-oriented museum, the first ever dedicated to the history of Chinese Americans. The award-winning permanent exhibition, entitled "Where Is Home?," features a moving collection of memorabilia, photographs, and commentary exploring the diverse identities and experiences of Chinese Americans.

70 Mulberry St., 2nd fl. (at Bayard St.), 619-4785, Cash Only, Admission: $1, Open: Tu-Sa, noon-5pm, ❶❿❻❻❷❻ to Canal St.

Columbus Park

There's more asphalt than grass at this bustling niche: pick-up basketball games and bladers share the space with Chinatown's elderly, who gather to play cards and mahjongg — how do you play mahjongg anyhow? — gossip, and sun themselves.

Between Bayard, Worth, Mulberry and Baxter Sts., ❶❿❻❻❷❻ to Canal St. ♿

Good Field Trading

A literary niche with an Eastern kick, this place is not for the wide hipped; still, the narrow aisles yield a varied selection of pens, stationery products, Chinese greeting cards, magazines, and writing tablets.

74 Mott St. (bet. Canal and Baxter Sts.), 431-4263, Cash Only, ❶❿❻❻❷❻ to Canal St.

K & W Books and Stationary
One of the biggest Chinese bookstores, K & W carries Hello Kitty toys and a large selection of books in Chinese and in English on topics like martial arts, bonsai care, Buddhism, and knife throwing.
131 Bowery St. (bet. Grand and Broome Sts.), 343-0780, Cash Only, ⑥⑩⑩⑩®②⑥ *to Canal St.*

Eastern States Buddhist Temple
The devout flock here daily to kneel and burn incense before the imposing porcelain Buddha. Pick up trinkets at the gift shop. *64 Mott St. (at Bayard St.), 966-6229,* ⑥⑩⑩⑩®②⑥ *to Canal St.* ♿

Zakka
Who says Chinatown is all about China? This impressive mecca of Japanese pop culture is evidence that New York is truly a melting pot, even if each ethnicity doesn't get a neighborhood named after it! (Maybe Zakka will become the epicenter of a newly dubbed neighborhood—Japanica!)
147 Grand St. (at Lafayette St.), 431-3961, MC, V, AmEx, ⑥⑩⑩⑩®②⑥ *to Canal St.*

The Year of the Dragon, 1985
This movie's violence rose to unprecedented levels, dealing with the New York Chinese mafia and biased police. Conflict between the head of the Chinese mafia and a decorated but anti-Asian cop comes to a head in an inevitable and bloody scene.

Mysterious Mr. Wong, 1935
The title character, a megalomaniac, is determined to complete his collection of the twelve gold coins of Confucius in order to have the power to own a large province in China. On his quest he captures a reporter who had been investigating a series of Chinatown murders.

@ *saturday*
IN CHINATOWN

Golden Unicorn

Start your day off with some
of the best dim sum in
Chinatown. Be adventurous
and try one of everything,
but be careful not
to get run over by the
food carts.

(see Restaurants)

Shop on Mott and Pell Streets

Head over to the commercial
center of Chinatown and either
shop 'til you drop or just look
at the wild assortment of
merchandise. You'll find
everything here from Walkmans
to kimonos. But be careful!
Just because the electronics
say Sony doesn't mean
they're made in Japan.
Ⓙ Ⓜ Ⓝ Ⓡ Ⓩ Ⓖ to Canal St.

[Map of Chinatown showing streets including Spring St, Delancey St, Broadway, W Broadway, Wooster St, Greene St, Mercer St, Crosby St, Lafayette St, Kenmare St, Broome St, Chrystie St, Bowery, Forsyth St, Grand St, Mulberry St, Mott St, Elizabeth St, Hester St, Canal St, Howard St, Lispenard St, Walker St, White St, Cortland Alley, Franklin St, Leonard St, Centre St, Baxter St, Bayard St, Pell St, Doyers St, Worth St, Thomas St, Pearl St, Park Row, James Pl, Division St, Duane St, Reade St, Trimble Pl, Church St, Catherine St, Chambers St, Centre St, Canal St]

Museum of Chinese in the Americas

Learn all about the heritage of one of the city's
largest ethnic populations for only $1.

(see Sites & Parks)

Chinatown Ice Cream Factory

Treat yourself to an ice cream taste sensation
with flavors like lychee, ginger, mango, and almond cookie.
And to think the choices used to be limited to
chocolate, vanilla, and strawberry. Heaven forbid!

(see Cafés)

Oriental Dress Company
For a truly exotic fashion
experience, get fitted for a
slick, silk Chinese dress —
or help a friend pick out
the right fabric, if you're not
the dress-wearin' kind.
(see Shopping)

Chinatown Fair
Even if you're not a video
game fanatic, you'll find
something to interest you
at this arcade at 8 Mott St.
You can play tic-tac-toe
with a chicken or get your
picture taken in a photo
booth with a friend.
*8 Mott St. (bet.
Mosco St. and Park Row),*
 to Canal St.

Bo Ky
Settle into a light end to an active day
at this excellent Chinese restaurant
which specializes in noodle soups.
Like most things in Chinatown,
you'll find it's a bargain.
(see Restaurants)

Noodle Stands
For less than it costs to do your laundry, you can enjoy
a big container of lo mein or a handful of egg rolls
bought at one of the food carts lining Canal St.
Craving Chinese food? There is no faster way
to satisfy your hankering for it!
*Canal St. (bet. Lafayette and Mulberry Sts.),
Cash Only,* ⒿⓂⓃⓇⓏ❻ to Canal St.

little italy

Once home to Italian and Irish newcomers whose transatlantic journey at the turn of the century landed them in tenements lining narrow streets, Little Italy is now getting littler and littler.

Mulberry St. and the Italian flags that wave above it, scores of restaurants with a choice of white or red sauce, and the few remaining specialty food shops that still carry stuffed peppers, black olives, and cannoli dripping with ricotta, are the only vestiges of the neighborhood's prior incarnation as an actual ethnic enclave that once stretched as far east as Orchard and Ludlow Sts., and as far west as Broadway. Chinatown is crowding in from the South and East and you might be hard pressed to find any Italians still living here.

If it's Mama Leone you're looking for, you might do better to visit Bensonhurst, Brooklyn or Belmont in The Bronx, where Italian communities flourish. In order to get the gist of what the neighborhood used to be like, you can watch Martin Scorsese's *Mean Streets* and Francis Ford Coppola's *The Godfather Part II*.

The neighborhood rallies during the 10-day festival of San Gennaro, the patron saint of Naples. Mulberry St. shimmers under twinkling lights and you might find yourself humming "That's Amore." Enjoy the festival by having some Italian "specialties" at stands selling sausage, zeppoles, Italian ice, and fried calamari. Of course, this street carnival only contributes to an atmosphere that more resembles the Italian section in Epcot Center than the Little Italy of yesteryear. But, after you feel as if you've eaten your way through Sicily and won a bear for your girlfriend, consider the advice of every fledgling mobster who's ever said, "If you can't beat 'em, join 'em." Don't offend anyone while having a good time though, or you might end up like Joey Gallo, who was gunned down at Umberto's Clam House on his birthday after he allegedly bad-mouthed a rival family.

It's early autumn, and for some weird reason you're instinctively geared up for fried dough, Italian sausage, and some good fun in the old fashioned, amusement park type of way. If you know what's what, you'll land a piece of sidewalk at the always cramped **San Gennaro Festival** in Little Italy, where greasy food and over-sized teddy bears are the way of the street.

The Feast of San Gennaro attracts over 3 million people every year, and is the oldest, largest, and liveliest festival in New York City. Maybe it's because San Gennaro is the patron saint of Naples, or maybe New Yorkers will use any excuse to take to the streets and party.

The Festival began in 1926 and has been attracting locals and tourists in hoards ever since. Officially, it is held down the stretch of Mulberry St. south of Houston, but when you need a break from all the action, slip down a side street and find one of the many small and sometimes authentic Italian restaurants where you can have a romantic dinner in a garden or hold a party gathering at the tables sprawling into the streets.

While San Gennaro is always a fun event to bring the kids to, the games attract everyone from bee-bee gun shooters to basketball hoopsters to those trying to loop a ring around a coke bottle. And though it may seem at times as if you've landed in a cheesy, 1970s carnival of kitch, the thousands of Italian-Americans present indicate that you're engaged in a timeless celebration that has everything to do with Italian and New York culture, replete with traditional artery clogging.

As long time Little Italy resident Sophia says "I wouldn't miss the San Gennaro festival for anything. I don't eat for a whole week beforehand, and my whole family comes down from the Bronx. Mama Mia!"

H I S T O R Y

When celebrated Italian-American filmmaker Martin Scorcese was growing up here in the 1940s and '50s, the neighborhood was still an Italian stronghold, anchored by the old St. Patrick's Cathedral on Mulberry St. Nowadays, the name suggests an ethnic population that, for the most part, no longer resides here.

On Mulberry St. between Prince and Spring Sts., a designer boutique stands in place of the Ravenite Social Club, a former hang-out of John Gotti and other wise guys, and surprisingly Soho-esque cafés and bars join sleek restaurants as the area's new merchant population. However, there are still remnants of the old Italian community: Head south of Houston St. on Mott or Mulberry Sts. and you'll find a string of gelati stands, gloppy Italian restaurants, and some souvenir shops where you can still buy Louis Prima tapes or "Kiss Me I'm Italian" t-shirts. The latter are the apparel of choice for the huge, glutenous autumn festival of San Gennaro, where attractions include piping hot zeppoles, fried dough, and oversized teddy bears.

Meanwhile, on West Houston St. between Thompson and Sullivan Sts., The Church of Saint Anthony of Padua honors its eponymous saint with an annual festival in June.

Additional neighborhood attractions include the old Police Headquarters at Centre and Grand Sts.. The huge dome at the top of the building was the site of Theodore Roosevelt's office when he was president of the police board under Mayor William L. Strong, beginning in 1895. Recently, a string of offbeat art galleries sprung up on Broome St., a further sign of Little Italy's "de-ethnicitation."

Elizabeth Street Company Garden Sculpture

Most Manhattanites couldn't even fit these sculptures in their living rooms, let alone any "garden" to which they may have access. However, this patch of green off of Elizabeth St. is the perfect place to escape the bustle of Houston and to dream of the English countryside.

Elizabeth St. (bet. Prince and Spring Sts.), ⑥ *to Spring St.* ♿

St. Patrick's Old Cathedral

Though it's difficult to tell now, the church was New York's first Gothic Revival structure, built in 1815 by Joseph Mangin. A fire in 1866 destroyed the historic façade, necessitating Henry Englebert's 1868 renovation. The parish consisted of a predominantly Irish immigrant population after the consecration of the new St. Patrick's Church at Fifth Ave. and 50th St. in 1879.

264 Mott St. (bet. Prince and Houston Sts.), *226-8075,* ⑥⑥ *to Prince St.,* ⑥⑥⑥⑥ *to Broadway-Lafayette St.* ♿

St. Michael's Russian Catholic Byzantine Church

This Orthodox church adds a distinctively Eastern flavor to the area, complementing its better-known Catholic neighbor.

266 Mulberry St. (bet. Prince and Houston Sts.), ⑥⑥⑥⑥ *to Broadway-Lafayette St.*

The Police Building

The domed edifice built in 1909 by Hoppin and Koen served as the city's main police headquarters for nearly 65 years. Its new copper dome was crafted by the same French artisans who restored the Statue of Liberty's flame and now shelters 55 co-op apartments.

240 Centre St. (bet. Grand and Broome Sts.), ⑥ *to Spring St.*

Ferrara Bakery and Café

America's oldest espresso bar, the place has been around since 1892, but we hear the espresso they serve isn't nearly that old. Everything is homemade by the family that's owned it since its inception.

195 Grand St. (bet. Mulberry and Mott Sts.), 226-6150, MC, V, AmEx, D, Diners, ⑥⑥⑥⑥ ⑥⑥ *to Canal St.*

Former site of the Ravenite Social Club

Until recently, 247 Mulberry St. (just below Prince St.), was the site of the Ravenite Social Club, a longtime Mafia hangout. Even though the building's facade had been bricked up to evade FBI surveillance, the Feds somehow managed to bug the building and John Gotti was arrested there in December 1990. The ground floor's brick facade was recently replaced with a shiny glass storefront, and a boutique has opened.

247 Mulberry St. (at Prince St.), ⑥ *to Spring St.*

Former Y.M.C.A Building
Otherwise known as the Bunker, this building was built in 1884 and designed by architect Bradford L. Gilbert in the Queen Anne style, with arched windows and irregular details. It is one of the area's most interesting buildings, and it housed some of New York's legends — painter Fernand Leger lived there in 1940 and 1941; writer William S. Burroughs kept an apartment there from 1974 until his death in 1997; and Mark Rothko also lived there for a time.
222 Bowery (bet. Prince and Spring Sts.),
6 to Bowery, **JM** to Bowery

Most Holy Crucifix Church
How New York is this? A Roman Catholic church in Little Italy, smack up against an irreverent art gallery, which offers Sunday mass in English (10am), Chinese (11am) and Spanish (12:30pm), but not in Italian. Tri-lingual weekly services are also held regularly. The building itself is worth checking out, a stately stone structure set among more modernized warehouses, tenements, and a growing number of artists' spaces, the owners of which found either the rent or the atmosphere (or both!) of nearby SoHo too much to take.
378 Broome St. (bet. Mott and Mulberry Sts.), 226-2556,
6 to Spring St., **JM** to Bowery

movies & books

Donnie Brasco, 1997
"Everybody's hearda Lefty from Mulberry Street," says Lefty himself, played by Al Pacino. This true story of an FBI agent (the title character, played by Johnny Depp) and his immersive, two-year infiltration of Little Italy's organized crime scene, co-stars Michael Madsen, Bruno Kirby, and Anne Heche. Some say this is one of the best gangster flics out there.

That Old Feeling, 1997
This silly comedy with scenes in Little Italy stars Bette Midler and Dennis Farina playing a divorced couple who begin an affair at their daughter's wedding, much to their own surprise.

a 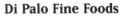 s a t u r d a y
IN LITTLE ITALY

Di Palo Fine Foods

You will swear you're shopping
in Italy when you enter this little
market run by gourmet Italians.
Di Palo is the perfect place to
find fresh mozzarella, mascarpone,
ricotta, and homemade sausages.
Pick up stuff for dinner or nibble
on some early morning treats.
(see Shopping)

Calypso

Walk north on Mott St. to this
funky boutique which attempts to
bring an international-island
aesthetic to Little Italy.
The prices all-too-closely
mirror those of fashion boutiques
only blocks away in SoHo,
but it's worth a glance at.
(see Shopping)

[cheap thrills}

Alleva Dairy, Inc.

For under $5, fourth-generation owner Bob Alleva
serves up hot and cold sandwiches authentic enough
to keep the idea of Little Italy respectable.
(see Shopping)

Di Palo Fine Foods

Especially cheap considering you'd have to
fly to Tuscany to find ingredients like these.
Choice items range from fresh mozzarella,
sun-dried tomatoes, sausages, bread, etc.
(see Shopping)

Strolling On Mulberry St.

Take an afternoon stroll down Mulberry St., admiring the plethora of little Italian restaurants and the variety of knickknacks being sold along the way.

The Big Cigar Co.

Where Mulberry St. intersects with Grand St. you'll find that fragrant tobacco lures the cigar-smoker into this store to gaze at the collection of fine smokes. *193A Grand St. (at Mulberry St.), 966-9122, MC, V, AmEx, Diners,* ❶❷❸ to Grand St.

Ferrara Bakery and Café

Relax with an espresso and Italian pastry at this neighborhood institution after a day of walking and browsing.
(see Cafés)

The San Gennaro Festival

Get yourself a glacier-sized Italian ice and ogle the macho men trying to win oversized stuffed animals for their girlfriends. Mingle with tourists, natives, and dancers along Mulberry St., during one of the last remnants of an authentic Italian pressence in this neighborhood.
(see Side Bar)

It's 10am and the sun is already beating down, serving up the first presummer scorcher. Clever Lower East Side locals adapt, setting up folding tables and chairs, and resume their Saturday morning activities. The residents compete for sidewalk space on the cluttered side streets of Essex and Norfolk, gathering in front of beaten-down chop shops and yellow-and-red-bannered bodegas. Some nibble at early lunches and mingle, and others play cards or dominoes, as salsa music pours out of windows and cars.

Up and down the main streets of the Lower East Side you'll find a string of shabby boutiques brimming with leather jackets and fabrics, frilly dresses and kids' clothing. Stepping onto Delancey St. is like stepping back in time; there are dime stores and lingerie stores still run by families who arrived in the U.S. fifty years ago.

The Williamsburg Bridge bestows on the area a transient feel, presenting the perfect metaphor as it shuttles passengers onto Delancey, reminiscent of the first major wave of immigrants who passed through Ellis Island and landed in the towering tenement landscape of the Lower East Side. The Lower East Side was once the most overpopulated, integrated neighborhood in world. One of the largest ethnic pockets was the Jewish one that, in 1920, was home to 400,000. Nowadays the Puerto Rican and Dominican presence dominates, but the Jewish culture lingers on in Yiddish theaters, and kosher delicatessens and food shops like Katz's Delicatessen and Kossars Bakery.

The Lower East Side was hit hard by drugs and other criminal activity in the '70s, and locals had to pool their strength and resources in order to reclaim "Loisaida." The Clemente Soto Vélez Cultural Center champions local Hispanic culture, housing theaters, art galleries, and studios for local artists, and is a stabilizing presence in the area, devoting much energy to improving the quality of life and instilling a sense of local pride. Thanks to their efforts, combined with those of local block associations, the crime rate and drug traffic have plummeted, making it a safer neighborhood. Evidence of this is the influx of trendy shops and night spots, mostly along Ludlow St. East of Essex, when the trendy bars and boutiques all but peter out, and the salsa music and smell of salt fish permeate the senses, you are reminded that the Lower East Side is not simply the latest area for the hipper-than-thou crowd to invade, but a diverse neighborhood with a long and interesting history.

For anyone seeking to understand the immigrant experience, the **Lower East Side Tenement Museum** is the requisite sequel to the Ellis Island Museum. Between 1863 and 1935, this building was home to 7,000 people from over 20 nations. Daily tour groups are kept small, under fifteen people, to preserve the intimacy of this heartrending look into the private lives of the families who lived here.

Visitors are shown the preserved, original flats, bleak and bare as they would have been when an immigrant family was first ushered into its new home. The tour then continues with a view of several apartments restored to a furnished incarnation. The visual reminders of the squalor and privations suffered by these immigrant families is supplemented by personal stories of each.

The museum also offers walking tours of the neighborhood, pointing out historical features which remain intact and those which survive onlyin memories and town records. For visiting families with children, the museum recommends a visit to the Confino family's apartment, an interactive experience with various costumed educators playing the part of Victoria Confino, a thirteen year-old Jewish immigrant, showing the way her life was lived and taking questions from the audience.

The popularity of this museum has grown recently. According to one museum employee, even the jaded denizens of New York City have found these tours enlightening. As the country's only tenement museum, it offers a unique perspective.

Amenities include free parking and admission to screenings of Lower East Side video histories. A gift shop features nostalgic New York curios and an impressive array of books about New York and the Lower East Side. Intriguingly, there is a comprehensive list of the families who once lived in the historically preserved tenement building. From this list, visitors may find themselves touched in ways even more personal way than they may have expected.

H I S T O R Y

For immigrants traveling from the provincial areas of Europe, the tenements which dominated the landscape of the Lower East Side must have been a chilling sight. Infamous for providing the worst housing conditions in the city, these five-story firetraps absorbed most of the first major wave of immigrants which passed through Ellis Island and could not afford anything better. During the last two decades of the 19th Century, the largely Irish population was joined by Italians and Eastern European Jews who crowded in by the tens of thousands.

New laws and housing plans failed to alleviate the situation. The first city housing project, built in 1936 as a last-ditch effort, portended the limited success of projects in general. But great spirit arose out of poverty and the neighborhood soon became as well known for its wealth of intellectual and artistic life as for its overcrowding. During the early part of the twentieth Century, Yiddish theater flourished along Second Ave., area newspapers grew into forums for intellectual debate, and many famous performers like George Gershwin, Irving Berlin, and the Marx Brothers cut their teeth here. The '50s and '60s saw revolutionaries, writers, and musicians populating the northern boundaries, an area that later expanded and became known as the East Village.

The Lower East Side fell into decline as rents once again decreased when crime, drug dealing, and dilapidated housing became prominent neighborhood features. In the '80s, however, the area stabilized somewhat after an influx of Latinos (who dubbed the area "Loisaida"), which led up to today's rapid resurgence.

East River Park

Every Saturday and Sunday in the warmer months, the park fills up with families from the nearby projects who come here to barbecue, fish, play ball, bike, or just hang out in the shadow of the Williamsburg Bridge. A walk through this riverside park reveals the romantically derelict urban landscapes of industrial Brooklyn. Don't venture here after dusk or on rainy days, when it can get a little sinister.
Montgomery to 12th Sts. (east of East River Drive), ❿Ⓜ❷ *to Essex St.,* ❻ *to Delancey St.* ♿

Eldridge Street Synagogue

Eastern European Jews erected the Lower East Side's first large-scale building in 1887. With its multi-hued stained glass windows, brilliant frescoes, and intricate woodwork, the synagogue stood out for many years amidst the notorious Lower East Side tenements. It fell into disrepair during hard times, but in recent years, the Eldridge Street Project has made significant renovations.
12 Eldridge St. (bet. Canal and Division Sts.), 219-0888, ❿Ⓜ❷ *to Essex St.,* ❻ *to Delancey*

Lower East Side Tenement Museum

These are permanent, interactive exhibits dubbed the "Confino Apartment" and the "Gumpertz & Baldizzi Apartments." The Confino is the exhibition of a Sephardic-Jewish immigrant family in 1916 and the others were restored to look like they did in 1870 and 1935.
90 Orchard St. (at Broome St.), 431-0233, MC, V, AmEx, Admission: $6-$8, Open: Tu-F 1pm-4pm, weekends 11am-4:30pm, ❿Ⓜ❷ *to Essex St.,* ❻ *to Delancey*

Esso

If there is a mien that suggests I-just-became-legal at a drinking establishment, then the artistic counterpart that suggests I-just-finished-art-school reigns at this funky downtown space, where pop art is reworked for a generation that grew up on the Smurfs and Atari.
191 Chrystie St., 6th Fl. (bet. Rivington and Stanton Sts.) 714-8192, ❻ *to Second Ave.* ♿

Ludlow St.

Grandma won't believe it — "chic" and "Ludlow St." used in the same sentence?!? Well, it's true. Between Houston and Delancey Sts., explore a trendy (albeit still a grimy) expanse of bars, boutiques, and vintage clothing and shoe stores. Hurry, before the world catches on and prices climb higher than the Chrysler Building.
❻ *to Second Ave.*

Nada

A storefront theater that in a few short years has acquired a wide-ranging reputation, including an Obie award. Catch a show almost every night.

167 Ludlow St. (bet. Houston and Stanton Sts.), 420-1466, Cash Only, **F** to Second Ave &

Collective Unconscious

Every possible configuration of campy art and anti-art event takes place at this downtown performance space. The hip, tongue-in-cheek crowd doesn't take anything very seriously — especially not the art world. Popular open mike at Reverend Jen's Anti-Slam, Wed. nights. 145 Ludlow St. (bet. Stanton and Rivington Sts.), 254-5277, Cash Only, **F** to Second Ave.

Storefront for Art and Architecture
Only open from March to November, this unique international gallery favors more abstract works, and often organizes its shows along geographical themes. The unusual name is, not surprisingly, derived from the gallery's unique facade; part of a growing number of art spaces located beyond the posh confines of SoHo and 57th St.
97 Kenmare Street (bet. Mulberry and Lafayette Sts.) 431-5795, **6** to Spring St.

movies & books

Hester Street, 1974
At the turn of the last century, a young Jewish immigrant joins her husband in New York City and finds he has forsaken the Old World and expects that she will follow suit. Carol Kane was nominated for an Academy Award for her stellar performance.

Crossing Delancey, 1988
Amy Irving stars as a woman who struggles as she falls in love with the proprietor of a pickle shop on Delancey St. This favorite as been called a "small but enjoyable celebration of the simple life." Catch a glimpse of the tenement houses lining the Lower East Side.

a *saturday*
IN LOWER EAST SIDE

Tonic
Stroll over to Tonic for
an early brunch of waffles
and fresh berries.
This cavernous spot
is equal parts café and
performance space.
(see Restaurants)

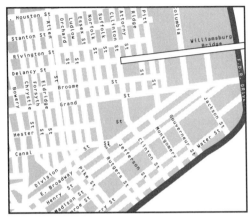

Vintage Shopping
There are some great vintage
clothing shops, especially on
Orchard St. (e.g. Cherry) and
on Ludlow St., where you can
find good deals on button-down
shirts, slips, and dresses.
Also try the Hester Street
Shoe Outlet on for size.
(see Shopping)

[cheap thrills}

Arlene Grocery
This amateur music stage is a key location for
checking out emerging talent. Admission is free,
so buy a brew or two to keep business booming.
(see Music)

Liz Christy Garden
Take a midday stroll with your paramour in this
most intimate and beautiful of Manhattan's flower gardens.
Northeast corner of Houston St. (at Bowery), **F** *to Second Ave.*

Economy Candy

Recharge with the
best selection of candy
this side of Willy Wonka's
factory. Everyone needs
a little sugar rush
to get them through
a New York City day!
The Turkish delight is said
to be especially divine.
Go basic, go exotic, just go!

(see Shopping)

Lower East Side Tenement Museum

Don't miss the free video
"South of Delancey" featured
in the gallery which tells all
about Lower East Side living.
For a more personal look
there is a guided tour for $8
($6 for students and seniors)
of several apartments in the
building that look as they
originally did from 1863
through 1935.

(see Sites & Parks)

Torch

Slip into one of the half-moon booths at this sexy '40s-style
French supper club. Sip on a Martini, have a fabulous meal,
and enjoy a live blues performance right in front of your table.
If there's a better way to end a busy day in Manhattan,
we don't know it. Sit back, relax, and please - enjoy!

(see Restaurants)

Delancey Street

Stores offering cheap, cheerful shoes and hip-hop gear along
this vibrant, if somewhat derelict, commercial stretch
make for an urban (not urbane) outing,
a throwback to an older New York.
🄵 to Delancey St., 🄹🄼🅉 to Essex St.

soho

Never, Never Land never looked so good, or cost so much!

Featuring cobblestone streets and converted warehouses surrounded by intricate mazes of wrought-iron fire escapes, landings, and steps, SoHo is far from the artists' refuge it was twenty years ago. While its real estate is still coveted, it is now reserved for those who can shell out lofty rental fees for its open areas. As a result, some consider SoHo an exorbitant fantasy world, more suited for those who pose as artists than the real thing. However, it is still the city's most prestigious artscape, where names are made and sold — though nowadays some of the biggest names are on the labels of clothing by designers like agnès b. and Marc Jacobs, rather than scrawled in the corners of paintings.

While the SoHo lifestyle is terrifically expensive, gallery browsing on Wooster and Mercer Sts. is conversely free as can be, one of the cities best cultural resources for those unable or disinclined to spend a bundle. The neighborhood now attracts a mass of shoppers with platinum cards and tourists eager to soak up New York City Bohemia and get some shopping done, all in one day. Weekends, traffic, both motorized and pedestrian, moves at a snail's pace, as both visitors and residents ogle the newest trends in fashion and art, or leaf through art books at outdoor stands. SoHo also features chic cafés and restaurants like Balthazar and Zoë, often with an appropriately Parisian flare, whose crowded spaces are packed with beautiful people, aloof and inaccessible to the average John or Jane.

While fitting into the glamourous SoHo scene is an understandable aspiration, it is not easily attained. What most of us think of as our Sunday best, so to speak, won't even raise an eyebrow below Houston, where fine fabrics and Florentine leather seem to be run of the mill, and everyone looks like they just stepped off the fashion runway. Better off beginning with a few day trips to see if your ego and your wallet can stand up to SoHo's demands.

Founded in 1986 by the venerable poet Stanley Kunitz, **Poets House,** an airy loft with floor-to-ceiling windows, houses one of the largest poetry collections in the country — boasting over 35,000 volumes — while still not making you feel like you're in a library. (For example, you can bring in food and talk at will without being constatnly hushed!) Comfortable couches and chairs, along with a very friendly staff, allow you to wile away your afternoon, taking in poetry from the well-known (Wallace Stevens, John Ashberry, Jewel) to the more obscure.

Poets House welcomes everyone to view their collection for free, with the motto "a place for poetry for everyone and by everyone." You can browse through new and old poetry without dealing with the insensative Grisham-reading crowd over at Barnes & Noble. Moreover, Poets House leads seminars throughout the year on various topics (such as "How Aspiring Poets Can Get Published"). In total, Poets House also has over thirty event/programs annually, including a Poetry Walk across the Brooklyn Bridge and a presentation of all new poetry published that year.

For those poetry detractors, Poets House Program Director Catherine Coy, herself a Columbia Writing Division Graduate, comments that "we operate according to the philosophy that if you hate poetry, you just haven't met the right match."

So whether for the skeptical or the already-converted, this house of endless volumes will provide friendly banter and new looks at the genre. The out-of-the-way second floor setting of the Poets House curbs the amount of meandering street traffic which passes through, making the experience all the more tranquil, enjoyable, and, well, poetic.

H I S T O R Y

Recently, southern Manhattan has seen the naming of mini-neighborhoods, such as NoHo and NoLita. The process of gentrifying and such acronymic identifying of areas started with chi-chi SoHo.

The region SOuth of HOuston, until about 30 years ago, was simply seen as the southern edge of Greenwich Village. Heading farther downtown, industry ruled until the western fringe of Chinatown, followed by Wall Street.

The district's buildings were legacies from the Civil War era; once the need for armaments subsided, foundry owners converted their rolling stock to the production of building materials, and the great cast-iron buildings they raised in the post-war industrial expansion now mark this neighborhood as one of New York's first and finest architecturally rich enclaves.

Attracted by the cheap, expansive, well-lit spaces, artists began moving into the neighborhood in the '60s. Word of mouth spread quickly, and a colony took root. Early SoHo pioneers liken the community's 'pitch-in-and-help' practice to barn raisings: With the help of friends, artists would install wiring, plumbing, and heating in non-residentially zoned spaces.

Eventually, galleries sprang up to showcase local work. By the mid-1980s, outsiders began to take note of the change, and bigger (and pricier) galleries, along with expensive designer boutiques, moved in. Nowadays, Broadway anchors a growing retail district, with nationally-known stores opening huge emporiums down the boulevard, while West Broadway hosts galleries, hot restaurants, and the area's first hotel, the chic Soho Grand.

The Puck Building

Erected in 1886, this building was originally a printing plant for Puck, America's first humor magazine. Today, the first floor hosts galas and the upper floors have been converted into apartments and offices, including those of the NY Press. Puck still grins from the northeast corner of the building.
295 Lafayette St. (at Houston St.), 274-8900, **BDFQ** *to Broadway-Lafayette St.* ♿

New York Open Center

A holistic learning center which offers lectures, workshops, and weekend retreats on topics ranging from screenwriting to flamenco dancing; call for a catalog. The meditation room is open to the public free of charge, pillows provided, if you forgot to bring your own.
83 Spring St. (between Crosby and Lafayette Sts.), 219-2527, **6** *to Spring St.* ♿

Poets House

This free reading room and resource center houses the largest collection of poetry books in the country. Current poetry and literary periodicals are available for browsing, and Walkmans are provided for listening. Call for information about programs.
72 Spring St. (bet. Crosby and Lafayette Sts.), 431-7920, **6** *to Spring St.* ♿

FIRE Museum

If a field trip to the fire station is a favorite childhood memory, don't miss this chance to relive it. The collection, housed in a renovated Beaux-Arts style firehouse from 1904, is the country's largest; it's full of all standard firehouse trappings, old engines and pump cars, and plenty of intriguing New York City fire history.
278 Spring St. (bet. Houston and Varick Sts.), 691-1303, MC, V, AmEx, Admission: $1-$4, Open: Tu-Su, 10am-4pm, **CE** *to Spring St.* ♿

Guggenheim SoHo

Opened in 1992, an ENEL virtual reality gallery and an electronic reading room with CD-ROMs are a couple of the ultramodern highlights of this downtown counterpart to its Museum Mile heavyweight. Though the architecture is hardly Frank Lloyd Wright, the SoHo building, designed by Arata Isozaki, is airy and conducive to the curators' ambitious programs, which re-examine 20th century innovators like Max Beckmann and showcase contemporary stars like media artist Bill Viola. Come Sundays at 2pm for a free tour of the collection.
575 Broadway (at Prince St.), 423-3500, Cash Only, Admission: $5-$8, Open: Su, W-F 11am-6pm, Sa 11am-8pm, **NR** *to Prince St.* ♿

The Drawing Center

This nonprofit organization has an extensive collection of works on paper, including lots of drawings by a variety of new and established artists. The operation has been so successful that a second space recently opened across the street.

35 Wooster St. (bet. Grand and Broome Sts.), 219-2166, Admission: free, Open: Tu-F 10am-6pm, Sa 11am-5pm, **Ⓐ**Ⓒ**Ⓔ** *to Canal St.* ♿

Joyce SoHo

All professional and aspiring dancers are familiar with this branch of the Joyce, the venue of choice for seeing all genres in a setting that's not stiflingly formal. Performances are Thursday-Sunday nights, with tickets available thirty minutes before curtain.

155 Mercer St. (bet. Houston and Prince Sts.), 334-7479, Cash Only, **Ⓝ**Ⓡ *to Prince St.* ♿

SoHo Grand Hotel

Currently the hottest hotel in New York, this newcomer made headlines and angered neighborhood residents as the first hotel in SoHo. Everything is in sync with the neighborhood: artsy, avant-garde types walk through the cutting-edge industrial lobby to their custom-designed digs. You can request a black goldfish to accompany you during your stay (and keep it if you want to when you check out!). In keeping with the cyber-sexy image, you can even make reservations on their website: http://www.SoHoGrand.com.

310 West Broadway (bet. Canal and Grand Sts.), 965-3000, MC, V, AmEx, Diners, D, Rooms: $334-$354, **Ⓐ**Ⓒ**Ⓔ** *to Canal St.* ♿

movies & books

Ghost, 1990

Ever had a dream of living in SoHo? Well get a taste of it through Sam and Molly's loft in this tear-jerker. Their renovated apartment has airy windows and polished wooden floors — not to mention a potters wheel to add just the right arty touch. This sappy romance about a love so strong that it defies death, stars Demi Moore and Patrick Swayze.

Great Expectations, 1998

This modern day version of Dickens' classic novel draws on the SoHo gallery scene. Ethan Hawke stars as the young man with "great expectations"— in this case that entails becoming an artist at the center of the New York City art world. Some may cringe at the "adaptation," but all in all, it's worth it. From the standpoint of City accuracy, Hawke oddly shuttles around downtown on the **Ⓖ**, the only subway line which in fact never enters Manhattan.

a saturday

I N S O H O

Jerry's

Get your butt out of bed,
pick up the *Times,* and get on
line for brunch at Jerry's as
early as possible, because everyone else in SoHo is doing it, too.
Once you've settled in, spread out
and stay awhile.
(see Restaurants)

Shopping

SoHo is one big shopping mecca,
with stores filled with everything
from designer clothes to expensive housewares to upscale cosmetics. The whole
of SoHo is worth exploring,
but Prince and Spring Sts. are
lined with premium shops. You'll
find everything from major chains
to independent boutiques.
NR to Prince St.

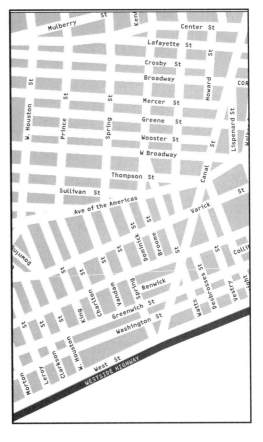

[cheap thrills}

The SoHo Grand Bar

Imbibe a fancy cocktail, as the glamour set
comes and goes. You'll fit in. Really.
(see Nightlife)

The New Museum of Contemporary Art

In the tradition of Museum Mile, this terrifically intriguing
museum, featuring contemporary work, lets you in
for free once a week: Thursdays, 6pm-8pm.
(see Visual Arts)

The Museum for African Art
SoHo is all about art, and this is a viable alternative to the Guggenheim SoHo and gallery scene, and a terrific entrée into folk art, sculpture, and more conventional media.
(see Visual Arts)

Zoë
Get here early and find a seat at the bar while you wait for your table at this elegant, welcoming hot spot. The menu changes seasonally and it's always right on.
(see Restaurants)

The SoHo Grand Bar
Show off your hot new outfit in this new hotel lounge for the hipper-than-thou crowd. Partake in a pretty postprandial cocktail and watch as your fellow fashionistas come and go.
(see Nightlife)

Gallery Hopping
You're in SoHo after all, so pick up a free copy of the *Gallery Guide* at any major gallery and spend the afternoon checking out the huge variety of art the district has to offer. Don't forget to nod appreciatively... *Wooster and Greene Sts. (bet. Prince and Grand Sts.),* 🄲🄴 to Spring St.

east village

Rents are up, the cell-phone set lines sidewalks looking for a signal, most of the squatters and artists are long gone and almost nobody remembers the 1988 riots in Tompkins Square Park. But while it takes more cash than it used to, the East Village is not quite over: it's a pathology that can be treated but not cured, still a hotbed of bars and street activity, even on cold winter nights. In the summer, it can be explosive.

If Tompkins Square Park is more genteel now than in the past, it still remains a stomping ground for Socialists, Pinkos, Reds, squatters, artists and other left-wingers. Though it's since moved to the West Side, Wigstock, the biggest drag fest of all time, began there — its camp, sass and political overtones a perfect match for East Village sensibilities. You can still find drag queens on Sundays at Stingy Lulu's, every evening serving food at Lucky Cheng's, on the street with girlfriends of both sexes, everywhere.

A scene from *Die Harder*, shot in the park a few years ago, forced a clean-up of sorts, though city workers are said to have found a pot plant near one of the park buildings since then. Most people think it was spurious, like volunteer corn sprouting in a field of soybeans, but others think it was more than a freak occurrence. Not coincidentally, "NYPD Blue" is set in the East Village; meanwhile, film school kids have probably shot every lamppost, fire hydrant, and phone booth ten times over.

This town is built on used-tos, and St. Marks used to be the hip street of the East Village. Not anymore. There you can get tattoos, cheap jewelry, used CDs and a few good meals, but Ave. A is now the vein of the East Village. Other streets such as 11th St. or First Ave. are included on maps, but they don't have the vibe, the tension, the cha-cha-cha that Ave. A has.

As the realtors who dubbed the East Village in the first place look for new hooks, subsections within the area have sprung up in recent years, all with snazzy nomenclature: Trendy NoHo fits between the Villages, bordered by Lafayette St. and Second Ave. to the west and east, and (go figure) Houston to the south. NoLita (North of Little Italy) describes the intersection of NoHo, the East Village, and the Lower East Side. While these acronymic derivatives still fit under the umbrella of East Village, they are growing too refined (not to mention pricey) to stay much longer under its auspices.

Performance spaces come in all shapes and sizes in NYC, including old public school buildings: downtown's hippest example of this phenomenon is **Performance Space 122**.

Mark Russell, executive director of P.S. 122 since 1983, has strengthened its identity as a showcase for daring work. Past and present artists include Japanese choreographer Min Tanaka, monologist Eric Bogosian, and puppet theater company The Elemantals. (P.S. 122 is a venue for the annual International Festival of Puppetry.) Russell sometimes invites established artists whose affiliation with P.S. 122 may go back a number of years. For instance, Spalding Gray workshopped his latest piece here in the fall of 1998, an invitation which stemmed from the fact that Russell felt Gray was "trying to stretch himself in a different way."

Controversy is no impediment to a spot in P.S. 122's schedule: Both Ron Athey and Karen Finley, survivors of political battles over their artistic funding, have drawn appreciative crowds here in times past. P.S. 122's own funding comes from a variety of sources, though not from the Feds anymore — Russell notes P.S. 122 has been "NEA-free" for two years.

P.S. 122 has a commitment to welcoming non-traditional audiences, which means in part making theater-going an accessible, affordable experience. This two-pronged attack on stuffed-shirt theater makes attending P.S. 122 shows fun. Many attend shows here because they know that, regardless of what's slated for a particular night, they know they're in for a lively evening. So while you're roaming the streets of the East Village, be sure to drop in at P.S. 122 and take in some cutting-edge art and performance — guaranteed your grade school never hosted the like!

H I S T O R Y

Long a haven for social dissidents, the East Village supports a cult of permissiveness. Much of the popular mythology of the neighborhood centers around a beatnik past and its cast of characters, including LeRoi Jones (now Amiri Baraka) and Charles Bukowski. The recreational drug use of literary luminaries like William S. Burroughs also set the stage for the East Village's darker side.

Drug traffic exploded during the economic plunge of the '70s, and led landlords to torch and abandon buildings, leaving the area depressed and undesirable. Drawn by the same low rents which attracted artists, anarchists, and squatters to Alphabet City, immigrants settled in the area. Puerto Ricans founded the community of Loisaida, which blurs the boundary between the East Village and the Lower East Side; Indians crowd around the mecca of 6th St., and an enclave of Ukrainians claims lower Second Ave.

The sense of community which these disparate groups have achieved is largely due to their joint efforts toward rebuilding their neighborhood, reclaiming it from drug dealers and prostitutes by planting gardens and founding community arts centers on the rubble of abandoned lots.

In the early '90s, the East Village was "discovered." Since then, its popularity has grown exponentially, and pricey restaurants and cyber cafés have followed the crowds. Now that the area has become economically viable, the city wants its property back to accommodate the upwardly mobile college kids and trendies who want to live in this bastion of "authenticity." Only time will bear out the results of this struggle, but the indomitable spirit which pervades the East Village will never go quietly into the night.

Community Gardens

Explore the nooks and crannies of Alphabet City and you'll be sure to come upon at least one of a number of community owned and operated gardens, such as the lovely retreat on 6th St. and Ave. B, where poetry readings, performances, and festivals are frequently held. When it's open during the day, take advantage of the shade.

Throughout Alphabet City, 🄕 to Second Ave., 🄛 to First Ave.

Tompkins Square Park

Major renovations in 1992 improved the park's facilities and safety, and the recreational courts, working bathrooms, and open green space attract families, tourists, and local oddballs alike, enlivening the park year-round. On any given weekend, you may stumble across a free concert or arts-and-crafts festival in the park, but the best events are spontaneous, like the drum circles, impromptu chess marathons, and the endless parade of East Villagers walking their dogs.

7th to 10th Sts. (bet. Aves. A and B), 🄕 to Second Ave., 🄛 to First Ave. ♿

Ukrainian Museum

This small museum highlights contemporary Ukrainian culture and history. Exhibits on the two floors rotate, so call ahead to find out what's on. Recent exhibitions have included student art, folk art, and Easter eggs.

203 Second Ave. (bet. 12th and 13th Sts.), *228-0110, Cash Only, Admission: $2-$3*, *Open: W-Su 1pm-5pm*, 🄛🄝🄡④⑤⑥ to 14th St. - Union Sq. ♿

Bullet Space

This "Urban Artist Collaborative," in a deteriorating building, showcases city artists known for political and challenging works. The stark gallery also has a musical space, community center, and residence space for artists. Open weekends 2pm-5pm, by appointment only.

292 East 3rd St. (bet. Ave. C and D), *982-3580*, 🄕 to Second Ave.

Cooper Union

An all expense paid college specializing in art, architecture, and engineering education, Cooper Union's standards are some of the highest in the country. The school houses the Houghton Art Gallery and the Great Hall, the site of an 1860 speech by Abraham Lincoln.

7 East 7th St. (at Third Ave.), *353-4100*, ⑥ to Astor Pl. ♿

Public Theater

Founded by the legendary Joseph Papp, "A Chorus Line" started here. The beautiful red brick Italian Renaissance style building was once the Astor Library and became the permanent home of the New York Shakespeare Festival in 1967. Along with the Bard

and other classics, the five stages here also host an eclectic mix of European imports, established, and up-and-coming American playwrights. New York's most venerable avant-garde theater, now featuring Joe's Pub, a performance space/bar featuring live music, dance, and spoken word.

425 Lafayette St. (bet. Astor Pl. and 4th St.), 539-8500, MC, V, AmEx, D, ⑥ *to Astor Pl.* ♿

Amato Opera House

Head downtown to see the divas of tomorrow paying their dues in an intimate setting. An alternative for opera lovers who lack the funds for nosebleed seats at the Met. One of Amato's goals is to foster opera appreciation by making it more accessible, so many performances are English translations of Italian operas.

319 Bowery St. (at 2nd St.), 228-8200, Cash Only, ⑥⑩⑤⑥ *to Broadway-Lafayette St.,* ⑥ *to Bleecker St.*

First Houses

Opened in 1935 these residences were the first completed projects of the New York City Housing Authority. The eight-building complex was later renovated, with courtyards and playgrounds, and was declared a city landmark in 1974.

138-180 East 4th St. (bet. 1st Ave. and Ave. A), ⑥ *to Second Ave.*

movies & books

200 Cigarettes, 1999

200 Cigarettes displays the funky style and flashy clothes of the East Village in the early 1980s. We follow the hip cast around as they take us on a personal tour of everything from darkened alleyways to local hot spots. Put on your New Year's Eve hats and get ready to party.

New York Stories, 1989

Made up of three different pieces, all set in New York City and all directed by famous movie makers: Woody Allen, Martin Scorsese, and Francis Ford Coppola. In "Life Lessons," Nick Nolte plays an artist struggling to hold onto Rosanna Arquette in downtown Manhattan. This short piece shows a great deal of the art culture in the East Village.

a *saturday*
IN EAST VILLAGE

Old Devil Moon
For a big plate of eggs, sausage, hash browns, biscuits, and grittiness all around, brunch here with the East Village grunge.
(see Restaurants)

The Russian Baths
For just $20 you can enjoy an afternoon in four kinds of high-temp, low-humidity Russian and Turkish steam rooms. Meanwhile, massages (costing $45 for an hour or $30 for a 1/2 hour) will leave you barely able to mumble "Spaceba."
East Village, 268 East 10th St. (bet. First Ave. and Ave. A), 505-0665, MC, V, AmEx, D, ❻ *to Astor Pl.*

[cheap *thrills*]

Free Theater
See hit show "Stomp," without buying a ticket, by watching the TV monitors outside of The Orpheum Theatre. *126 Second Ave. (bet. 7th and 8th Sts.), 477-2477,* ❻ *to Astor Pl.*

La MaMa etc.
Four small theaters offer new and experimental dance and theater. Shows are hit or miss, but cheap tickets make it worthwhile to test the odds.
(see Performing Arts)

Community Gardens

Explore the nooks and crannies of Alphabet City's community owned-and-operated gardens. The one on 6th St. and Ave. B has a famous sculpture standing four-stories high and lots of live performances. On Houston St. and Bowery, peek at the chock-full fishing holes amongst the greeery.

(see Sites & Parks)

First

Continue your day of decadence at a really hip joint. Martinis are the story at this chic East Village restaurant — orders come in tiny, individual shakers — as the glam of SoHo seems to sneak east.

(see Restaurants)

Vintage Shopping

Stroll east on 9th and 10th Sts. for some of the best vintage boutiques in the city. You never know when new little holes in the walls will open up, so keep your eyes peeled for these gems. Good tip — go early for the best selection; Find out when they re-stock, too!

❻ to Astor Pl.

greenwich village

Greenwich Village has earned its reputation as the elder statesman of hip, having housed generations of artists, revolutionaries, and writers like Dylan Thomas and Edna St. Vincent Millay. In addition to countless clusters of coffee houses, jazz and cabaret clubs, and taverns, the Village hosts New York University, perhaps the area's greatest cultural influence nowadays.

Bordered by two major downtown thoroughfares to the north and south (14th and Houston Sts., respectively), the Village is a limitless resource in a city of limitless resources. Its epicenter, flanked by Seventh Ave. South and Broadway, is constantly abuzz, though perhaps soft-core for some grittier urbanites. Shoe shops line 8th St. east of Sixth Ave., while record stores are ubiquitous along Bleecker and MacDougal Sts. Meanwhile, Washington Square Park is an open playground for residential and visiting masses alike, replete with live street shows, sun bathing, and chess. To the south and the east of the park, the shops which crowd the NYU area foist their schlocky wares upon the newcomers 365 days per year, be they tourists or the fresh crop of gawking freshman which arrives each fall. After dark, hip nightcrawlers ascend from the subway station at Sheridan Sq., thrust into the big city atmosphere of the Village's busiest and most confusing intersection, before dispersing into the various cafés, clubs, and theaters which fan out along the nearby streets.

However, Greenwich Village is not simply a commercial center and tourist destination. It's also one of the city's few neighborhoods which has artfully blended its past and present, supporting an ever more radical and diversified gay and artistic community while still accommodating the many families who quietly thread through the sea of tourists on their way to Balducci's to pick up bagels and lox. Just when nostalgic critics begin to arm themselves with accusations of the neighborhood having sold out, the Village reveals its authenticity. The area west of Seventh Ave. South, known appropriately as the West Village, is one of the most quiet and beautiful sections of the city. This cloistered neighborhood shelters a nest of tangled, tranquil streets, among which it's easy to lose yourself, literally. Lined with slender trees, fussy federal style doorways with fluted columns on either side, and flanked by ornamental windows webbed with ivy, residential streets like Barrow, Commerce, Jane and Perry have held true to their roots as genteel enclaves, remaining remarkably settled and serene. Meanwhile, these routes, architecturally reminiscent of the narrow nooks of Amsterdam, are peppered with some of the most romantic restaurants the city has to offer.

Strolling down Sixth Ave. in Greenwich Village, you may pass by two important architectural and literary landmarks without even knowing it. Built in 1848 and 1852 respectively, **Patchin Place** (entrance on 10th St., just west of Sixth Ave.) and **Milligan Place** (entrance on Sixth Ave., just north of 10th St.) remain in much the same condition as they were originally: cobblestoned, separated from the hubbub of the Village by iron gates bearing their respective names in unadorned wrought-iron cursive. The easy-to-miss residential sidestreets, were once home to such notables as e.e. cummings, O. Henry, Edna St. Vincent Millay, John Reed, and Djuna Barnes, among others. These homes provide a remarkably relaxing sanctuary for their residents; one in-house tenant-psychiatrist comments, "It's so serene I'm able to treat my patients more effectively."

These eminent alleys are often overlooked due to both their obscure location and the lack of publicity that goes hand-in-hand with their peace and quiet. In 1963, however, they made the news when a new owner attempted to tear down Patchin Place and Milligan Place to replace them with a more modern apartment building. Residents rallied against him and had the two declared historical landmarks.

The occupants of Patchin and Milligan Places have access to private atria, hidden from the intrusion of tourists. Residents make eclectic contributions to these quirky gardens. According to one tenant (who claims Marlon Brando used to live in his apartment), every summer the residents of Patchin Place dress in 1930s garb for a garden party. Inspirationally set, it's no surprise that the residences of Milligan and Patchin have their fair share of artists and free thinkers — just strolling by the discreet gates of these mews can hone one's sensibilities!

HISTORY

In the mid-19th Century, Greenwich Village became host to art clubs, private galleries, and literary salons, while hotels, shops, and theaters clogged lower Broadway. The Village yielded the development of a phenomenon for which the neighborhood would become world-famous: the Bohemian lifestyle. Experimental theater, galleries specializing in avant-garde art, and irreverent "little magazines" (forerunners of today's "zines") exploded onto the scene. Wild parties, candle-lit tearooms, novelty nightclubs, and bizarre boutiques soon followed.

Just prior to the Depression, "artistic flats" became the era's local euphemism for luxury apartments which displaced the longtime residents who had spawned the artistic revolution that first put the neighborhood on the map. Following the Depression, the Beat Generation arrived and the Village saw its first stirrings of gay culture, which soon became integral to the neighborhood. Again, writers and artists of all kinds congregated here, helping to fuel the genesis of the hippie movement and the gay revolution. Novelist Norman Mailer started the *Village Voice* in 1955, a paper which remains a lead-

ing instrument of the left wing throughout the city, and beyond.

The 1990s has seen the continuation of widespread gentrification in the Village. The city and New York University have combined to decrease crime and drug use, especially in and around Washington Square Park. Meanwhile, corporate America has begun taking over, with multiplex cinemas replacing smaller art houses and Starbucks supplanting intimate cafés. In spite of this influx of big bucks and gaudiness, Greenwich Village retains much of its bohemian flavor, and remains an artistic center.

Grace Church
Designed and built by James Renwick, Jr. from 1843-46, this Episcopal church is in a Gothic-Revival style. NYU students in the residence hall across the street whose windows face Broadway can wake up in the morning to the sight of the church's white spire.
802 Broadway (at 10th St.), 254-2000, ⓝⓡ to 8th St.-NYU ♿

The Jefferson Market Regional Library
High Victorian Gothic pinnacles, gables, and a patterned slate roof crown this former courthouse, erected near the site of the former produce market for which it is named. Voted one of the country's most beautiful buildings in the 1880s, it served as a police academy and temporary housing for the Census Bureau until the city decided to landmark it and convert it into a much-needed branch of the New York Public Library in the '60s.
425 Sixth Ave. (at 10th St.), 243-4334, ⓕ to 14th St., ⓛ to 6th Ave. ♿

Washington Square Park
The park is now almost unrecognizable as the public gallows and potters' field of its 1780 origins. Most of the surrounding 19th Century Federal-style brownstones have been taken over by NYU; the elegant houses known as "The Row" on Washington Square North, which now accommodate university administrators, once housed such talents as Henry James.
At the foot of 5th Ave., ⓐⓑⓒⓓⓔⓕⓖ *to West 4th St.-Washington Sq.* ♿

Judson Memorial Church
Originally constructed to bring together the poor populace living on the south side of the square and its upscale northern counterpart, the church was consecrated in 1890 and named for Adinirom Judson, a baptist missionary. The church was designed by McKim, Mead, and White; the 13 stained-glass windows were made by John La Farge.
55 Washington Square South (bet. Thompson and Sullivan Sts.), 477-0351, ⓐⓑⓒⓓⓔⓕⓖ *to West 4th St.-Washington Sq.*

Parsons School of Design
Get a sneak peek at this crucible of young talent at one of the two exhibitions open to the public or by attending one of the ever-intriguing openings.
2 West 13th Street (at Fifth Ave.), 229-8900, ⓛⓝⓡⓠ④⑤⑥ *to 14th St.-Union Sq.* ♿

Sheridan Square

A major hub of the West Village, noisy and raucous on the weekends when its subway stop starts hatching night crawlers.
Among Seventh Ave. South, Christopher St., West 4th St., and Grove St.
①⑨ to Christopher St.-Sheridan Sq. ♿

Stonewall Memorial Statues
General Sheridan calmly gazes down upon a standing
gay male couple and a sitting lesbian couple which
commemorate the 1969 gay rights riots at the
Stonewall Inn.
Christopher and Waverly Sts. (in Christopher Park),
①⑨ to Christopher St.-Sheridan Sq. ♿

Church of St. Luke in the Fields
A church that remembers a time when there were
fields. You can still get a taste of old-time Village life
within the church when the adjacent elementary
school is not in session.
*487 Hudson St. (bet. Grove and Christopher Sts.),
924-0562,* **①⑨** to Christopher St.-Sheridan Sq. ♿

Casa Italiana Zerilli-Marimò
The former home of General Winfield Scott, hero
of the Mexican-American War and Chief-of-Staff
of the U.S. Army in the 1850s. Call for information
about free lectures, films, and art exhibits that
focus on Italian culture.
*24 West 12th St. (bet. Fifth and Sixth Aves.), 998-8730,
Admission: free, Open: Tu-F 10am-6pm, Sa 11am-5pm,*
Ⓕ *to 14th St.,* **Ⓛ** *to Sixth Ave.*

movies & books

The Age of Innocence, 1920
Greenwich village may
not look today the way
it was depicted in Edith
Wharton's novel on early
20th Century life in New
York, but travel back
to a time where women
still wore corsets and
New Yorkers traveled
on bumpy dirt roads.

Washington Square, 1881
Henry James' novel about
the upper classes of the
1830s and 1840s was based
on experience: as a child
he lived in his grand-
mother's house on
Washington Square Park.

The Freshman, 1990
Matthew Broderick co-stars
with acting heavy Marlon
Brando in this spoof of *The
Godfather* set in and around
the NYU campus. If you
ever wondered what a
part-time job working for
gangsters would be like,
watch this one.

a *saturday*
IN GREENWICH VILLAGE

Cowgirl Hall of Fame
"Breakfast" tacos are a mis-
nomer here; you won't need
to eat for a week afterwards
at this off-beat, down home,
rootin' tootin' girly joint.
The 32-ounce beverages should
help you wash it all down.
(see Restaurants)

**Patchin Place and
Milligan Place**
Be among the few
to notice these quaint
architectural gems,
home to some of the
20th Century's most
famous literary figures.
(see Side Bar)

Balducci's
Just down Sixth Ave., find perhaps the city's best offering of gourmet delicacies, with prices to match.
(see Shopping)

Washington Square Park
You can't go to the Village on a Saturday without taking a walk through Washington Square Park. Stop and watch the grumbling chess players, as preschoolers climb the slide, then wander over and listen to guitar players strum; or just lie down under the shade of a tree and close your eyes for awhile.
(see Sites & Parks)

Pó
Book a table here earlier in the week, or show up and be prepared to wait at Mario Batali's ultra popular, diminutive Italian eatery.
(see Restaurants)

Bar d'O
As dark and sultry as a lounge gets, this cool, leathery hideaway also has its fair share of flamboyancy among its clientele. Cabaret is featured periodically, often by luscious drag queens.
(see Nightlife)

Hoops at The Cage
This claustrophobic den of dunks is good for some ooohs and ahhs, even if you don't got game yourself.
Sixth Ave. (at 3rd St.), **ⒶⒷⒸⒹⒺⒻⓆ** to West 4th St.-Washington Sq.

Quels frites!
The cobblestoned crossroads of 14th St. and Ninth Ave., known as Little Belgium, serves fries at places like Petite Abeille.
(see Restaurants)

When Sinatra belted out "I want to be a part of it — New York, New York" he wasn't talking about Gramercy Park. But even Old Blue Eyes would have been pressed up against the bars of this private oasis unless he had a pad in one of New York's most elite areas of real estate. Only those living along the park itself receive a key to the serenity resting snugly behind its gates.

Of course, there's more to the area than just the park. The region between Union and Madison Squares — known now as the Flatiron District after the triangular building at the intersection of Broadway and Fifth Ave. — sits between Gramercy and Chelsea, and is full of bars and shops, some with a slightly more laid-back atmosphere than in Gramercy proper. What's more, this formerly commercial zone has a surplus of converted warehouses, now used for expansive (i.e. expensive) residences. According to disgruntled Flatironer Evan, a journalist, the neighborhood has assumed a "see-and-be-seen" air, similar to that of its neighbors to the west and east, filled with "rich kids with as much space between their ears as between the first and last digits of the their trust funds."

Gramercy has become a hub for fashion models and photographers, as well as for an eyeful of young celebs; at the right moment, you might catch an informally dressed Winona Ryder on her way to one of the spacious, pricey restaurants that fill up for brunch on Sundays. With a literary history including Herman Melville and Edith Wharton, Gramercy has maintained its patronage for the arts. Though the area may seem indifferent to the world outside, it makes a point of taking care of its creative institutions; the National Arts Club and the Poetry Society of America are both housed in the stately building at 15 Gramercy Park South.

Though perhaps an ideal urban landscape — clean, residential sidestreets crossing elegantly commercial avenues — Gramercy may feel to some more like a fantasy land. Still, it's impossible not to admire its beauty, best taken in on a walk up from the bottom of Irving Pl. at 14th St., where charming houses (alas, no key included) sit alongside prim restaurants and markets. Unfortunately, once you reach the top of the street, blooming out into the square around the Park itself, you may feel as though you've walked the yellow-brick road, only to find the doors of Oz closed to the public.

Virtually all the buildings surrounding Gramercy Park are historical landmarks, and **The National Arts Club**, founded in 1898, is no exception. The building itself exudes a tradition of appreciation for the arts, embroidered by 19th Century iron filigree, bay windows, and a well-tended few feet of flower garden between a black, cast iron fence and the stone facade of the townhouse. It is therefore no surprise what prominent names grace the building's plaques: Frederick Remington, Robert Henri, Theodore Roosevelt, and other members of the Ashcan School of early 20th Century American painting.

The galleries are the only part of The National Arts Club officially open to the public, but the thickly carpeted staircase leading to the Clubs private facilities (an additional gallery, a dining room and bar) has no stern, suspicious security guards or chained-off rooms. If your curiosity gets the best of you, climbing a few extra flights of lightly creaking steps will give you a better view of the gorgeous stained glass skylight over the apex of the staircase. The walls are lined with portraits of those who have had an impact on the club's development, including Leonard Bernstein, Alice Tully, Tennessee Williams, and Roy Lichtenstein.

The galleries and the integrity of their paintings testify to the Club's mission: to broaden enlightened appreciation of the art form. Still, the traditions of The National Arts Club do not exclude the nontraditional — the paintings in this particular exhibit were varied, from a colorful, realist passageway to a mud colored nude portrait of an emaciated woman. Overall, in spite of its posh setting, The National Arts Club gives the impression of sublime seclusion, not elitist exclusion. In fact, it's one Club that is happy to receive new members.

H I S T O R Y

Although originally a swamp, the area surrounding Gramercy Park has long been one of the most fashionable addresses in New York. Thanks to its intellectual residents at the turn of the 20th Century, the historical Gramercy has been called "an American Bloomsbury." Past residents include James Harper (founder of the HarperCollins publishing house), Theodore Roosevelt, Edith Wharton, and Eugene O'Neill. O. Henry, who wrote *The Gift of the Magi* in a local restaurant, also called Gramercy home.

In 1831, Samuel Ruggles, longtime trustee of Columbia College, drained the swamp and laid out 66 English-style lots around a private park, still standing as the neighborhood's famed Gramercy Park. By the late 1920s, the development of high-rise apartment buildings, the extension of the Third Avenue El, and the onset of the Depression meant that an address around Gramercy Park was no longer as desirable as it once was. The neighborhood's majestic mansions crumbled a bit, and the turn-of-the-century elite shopping mecca dubbed "Ladies' Mile" became the "temple of love" after an influx of brothels. On the heels of capital flight came a vibrant population of leftists and artists, including Andy Warhol, who instituted his legendary Factory. Gramercy became an enclave for groups of rebels, ranging in identity from communists to junkie divas, and heavy drug traffic and drifters plagued the area.

Today, the revitalization which has spurred development in most of the downtown area has returned much of the old panache to Gramercy, and a Union Square address is desirable once more.

Flatiron Building

While 21 stories barely constitutes a sky-scraper in modern parlance, this triangular office building at the intersection of Fifth Ave. and Broadway, erected in 1902 by Daniel H. Burnham, certainly impressed turn-of-the-century tourists; the men were especially eager to see if the unusual flow of air created by the building's angle really did lift ladies' skirts above their ankles.

For many, its rusticated lime-stone facade and steel frame symbolized the dawn of the skyscraper era. *175 Fifth Ave. (at 23rd St. and Broad-way)*, **N R** to 23rd St.

Madison Square Park

Dog walkers and baby-sitters bask in the serenity, just as Edith Wharton and Theodore Roosevelt once did, on the site of the original Madison Square Garden. *23rd to 26th Sts. (bet. Fifth and Madison Aves.)*, **N R** to 23rd St. &

Theodore Roosevelt's Birthplace

Saturday afternoons are the best time to visit the birthplace of our 26th President for a spin around his childhood home, a couple of museum galleries, and admission to a chamber music concert. Ask about Roosevelt's playboy uncle Robert, who lived in the brownstone next door. *28 East 20th St. (bet. Park Ave. So. and Broadway)*, 260-1616, *Cash Only, Admission: $2, Open: W-Su 9am-5pm*, **6** to 23rd St.

Gramercy Park

Only the crème de la crème of Gramercy possess a rusty key to the gate of this manicured private park, where time seems to stand still. The park is opened once a year to the general public, but for the other 364 days, membership is a privilege. If it's not too depressing for you, peek through the bars — the toddlers you see puttering around inside probably make more in inter-est annually than you do! *20th St. and Irving Pl.*, **6** to 23rd St. &

Union Square Greenmarket

On Mondays, Wednesdays, Fridays, and Saturdays, one of the city's largest — though not cheapest — green markets, chock-full of farm-fresh produce and non-green goods like used books and fat pretzels made from scratch, commands the park's western edge. *14th to 17th Sts. (bet. Broadway and Union Sq. West)*, **L N R 4 5 6** to 14th St.-Union Sq. &

American Ballet Theatre

Drop-in classes, with fees to the tune of $12 a pop ($110 buys ten classes), for aspiring prima donnas at one of the country's pre-mier studios. Alaine Haubert and Diana Cartier teach regularly, though guest instruc-tors from the ABT Artistic Staff occasionally fill in. Advanced dancers should stop by at

10am Monday, Wednesday, or Friday, while intermediates will be best served by the 6pm weekday classes.
890 Broadway (at 19th St.), 3rd Floor, 477-3030, ❶❻❽❹❺❻ to 14th St.-Union Sq. ♿

Pete's Tavern

An honest-to-God neighborhood establishment (and an

Irish one, at that!) Pete's has been a gathering place in Gramercy since 1864 — in fact, it's holds the distinction of being the oldest continually operating bar in the New York. This place has provided inspiration for writers (O. Henry) and filmmakers (Milos Forman) alike, as well as good cheer for all.
129 East 18th St. (at Irving Pl.), 473-7676, AmEx, V, DC, ❶❻❽❹❺❻ to 14th St.-Union Sq. ⤶

School of Visual Arts

Founded in 1947 as a school for cartoonists and illustrators, this private arts college has become one of the country's most prestigious producers of artsy-farsty types — you can almost inhale the creative energy just hanging around the school's environs! In addition to operating a professional gallery in SoHo, the school operates six student galleries at this main campus; check them out and jot down names, so that in ten years you can say you saw so-and-so when he or she was just a starting out.
209 East 23rd St. (bet. Second and Third Aves.), 592-2000, ❻ to 23rd St.

Manhattan Murder Mystery, 1993

Diane Keaton and Alan Alda sip wine in The National Arts Club, overlooking Gramercy Park. This delightful Woody Allen comedy follows unlikely detectives as they search for the truth about a neighbor's death.

Endless Love, 1979

In this Scott Spencer bestseller, the well-meaning yet misguided David Axelrod, in search of his ex-girlfriend Jade, tracks down her mother, whose house he has burned down, at her new apartment at Park Ave. South and 22nd St. Forty pages of psychosexual tension follow. A word to the wise: read the book, skip the movie (a mega-flop starring Brooke Shields).

Friend of a Farmer

You don't need to wake when the rooster crows to chow down on an honest-to-goodness farm-style brunch at this little slice of Vermont. Actually, "little" is the wrong way to describe both the portions or the wait here; the hearty fare on the other end of the line is worth standing around for.

(see Restaurants)

The National Arts Club

See what's on display in this beautiful architectural specimen. Upstairs is the Poetry Society of America, solidifying Gramercy's role as patron of the arts.

15 Gramercy Park South (bet Irving Pl. and Gramercy Park West), 475-3424, ❻ to 23rd St.

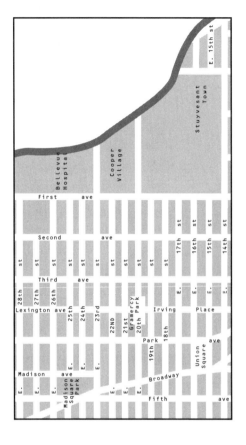

Drink at the oldest bar in New York

If you want to check out a historical New York site, but have had it with museums and churches for the day, then go the Pete's Tavern and have a beer at the oldest bar in the city. While you're there, you can check out the spot O. Henry supposedly started *The Gift of the Magi*.

(see Nightlife)

Union Square Greenmarket

Walk west to Park Ave. South and down to Union Sq., where the outskirts of the park will be filled with, among other things, a thriving market of produce and baked goods (though you can't possibly be hungry yet, after the brunch at Farmer's!).

(see Sites & Parks)

Theodore Roosevelt's Birthplace

Strange that a Rough Rider like Teddy was born in genteel Gramercy, but sure enough, his childhood home is marked by a five-room display, with a guided tour for $2; located just up Broadway from Union Sq.

(see Sites & Parks)

Union Square Cafe

Doesn't life sometimes seem like it's all about biding time until the next meal? A wonderful way to close out your day, New York dining doesn't get better, or more popular. If you don't believe us, check in Zagat.

(see Restaurants)

Movie Filming at the National Arts Club

During the summer months, movies seem to be shot on a near weekly basis in or around the National Arts Club at Gramercy Park. Hang nearby with a pen and wait for autographs.

(see Side Bar)

Shakespeare & Co.

In this most literary of neighborhoods, spend some time browsing through the Bard's unofficial bookstore, one of four branches located in Manhattan.

(see Literature)

chelsea

Of all of the neighborhoods in New York which have made the climb from rags to riches, Chelsea's has been perhaps the least meteoric and, therefore, the most profound. While it has become known as a residential center for gay men, it in fact has a huge variety of inhabitants and is shaping up as a stylish, diverse district. Grittier than Greenwich Village to the south, Chelsea has nonetheless developed a remarkable restaurant scene.

Uprooted by high rent and close quarters, a number of art galleries have quietly resettled not just north of Houston but north of 14th St. near the Hudson River. The social scene on Eighth Ave. (Mom, why are there no women in that bar?) compliments nicely the shopping on Sixth Ave. and regal townhouses between Ninth and Tenth Aves., making Chelsea as varied and interesting a neighborhood as you'll find. Plus, it's one of the friendliest places in Manhattan, with its eateries spilling out into the streets, creating a sense of common space and community.

Spending time in Chelsea will force you to watch your waistline. The gym scene is huge here and you can see (from the street) the abs of iron on the men sweating it out during window-front workouts. Chelsea after dark possesses many activities for folks of partying persuasions, replete with eclectic dance clubs, eccentric bars, and a pervasive, in-your-face singles scene. That Chelsea, along with Greenwich Village, is home of the old meat-packing district serves an appropriate social metaphor.

Finally, Chelsea is a neighborhood of interesting architecture, including the London Terrace, a glorious block-long expanse on 23rd St. between Ninth and Tenth Aves., and The Chelsea Hotel, site of myth and mischief, scene of the death of Nancy by Sid's hand, and the New York address for Leonard Cohen and Dylan Thomas, among others.

Parts of Chelsea may be too "exuberant" for some, but by and large this section of town has found its niche. Between an ethnic pocket right out of bygone Spain, the flower district on 28th St., an enormous movie multiplex, and enough restaurants to challenge the flattening effect of those plentiful gyms, Chelsea has muscled its way into being an integral part of New York City life. Taking the weight off of the Village as another gay-friendly section of town, it would be a shame to look at Chelsea as one-dimensional: Although the Chelsea boys do thrive, God bless 'em, bringing the average body-fat percentage down a point or three, they make up just one aspect of a neighborhood bursting at the seams.

After only several years on the art scene, Chelsea has staked out a name for itself as a stomping ground for exciting contemporary art. As SoHo began to move away from its Bohemian roots, nearby Chelsea was a logical alternative for cutting edge art. Gallery owners looking for a calmer atmosphere, lower rents, and a more democratic environment have tucked themselves into resurrected warehouses, soaking up the great light, great views, and pioneer spirit of the neighborhood.

With today's SoHo covering a broader gamut of the art market, Chelsea offers gallery goers innovative, emerging talent, and riskier exhibits. The work varies widely in media, offering a full-spectrum experience in a non-intimidating environment.

Since Chelsea remains a diverse residential neighborhood, it's unlikely that the art scene will loose its adventurous feel anytime soon. While trendy Italian sandwich shops are spreading like wildfire and Comme Des Garçons, the French fashion avant-garde staple, unveiled a monster flagship store in the neighborhood, the area is still a ways from becoming a mecca for mainstream consumers. The old and the new mix well here, offering a good backdrop for the creative processes on display along the increasingly expansive gallery trail.

A Sampling of Chelsea galleries:

Annina Nosei Gallery
528-530 West 22nd St., 2nd Floor, 741-8695
Barbara Gladstone Gallery
515 West 24th St., 206-9300
Dia Center for the Arts
548 West 22nd St., 989-5566
Greene Naftali
526 West 26th St., 8th floor, 463-7770
Linda Kirkland
504 West 22nd St., 2nd fl., 627-3930
Matthew Marks
523 West 24th St., 243-0200;
522 West 22nd St., 243-0200
Metro Pictures
519 West 24th St., 206-7100
Pat Hearn Gallery
530 West 22nd St., 727-7366
534 West 21st St., 255-1105
Paula Cooper Gallery
534 West 21nd St., 255-1105

H I S T O R Y

The core of the area known today as Chelsea was originally Thomas Clarke's family estate, which was subsequently divided into homogeneous blocks of one-family residences. Warehouses, factories, and piers later shot up along the Hudson as the economy shifted from agriculture to industry in the 19th Century. At the end of the Civil War, the area between 14th and 23rd Sts. on Sixth Ave. constituted the city's shopping nexus, but construction of major department stores nearby lured consumers away. The creation of the fur trading market has remained a vital segment of the economy through the '40s.

Shortly before completion of Pennsylvania Station, the firm of McKim, Mead, and White was asked to design a post office to complement the beautiful new railroad station whose grandeur rivaled that of Grand Central. Their answer was the elegant white-columned, structure that still stands opposite the site of the original Pennsylvania Station, marking the height of New York City's architectural Golden Age.

Today, the historical flourishes in the neighborhood still contrast with the modern accents. The '80s ushered in a renaissance of commercial prosperity with the arrival of superstores; in the last decade, entrepreneurs capitalized on Chelsea's bevy of vacated warehouses to create monster dance emporiums, attracting sex-and-drug trades to the area. Depreciated land values by the Hudson River led to low rents, attracting galleries as SoHo prices began to soar. The neighborhood has greatly benefited from the conversion of many of its abandoned piers into the city's premier sports and recreation center, unoriginally dubbed Chelsea Piers.

The Chelsea Hotel

From its opening, this hotel has lured literati and pop-culture icons to its famed halls: Mark Twain, Dylan Thomas, William S. Burroughs, Vladimir Nabokov, and Arthur Miller all crashed here at some point. Even sometime-girlfriend of Sex Pistols front man Sid Vicious, Nancy Spungen, met her untimely end here, allegedly at the hands of hunting-knife-wielding Sid himself. Rooms aren't readily available, but swing by and survey the plaques commemorating the most venerated guests and gaze at the residents' artwork, which crowds the walls.

222 West 23rd St. (bet. Seventh and Eighth Aves.), 243-3700, ❶❾ *to 23rd St.* ♿

Little Spain

Though the population of Spanish sailors that burgeoned after the Civil War has since waned, snatches of Spanish still drift by on the streets, salsa music pours from the windows, and a few bookstores and restaurants persist as remnants of the past.

14th St., west of Sixth Ave., ❶ *to 14th St.,* ❶ *to Sixth Ave.*

Chelsea Piers

Restless New Yorkers recreate at this insular arena of sports and recreation facilities: Indoor soccer, the sky rink, and an open-air roller rink help city-dwellers relive starry-eyed junior-high romance. Boutiques galore and restaurants, too.

Piers 59-62, Twelfth Ave. (at 23rd St.), 336-6800, ❶❶ *to 23rd St.* ♿

General Post Office

A beautiful example of McKim, Mead, and White architecture, circa 1913, this imposing, columned structure on the cusp of Chelsea and Clinton bears the famous postal slogan ("Neither snow nor rain..."). Open to the public 24 hours a day.

421 Eighth Ave. (at 30th St.), 967-8585, ❶❶❶ *to 34th St.-Penn Station* ♿

Chelsea Flower District

Sunrise heralds the aroma of roses and snapdragons wafting along this stretch of Sixth Ave. where vendors meet the horticultural needs of every urban green thumb.

Around Sixth Ave. and 27th St., ❶❾ *to 28th St.*

s i t e s +

General Theological Seminary Gardens

An enclave of serenity hides behind the wall of this Episcopalian seminary. Afternoons, the garden is open to backyard-deprived urbanites.
175 Ninth Ave. (bet. 20th and 21st Sts.), 243-5150, Open: M-F noon-3pm, Sa 11am-3pm, ©© to 23rd St. &

Dia Center for the Arts
Dia opened its main exhibition facility in a four-story renovated warehouse in 1987, dedicating it to large-scale, long-term exhibitions, offering artists the opportunity to develop new work or a focused presentation of work on a full floor of the building.
548 West 22nd St. (bet. Tenth and Eleventh Aves.), 989-5566, ©© to 23rd St. &

Barbara Gladstone
This enormous space has tall ceilings and two levels displaying contemporary and modern art in various media, including rotating painting, sculpture, video installations, and photography.
515 West 24th St. (bet. Tenth and Eleventh Aves.), 206-9300, ©© to 23rd St. &

Picture Perfect, 1997
Just like the title, the movie's view of Chelsea is "picture perfect." You can spot many local hangouts like Bendix Diner and Man Ray located on Eighth Ave., or kick back and relax in Jennifer Aniston's walk-up brick apartment building. Finding true love in New York City is always hard, but this romantic comedy makes it appear enjoyable.

9 ½ Weeks, 1986
This erotic drama with Mickey Rourke and Kim Basinger features scenes outside The Chelsea Hotel. The movie follows Basinger and Rourke's obsessive sexual relationship. It's a crash course in hot sex, so maybe wait till the second or third date.

Rocking Horse Cafe Mexicano
Start your day with a little bit
of spice at this popular,
experimental Mexican joint.
(see Restaurants)

Chelsea Architectural Tour
Heading west on 20th St. affords
views of some of the city's most
striking 19th Century buildings.
Between Eighth and Ninth Aves.,
the gothic style soaks up most of
the attention, while a block west,
gorgeous Greek-style townhouses
line the north side of the street.
Swing up Tenth Ave. and back east
on 23rd St., where the London
Terrace Apartments regally occupy
the entire block. Also on 23rd St.,
between Seventh and Eighth Aves. is
The Chelsea Hotel, more impressive
for its lore than its design.
CE to 23rd St.

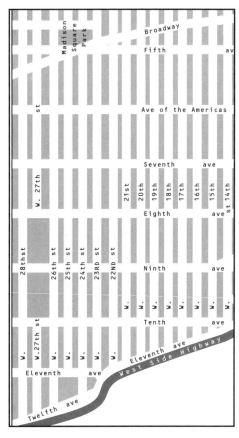

Blading by the Hudson
The outer rink on the water is fun,
but avoid crowded times when the slow-moving,
flat-footed folk turn into so many bowling pins.
23rd St. at the Hudson River, CE *to 23rd St.*

Enjoying Some Silence
Read amidst General Theological Seminary's greenery;
no charge for admission.
Ninth Ave. at 20th St., CE *to 23rd St.*

Chelsea Flower District
A sweet-smelling addition to your day, don't wait too long
after rosy-fingered dawn to get the full effect.
For obvious reasons, spring is the best time of year to visit here.
(see Sites & Parks)

Alley's End
This wonderful hideaway is
a less hectic way to approach
the frenetic Chelsea meal scene.
Cute, contemporary, and
relatively cheap, it's getting
more and more popular, to the
point where there's actually
a wait on weekends.
(see Restaurants)

Barracuda
End your day at this funky lounge
complete with lava lamps.
Order a Cosmopolitan, or any other
urban cocktail of your choice,
and kick back. A nice group gathers
after dinner to chat and be merry.
(see Nightlife)

Free Flics at A Different Light
This landmark gay and lesbian bookstore
offers free movies, including popcorn,
on Sundays. While you're there, if you happen
to pass through the store's noteworthy
erotica section, you may find yourself
hurrying home to your honey...
(see Literature)

midtown

From grandiose to gaudy, Midtown is the New York many New Yorkers know least about. The 25 or so blocks below Central Park include the city's famous theater district; Restaurant Row on 46th St.; a gussied-up Time Square, between the country's most famous meat market and the seedy Port Authority Bus Terminal; and the no-nonsense corporate world to the east, which sidles up to the United Nations' often chaotic sphere of diplomacy and diplomatic immunity.

While these are the most famous aspects of Midtown, pockets of residential areas have become popular as people scramble from the high costs of living both up and downtown. The area between West 34th and 59th Sts., Hell's Kitchen, has gone from a disjointed refuge to a bustling neighborhood. Tenth Ave. in the 50s buzzes with television studios while glam hipsters pour in and out of loud, dark, lounges. A variety of Indian restaurants on one Midtown stretch Ninth Ave. in the 40s has prompted a new sobriquet: Little Calcutta.

Across town is Murray Hill. Centered around Third Ave. in the 30s, some of the city's most well-preserved brownstones are there for the gawking. The neighborhood, though, isn't exactly a social mecca. Its primarily yuppie denizens tend to keep to themselves. "There are these beautiful brownstones, which I never see anyone coming in or out of," regrets one less professional dweller.

Stroll down Madison and Fifth Avenues to window-shop at some of the city's most luxurious stores. Meanwhile, on the West Side by the Hudson, sits the Jacob K. Javits Convention Center, with trade shows of everything from Studebakers to greeting cards. For sports fans, there's the "world's most famous arena," Madison Square Garden, home of the Knicks, basketball's reigning Eastern Conference champs, as well as hockey's Rangers. For the artier at heart, look for the row of standout art galleries west of Fifth Avenue on 57th St.

With no shortage of distractions, Midtown is virtually inexhaustible, if you don't mind thick crowds and the frenzied pace of Midtown city life. One way or another, though, mind your wallet — if Time Sq.'s pickpockets-in-residence don't get it, the cashiers at Saks Fifth Avenue will.

To paraphrase one of his biographers, before there was the Federal Reserve, there was J. Pierpont Morgan. For decades, the titanic financier of turn-of-the-century America was the go-to guy when something went wrong with the nation's economy. So when the Panic of 1907 hit absolute crisis mode, it was Morgan who stepped in to change the way the country handled its banking business forever. He corralled Wall Street's leading investors into the plush, stately confines of his own personal library and he locked the doors. Morgan then rallied his hostages to sign an emergency bailout package that would save the economy and set the stage for the creation of a central banking system. The night was, appropriately, one for the books.

Today **The Morgan Library**, a national historic landmark, is open to the public. Inside the East Room — the original showcase for Morgan's tremendous collection of rare books, Renaissance manuscripts, fine gilt bindings, master drawings and autographed

letters from English and American literary giants — you can soak up the history of Western civilization just by peering at the massive volumes that line the walls.

The Bible in Gaelic, la Bible en français, la Bibla... the library has stacks of exquisite Bibles, including three versions of the famous Gutenberg edition, one of which is always on display. The collection includes other masterpieces such as Milton's Paradise Lost, Albrecht Dürer's Adam and Eve, and the score of Mozart's Haffner symphony, as well as the Ninth Century Lindau Gospels, the Hours of Catherine of Cleves and etchings from da Vinci, Rubens and Degas.

The Morgan Library is both a museum and a center for scholarly research. Spending an afternoon there is like stepping back into turn-of-the-century America with the richest, most insatiable arts patron in the country — only better: nowadays, the domineering patriarch can't lock you in.

29 E. 36th St. (at Madison Ave.), 685-0610, Open: Tu-Th 10:30am-5pm, F 10:30am-8pm, Sa 10:30am-6pm, Su noon-6pm, ⑥ to 33rd St. ♿

H I S T O R Y

Once the section of Broadway that runs through what we now know as Midtown was just a dusty road. All that began to change in 1811, when, under the Commissioner's Plan, the city bought estates, subdivided them into city blocks and resold the lots. Then the New York and Harlem Railroad pushed north. When Cornelius Vanderbilt, who ran the company, was warned he was staking money on a losing game, he replied "Put the road there, and people will go there to live."

Vanderbilt was right. What's more, along with a residential population came all the service industries that accompany it.

The city's retail trade advanced from Union Sq., marking first Sixth Ave. and then Herald Sq. as mercantile districts. In 1904 *The New York Times* relocated to, and shared its name with, a dull area known as Long Acre Square; the move was announced on December 31st with a fireworks show at midnight and a New Year's Eve tradition was born. Meanwhile, Tin Pan Alley, on Broadway in the 40s and 50s, was the heart of the country's music publishing industry in the first half of the 1900's, supporting songwriters such as Cole Porter, the Gershwins, and Irving Berlin.

During the 1930s the business district saw the rise of the great modernist edifices that still draw tourists today. Rockefeller Center began to integrate art into its plans. The rough traditions of Hell's Kitchen died hard: though the Irish gang, the Westies, were still running things up until the '70s, gentrification proved more resilient than the local toughs. Nervous real estate agents renamed the area "Clinton;" still, it's fair to say that this area still remains grittier than other "improved" neighborhoods — just ask the late-night bar crowd at the local Blarney Stone.

Columbus Circle

Reminiscent of Parisian traffic circles, complete with anti-pedestrian sentiment, endless honking, and maniacal motorists. Christopher Columbus is the American touch, presiding over the madness which grew out of his expedition. Donald Trump's gaudy tower of overpriced condos, completed in 1996, and identified by the burnished replica of Queens' Unisphere out front, dwarfs everything in the vicinity.

Intersection of 59th St., Central Park South, Broadway, and Eighth Ave., **ABCD19** to 59th St.-Columbus Circle

Intrepid Sea Air Space Museum

Marvel at the ingenuity of the Masters of War and the military-industrial complex at this World War II aircraft carrier, now parked permanently on the Hudson and open to the public. A Stealth bomber, a guided missile submarine, and an Iraqi tank are among the goodies on display.

Pier 86, Twelfth Ave. and 46th St., 245-0072, MC, V, AmEx, Admission: $5-$10 Open: M-F 10am-5pm, weekends 10am-6pm, **ACE** to 42nd St. &

Madison Square Garden

As "The World's Most Famous Arena," the Garden is home to the Knicks, Rangers, college basketball, and the Paramount Theatre. The complex underwent massive renovations in 1991, including the addition of 89 corporate box suites. The original arena was on 26th St. and Madison Ave., where turn-of-the-century New Yorkers packed themselves in like sardines to watch boxing, horse racing, and live cabaret.

4 Penn Plaza (Seventh Ave. and 32nd St.), 465-6000, **1239** to 34th St.-Penn Station &

Theater District

Home to bloated musicals like "Cats" as well as the more innovative productions that keep it respectable; the heart of it all is Times Square. Skip McDonald's and check out Restaurant Row on 46th St. between Eighth and Ninth Aves. for great deals on pre- and post-theater prix fixe dinner menus.

West 40s (bet. Broadway and Eighth Ave.), **NRS123679** to 42nd St.-Times Sq.

Pennsylvania Station

McKim, Mead, and White modeled the original station (commissioned by the Pennsylvania Railroad), on the Baths of Caracalla in Rome, intending to upstage Grand Central and put another feather in the City Beautiful movement's cap. Completed in 1911, its subsequent demolition in 1965 prompted the formation of the Landmarks Preservation Council to ensure that buildings would no longer be sacrificed to the postmodern aesthetic. Today's Penn Station recently got a facelift and is as busy as ever, serving up to one thousand passengers every 90 seconds.

30th to 34th Sts. (bet. Seventh and Eighth Aves.), **1239** to 34th St.-Penn Station, **ACE** to 34th St.-Penn Station &

Times Square

Huge efforts to transform this notoriously sleazy strip of 42nd St. into a family-oriented funland have been a hallmark of Mayor Guliani's New York. A seedy aura still clings to the area, especially at night, despite the throngs of tourists, dazzled by Broadway's lights, and the towering underwear ads. Grittier outposts of hustling and dealing remain, though they're much subtler.

42nd St. (at Broadway), **NRS123679** to 42nd St.-Times Sq.

Bryant Park

Strangely enough, in a city where everything not bolted down disappears, the elegant movable chairs never stray far from their designated spots. Summers, classic movies projected onto a large screen draw after-work crowds toting cheap

wine and blankets; the outdoor bar abutting the park is also a scene.
40th to 42nd Sts. (bet. Fifth and Sixth Aves.), behind the New York Public Library,
B D F Q to 42nd St.,
7 to Fifth Ave.

Rockefeller Center

The 19 commercial buildings and a subterranean network of shops and tunnels are dwarfed by attractions immortalized in the popular lore of New York: Seasonal highlights include the ice rink and the tree lighting, at which thousands fenced in by the NYPD stand around with their kids, muttering "When are they gonna light the goddamn tree?" Also, in the winter, slip and slide among twirling would-be Ice Capades at the skating rink or just park yourself on the sidelines and take in the scene while sipping a cup of hot cocoa.
49th to 52nd Streets (between Fifth and Seventh Aves.),
B D F Q to 47th-50th Sts.-Rockefeller Center

Radio City Music Hall

The Rockettes' kicking grounds opened in 1932 with a gala performance by the decidedly classier trio of Martha Graham, Ray Bolger, and Gertrude Niesen. The brainchild of Samuel Rothafel, the hall was designed by Donald Deskey, whose flair for art deco opulence continues to astound tourists much as it did Depression-era theatergoers. These days, everyone from the Moscow Circus to Michael Jackson has graced its stage; the annual "Radio City Christmas Spectacular" is a New York tradition. "The Grand Tour" costs $13.75 and leaves every half hour, 10am-5pm, Monday through Saturday; 11am-5pm on Sunday.
1260 Sixth Avenue (at 50th St.), 247-4777,
B D F Q to 47-50 Sts.-Rockefeller Center

movies & books

Who Is Harry Kellerman and Why Is He Saying These Terrible Things About Me?, 1971

With scenes at the GM Building (58th St. and Fifth Ave.) and in the Midtown Tunnel, this movie tells the oh-so-familiar sob story of a songwriter who can write about love but not experience it himself.

Vanya on 42nd Street, 1994

Actors gather at a Midtown theater to rehearse David Mamet's adaptation of Andre Gregory's rendition of Anton Chekov's "Uncle Vanya." Part documentary, part re-creation, this film is a breath of fresh air for intellectuals who cringe at the constant barrage of big-scale summer blockbusters.

 *@ saturday*
I N   M I D T O W N

Bryant Park Grill
Begin your Saturday with
brunch in this beautifully laid
restaurant facing the eponymous
park and situated on the back side
of the New York Public Library.
(see Restaurants)

New York Public Library
One of the City's ultimate resources,
the library's newly resigned reading
room will send you scampering
for a book to curl up with.
(see Visual Arts)

Screenings at Bryant Park
In the summer, free classic movies on Mondays at dusk,
and afternoon and evening concerts entertain
in this charming and tranquil oasis.
(see Sites & Parks)

Marriott Marquis Hotel
Check out the vertigo-inducing glass elevators,
which shoot up to the 48th floor.
1535 Broadway (bet. 45th and 46th Sts.), 398-1900,
N R S 1 2 3 7 9 to 42nd St.-Times Sq. ♿

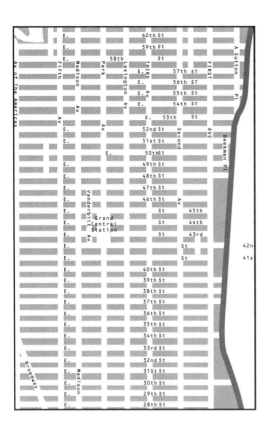

Window-shopping
Check out some of the most
expensive stores in Manhattan,
in the 50s along Fifth Ave.
Unless you've got a gold card with
lots of room, don't even think
of going inside Chanel.
(see Shopping)

**Michael Jordon's Steakhouse
at Grand Central Station**
Enjoy the view of the historic,
recently renovated train station,
its starry ceiling, and the passers-
bys below. As glitzy as this place is,
the cost of entrées is actually
a bit less than other elite
steakhouses in the City.
(see Restaurants)

Empire State Building
Head down Fifth Ave. to the Empire State Building. At the top, snap pictures
of Manhattan's spectacular nighttime cityscape. At 1250 feet in height,
this is the world's most famous skyscraper. A good opportunity for romance.
Fifth Ave. (at 34th St.), **B D F Q** to 34th St.

New York Public Library
The main branch of the NYPL offers free exhibits, lectures,
and programs year-round. Pick up a calendar of events
in the entrance hall, and get yourself a membership card
while you're there, one of the city's cheapest, most
thrilling opportunities.
(see Visual Arts)

upper east side

Fifth Avenue, Madison Avenue, Park Avenue — How often do streets become household names, so to speak, synonymous with wealth, corporate power, and exclusivity?

In the late 19th and early 20th centuries, the Upper East Side was home to the Astors, Carnegies, and Fricks, among many other wealthy families. Their palatial residences have, in some cases, been converted into foundations, galleries, and museums. Manhattan's Gold Coast, above 60th St. and west of Lexington Ave., is home to luxurious apartments with price tags that might make even Donald Trump hesitate, opulent restaurants that don't bother to list something as crass as menu prices, and clubs like the Knickerbocker, so exclusive it discourages any publicity or recognition.

Exploring the Upper East Side can be an intimidating experience for the uninitiated. Gloved doormen still hail cabs, caterers still have their own entrances, nannies still take the kids out strolling, and adolescents in navy blue suits still get shuttled to exclusive private schools where they are groomed for inheritance. Gradually, however, the luxury of Fifth, Madison, and Park Aves. begins to vanish after crossing Lexington.

Despite all its associations with old money and power, the Upper East Side is ultimately a neighborhood of many minds. The area beyond Third Ave. has a decidedly middle-class charm, which becomes intermittantly blue collar near the East River. Many Eastern European and German immigrants reside in this modest area called Yorkville. This neighborhood within a neighborhood still boasts an active Hungarian patronage, old-world delis, and moderately priced ethnic restaurants. Long-time Yorkville resident Bridget promises, "It's easy to feel comfortable on the Upper East Side. All my neighbors are warm and friendly, and I've never felt excluded because I earn a modest income." Indeed, an area as large as the Upper East Side has, as Bridget says, "a lot to offer, and room for everyone. You be sure to print that!"

In 1870, the Union League Club, a socially-minded group whose adherents included such men as William Cullen Bryant, proposed a public art museum for the purposes of education and moral enlightenment. The city raised $500,000 for the construction, and in 1880 The Metropolitan Museum of Art opened its doors. This was the inception of **Museum Mile**, now an idyllic stretch of Fifth Avenue attracting visitors as diverse as the treasures they come to view.

The social and financial success of The Met encouraged sponsorship for other institutions of art of culture. New museums bloomed along Fifth Ave., many from privately held collections. Prominent industrialist Henry Clay Frick had maintained his collection of European paintings and sculptures in his residence, aptly named the Frick Collection. In 1935, after both Frick and his wife had passed away, the mansion's impressive display was opened to the public.

Not all the museums of Museum Mile were indigenous to Fifth Ave. Transplanted from Gracie Mansion in 1932, the Museum of the City of New York was established for the preservation of local history. It amassed colorful, local artifacts, colonial-era costumes, portraits, and detailed models of clipper ships and fire engines.

By the "Roaring Twenties," several collections wanted to promote modern artists. The Whitney Studio was founded by Gertrude Vanderbilt Whitney. In 1930, her private collection became the basis of The Whitney Museum of American Art. Another aficionado of modern art was Simon R. Guggenheim. With the help of collector Hilla Rebey, Guggenheim began amassing avant-garde works by twentieth century artists. By 1939, the collection had evolved into the Museum of Non-Objective Painting, residing in rented quarters before moving to its permanent, current location, where architect Frank Lloyd Wright had prepared the Simon R. Guggenheim Museum, itself a work of modern art.

the whitney museum

H I S T O R Y

Until Central Park opened in 1859, much of Manhattan's uptown landscape resembled an affluent countryside. However, as the city expanded northward it quickly became dotted with various buildings and attractions.

The eastern section of the region developed rapidly as the Second and Third Avenue elevated train lines, completed in 1879, facilitated transportation between the city's urban center and outlying regions, attracting Irish and German immigrants who settled in the brownstones and tenements lining the area that would become Yorkville.

The development that earned the area its elite reputation, however, was constructed astride the park, along what would become the luxurious Fifth, Madison, and Park Aves. From Astor to Tiffany, NYC's wealthiest barons erected parkside mansions. Although most were later demolished, the Carnegie's and Frick's survive as the Cooper-Hewitt Museum and the Frick Collection, respectively.

Park Ave.'s glamorous reputation developed after the New York Central Railway buried its elevated tracks. Elegant apartment buildings lined the newly cleared blocks while Madison Ave.'s wealthy inhabitants attracted opulent boutiques and gourmet grocers to the ground floors of the street's row houses. The Upper East Side cemented its reputation for both ethnic diversity and upscale living with the construction of high-rises, as even the former working-class, immigrant-packed Yorkville area became a desirable address in the 1950s. Upper-class immigrants from Europe and Asia arrived in the '80s, underscoring the area's position as one of the most exclusive and expensive zip codes in the United States.

Carl Schurz Park

Picturesque views of the East River, Queens, and the Triboro Bridge are the draw of this verdent locale, not to mention Gracie Mansion. Get a feel for the East Side amidst the rollerbladers, joggers, and well-groomed dogs that frequent this site.
East End Ave. (bet. 84th and 90th Sts.), ❹❺❻ *to 86th St.*

Gracie Mansion

Constructed in 1799 by merchant Archibald Gracie, this retreat from the urban gridlock of the city continues to stand as an elegant reminder of a bygone New York elite. Bought by the city in 1896, it became part of Carl Schurz Park and housed the Museum of the City of New York from 1924-32. Since the 1940s it has been the official residence of New York mayors. Tours are conducted Wednesdays, March through November; call in advance for times and reservations.
East End Ave. (at 88th St.), 570-4751, Cash Only, Admission (suggested): $4, Open: W 10am, 11am, noon, ❹❺❻ *to 86th St.* ♿

Henderson Place

Rumor has it that the 24 surviving Queen Anne-style townhouses built in 1882 by fur importer John Henderson are haunted, either by ex-residents or by vengeful beavers.
86th and 87th Sts. (bet. East End and York Aves.), ❹❺❻ *to 86th St.*

Asia Society

America's preeminent organization celebrating Asian cultural awareness with notable film series, lectures, and a Pan-Asian art collection featuring sculpture, paintings, ceramics, prints and bronzes. Prominent authors and public leaders speak regularly here; other programs for the public include dance performances, well-attended art exhibits usually gathered from private collections, and receptions involving community and professional organizations.
725 Park Ave. (at 70th St.), 288-6400, MC, 'V, AmEx, Admission: $4, Open: Tu-Sa 11am-6pm, Su noon-5pm, ❻ *to 68th St.-Hunter College* ♿

The International Center for Photography

Founded in 1974, one of the youngest members of Museum Mile showcases over 45,000 photographs and serves as a learning center for budding photographers of all levels of expertise.

1130 Fifth Ave. (at 94th St.), 860-1777, Cash Only, Admission: $4-$6, Open: Tu 11am-8pm, W-Su 11am-6pm, ❻ *to 96th St.* ♿

Jewish Museum

The largest collection of Judaica in the world outside of Israel, housed in an imperious French Renaissance structure, boasts over 27,000 works in its permanent collection. Works detail the Jewish experience throughout history and feature archeological pieces, ceremonial objects, modern masterpieces by Marc Chagall and Frank Stella, and even an interactive computer program based on the Talmud. The first two floors host temporary installations and exhibits. Admission is free for children under 12 and for everyone Tuesdays 5pm-8pm.

1109 Fifth Ave. (at 92nd St.), 423-3200, MC, V, AmEx, Admission: $5.50-8, Open: M, W, Th: 11am-5:45pm, Tu 11am-8pm, **6** *to 96th St.* &

92nd Street Y

One of New York's most valuable cultural resources serves as an umbrella for a multitude of classes, workshops, and speaking and reading series. The Unterberg Poetry Series is by far the city's most star-studded, consistently drawing the finest poets and authors, both national and international, established and emerging.
1395 Lexington Avenue (at 92nd St.), 996-1100, **6** *to 96th St.* &

---

movies & books

Everyone Says I Love You, 1997

Though people may not normally break out into song in the middle of Lexington Ave., this movie still gives a delightful view of the charmed life of the Upper East Side. Directed by Woody Allen and staring Edward Norton, Alan Alda, and a lip-synching Drew Barrymore.

Breakfast at Tiffany's, 1961

Audrey Hepburn plays Holly Golightly, a woman who believes that nothing can go wrong at Tiffany's & Co. (57th St. and Fifth Ave.) Sometimes after a night out, she arrives at the store with breakfast in hand and window shops. Otherwise, she spends her days in her Upper East Side apartment.

Le Pain Quotidien
For the freshest, flakiest,
Frenchest — okay,
it's not French, it's Belgian...
But croissants and café
are a good way to go at
this neighborhood favorite.
(see Restaurants)

Gracie Mansion
The New York mayor's private
residence since the 1940s is in
Carl Schurz Park. There are tours
only on Wednesdays, but you can
view the exterior of building
anytime you desire.
(see Sites & Parks)

[cheap thrills]

Iris B. Gerald Cantor Roof Garden
May thru November, the Met's roof garden caters to a
white-wine-sipping, after-work crowd and others
just admiring the gorgeous view.
1000 Fifth Ave. (at 82nd St.), 535-7710, ❹❺❻ *to 86th St.*

Pay-What-You-Wish Days
The museums along Museum Mile, as well as
the Museum of Modern Art, host "free" nights approximately
once a week with hours into the evening.
(see Visual Arts)

Frick Collection

From one mansion to another, visit one of the most intimate museums on Museum Mile, with art displayed in an actual residence, albeit a palatial one.
(see Visual Arts)

Museum of the City of New York

Not as classy as the Frick, this often-overlooked institution is nonetheless worth a look for its exhibits on local arts and culture.
(see Visual Arts)

Match Uptown

Lively and candle lit, this popular uptown restaurant serves excellent, eclectic New American cuisine and is as much a place to see and be seen as its SoHo parent. Dress up and walk in with attitude.
(see Restaurants)

The Roosevelt Island Aerial Tramway

Pay just a token to dangle precipitously from the exoskeleton of the Queensboro Bridge for spectacular views of Midtown.
Second Ave. (bet 59th and 60th Sts.), 832-4543,
6am-2am weekdays, until 3:30am F-Sa,
④⑤⑥ to 59th St., **⑭⑮** to Lexington Ave.

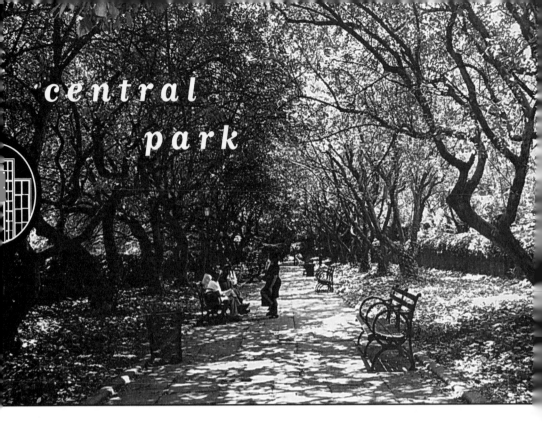

central park

Central Park is a place where bronzed, scantily clad sunbathers attempt deeper shades. It is where every kind of in-line skater, from the seamless gliding expert to the tentative novice, enjoys a long afternoon of blading. Necktied businessmen chat with dredlocked Rastas. Musicians open their guitar cases and serenade crowds reclining on gently sloping hills. Lovers curl together in the Park's intimate enclaves. Statues of *Alice in Wonderland* characters hold court, and a poignant memorial, Strawberry Fields, reminds us of John Lennon's legacy. Central Park is everything that is magical about New York, condensed into 10 million cart loads of rock and soil, 843 acres carefully landscaped over 20 years.

It is difficult to fathom any trip to New York City without a trip to this Arcadia. An estimated 20 million people visit every year. "It's such a beautiful place," smiles 17 year old Ashley. "My family and I come here every weekend during the spring and summer for a picnic, and we walk around for hours." Miles of paved and unpaved paths allow hiking, biking, skating, and jogging enthusiasts to get their share of exercise. "There's something for everyone here, not only for the athletically inclined," says John, a park ranger

for the past nine years," but for the aesthetically inclined as well. Some of city's most striking apartment houses have been built along the Park's perimeter, so the skyline is really spectacular, especially when the sun begins to set behind the buildings."

In a city that's notorious for draining cash flow, Central Park is a welcome relief. While the antique castle carousel costs 90¢ per ride, almost all the Park's attractions and events are free, including Belvedere Castle, the Swedish Cottage Marionette Theater, The Conservatory Garden, and Shakespeare in the Park.

The Park is also a popular place for bird watchers. The Baltimore Oriole spends summers nesting in the Park and the stark winter brings the yellow rumped Warbler. Even swarms of Monarch butterflies drift through the Park in autumn before embarking on their long journey to Mexico. The contrast between Manhattan's overwhelming concrete-and-steel and Central Park's earthy communion of soil and water is a reminder that although city business and commerce are crucial to New York's survival, humans cannot survive without places to retreat, reflect, and relax.

movies & books

Big Daddy, 1999

Adam Sandler teaches cute-as-a-button "Julian" to trip unsuspecting park rollerbladers with a stick. The whole movie is set in Manhattan so keep your eyes open for other landmarks.

When Harry Met Sally, 1989

For a whole lots of laughs (and several walks through Central Park), this Rob Reiner romantic comedy is it. Listen to Harry and Sally bicker, bicker, bicker, then fall in love. A classic nowadays, Meg Ryan and Billy Crystal have immortalized the question: Can men and women simply be friends?

Eloise, 1955

Eloise is a precocious little girl living in and wreaking havoc on the Plaza Hotel (on Central Park South). This now-classic children's book is available in, among other places, the hotel's gift shop. We suspect the staff of this posh parkside establishment is not nearly as tolerant of children's antics as they are in this story.

HISTORY

In the 1800s, the beautiful sanctuary, now know as the Park was predominantly undeveloped camp territory known as Squatters' Sovereignty, a residence-by-default for poor immigrants, blacks, and American Indians, all of whom dwelt in shacks, huts, and caves alongside livestock. This social and geographical wasteland (as it was seen by wealthy citizens and government) was soon deemed better suited for social reform as a center for leisure and recreation. The conception of the Park was inspired by the public grounds in London and Paris and, in 1857, a contest was held to choose a design. The winning entry, submitted by Frederick Law Olmsted called the "Greensward Plan," con-sisted of a pastoral, romantic, English landscape which combined picturesque and formal elements. In building the park, over 270,000 trees, shrubs, and vines were planted while 1,600 shantytown residents were displaced, among them Irish pig farmers, German gardeners, and the black Seneca Village population. The project took sixteen years and the modern equivalent of $20 million to realize.

Although the designers opposed the idea, ball fields were introduced in the 1860s and public sculptures installed, though only Bethesda Fountain was included in the original design. Grazing in Sheep Meadow was discontinued in 1934 and the sheepfold became Tavern on the Green. In 1965, the park was declared a national historic landmark, and as a part of urban renewal and countercultural movements during the '60s, the park hosted rock concerts and "be-ins." Deterioration during the 1970s led to a revival of the Greensward Plan by the Central Park Conservancy in the 1980s, reinstating the park as the public respite it was constructed to be.

Belvedere Castle

One of the main attractions at the Castle, apart from the view, is the Henry Luce Nature Observatory, which identifies local bird and plant life. Also located here is the Weather Center, the source for New York local weather forecasters.
Mid-park near 79th Street, ⑥ to 77th St., ⑧⑥ to 81st St.-Museum of Natural History

The Carousel

Open for slow-paced spinning year round.
Mid-park at 64th Street, 879-0244, ⑥ to 68th St.-Hunter College, ①⑨ to 66th St.-Lincoln Cntr.

The Conservatory Garden

This garden is one of New York's best examples of formal landscaping in the European tradition, with fountains, flowers, and shaded pathways.
East Side, near 105th St., ⑥ to 103rd St.

Charles A. Dana Discovery Center

A performance space for multicultural dance and music where the Harlem Meer Performance Festival is held.
110th St. and Fifth and Lenox Aves., 860-1370, ②⑨ to 110th St. (Central Park North) ♿

Delacorte Theater

Shakespeare in the Park lures stars like Patrick Stewart and Andre Braugher to its leading roles. Tickets are free at the box office at 1pm on the day of the show. Be prepared to arrive as early as 4am on weekends for the most popular shows, though you can sleep later on weekdays.
West side near 81st St., 861-7277, ⑧⑥ to 81st-Museum of Natural History

The Harlem Meer

The Meer is a haven for locals, many of whom have fished there for as long as they can remember. The Charles A. Dana Discovery Center is situated on its northern bank and to the south and west lies the pool, with its lush greenery, a running stream, and even a small waterfall.
Northeast corner of the park, ⑧⑥ to Cathedral Parkway (110th St.)

The Reservoir

The Reservoir lies directly to the north of the Great Lawn, recently refurbished by the Parks Dept. It is circled by the park's main running track, which is about a mile-and-a-half around and named for New York icon and philanthropist Jacqueline Kennedy Onassis.
Mid-park between 86th and 96th Sts., ④⑤⑥ to 86th St., ①②③⑨ to 96th St.

The Mall

A stately avenue lined with trees and statues of great literary figures leads up to the band shell and fountain at Bethesda Terrace.
East side of the park, bet. 65th and 72nd Sts., ⑥ to 68th St.-Hunter College

Metropolitan Opera

Bring wine and a picnic basket in June and listen to arias as the stars come out and the skyline lights up; arrive early fora good seat. People seated farther from the stage treat the opera as background music for conversations so be prepared to shush. Admission is free.
Great Lawn, 362-6000, ⑧⑥ to 81st St.-Museum of Natural History

The Ramble

This 37-acre natural woodland has winding paths and open lawns; the perfect place to bring a book and read in the shade.
Northeast side of the lake, ⓑⓒ to 72nd St.

The Shakespeare Garden

Leading upwards to Belvedere Castle, The Shakespeare Garden is reminiscent of the villa gardens of Northern Italy. In this formal garden grows every species of flower or plant mentioned in Shakespeare's plays.
West side of the park, at 80th Street,
ⓑⓒ to 81st St.-Museum of Natural History

Sheep Meadow

The hot spot for sun-worshippers, Frisbee-players, and kite-flyers of all ages, sizes, and shapes. On sunny afternoons in summer, the grass cannot be seen for all the bodies, hence the Meadow's vaguely distasteful nickname, "Gettysburg."
West side of the park, mid-60s, ①⑨ to 66th St.-Lincoln Center.

Strawberry Fields

The heart-shaped grove, a memorial to John Lennon, is right across from the Dakota where Lennon was shot.
West side of the park, at 72nd St., ⓑⓒ to 72nd St.

SummerStage

A summer-long program of concerts, poetry readings, modern dance shows, and other events.
Rumsey Playfield, mid-park at 72nd St., 360-2777,
ⓑⓒ to 72nd St.

Swedish Cottage Marionette Theater

Performances take place on Saturday afternoons; call for reservations.
West park at 84st St., 988-9093, Cash Only, Admission $4-$5,
ⓑⓒ to 86th St.

The Wildlife Conservation Center

Open year-round, this zoo features fun not just for kids but for the whole family.
Fifth Ave. and 64th St. 861-6030, ⓒ to 68th St.-Hunter College

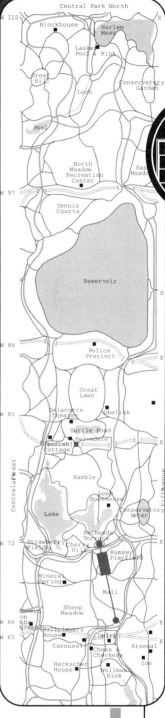

upper west side

"We're a kind of grown-up Greenwich Village," says 32-year-old Peter about the neighborhood where he has lived for the past four years. "Life up here seems more leisurely and mature than in the Village. It's also domestic, so much so that I'm always side-stepping baby carriages."

At night, the Upper West Side's stretch of Broadway pulses with activity, but its shine is friendly. Taxis make their way along the avenues, shuttling uptowners between historic restaurants, like Café des Artistes, and the city's most esteemed venue for the arts, Lincoln Center. The Center's enormous illuminated fountain reflects the glow of surrounding theaters, as well as the beckoning neon of bars and restaurants clustered across its expansive plaza. At the same time, collegiates barhop along Amsterdam Ave., while those with a more refined palate sample tortes and ladyfingers at the superb dessert cafés tucked away in sidestreet brownstones.

During the day, young professionals grab a cup of coffee at Zabar's before catching the subway to work. Parents drop off kids at progressive private schools. Lucky stiffs who have the day off can spend the afternoon in either Riverside or Central Park, or browse through one of the area's many boutiques.

While the Upper West Side has traditionally been associated with moderate-to-liberal intellectuals with a soft-spot for politically correctness, investment bankers and account executives climbing the rungs of the corporate ladder also populate the area. Ambitious singles have also come to inhabit the leviathan apartment buildings of Broadway and West End Ave., as well as the beautiful cross-streets between the two, from Lincoln Center on up to Straus Park at 110th St. Riverside Dr. features gorgeous architecture and views of its park, the Hudson River, and New Jersey.

With its strong community spirit, the Upper West Side strives for a balance between a tight-knit neighborhood and a sophisticated part of a massive metropolis. While not as hypersocial as Greenwich Village, this highly respectable niche of New York replaces some of downtown's pace with what its residents consider a more mature mix of work and play.

For five weeks each summer, the Fountain Plaza at Lincoln Center, snug between the Metropolitan Opera House, Avery Fisher Hall, and the New York State Theater, is dedicated to the **Midsummer Night Swing dance festival**. For less than $3 a night you can introduce yourself to everything from cajun to tango.

Different bands, many famous, come to play from Tuesday to Saturday. Teachers from the best dance schools in the city lead the crowd through basic steps; performers present athletic demonstrations, many of which put GAP ads to shame; and then everyone plunges into a mayhem of shuffles, spins, turns and dips.

A hallmark of the avant garde (yet simultaneously retro, reviving the jitterbug craze of the '30s and '40s when Frankie Manning and Willie Posey first learned the dance), swing is perhaps the hottest partner dance in New York. While the scene is still divided fairly sharply between the Lindy Hop tradition and the smoother West Coast movement, more dance clubs try to cater to both styles on different nights. Most clubs have free lessons for an hour before the band starts playing. Some of the most popular include:

The Greatest Bar on Earth

The spectacular view compensates for the small dance floor.
Windows on the World, 1 World Trade Center, 107th Floor, 524-7105

Irving Plaza

The most eclectic, friendly venue — Swing on Sundays only, hosted by the New York Swing Society
17 Irving Place, 777-6800

China Club

The main artery in an network of supper clubs hosting swing events, this is a den of traditional extravagance, dominating by professions and aspiring professionals.
268 West 48th St., 398-3800

Swing 46

Younger, more casual, and more of a bar than a dance hall.
349 W 46th St. 262-9554

For other supper club swing events, with varying cover charges, bands, and venues, call the Swing City Hotline (which also may offer discount passes) at 462-3250.

HISTORY

Though difficult to envision nowadays, the Upper West Side was once a distant suburb of New York City. Before the completion of the Ninth Ave. elevated train line in 1879, the area, known then as Bloomingdale, was a popular refuge from the crowded city. The Dakota, the famous West Side apartment building, received its name in the late 19th Century because residents felt it was so far from downtown that it might as well have been in the Dakotas.

The area did not truly become the Upper West Side until the development of Central Park, from 1856 to 1873. Its completion spurred a wave of construction, and by the turn of the 20th Century, notable cultural institutions such as the American Museum of Natural History moved into the neighborhood along the Park's exterior. The extension of the Interborough Rapid Transit in 1904 spurred the construction of many new residential buildings. The population of the area skyrocketed over the subsequent 25 years.

In the 1960s, a successful attempt at urban renewal trans

formed the area with the construction of Lincoln Center. The neighborhood became known for its social tolerance and political activism. Fashionable boutiques and restaurants opened along Columbus and Amsterdam Aves. As real estate prices rose, luxury apartment towers began springing up in the 1970s and '80s. Today, the Upper West Side grapples with Donald Trump's development proposal at the West Side Rail Yards. Running from 59th to 72nd Sts. along the river it is the last undeveloped plot of land in this former country retreat.

Pomander Walk

This private fairy-tale street of quaint Tudor houses, complete with flower-lined walks, old-fashioned lampposts, and colorful trim, was built to resemble the set of an eponymous play by the same name; tough-guy Humphrey Bogart is said to have been a resident.

94th to 95th Sts.(bet. Broadway and West End Ave.), ❶❷❸❾ to 96th St.

Soldiers' and Sailors' Monument

This 100-ft. tall memorial was erected in 1893 in memory of fallen military heroes. Declared a municipal landmark in 1976, the monument stands in the center of a cannon-lined, leafy esplanade in Riverside Park.

Riverside Drive at 89th Street, ❶❾ to 86th St.

The Ansonia

Completed in 1904 with the intention of bringing Parisian architecture to the Upper West Side, the building's interior has since been drastically altered. Most of the grand, irregularly shaped rooms have been subdivided. The ornate exterior is still intact and a landmark.

2109 Broadway (bet. 73rd and 74th Sts.), ❶❷❸❾ to 72nd St.

New York Historical Society

Established in 1804 in an effort to preserve and document the history of New York and the United States, a vast collection of art, Americana, crafts, printed material, and artifacts are available on display here at the oldest continually operating museum in the country.

2 West 77th St. (at Central Park West), 873-3400, ❽❾ to 81st St.-Museum of Natural History ♿

The Apthorp

Commissioned by William Waldorf Astor, who dreamed of a new, monumental style of building in New York, this enormous limestone structure was built around an elegant courtyard which is only open to tenants.

2211 Broadway (bet. 78th and 79th Sts.), ❶❾ to 79th St.

The Dakota

The turrets and shutters were more imposing when the whole building was black with over a hundred years of soot. After its recent bath, it is harder to picture it as the haunting backdrop for the film *Rosemary's Baby*. As one of four famous twin towered buildings so distinctive on Central Park West — the others being the Majestic, San Remo, and Eldorado — this exclusive apartment building attracts celebrity residents. Since 1980, the doormen have spent most of their time answering questions about the exact spot where John Lennon was assassinated.

1 West 72nd St. (at Central Park West), ❽❿ to 72nd St.

Public Plaza at Fordham University

Built by Robert Moses, the Upper West Side branch of the Bronx university was established in the early '60s in an effort to revitalize the area. Located above street level, this quiet sunny plaza has a marble wall and a sculpture of St. Peter casting his net.

60th to 62nd Sts. (bet. Columbus and Amsterdam Aves.), ❶❷❸❿❶❾ to 59th St.-Columbus Circle

Riverside Park

Frederick Law Olmsted, co-creator of Central Park, also designed this less crowded three-tiered neighborhood retreat. Courts, playing fields, and a half-pipe are available for public use.

Riverside Drive (bet. 72nd and 125rd Sts.)

New York Society for Ethical Culture

This secular humanist association began in 1876 on the philosophical basis of ethical idealism. The group is dedicated to bettering human relations in the city. Active social and political reformers, the society's members have advocated rights for workers, women, and the poor; it is right at home in the traditionally liberal Upper West Side.

2 West 64th St. (at Central Park West), 874-5210,
Ⓐ Ⓑ Ⓒ Ⓓ ① ⑨ to 59th St.-Columbus Circle ♿

Lincoln Center

San Juan Hill, the setting for West Side Story, was leveled in the '60s to make way for the city's cultural heart, which now draws over five million people a year. The New York State Theater, Avery Fisher Hall, the Metropolitan Opera House, the Juilliard School, the Performing Arts branch of

the New York Public Library, and the Walter Reade Theater are all housed within the complex, designed by Robert Moses and funded largely by the Rockefellers.

62nd to 66th Sts. (bet. Columbus and Amsterdam Aves.),
① ⑨ to 66th St.-Lincoln Center ♿

West Side Community Garden

Paths lined with benches and all kinds of flora surround this old-fashioned patch of greenery. The park extended over the entire block until ten years ago, when developers moved in with high-rise apartment buildings. There is a waiting list for plots in the vegetable and flower garden.

89th to 90th Sts. (bet. Amsterdam and Columbus Aves.),
580-1399, ① ⑨ to 86th St. ♿

movies & books

Rosemary's Baby, 1968

Director Roman Polanski's breakthrough, starring Mia Farrow as a housewife whose husband makes a creepy Faustian bargain; filmed in The Dakota (1 West 72nd St.; called The Bramford in the film).

West Side Story, 1961

This modern day Romeo and Juliet was filmed in the tenements in the lower 60s, before they were razed to build Lincoln Center.

You've Got Mail, 1998

Tom Hanks and Meg Ryan fall in love on-line against the backdrop of the Upper West Side and the shops, parks, and restaurants that are the pride of its residents.

parks

a s a t u r d a y
IN THE UPPER WEST SIDE

Good Enough to Eat
Get here promptly and get in line
for one of the best brunches
the Upper West Side affords.
Locals just can't say enough about
the stuff this place serves up.
(see Restaurants)

American Museum of Natural History
Feel like a kid on a field trip
as you circumnavigate dinosaur bones
and then continue your tour of
historic apartment houses.
(see Visual Arts)

[cheap thrills}

Student Discount Tickets at Lincoln Center
Check the box office at the City Opera a few hours
before evening performances for dirt-cheap
student rush tickets. You may get to sit in
the front row for your favorite opera,
content with the knowledge that you paid $50 less
than the person sitting a few seats over.
Lincoln Center, ❶❾ to 66th St.-Lincoln Center ♿

Upper West Side Architecture Tour
This neighborhood features some of the City's most interesting buildings, including The Apthorp, The Ansonia, and The Dakota. The last of these in particular has played an important role in the city's cultural and cinematic history.
(see Sites & Parks)

Gabriel's
The perfect blend of class and casual, the menu here makes great seasonal adaptations, making it worth a trip at least four times a year.
(see Restaurants)

Shark Bar
This rowdy and culturally flavorful haunt is an excellent place to scope for celebrities and end your day on an upbeat note. They also serve food, so if you skip Gabriel's and have a taste for soul food, this may be your best bet.
(see Nightlife)

Symphony under the Stars
Lincoln Center offers free summer concerts in Damrosch Park.
Lincoln Center, 546-2656, ❶❾ to 66th St.-Lincoln Center ♿

$3.50 Movies
The Loews Cineplex Worldwide Cinema offers first-run films at discounted prices about two to three months after opening.
Call for listings.
340 West 50th St. (bet. Eighth and Ninth Aves.),
246-1560, ❶❾ to 50th St. ♿

morningside heights

Morningside Heights is a small town in the big city. As removed from Manhattan's exceedingly developed urban core today as it was at the turn of the century, the neighborhood lies outside the perimeter of most sightseers' travels and affords a welcome reprieve from expected city noise and congestion.

Here the business of education harmonizes with the restful quietude of a largely residential area. Many small communities exist within the larger academic ones of Columbia University, Barnard and Bank Street Colleges, and the Jewish and Union Theological Seminaries. A congenial air pervades the neighborhood. Even the many panhandlers become familiar faces though sobering reminders of the urban blight that creeps around Morningside's edges.

Sandwiched between two parks, Morningside and Riverside, Columbia University is the neighborhood's largest landholder. The University has been instrumental in influencing the character of Morningside Heights, not only because of its intellectual presence, but also its sweeping control over residential property.

During the week, bookbag-toting students with busy schedules rush into Columbia Bagels, Tamarind Seed, or other popular eateries for a meal-on-the-run between classes. Area businesses range from bars that draw both working-class crowds and local bookworms, to street vendors peddling plastic sunglasses and inexpensive dog-eared books.

Columbia University's Campus Walk interrupts 116th St. between Broadway and Amsterdam Ave. and is a great place to people-watch. The steps outside Low Memorial Library provide lounge space for students on a break from classes. Riverside Park, the neighborhood's largest, is often packed with sun-worshippers during the spring and summer, and remains a perennial favorite place to walk the dog or go running.

Morningside Heights also supports a thriving and highly visible Hispanic community, whose restaurants, barber shops, botanicas, and other businesses flourish several blocks south of 110th St. on Amsterdam Ave.

In the summer, when most students are on vacation, the area often seems deserted. Locals who normally avoid student hangouts reclaim their turf, giving the neighborhood an equally pleasant, but refreshingly different atmosphere until classes resume in September.

There's a party going on beneath the steel arcades of Riverside Drive. You could almost call it a free-for-all. Olive lovers mingle with coffee connoisseurs, Belgian beer enthusiasts mix with caviar fiends — the invite-list includes all types. And the occasion? No occasion. The event runs from eight in the morning till eleven at night, 364 days a year (the revelry pauses on Christmas). And get this: there is no waiting in line, unless you count the checkout stand.

The owners of **Fairway** on 12th Ave. (bet. 132nd and 133rd Sts.) cordially invite you to shop your heart out in their 35,000-square-foot extravaganza of edibles, New York's number one food warehouse. "This is rock-n-roll for the food business," says Steven Jenkins, General Manager of the second Fairway to feed the greater New York area (the original is on West 74th St.). But the only beet you'll find is cooked, peeled and delivered directly from France. ("It's not sold anywhere else in the city," Jenkins says of the gourmet root his three-

year-old market imports.) Fairway's other products are no less distinct: Sixteen varieties of olives, an extensive selection of kosher meats and oodles of fine imported caviar — "Fairway is caviar central" reads a store banner — are just a few of the items to grace the shelves, and there are thousands more. But don't be fooled by all the gourmet fare; there is plenty of standard stuff like orange juice — in fact, five overhead carts are devoted to Tropicana alone. Chances are, if you crave it, Fairway's got it, and in mass quantity. The produce section, with its enormous stock of fruit, could engulf your corner market. There are enough packages of tenderloin and rib-eye steak in the meat department to stuff a regiment of Sub-Zero refrigerators. There's even a parking lot for epicures whose eyes are bigger than their carts. These days, Manhattan's culinary ante is up — uptown, to be exact — and it won't be easy to improve upon. "Comparisons are odious," Jenkins boasts, justifiably. "We don't follow trends, we set them."

H I S T O R Y

The ridge that gives this neighborhood its name becomes noticeable at 110th St., or Cathedral Parkway, so named for the as-yet-incomplete Episcopal Cathedral of St. John the Divine. This local institution serves as a focal point for both religious and community activists; one favorite tradition that unites both parties is the popular Baptism of animals on St. Francis of Assisi, during which pet-owners can have their loved ones consecrated. Behind the cathedral runs Morningside Park, formed by the narrow strip of rocky cliff that runs from 110th to 123rd Sts. Towards the west, overlooking the Hudson, stands Riverside Church, which recalls France's Cathedral of Chartres in its design. Near that is Grant's Tomb, constructed in 1897.

But the neighborhood is best known as the home of a certain Ivy League Institution: Barnard and Columbia Colleges banded together to become Columbia University in 1896. Later, such institutions as Teacher's College and the Jewish and Union Theological Seminaries came under Columbia's auspices. In 1897, the school established a permanent home on the McKim, Mead, and White-designed Morningside Heights campus, and has since put its unmistakable stamp, for better or for worse, on the neighborhood. Until recently, the campus gates marked more than just a physical divide between the academic and local populations. New building initiatives around the campus and in the neighborhood are seeking to serve both groups, proof that the administration has realized the value of giving back to the neighborhood as much as it draws from it.

Cathedral of St. John the Divine

The largest Gothic cathedral in the world and principal church of the Episcopal Diocese of New York, it is both a place of worship and the host to a multitude of community events, including a 4am Winter Solstice celebration, an all-night recitation of Dante's Inferno, a Halloween showing of Nosferatu, as well as the more traditional chamber music and candlelight Vespers.
1040 Amsterdam Ave. (at 112th St.), 316-7540, **①⑨** *to 110th St.* ♿

Postcrypt Coffeehouse in St. Paul's Chapel

Although the setting of this unique venue — gothic, solemn, vaguely vampirical — might seem to lend itself primarily to organ music, with an occasional interruption by one of The Cure's less cheery songs, the Postcrypt Coffeehouse actually offers an expansive variety of folk, jazz, and even country music; as long as it's "un-plugged," you can find it here, while checking out the architecture of Columbia University's St. Paul's chapel in the process. For no charge, it's a great chance to see some future stars; Suzanne Vega played some of her first gigs here!
Columbia University (at 116th St. and Broadway), 854-1953, www.columbia.edu/~crypt/, Cash Only, No cover, Open: F-Sa 9pm-12am (during school year only), **①⑨** *to 116th St.-Columbia University*

Columbia University Campus

Architecturally and financially the centerpiece of the neighborhood, this heavily symmetrical creation of McKim, Mead, and White appears uncannily like a walled city from the outside; recent construction and renovation projects solidify this Ivy's presence just under Harlem. Low Library (now an administrative building) was once voted one of the most beautiful buildings in North America. The "Steps," one of the best hangouts in NY, is a great spot for people-watching and lazing in the sun. The plaza below is a grassy playground for co-eds and families alike.
From 114th to 120th Sts. (bet. Broadway and Amsterdam Ave.), 854-1754, **①⑨** *to 116th St.-Columbia University* ♿

Manhattan School of Music

Prodigies at one of the country's most prestigious music conservatories perform, usually for free, in the school's plain looking (but great sounding) home, a building which housed the Julliard School (now at Lincoln Center) for the better part of this century.
120 Claremont Avenue (at 122nd St.), 749-2802, Cash Only, **①⑨** *to 125th St.* ♿

General Grant Ashley Memorial
America's largest mausoleum, this tomb, once marred by graffiti, is now in prime condition. Recently, residents of the neighborhood fought to preserve mosaic benches around its perimeter.
Riverside Drive (at 122nd St.), 666-1640, ❶❾ to 116th St.-Columbia University

New York Buddhist Temple
This branch of the Japanese Buddhist sect Jodo Shinshu welcomes all visitors to the Sunday services, which are conducted in both Japanese and English, and to meditation workshops.
331-332 Riverside Drive (bet. 105th and 106th Sts.), *678-0305,* ❶❾ to 110th St.

Riverside Church

Modeled after the celebrated Cathedral at Chartres, this interdenominational church boasts spectacular stained-glass windows, the world's largest carillon, and an impressive view of the city from its tower. (Take a free ride to the top on Sats.) If you're in the area at night, look up - if the church is illuminated, you'll be glad you did. Lectures and concerts are held regularly; call for information.
490 Riverside Dr. (at 120th St.), *870-6700,* ❶❾ to 116th St. Columbia University ♿

Miriam and Ira D. Wallach Art Gallery
Columbia's gallery presents exhibitions throughout the year, curated by professors and students who ensure an academic tilt to the line-up. Lectures and receptions are often sponsored in conjunction with exhibits.
2960 Broadway (at 116th St.), 854-7288, ❶❾ to 116th St.-Columbia University ♿

movies & books

Hannah and Her Sisters, 1986
Barbara Hershey takes an adult education class, and in her spare time she hangs out with her new friend on the majestic Low Library steps. As is often the case in Woody's films (and life), Hershey's character marries an older mentor, a Columbia professor.

The Mirror Has Two Faces, 1996
Barbra Streisand and Jeff Bridges play Columbia University professors who fall in love, though not without their share of trauma. If you can stand the cheese, it's worth seeing all the scenes that are filmed on and around the serene campus.

Amsterdam Café

Much of the crowd here is local and older, but students can still be seen, particularly on the weekends. Friendly neighborhood feel with a good menu of classic bar items and pastas. Their weekend brunch for $4.95 is the best deal in the area.
(see Restaurants)

Cathedral of St. John the Divine

This is the largest Gothic cathedral in the world, with an interior composed of 14 bays depicting mankind's vocations, and 7 chapels, each paying tribute to a different ethnic group.
(see Sites & Parks)

[cheap thrills}

Opera Night at Caffé Taci

Friday and Saturday nights are a raucous good time as opera singers, often students from nearby Manhattan School of Music, raise their voices amongst late-night diners, bar dwellers, and coffee sippers.
(see Restaurants)

Free Folk Music and Popcorn

The Postcrypt Coffeehouse at Columbia University offers free live folk music on Fridays and Saturdays starting at 9pm (during the school year only).
(see Sites & Parks)

General Grant Ashley Memorial
Someone's buried here.
We're not sure who, but would you
let us know once you find out?
On the way, you'll pass through
scenic Riverside Park with its
views and dog walkers.
(see Sites & Parks)

Book Tour
Due to its academic denizen,
Morningside Heights has
more than its share of
book dealers. Papyrus,
Labyrinth Books, and
Bank St. Bookstore should
give you more than
enough to leaf through.
(see Literature)

The West End
For dinner, head over to this old stand-by
for Columbia students — indeed, it's
always been a favorite nightspot. Perhaps
that's because of its proximity to the
main campus and its versatility as bar,
restaurant, theater, and concert hall.
(see Nightlife)

Peacock Watching at St. John the Divine
Just about the most unexpected phenomenon in
Morningside Heights could very well be
a glimpse of these exotic birds
strutting and sunning amongst the foliage.
New York City is nothing if not full of surprises!
(see Sites & Parks)

harlem

In the collective imagination, Harlem has two identities: its glorious heritage as the intellectual, political, spiritual, and artistic capital of Black America, and its tragic recent history as a community besieged by poverty, crime, drugs, racism, and political disempowerment. In truth, Harlem accommodates these images, but also many in between. Absorbing not only the African American populations for which it is most famous but also increasing numbers of Cubans and Dominicans, trying to balance the needs of the upwardly mobile with the realities of deeply rooted poverty, Harlem is undergoing radical economic and cultural transformations.

The largest neighborhood in all of Manhattan, stretching from the Hudson River and West Harlem to Spanish Harlem and the East River, Harlem's diversity is inscribed in its buildings and on its streets. Many of the area's row houses and brownstones are beautifully restored, pristinely kept while a fraction the price of those on the Upper West Side. Others, though, are derelict and abandoned. Twelfth-generation Americans mingle with first-generation immigrants in both housing projects and historic, genteel brownstones in Striver's Row, Hamilton Heights, and Sugar Hill. Upscale restaurants, supper clubs, boutiques, and other small businesses are sprouting up amidst fast-food joints, thrift stores, bodegas, and lush public gardens that function as neighborhood gathering places.

Racism and the economic and political disenfranchisement which generally accompany bigotry have reinforced physical and psychological boundaries, rendering Harlem a city unto itself. Many Harlemites lament that the closest many tourists (and even native New Yorkers) dare to come to their community is to admire the panoramic view from the other side of that seemingly impassable threshold of Morningside Park.

Fortunately, through the efforts both of the city and its native sons and daughters, Harlem is currently experiencing an economic and social resurgence. Harlem's club scene in particular is experiencing a renaissance the likes of which it hasn't seen since the '50s. Nocturnes will relish Harlem's jazz clubs, such as Showmans and the Lenox Lounge. But regardless of the attractions Harlem may boast, it is first and foremost a place where people live.

While **The Boys Choir of Harlem** might be young, uptown's most famous group of singers is anything but inexperienced. In fact, with three hours of rehearsal daily and two years in a Preparatory Choir prior to entrance, these boys have logged more hours singing on stage than many do in a lifetime of showers.

Founded in 1968 by artist/educator Dr. Walter J. Turnbull as a way for inner city kids to escape the depressing situations many of them found on the streets, The Choir started with a group of twenty boys from Ephesus Church. It has since grown to be a body celebrated by the world at large. As time went on, the Choir developed a reputation for the energy and spunk of its performances, a reputation which earned it its first European tour in 1979. The tour was filmed as an Emmy Award winning television special "From Harlem to Haarelm: the story of a Choir Boy."

The Boy's Choir of Harlem is known not only for the quality of its training but the variety in its songs. It performs numbers from classical, jazz, contemporary, gospel, and spiritual music on its international touring schedule of over 100 annual shows to a combined live audience of over 150,000 people. The Choir has performed with artists like Stevie Wonder, and with orchestras such as the New York Philharmonic. It has also sung repeated-

ly at The White House and was recently awarded the National Medal of Arts.

But hearing is believing. So catch the current members of The Boys Choir of Harlem to learn what all the noise is about.

H I S T O R Y

In 1925, when Alain Locke edited *The New Negro*, an anthology of poetry and prose by up-and-coming black artists, he wrote, "I believe that the Negro's advantages and opportunities are greater in Harlem than in any other place in the country, and that Harlem will become the intellectual, cultural, and the financial center for Negroes of the United States, and will exert a vital influence upon all Negro peoples."

The Harlem Renaissance of the late 1920s proved Locke correct, but Harlem's population in the early part of that decade was by no means entirely black.

The area was originally settled by the Dutch, who named it Nieuw Haarlem since it was so far from the settled areas of New York. Many immigrants from Ireland and Germany settled around 125th St. As more and more blacks moved into the area, however, whites began to leave. The combined effect of white flight and black migration from the south helped solidify the development of black Harlem.

This new concentration of blacks spurred on the Harlem Renaissance, as many wealthy Harlemites began entertaining and organizing literary and social clubs. At these gather-

ings, authors and poets such as Countee Cullen, Langston Hughes, and Zora Neale Hurston read from their works, and locals discussed politics and arts.

The Depression sent the area into decline, and racial tensions erupted in several large-scale riots. Today, business and rebuilding efforts from within the community are helping restore Harlem to its former glory, and prominent members of the black community live in the area. Perhaps that's why soon-to-be-former South African president Nelson Mandela called Harlem, "the capital of the black world."

Abyssinian Baptist Church

Pastor Adam Clayton Powell, Sr. built this church from 1920-23 to serve the needs of the growing numbers of blacks on the Upper West Side, naming it for its first worshipers, Abyssinian merchants wanting to maintain their connection with Africa. The congregation has grown to over 4,000 and is known for its community involvement.
132 West 138th St. (bet. Adam Clayton Powell, Jr. and Malcolm X Blvds.), 862-7474, **2&3** *to 135th St.* ♿

Hamilton Grange National Memorial

When Alexander Hamilton commissioned this house from one of City Hall's architects, John McComb Jr., the location was far removed from the heart of New York. Today, it serves as a public museum operating under the auspices of the National Park Service in the heart of Hamilton Heights.
287 Convent Ave. (at 141st St.), 283-5154, Open: F-Su 9am-5pm, **A&B&C&D** *to 145th St.*

Jackie Robinson Park

Oak-lined walkways, an Olympic-sized pool, bandshells, and pick-up basketball make this oasis in Harlem's St. Nicholas district one of the area's best-equipped parks. Originally known as Colonial Park, in 1978 it was renamed after the Brooklyn Dodger legend.
145th to 152nd Sts. (bet. Edgecombe and Bradhurst Aves.), 234-9607, **A&B&C&D** *to 145th St.* ♿

Marcus Garvey Park

The "Back to Africa" spokesman and noted civil rights leader was honored by the 1973 renaming of Mt. Morris Park. The park boasts an iron frame bell tower built in 1956, as well as a manmade bed of rocks in the center of the park which offers one of the city's best vistas.
120th to 124th Sts. (bet. Fifth and Madison Aves.), 410-2818, **2&3** *to 125th St.* ♿

Riverbank State Park

Uptown's sprawling athletic facility is free and open to the public. Swim, run laps around the outdoor track, or take in a soothing view of the Hudson from the high terrace.
679 Riverside Dr. (bet. 137th and 145th Sts.), 694-3600, **1&9** *to 145th St.*

Sugar Hill

By 1919, this area supported a wealthy enclave among its sizable working-class and middle-class contingents and was dubbed Sugar Hill to reflect the "sweet life" of its residents. W.E.B. Du Bois and Thurgood Marshall resided at this area's most well-known address, 409 Edgecombe Avenue, which has since been designated a landmark.
145th to 155th Sts. (bet. Edgecombe and St. Nicholas Aves.), **A&B&C&D** *to 145th St.*

s i t e s +

Malcolm Shabazz Masjid (Mosque of Islam)

Founded by Malcolm
X in the 1950s, this
silver-domed mosque
has become the coun-
try's most renowned
Black Muslim place
of worship.
102 West 116th St.
(bet. Adam Clayton
Powell, Jr. and
Malcolm X Blvds.),
662-2200,
❷❸ *to 116th St.* ♿

El Museo del Barrio

Located at the tippy top of Museum Mile, this museum
establishes a forum that preserves and projects the cultural
heritage of Puerto Ricans and all Latin Americans in the U.S.
The museum hosts bilingual public programs, educational
activities, and festivals.
1230 Fifth Ave. (at 104th St.), 831-7272, MC, V, AmEx,
Admission (suggested): $2-$4, Open: W-Su 11am-5pm,
❻ *to 103rd St.* ♿

Schomburg Center for Research in Black Culture

World-famous for its extensive research facilities, this branch
of the New York Public Library is an invaluable resource for
scholars of black history and culture.
515 Malcolm X Blvd. (at 135th St.), 491-2200, Open: M-W
noon-8pm, Th-Sa 10am-6pm, Su 1pm-5pm, ❷❸ *to 135th St.* ♿

St. Nicholas Park

On a rainy day, this lush park seems more like a rain forest
than an urban oasis. Well-preserved paths wind through a
refreshing landscape linking City College, Sugar Hill,
Hamilton Place, and Convent Ave.
127th to 141st Sts. (bet. St. Nicholas Ave. and St. Nicholas
Ter.), ❽❷ *to 135th St.*

p a r k s

movies & books

The Street, 1946

This was the first novel
written by an African-
American woman to sell
over a million copies. Author
Ann Petry's depiction of life
in Harlem and her ability to
look closely at the issues
facing her community there
won her critical acclaim.

Underworld, 1997

On October 3rd, 1951,
Bobby Thomson of the
New York Giants hit the
most famous home run in
New York City history. Don
DeLillo's epic traces the
"shot heard 'round the
world" from the center field
bleachers in Harlem's Polo
Grounds through America's
history in the second half
of the 20th Century. The
Polo Grounds, one of the
country's most eccentric ball
fields, was demolished in
the spring of 1964.

Well's

Do homemade cornbread and strawberry butter perk your breakfast antennae? Since 1938, Harlemites have swooned over this family-run legend.
(see Restaurants)

Sugar Hill

Take a stroll in this historic district. The stretch between 145th and 137th Sts. is lined with beautiful, historic brownstones. Make sure to see W.E.B. Du Bois and Thurgood Marshall's former home at 409 Edgecombe Ave.
(see Sites & Parks)

[cheap *thrills*}

Dance Theatre of Harlem

On the second Sunday of every month from November to May, the Theatre hosts an open house to showcase its excellent dancers. Equally thrilling, if more expensive, are its renowned dance classes, offered in African, ballet, jazz, and other forms, and geared towards dancers of various levels.
466 West 152nd St. (bet. Amsterdam and St. Nicholas Aves.), 690-2800, **Ⓐ Ⓑ Ⓒ** *to 155th St.*

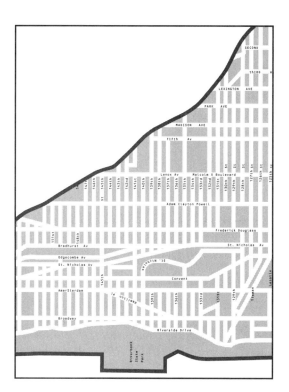

Studio Museum in Harlem
Soak up a little culture at this innovative setting for arts of Africa and Black America. (Saturday tours aren't all corn-bread and pretty buildings!)
(see Visual Arts)

Mart 125
Feed your eyes browsing among handicrafts from all different cultures, then take care of your stomach with something from the food court upstairs.
(see Shopping)

Londel's
A night in Harlem wouldn't be complete without visiting one of the supper clubs for which it is famous. Although Londel's is new, its classy musical and gastronomic acts are certainly reminiscent of the neighborhood's glory days.
(see Restaurants)

Lenox Lounge
Superb live jazz jam session, with no cover for the second set every Monday (around 10:30pm).
288 Lenox Ave. (bet. 124th and 125th Sts.),
427-0253, ❷❸ to 125th St.

Studio Museum in Harlem
For just $5, experience this pioneering museum, focusing on arts from Africa and Black America.
(see Visual Arts)

washington heights

Of all the neighborhoods in New York City undergoing a renaissance, Washington Heights is perhaps the most deserving and overdue. Throughout the late 1970s and into the '80s, its name served as a synonym for crack-cocaine, after then-U.S. District Attorney Rudy Giuliani and future U.S. Senator Alfonse D'Amato went undercover to prove how easy such purchases were. This event, immortalized on the front page of the New York Post, has dogged the area's image for years.

Now Washington Heights, its reputation on an upswing, is on the cusp of trendiness. A walk through the hopping shopping districts of 181st St. and 207th St. confirms just how vibrant and healthy the area can be. Inwood, Manhattan's northern-most neighborhood, continues onward from 207th St. up to the Harlem River Ship Canal, just north of Fort Tryon Park, home to the Cloisters (the Metropolitan Museum of Art's medieval art complex), as well as stunning vistas to the west, towards the New Jersey Palisades. Nestling in the northeastern reaches of the island is the wild and woolly Inwood Hill Park, where you can still find artifacts from the Algonquin village that once stood here.

For much of the 20th Century, Washington Heights and Inwood have welcomed large and lively immigrant communities. German, Irish,

Jewish, and Greek settlements strung along Broadway have recently been joined by Latin (mostly Dominican) ones, as well as refugees from the overpriced neighborhoods of southern Manhattan. This last influx has led real estate agents to cynically rename the area west of Fort Washington Ave. as "Hudson Heights," attempting to circumvent negative associations with Washington Heights.

Dominating the eastern section of the mid-Heights is Yeshiva University, founded as the first Jewish parochial school in the country. Ten blocks to the south is High Bridge Watch Tower, an architectural leftover from the city's Roman-inspired 19th Century aqueduct system. The tower's analog on the west side of the island is the mighty and graceful George Washington Bridge, the only bridge linking New Jersey and Manhattan. Another Heights features is the newly developed Audubon Biomedical Science and Technology Park, built behind the preserved facade of the Audubon Ballroom, site of Malcolm X's assassination.

This area has always accommodated the blend of middle- and working-class, old world and new, urban and parkland, a scene which is leading out-siders to understand what locals have always known — Washington Heights and Inwood are an authentic microcosm of the city experience.

A little-known cultural gem in Washington Heights, the **Audubon Terrace Museum Complex** is a cluster of museums and cultural institutions built around an eclectic courtyard. In addition to housing Boricua College and the American Numismatic Society, the complex is home to the prestigious American Academy of Arts and Letters and The Hispanic Society of America.

The American Academy was founded in 1904 by the National Institute of Arts and Letters to recognize achievements in the arts, with artists admitted to its select membership by a process of peer review — past members include Mark Twain and Duke Ellington, and current ones include Jasper Johns and Toni Morrison. The Academy presents three exhibitions a year on the arts and literature, drawing on its library's resources (over 25,000 books and 2,000 manuscripts, paintings, and photographs) and works by and about its members and award recipients.

Meanwhile, The Hispanic Society is the Complex's real spectatorial treat. Founded in 1904, it is now home to the country's largest collection of Iberian, Latin American, and Filipino arts, literature, and culture. Particular strengths lie in the Spanish Golden Age (1550-1700); late 19th and early 20th Century materials, including paintings by masters such as El Greco, Goya, and Velázquez; sculpture; decorative arts (highlights are Hispano-Moresque and Mexican ceramics and both sacred and secular gold and silver works); textiles; and archeological artifacts. The Society's library contains manuscripts and rare books from such literary luminaries as Mexico's Sor Juana Inés de la Cruz.

Like Washington Heights itself, the area's cultural landmarks have been slow to catch on as major attractions. As the neighborhood grows in stature, the Audubon Terrace Museum Complex is sure to be among its most appealing draws. *155th St. and Broadway,* ❶ *to 157 St.*

H I S T O R Y

Until the turn of the twentieth century, the region of Washington Heights was still a largely undeveloped countryside, dotted with wealthy estates boasting spectacular views of the Hudson River. This condition changed abruptly in 1904 with the arrival of the IRT subway line which, within two years, had reached the tip of Manhattan and points north.

This development in transportation led to a sharp class divide along Broadway, with poorer residents to the south and east segregated from more prosperous communities to the north and west. Many Greeks and Irish settled in the poorer areas and were soon joined by an influx of Jews, an increasingly ubiquitous people as its refugees fled Germany. Quick population shifts unfortunately resulted in the predictable ethnic tensions: Right-wing groups and gangs vandalized synagogues and assaulted young Jews during the '30s and '40s, and many immigrants became disenchanted with this neighborhood that was ideally supposed to offer escape from foreign persecution and bigotry.

By the '60s, the area was largely abandoned by the Irish and Jewish settlers and became home to a predominantly black, Puerto Rican, and Cuban population. The 1965 assassination of Malcolm X in the Audubon Ballroom was simultaneously a reminder of earlier conflict and a harbinger of the crime wave that was to hit the city, in general, and Washington Heights, in particular, during the '80s.

The immigrant population continued to change, with Dominicans coming to outnumber other residents; by 1990, there were more Dominicans in Washington Heights than in any other U.S. community. District lines were eventually redrawn to offer residents better government representation, and in 1991, Guillermo Linares became the country's first elected official of Dominican descent.

Baker Field

After student rioters in the '60s effectively canceled plans for a massive recreational facility in Morningside Park, Columbia built here instead, in the midst of a neighborhood of beautiful brownstones. Now that C.U. football has ended decades of losing seasons, crowds have begun to make the trek to Manhattan's northern tip.
Broadway at 218th St., ❶ *to 215th St.*

Dyckman Street Marina

This marina at the western end of Dyckman St. — the only point above 145th St. where river access isn't blocked — is one of the latest steps in recent revitalization plans for the waterfront. The marina development has sparked a clean-up movement — rumor has it, Bette Midler has recently rolled up her sleeves and joined the litter patrol!
Dyckman St. on the Hudson River,
❶ *to Dyckman 200 St.*

Fort Tryon Park

Home to the Cloisters, the entire park sparkles with the sheen of maintenance: well-manicured flower beds, shady hilltops, and winding paths all make the park ideal for picnicking.
Entrances at 191st and 200th Sts., 360-1311,
Ⓐ *to 190th St.*

Inwood Hill Park

This uptown expanse of woodland boasts cross-country ski trails, caves that were once inhabited by a local tribe, and the island's last remnant of primeval forest. Park Rangers organize tours of the caves during the summer; safety concerns dictate that you not explore them alone.
Entrance at 207th St. and Seaman Ave., 360-1311, Ⓐ *to 207th St.*

Trinity Church Cemetery

Once part of John J. Audubon's farm, the gentle hill cresting at Amsterdam Ave. holds the rural cemetery of the Financial District's Trinity Church. The church, boasting 13th Century glass window-panes, overlooks the Hudson.

153rd to 155th Sts. (bet. Riverside Dr. and Amsterdam Ave.), 368-1600, ⒶⒷⒸ *to 155th St.,* ❶ *to 157th St.* ♿

Dyckman Farmhouse Museum

A museum of 18th Century farmhouse life, located in one of Manhattan's oldest residences, reminds you that the city did not spring from the soil full-grown. Period furnishings and quiet gardens maintain the mood. Benches out front are ideal for catching rays or hanging out with the area's elderly (and no, none of them lived here).
4881 Broadway (at 204th St.), 304-9422, Admission: free, Open: Tu-Su 11am-4pm,
Ⓐ *to 207th St.*

Morris-Jumel Mansion

Down from the remaining farmhouse is the area's extant Georgian mansion, built in 1765, where General Washington, among others, kept his headquarters during the Revolution. It subsequently became a tavern before it was bought in 1810 by the Jumels, one of the wealthiest families of mid-19th Century America.
65 Jumel Terrace (at 160th St.), 923-8008,
Cash Only, Admission: $3, Open: W-Su 10am-4pm,
A **B** **C** to 163rd St.-Amsterdam Ave.

The Cloisters

A smorgasbord of old-style European glories, not to mention the finest picnicking in the city. The Met has its famed medieval collection here, including the breathtaking Unicorn tapestries, and medieval-themed readings and concerts keep hobbyists and scholars busy.

The Cloisters themselves are a collection of European chapels and buildings in the Gothic and Romantic styles that were disassembled and shipped overseas stone by stone by John D. Rockefeller, Jr. and George Barnard, then reassembled way uptown.
Fort Tryon Park, 923-3700, Cash Only, Admission (suggested): $5-$10, Open: Tu-Su 9:30am-5:30pm,
A to 190th St.

movies&
books

A Perfect Murder, 1998

In this 1998 remake of Alfred Hitchcock's *Dial M For Murder*, humane heiress Gwyneth Paltrow searches for answers at the derelict Washington Heights home of a man she killed when he broke into her sprawling Museum Mile apartment.

The Little Red Lighthouse and the Great Gray Bridge, 1942

One of those children's books that has developed a large cult of nostalgia, this charming story features the eponymous lighthouse, still extant and set in Fort Washington Park along the Hudson, and its new neighbor, the great, gray George Washington Bridge.

Fort Tryon Cafe

Delicious pastries, divine coffee and heavenly soups are standard fare at this charming café, conveniently located near The Cloisters. Good to get you started before checking out the monastery itself.

(see Cafés)

The Cloisters

Enjoy the art and atmosphere at one of the city's most peaceful (and medieval) spots.

(see Sites & Parks)

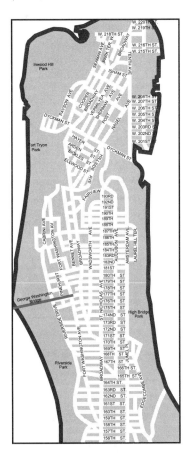

[cheap *thrills*]

Ropa 203

If you're patient enough to sort through acres of vintage clothes, you'll leave with some of the best deals in the city.

(see Shopping)

George Washington Bridge

With a bike or a pair of good walking shoes, crossing the Hudson from way up high guarantees a thrill for free.

🅐 to 175th St.

Audubon Terrace Museum Complex
A host of cultural institutions,
including the American Numismatic
Society and The Hispanic Society
of America, make this a valuable,
enlightening spot to spend
a couple of hours.
(see Side Bar)

George Washington Bridge
Follow the sun toward
Jersey and watch the tugboats
steaming along the Hudson
River. After your leisurely
afternoon, a walk across
"the most beautiful bridge
in the world" will work you
up an appetite and prepare
you for venturing back
into modernity.
Ⓐ to 175th St.

El Nuevo Sambuca Restaurant
Heat up as the day cools down
at this Heights hot spot,
complete with piano bar
and many mirrors.
(see Restaurants)

Butterfly Watching in Sumac Meadow
Inwood Hill Park affords numerous outdoor spectacles,
including this hot-bed of lepidoptery.
(see Sites & Parks)

Irish Brigade Pub
An authentic dive, not one of those East Village wannabes —
beers start at $1.50, unheard of in a city that often
charges thrice that for a pint.
(see Nightlife)

the bronx

The Bronx is a borough defined by contrasts. With acres of parkland, what many outsiders envision as a concrete desert is in fact one of New York's greenest boroughs. In spite of this overlooked prevalence of flora, the South Bronx represents the closest thing to the asphalt jungle Hollywood often portrays.

In contrast to the economic hardships of the South Bronx, Riverdale lies tucked away west of Van Cortlandt Park. One of New York's richest areas, opulent mansions line Fieldston Rd. and Riverdale Ave; people often bike through the neighborhood to catch a glimpse of its luxurious houses. Riverdale is also home to Manhattan and Mount St. Vincent colleges.

Southeast of Riverdale, the Fordham area is the geographical and demographical center which holds the Bronx together: Latino, Afro-Caribbean, and African-American cultures are found here, allowing meringue to mix with hip-hop, providing the soundtrack for the area's cultural convergence. Add a few Fordham students from Long Island and the mix is complete.

Caribbean rhythms dominate the Williams-bridge and Woodlawn sections of The Bronx, giving visitors urban island flavor in a middle-working-class community directly adjacent to Westchester's Mount Vernon. Other notable areas include Belmont's Little Italy, where Italian authenticity remains relatively unscathed due a the lack of tourism. Here you'll find bakeries, butcher shops, restaurants and produce markets concentrated on Arthur Ave. between Fordham Rd. and 183rd St., and on 187th St. between Third Ave. and Southern Blvd.

More sterile is Co-op City, a large housing development in Baychester, The Bronx's north-eastern corner. Constructed between 1968-1970, it now consists of 35 mostly high-rise buildings. 60,000 people live in its 15,372 apartments, making it one of the largest housing complexes in the country. Contrastingly, nearby City Island offers maritime aesthetics with a small-town feel, proclaiming itself on advertisements as "A little bit of New England in New York City." If you came to "rumble," you might be disappointed: Popular image aside, The Bronx is as filled with different faces like any other borough.

L ooking for a little small town fun in the big city? Well, catch the Bx 29 bus and head on over to **City Island**. Located just beyond Pelham Bay Park in The Bronx, City Island is a real slice of provincial life. As you drive over the bridge, you feel as if you have just dropped in on a New England seaside village. To the left sits a Marina, while the quaint main street stretches out, boasting an array of shops, none more than three stories high. Still, if you look a little farther along the horizon you see the skyscrapers of the Bronx and you can't help but wonder how this small town is part of New York City.

If you're craving some good maritime eateries City Island will be sure to provide. There is an abundance of restaurants with names like Sammy's Fish Box, King Lobster, and Ketch 22. If you prefer something that dwells on land there are other kinds of restaurants as well — check out Portofino, which locals highly recommend. City Island has a collection of art galleries and museums which display the island's rich nautical history. It also hosts many special events in the spring and summer months, like the annual Arts and Crafts Fair and Fleet Weekend (which includes a chowder eating contest!). Hot weather tends to bring tourists, along with events and celebrations. As one local resident explains, City Island really gets "slammed" as people head out to its beaches. (While the Island has many private beaches — one at the end of each street — the public Orchard Beach is nearby as well.) You can also take a stroll down the boardwalk which starts at the northern tip of City Island and runs to the even smaller High Island. You won't be seeing a McDonald's or an A&P on City Island but this might be a welcome relief. So take a clue from an island realtor who lives 10 minutes away off-island — "I want to move here," she exclaims. "I have always loved City Island!" — and escape to this little wonder by the water.

H I S T O R Y

The Bronx is the only NYC borough named after a person, Jonas Bronck, a Swedish sailor who cleared 500 acres and built a farmhouse. By 1700, Bronck's farm was destroyed and most of the land was split between four large manors: Pelham, Morrisania, Fordham, and Philipsburg.

The Bronx became famous for its landscaping attractions. In the late 19th Century, the Grand Concourse was built, modeled after tree-lined French boulevards. In 1891, the New York Botanical Gardens opened, followed by the Bronx Zoo; at 2,764 acres, Pelham Bay Park is still the city's largest oasis.

The borough was consolidated into New York City in 1898, and immigrants flocked there after 1904, when the first subway connecting The Bronx with Manhattan was completed. Droves of Yugoslavians, Armenians, and Italians arrived, as well as many Jews from central and eastern Europe. Business in the borough took off, with the Hub and Fordham Rd. becoming major shopping centers. Yankee Stadium, the "House that Ruth Built," was opened in 1923 and the Bronx Bombers soon became the world's most famous baseball team, dominating the sport through the '50s and reassuming this potency in the '90s..

After World War II, wealthier residents moved to luxury apartments in Riverdale or the suburbs in Westchester. An influx of poor people, displaced by urban renewal in Manhattan, moved to the southern neighborhoods, and poverty grew. While other parts of The Bronx continued to prosper as residential communities, the South Bronx declined. Continuing rumors that the Yankees may leave does not bode well for that part of the borough. However a 10-year billion-dollar program to build low-income housing has recently been instituted by the city, perhaps suggesting a potential rebound.

Bronx Museum of the Arts

True to its slogan,"It's more than just a museum," the space serves not only as a site for visual arts exhibitions, but also as a performance space, an artists' forum, and a center for "art making workshops." Its commitment to multicultural programming is evident in its diverse array of shows and weekly events.
1040 Grand Concourse (at 165th St.),
(718) 681-6000, Admission (suggested): $1-$3,
W 3pm-9pm, Th-F 10am-5pm, weekends noon-
6pm, ❹❺❻ *to to 161st St.-Yankee Stadium* ♿

Bronx Zoo/Wildlife Conservation Society Park

Four thousand animals observe visitors with an air of profound boredom as members of the earth's single most absurd species whistle, dance, and gesticulate. Stone monuments and naturalistic landscaping contribute to the theme-park atmosphere. The monorail brings you within feet of a red panda or a tapir, with nothing between you and them. Many exhibits are individually ticketed, even on "free" Wednesdays, so be prepared to spend $7 or $8 per person over the regular price of admission.
Bronx River Parkway and Fordham Road,
(718) 367-1010, Cash Only, Admission: $3-$7.75,
Open: 10am-5pm, ❷❺ *to Pelham Pkwy.* ♿

City Island

This former fishing village is still largely residential, housing a large portion of the city's small boat population and shipyards, bait-and-tackle shops, and restaurants like Sammy's Fish Box. From Manhattan, it's a trek: allow an hour and a half if traveling by public transportation.

Edgar Allan Poe Cottage

Situated on little more than a median strip, this tiny cottage where the godfather of gloom lived out the last years of his life and penned "Annabel Lee" and "The Bells" will nonetheless delight Poe admirers. Open only on weekends, or by appointment; the tour includes a video presentation.

Grand Concourse and East Kingsbridge Road,
(718) 881-8900, Cash Only, Admission $2,
❹❺ *to Knightsbridge Rd.*

The New York Botanical Gardens

New York's largest and most magnificent gardens include both cultivated exhibits and 40 acres of pristine forest. An extensive botanical library is available to the public, and classes, sales, and events fill the calendar year-round. Weekdays afford remarkable quiet and solitude. The Garden Cafe offers sandwiches and snacks, but visitors are welcome to bring a picnic basket. Admission is free for everyone on Wednesdays and Saturday mornings 10am to noon; on-site parking is $4.

200th St. and Southern Blvd., (718) 817-8705,
Cash Only, Admission: $2-$10, Open: Tu-Su
10am-6pm, ❹❺ *to Bedford Park Blvd.* ♿

Van Cortlandt Park

The Bronx's answer to Central Park, "Vannie" is occupies 1146 acres near Riverdale, a massive center for recreation, nature, and sight-seeing. The main parade ground hosts numerous soccer, softball, cricket, and football games every day but is just as nice for Frisbee and a blanket. Among the trees surrounding the perimeter are plenty of trails for nature hikes and biking, as well as one of the nation's best cross-country courses and the first municipal golf course in the country.
❶❾ *to 242nd St.-Van Cortlandt Park*

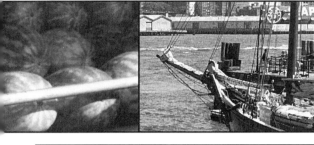

Wave Hill

This Riverdale estate and public garden is one of New York's best-kept sight-seeing secrets. Overlooking the Hudson River and the Palisades, Wave Hill offers a number of breathtaking views to inspire even the most jaded New Yorker. Within its 28 acres are meticulously manicured gardens and nature trails highlighting the estate's diverse flora. Guided walks are offered every Sunday; art and nature are celebrated year-round with concerts, nature hikes, and educational programs. *675 West 252nd St. (entrance at West 249th St. and Independence Ave.), (718) 549-3200, Cash Only, Admission: $2-$4 (free Nov.-March, Tuesday year-round), Open: Tu-Su 9am-5:30pm (Oct.-Apr. closes 4:30 pm),* ❶❾ to 231st St.

Woodlawn Cemetery

Filled with a staggering variety of trees and gargoyled mausoleums, the rolling landscape of Woodlawn Cemetery has been compared to Père La Chaise in Paris. Thanks to the trees, this resting place is also a roosting place for almost 200 different species of birds; even bald eagles have been spotted. Among the cemetery's deceased residents are Juilliard, La Guardia, Macy, Duke Ellington, Miles Davis, and W.C. Handy. *Webster Ave. (at 233rd St.), (718)920-0500,* ❹ to Woodlawn

Yankee Stadium

"I don't know what your name is or where you come from, but you're wearing pinstripes so I love you'se — now hit the effin' ball!" Big games fill the seats in this 56,000 capacity stadium, and these days, they all seem pretty big, with two World Series titles and three, count 'em - three, no-hitters in three years. Hot dogs go for $3, beer is $5, and tickets in the bleachers can go for as little as $6. Monument Park, a gallery of Yankee greats, closes 30 minutes before game time, so go early and enjoy the park's history. *River Ave. and 161st St., (718) 293-6000,* ❹❺❻ to 161st St.-Yankee Stadium ♿

A Bronx Tale, 1993

Robert DeNiro's directorial debut is set in the Fordam section of The Bronx and is produced by DeNiro's TriBeCa Films, a borough away. The plot involves a young boy in the 1960s torn between respect for his father (DeNiro as a bus driver) and the glamour of the life of a mob boss (Chazz Palminteri, who wrote the screenplay, based on his play).

The Devil's Own, 1997

This drama stars two of the hottest actors out there today. Follow Brad Pitt, playing a northern Ireland IRA terrorist, as he escapes to New York and finds shelter in the home of a police officer, played by Harrison Ford. Things get complicated as Ford becomes suspicious of his houseguest's identity.

parks

a *saturday*
IN THE BRONX

The New York Botanical Gardens
Admission is free from 10am-noon
on Saturdays, so get up early and
see some of the nature The Bronx
has to offer. Bring a thermos of
coffee and a newspaper to relax
in the gardens, spend a few hours
surrounded by gorgeous flora,
and grab a bite of late breakfast
in the café on the grounds.
(see Sites & Parks)

Bronx Zoo/
Wildlife Conservation Society Park
After you've checked out plants, immerse
yourself in New York's best animal
watching experience. The world-renowned
zoo tries its best to give the animals a
natural habitat, but watch out for
gum-spewing little kids who think it's
funny to toss lollipop sticks at the seals.
Don't miss the 6.5 acre Congo Gorilla
Forest - it just opened in July 1999!
(see Sites & Parks)

fordham

Yankee Stadium
Go and root for the players in the house that Ruth built! With some tickets cheaper than the cost of movie admission, this is some "can't miss fun." Grab yourself an Italian sausage and spend the afternoon full of real New York pride.
(see Sites & Parks)

Bronx Museum of the Arts
The diverse array of shows and weekly events are sure to make a late afternoon trip to this Bronx standby a perfect treat.
(see Museums)

Jimmy's Bronx Café
With the upstairs serving seafood and the downstairs set up as a dance floor, you can have yourself some dinner and dance into the wee hours of the night at this "Latin Restaurant and Entertainment Complex."
(see Restaurants)

riverdale

Bronx Museum of the Arts
11,000 square feet of galleries, classrooms, and an auditorium all open to the public. Special programsand technology-oriented classes are routinely offered to all ages andgroups. Who says da Bronx is all about tough guys?
(see Sites & Parks)

The most ethnically diverse borough of the most ethnically diverse city in the world, Queens boasts residents belonging to 100 backgrounds, speaking over 120 languages in all. Enclaves still house immigrants who bring with them the most vibrant aspects of their homelands, many of whose children choose to remain in Queens. Forest Hills, Kew Gardens, and the Rockaways have long been predominantly Italian and Jewish, while Woodside and Long Island City harbor Irish; Astoria constitutes a little Greece; Jamaica and Elmhurst boast the borough's largest black population; and Jackson Heights supports communities of both Latin Americans and South Asians.

It is fitting, then, that the borough acts as a gateway to New York for the rest of the world: With two major airports, the Brooklyn-Queens Expressway, and the termination of the **ⒶⒺⒻⒼⒿ ⓂⓃⓄⓇⓏ** and **❼** subway lines, virtually every resident of New York has visited Queens for some reason or another, whether they've meant to or not. Although Queens lies among all the airplanes, highways, and subway lines, its life offers a less hectic pace and a more family oriented environment than Manhattan.

The common ground shared by the borough's residents is their middle- and working-class status; Queens residents affirm it is a reasonably inexpensive and pleasant place to live, work, and play. They mix freely at Shea Stadium to cheer on the Mets, picnic in Flushing Meadows Corona Park, bargain shop on Steinway St., and enjoy the nightlife on Queens Blvd. Queens boasts the comforts of suburbia while retaining an urban consciousness; college student and long-time Rosedale resident Latressa proclaims, "I simply love it here. I can't imagine ever living anywhere else!"

Looking for a little adventure? Trying something outside of Manhattan for a change, and head on over to **P.S.1.** in Long Island City — it will be worth the trip. This museum is housed in an old school building — the first one in Queens — and finding the art can be half the fun. Exhibits are displayed everywhere from cracks in the floor to the dark corners of a boiler room. "Things are hidden and you have to explore for yourself," says Chloe Stromberg, the museum's Press Officer. P.S.1 has no permanent collections so its 125,000 sq. feet of space is constantly changing. In fact, that is one of its known functions in the art world — to produce a lot of new work.

P.S.1 recently reopened to the public in 1997 after a renovation which expanded and redesigned the facility. In January 1999 they announced an intent to merge with MoMA — a deal still in the works. The deal was born out of a friendship between the directors of the two establishments — Alanna Heiss at P.S. 1 and Glenn D. Lowry at MoMA — in order to enhance each institution's functions.

True to its name, P.S.1 also offers a variety of educational classes, among which are a summer art camp and a program called "From High School to Art School" — a preparatory class for high school students. The museum also has a café which offers a variety of delectable looking desserts and drinks. There is no gift shop, but don't be alarmed — P.S.1. sells its own publications at the front desk.

The art at P.S.1. is definitely contemporary: Exhibits range from detailed paintings to foam sculptures to a room that is simply blue, a piece by Joachin Koester. Conservatives, don't be scared, Stromberg says, since "P.S.1. is a space where people can come and understand contemporary art." The art is "user-friendly," as many exhibits are interactive: The Patrick Killoran Observation Deck features a plank on which participants lie down and are rolled halfway out a window!

So come take a lesson from P.S.1 on the joys of contemporary art, and follow the advice of de la Vega, quoted in adhesive tape by the entrance: "Be free my son be free."

H I S T O R Y

When Queens was consolidated into New York in 1898, much of it was still fenced off into farms, and in the eastern sections of the region, there was little desire to become a part of any city, much less one of the largest in the world.

This lack of a distinct borough community was mitigated by the secession of far eastern areas toward Nassau County as well as increasing urbanization closer to Manhattan. Much of the original identity crisis remains today — neatly symbolized by Northern Blvd., laid over old country pathways which led to the once-rural eastern areas of Long Island. By the '20s and '30s, Queens was beginning to develop its current character, with tree-lined rows of modest brick and wood-frame houses.

The 1939-40 World's Fair solidified Queens' role as one of New York's primary locales for recreation, arenas, and beautiful parks. Preparation for the Fair converted Flushing Meadows from a dump site to the city's largest landscaped recreation area after Central Park. La Guardia Airport and bridges were built, streets were widened, and sports stadia were constructed.

Queens has become the borough of choice for immigrants since the 1960s. In 1990, first-generation immigrants made up more than one-third of the two-million plus population of Queens, the greatest percentage in the any of five boroughs.

Queens is also the most ethnically diverse borough in NYC; although certain neighborhoods are identified with predominant ethnic groups, the extent to which these areas interact and overlap demonstrates that diversity itself acts as the borough's unifying force.

Bowne House

Historic home of John Bowne, whose trial for holding Quaker meetings and whose subsequent acquittal helped establish religious freedom in America. The oldest building in Queens, it dates back to 1661. *37-01 Bowne St. (bet. 37th and 38th Aves.), Flushing, (718) 359-0528, Cash Only, Admission $2-$4, Open: T, Sa, Su 2:30pm-4:30pm,* ❼ *to Main St.-Flushing* ♿

Socrates Sculpture Park

A prime example of what beautiful things you can make with what others might consider junk, this odd yet somehow serene collection of industrial sculptures seem appropriate with the East River and Manhattan as an equally industrial backdrop. Crumpled, bent, and molded steel make up the bulk of this amalgemation, amazingly geometric considering how unmalleable the medium is. *Long Island City, Broadway (at Vernon Blvd.), (718) 956-1819, Open 10am-sunset year-round,* ❶ *to Broadway*

Kaufman-Astoria Studios

Valentino, the Marx Brothers, and Paul Robeson have all made films at this popular studio, which has been at the heart of New York's movie industry for years. *34-12 36th St. (bet. 34th and 35th Aves.), (718) 392-5600,* ❶❶ *to Steinway St.*

King Manor Museum

Home of Rufus King, delegate to the Constitutional Convention. The oldest house in southeast Queens has been restored to reflect the King family's tenancy in the early 19th century. Visitors can tour King's library and read pages from his diary, account books, and letters; guided tours are available in English and Spanish. Exhibit galleries are devoted to local history and to village life in Jamaica during the early 1800s. *King Park/Jamaica Ave. (bet. 150th and 153rd Sts.), (718) 206-0547, Cash Only, Admission: $2, Open: March-Dec. weekends noon-4pm,* ❶❶❶ *to Jamaica Center-Parsons/Archer*

Weeping Beech Park

Created in 1847 by Samuel Parsons, this park is a NYC "living landmark." The first weeping beech tree in North America died here and was cut down in Feb. 1999, though eight offspring remain. *143-35 37th Ave. (bet. Parsons and Bowne), (718) 939-0647,* ❼ *to Main St.-Flushing*

World's Fair Ice Skating Rink

Near the Unisphere at Flushing Meadows Corona Park (of *Men In Black* fame), this is a popular attraction for kids of all ages, as well as thouse ludites who raise their noses at the in-line trends of the spandex generation. Great skating music, but the snack bar and vending machine food are a bit pricey.

Flushing Meadows Corona Park, (718) 271-1996, Cash Only, Admission: $7, Open: Oct.-March, ❼ *to 111th St.*

The Isamu Noguchi Garden Museum

More than 300 works in granite, steel, and marble, including the famous Akari paper light sculptures by Isamu Noguchi, who also designed the twelve galleries and the outdoor sculpture garden. Open April to October. A shuttle runs from 70th St. and Park Ave. on weekends.

Long Island City, 32-37 Vernon Blvd. (at 33rd Rd.), (718) 204-7088, Cash Only, Admission: $2-$4, W-F 10am-5pm, weekends 11am-6pm, ❿ *to Broadway* ♿

Shea Stadium

A good example of the sort of gaudy, lunar-minded ballparks built in the mid 1960s, Shea has seen the best of times (1969, 1986) and the worst of times (1962, 1977, 1992) over the Mets' up and down history. Having served as stomping grounds for names like Thronberry, Seaver, Staub, Gooden, Carter, and Hundley, the fate of this thirty-six year-old has been sealed, as the Mets are plannng to build a new facility across the street, modeled after Brooklyn's old Ebbett's Field. In the meantime, the Amazin's are busy putting together an honest-to-God threat to the Atlanta Brave's supremecy in the National League East. Can you say "subway series?"

Flushing, 123-01 Roosevelt Ave. (at 126th St.), (718) 507-8499, MC, V, AmEx, D, Tickets: $10-$30, ❼ *to Willets Point-Shea Stadium* ♿

movies & books

Maus, 1986

This is Art Speigelman's Pulitzer Prize winning graphic novel about his father's experiences in Auschwitz. Vladek Speigelman, as an old man, lives in Rego Park, Queens on Carlton St. off of 63rd Ave. The stark contrast between Queens and Poland, present and past, reveal this to be a memoir of all generations of the Speigelman family and the effect of history on today.

Coming to America, 1988

Eddie Murphy plays an African prince in search of a "True Love" to be his princess. Upon arriving in New York, he heads straight for Queens where he finds work in a McDonald's knock-off and, happily, the woman of his dreams.

parks

Astoria Pastry Shops
In Little Greece, centered around 31st St. and Ditmars Blvd., stop in at any of the street side cafés for Greek coffee and pastries before further exploring this fascinating ethnic pocket.

Ⓝ *to Ditmars Blvd.- Astoria*

astoria

Socrates Sculpture Park
Large-scale outdoor sculptures by artists from all over the world are free, as are public concerts, performance art, film, etc.
Long Island City, Broadway (at Vernon Blvd.),
(718) 956-1819, Open 10am-sunset year-round, Ⓝ to Broadway

Unisphere
Created for the 1964 World's Fair, the Unisphere is an impressive model of our planet; its fountains provide welcome relief on a hot day.
Flushing Meadows/Corona Park, ❼ to Willets Point

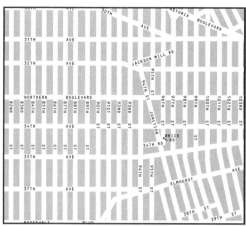

jackson heights

The Isamu Noguchi Garden Museum

An outdoor exhibit like you'd never find in packed Manhattan, this is an exhilarating, artistic way to spend your postprandial hours. Open April to October.

(see Sites & Parks)

American Museum of the Moving Image

Long Island City was once the heart of Queens' old movie district, which makes it a fitting location for this gem of archives, exhibits, and over 500 screenings annual. One of Queens' cultural treasures.

(see Visual Arts)

Elias Corner

You get right down to business at this no frills local legend, feasting on fish and washing it down with good white whine. An alternative to the relatively high-brow eating experiences across the East River, this represents some of best of New York's Hellenic heritage.

(see Restaurants)

Free bleacher seats at Shea Stadium

Friday nights during the baseball season, the first 800 people to show up at the entrance of the Pepsi Picnic Bleachers with an empty bottle of Pepsi get in free. Drink up and head out to the ball game. Bonus - you could be the lucky recipient of a Piazza/Ventura/Olerud homerun ball if you situate yourself carefully and work the elbows.

(see Sites & Parks)

brooklyn

Although many New Yorkers thought Brooklyn went west with the Dodgers, the County of Kings is taking its place atop the city's royalty. The combination of parks, arts, and cheap(er) apartments makes Brooklyn much more than the former home of Ebbets Field.

Summing up its residents is as easy as summing up a party of United Nations delegates. While the Italian stick-balling areas depicted in film do exist, Brooklyn is ethnically and economically diverse. Brooklyn Heights, made famous by Walt Whitman, has stunning views of the Manhattan skyline. Head south through the Hills (Cobble and Boerum) or east to Fort Greene and Clinton Hill, to find beautifully restored neighborhoods where handsome townhouses are selling for one-third the price of those in the West 80s in Manhattan. Fort Greene, recently dubbed the "Black East Village," is also home to the Brooklyn Academy of Music (BAM) which, with its renovated café and terrific schedule of symphony, dance, and opera — as well as its new art-house movie theater — has helped put Brooklyn back on the proverbial map.

Park Slope, long a melting pot of artists and businesspeople of all colors, is now a bastion for the up and coming, all of whom seem to have a toddler in one hand and a dog on a leash in the other. Its bistros, cafés, and bakeries, as well as its proximity to Prospect Park, the Brooklyn Botanic Gardens, and the Brooklyn Museum of Art, make the surge of the young and successful understandable.

Head to Williamsburg to find a burgeoning artsy enclave. But be forewarned — the word on this newest Bohemia is definitely out; rents are rising. For those unbearable New York Augusts, Brooklyn is home to the City's longest shoreline this side of the Verrazano Narrows Bridge. Pick up a few 'dogs at Nathan's Famous on the Coney Island boardwalk, while trying to spot Woody Allen's alleged childhood home under the roller coaster. In addition to swimming, Brighton Beach features a collection of outrageous Russian dinner theaters.

Yellow cabs are scarce in Brooklyn, but car services are just a phone call away and aren't more expensive. Getting around this borough takes time. It may take months to make it up to Greenpoint for pierogi but it's worth the exploration. One old-timer recently exclaimed: "I don't get why anyone goes to that other borough — what's it called? — ya know, where the Giants used to play?"

Construction may have been plagued with difficulty, but the **Brooklyn Bridge** is arguably the most inspiring in New York. Plans for the bridge began as early as 1802, but construction didn't start until 1870, and it wasn't completed until 1883. This, the world's first steel suspension bridge, was designed by German engineer John Augustus Roebling. Roebling, however, died during construction when a ferry toppled onto him from a waterfront piling. His son, Washington, assumed the job, but was struck down with caisson disease — "the bends" — and was forced to direct operations from his home, viewing them through a telescope, while his wife, Emily, served as a go-between. Many deaths, not to mention a disastrous fire, resulted from the bridge's fourteen year construction. At the time of its completion, the Brooklyn Bridge was the longest bridge in the world.

Today, this famous link between Brooklyn and Manhat-

tan is often clogged with commuter traffic. It's also a popular spot because of the stunning views one can catch from the bridge. Looking north, you can see Midtown, including the Empire State Building, about two miles away. Both cyclists and pedestrians are free to enjoy the bridge's elevated wooden walkway. People often walk across the bridge, an activity considered very safe, even in the evening. In fact, the greatest threat pedestrians face is mostly likely from the occasional inconsiderate cyclist. From Manhattan, you can enter the walkway off Park Row; from Brooklyn, enter off of Cadman Plaza West. If you want to simply admire the bridge rather than crossing it, go to the top of Pier 17 at the South Street Seaport after a day of shopping. In Brooklyn, Pier 1 at the Fulton Ferry Landing also provides a beautiful shot of the bridge.

Most New Yorkers agree, however, that nothing can match walking across the bridge on a clear summer evening.

HISTORY

Like Manhattan, the borough of Brooklyn was originally settled by Dutch explorers. When they purchased land from the Canarsie natives and linked together three villages in 1642, the new community called itself "Breuckelen" or "Broken Land."

Brooklyn remained rural until the 1800s, when many immigrants began to settle in the area. By 1814, Robert Fulton's steamboat service established regular transportation to Manhattan and helped develop stronger commercial links between the two island communities.

In 1833, Brooklyn was asked to join New York, but refused and incorporated itself as a separate city the next year. It remained an independent city even after the opening of the Brooklyn Bridge in 1883, an event which altered Brooklyn's social and economic geography more than any other. Brooklyn became a borough of Greater New York in 1898, a decision called "The Great Mistake" by writer Pete Hamill.

Brooklyn witnessed a severe decline in the decades following World War II. Largely due to industry and manufacturing moving away from the borough, massive job losses depleted

many neighborhoods. The Brooklyn Navy Yard was shut down by the federal government in 1966, and by the 1970s, entire areas of Brooklyn had been abandoned. However, the area has begun a revival in recent decades.

Brooklyn remains New York's most populous borough and maintains its own flavor and symbolic autonomy. This sense of self has nonetheless been subject to many vicissitudes, emblemized by the fate of Brooklyn's beloved Dodgers, who won the World Series for the first time ever in 1955 only to depart for Los Angeles two years later.

Brooklyn Heights Promenade
Room for roller blading and benches draw crowds of all ages, but the main attraction is the stunning view of the Manhattan skyline.
Montague Terrace, ⓜⓝⓡ *to Court St.,* ❷❸ *to Clark St.* ♿

Brooklyn Bridge
Bike, blade, or walk across the bridge on the well-maintained pedestrian path high above the traffic; the spectacular views of the downtown skyline never fail to stun both visitors and New Yorkers alike.
ⒶⒸ *to High St.-Brooklyn Bridge,* ❹❺❻ *to Brooklyn Bridge-City Hall* ♿

Coney Island Boardwalk

The quintessential urban getaway by the shore. A stroll down the famous boardwalk presents a stunning view of the Atlantic shore and visions of scantily clad women in heels, Speedo-sporting men, wizened old Russian card-players, and shrieking children waving corn dogs. Walk out onto the pier, where fishermen haul in ocean fish and spiny crabs; the beach is passable, but trash mars the effect on busier days.
ⒷⒹⒻ *to Stillwell Ave.-Coney Island* ♿

Astroland Park
Thrills and amusements abound at this colorful park, boasting kiddie rides and heart-stopping action for adults. Foremost among these thrills is Astroland's famous Cyclone roller coaster, not for the faint of heart.
Surf Ave. and West 10th St., (718) 372-0275, ⒹⒻ *to West 8th St.-NY Aquarium*

New York Aquarium
Various exhibits and habitats present marine life in both indoor tanks and outdoor pools. Replicas of an ocean habitat, the Gulf Stream, and the rocky Pacific seacoast house wildlife ranging from penguins to sea otters.
West 8th St. and Surf Ave., (718) 265-3474, Cash Only, Admission: $4.50-$8.75, Open: 10am-6pm, ⒹⒻ *to West 8th St.-NY Aquarium* ♿

Marine Park
With a playground, lush and grassy fields, and facilities for baseball, basketball, and tennis, Marine Park is an ideal place for gatherings and field events.
Fillmore and Ave. U, Ⓠ *to Ave. U* ♿

Floyd Bennett Airfield
Now that the air traffic doesn't come through, this spacious airfield is used mostly for biking and blading. The hangar has become an exhibition hall, and visitors can golf, mini-golf, and use batting cages at the nearby Gateway National Recreation Area.
At Gateway National Recreation Area, (718) 338-3799, Ⓠ *to Ave. U*

Prospect Park

Brooklyn's expansive central park borders many different neighborhoods whose residents fill the park for cookouts, sports, fishing, and tailgating; there are also secluded meadows for quiet reflection and picnicking. In June, the "Celebrate Brooklyn" festival holds weekend events in the Prospect Park bandshell, where a $3 "contribution" grants admission to concerts by the likes of David Murray, Dee Dee Bridgewater, Allen Toussaint, and Don Byron.
Bordered by Prospect Park West, Prospect Park Southwest, Parkside Ave. and Washington Ave., (718) 965-8950, ❷❸ to Eastern Pkwy.-Bklyn Museum, ❶❷❻ to Prospect Park &

Brooklyn Botanic Gardens

Unwind after a busy day of sightseeing at one of the many gardens situated on the 52 acres, including the Shakespeare and Conservatory Garden, the Japanese Garden, the Pond Garden, and Celebrity Park's Herb Garden.
Entrances at Flatbush Ave. and Empire Blvd. and at Washington Ave. and Eastern Pkwy., (718) 623-7200, Cash Only, Admission $1.50-$3, Open: April-September Tu-F 8am-6pm, weekends and holidays 10am-6pm; October-March closes at 4:30pm, ❷❸ to Eastern Pkwy.-Bklyn Museum &

Fort Greene Park

A trip through this park is both relaxing and historical. Visitors can view Prison Ship Martyr's Monument, designed by Stanford White and dedicated to Continental soldiers on British prison ships in Wallabout.
Myrtle and DeKalb Aves., and St. Edwards and Cumberland St., ❶❷❸❻❼ to DeKalb Ave. &

Brooklyn Academy of Music

Offering contemporary performing arts and cinema, this glorious building, erected in 1908, attracts audiences from across the metropolitan area. The Brooklyn Philharmonic is the resident orchestra and The New Wave Festival, an avant-garde series, takes place here. Call to verify performance times; be aware of the wide price range.
30 Lafayette Ave. (at Ashland St.), (718) 636-4111, ❶❷❸❷❹❺ to Atlantic Ave., ❽❶❷❸ to Pacific St. &

movies & books

Do the Right Thing, 1989

Set in the Bedford-Stuyvesant neighborhood, on "the hottest day of the summer." Spike Lee stars as Mookie, the pizza delivery man who wears a Jackie Robinson Brooklyn Dodgers jersey as he makes his rounds.

The Boys of Summer, 1972

Roger Kahn's classic then-and-now report on the Brooklyn Dodgers remains the best book written about the borough's beloved team, and what it meant to its fans.

Saturday Night Fever, 1977

The movie that brought us polyester suits and disco wouldn't have been the same if it wasn't set in Brooklyn. It features an studly John Travolta and a very tense scene on the Verrazano Narrows Bridge.

parks

@ *saturday*
IN BROOKLYN

New Prospect Café
One of the best brunches in Brooklyn, it's also becoming one of the most popular. The food, service, and proximity to Park Slope make it well worthwhile.
(see Restaurants)

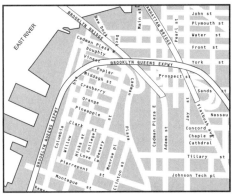

brooklyn heights

Prospect Park
Just as integral a part of Brooklyn as Central Park is to Manhattan, and just as social too. You could easily spend your whole day here.
(see Sites & Parks)

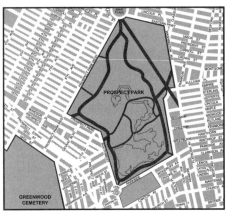

park slope

[cheap thrills}

Gallery Hop
Williamsburg is a burgeoning artists' neighborhood with funky galleries to explore and cute cafés for replenishment.
L to Bedford Ave.

Promenade on the Promenade
One of the many places that keeps New York City from being just another big city. A great place to take (or pick up!) a date. Arrive at sunset to watch the lights go up over Manhattan.
2 **3** to Clark St.

The Brooklyn Museum of Art

A short stroll to burn off brunch
will whirl you to one of New
York's best-kept secrets which
probably wishes it weren't.
A wonderfully curated institution
with exhibitions ranging from
"Monet's Mediterranean" to
"Jewels of the Romanov's."
(see Visual Arts)

Oznot's Dish

A shift from posh Park Slope
to bohemian Williamsburg
may seem jarring, but this
great restaurant will help
ease the transition, as will a
couple of glasses of wine
from its extensive cellar.
(see Restaurants)

Ocularis

Try out the bar at this hip
sometimes-cinema
and pick up a schedule for
the Sunday night movie series.
(see Film & TV)

Cocktails at River Cafe

Now you don't have to eat at fancy restaurants —
you can just look like you do!
The indoor/outdoor lounge at this prestigious
restaurant serves drinks ($10 minimum),
and the view is perhaps the city's best.
Make sure to call ahead to make sure the lounge is open.
(see Restaurants)

staten island

Combining close proximity to the urban with the tranquility of the suburban, Staten Island, with over 400,000 residents, is the city's smallest and quietest outer borough, one which most New Yorkers neglect. Though the butt end of more jokes than any place this side of Poughkeepsie, its plethora of fine restaurants, historical sites, and shoreline, contain some of New York's best-kept secrets.

Many neighborhoods on the south shore of the island are predominantly Italian, while the older neighborhoods on the north shore tend to have relatively diverse populations. Among the offerings for Staten Islanders and visitors alike are the Staten Island Mall and performances by the Staten Island Ballet Theater and the Staten Island Symphony.

Separated from Manhattan by the New York Harbor and the only borough not accessible by subway, Staten Island has maintained its own distinctive character, which has led to a long and intermittent fight for secession from the city by some residents. The situation has been exacerbated by the infamous Fresh Kills Landfill, New York's garbage dump until 2001, when the city will, supposedly, stop dumping. Staten Islanders will, no doubt, raise a stink of their own and demand that Manhattan keep its promise as their community enters the new millennium.

For many residents, Staten Island's divergence from the rest of the city and its residential character are the reasons they choose to live there. Like its neighbors to the north, Staten Island has its share of museums, historical sites and public spaces; though, unlike Manhattan, it can also claim the ups and downs of suburban culture, where communities are small, strip-malls line main boulevards, and hibachis outnumber hipsters by leaps and bounds.

Named (not surprisingly) after Alice Austen, a pioneering women in documentary photography in the late-19th and early-20th centuries, **The Alice Austen House** is a museum with a family history.

Austen first held a camera at the age of ten and taught herself how to operate the instrument and make prints. By the age of eighteen Austen was highly skilled in the field and was pursuing subjects from high society to new immigrants. However, not all of Austen's life was so picture perfect — her mother was abandoned by her father before Austen was born. So her mother moved into her parents' house, the house which now displays Austen's work.

The Alice Austen House was originally a one-room Dutch farmhouse built in 1690. In 1844 Austen's grandfather, John H. Austen, bought the property and renovated the house in a Gothic Revival style. He named it "Clear Comfort," a name that the house would be called for years to come. Austen lived in her grandfather's house even after losing her money in the stock market crash of 1929. Yet after a failed attempt to run a tearoom, she was forced to mortgage the house and move to the county poorhouse in 1945. Perhaps as a result, it was only in the last few years of her life that

Austen's work gained the recognition it deserved — as one of the finest records of turn of the Century American life.

At her death in 1952, Austen left behind nearly 8,000 negatives, 3,000 of which survive today. The Alice Austen House was bought by the city in 1975. In 1984-85 Austen's detailed photographs helped to restore the house so that it looked much like it did when Austen lived there in the 1890s. Her work is now displayed there in a variety of changing exhibits. A stroll through the house and the surrounding park (also converted to 1890s-style) yields a remarkable view of the New York Harbor and a sense of what life might have been like a century ago.

H I S T O R Y

Henry Hudson gave Staaten Eylandt its original name in 1609, when he sailed into the bay which now bears his name. In 1639, the Dutch opened Staten Island to colonization, but the area remained difficult to settle due to conflicts with indigenous inhabitants; there was constant warring between American Indians, who had been there for thousands of years, and the Dutch. The colony of Oude Dorp stabilized in 1661, but Staten Island became a province of New York after

the British took control in 1664. In 1683, the island became known as Richmond County, after the Duke of Richmond, a brother of Charles II.

Even after becoming part of New York, Staten Island was reachable only by private boat and remained largely a secluded place for fishing and farming until 1713, when a public ferry began carrying passengers to and from Manhattan and continues to do so today.

Today this is the most economically homogeneous and politically self-conscious

of the boroughs. The Island's independent streak has persisted ever since it joined New York City in 1898 and saw the watershed 1964 construction of the Verrazano Narrows Bridge, which connects it to Brooklyn. Fed up with garbage dumps filled largely with trash from elsewhere, the citizens of Richmond voted in 1993, albeit unsuccessfully, to secede from New York City. Perhaps the presence of a minor league affiliate of The Bronx's Yankees will inspire some interborough camaraderie.

Alice Austen House

This vine-covered Victorian cottage called Clear Comfort was home to Alice Austen, the Emily Dickinson of turn-of-the-century photography. Although Austen took more than 8,000 photographs of daily life from 1884-1934, she went undiscovered most of her life and died in 1952. The view from the gently sloping hill in Austen's front lawn is breathtaking.

2 Hylan Blvd. (at Bay St.), (718) 816-4506, Cash Only, Admission: $2, Open: Th-Su noon-5pm ♿

Snug Harbor Cultural Center

This National Landmark is one of the city's great quiet retreats, with historical buildings, gardens, and exhibition sites. The New House Center for Contemporary Art is an exhibition space and concert hall which hosts various art shows, performances, and flea markets. The Staten Island Botanical Garden contains butterfly gardens, a bonsai collection, and a fragrance garden. Gardens are open from 9am 'til dusk and admission is free for everything but special events.

1000 Richmond Terrace (bet. Tysen St. and Snug Harbor Rd.), (718) 448-2500, Open: 9am-dusk ♿

Historic Richmond Town

Staten Island's own version of Colonial Williamsburg, this indoor and outdoor exhibit documents local history and includes, among other historic buildings, the oldest surviving elementary school in America. Staff and volunteers dressed in early 19th-century costume reenact everything from candle-making to declarations of war.

441 Clarke Ave. (bet. Arthur Kill and Richmond Rds.), (718) 351-1611, Cash Only, Admission: $2.50-$4, Open: W-Su 1pm-5pm ♿

South Beach Park

The fourth longest boardwalk in the country is always packed with cyclists, but this is primarily a bathing beach for families and other sun worshipers admiring the great view of the Verrazano Narrows Bridge.

♿

Jacques Marchais Museum of Tibetan Art

Housed in a two-story stone building resembling a Himalayan Buddhist monastery and set in a terraced garden overlooking New York Bay, the museum features a permanent collection of Tibetan and other Buddhist art and ethnography. Notable past visitors include the Dalai Lama, who came in 1991.

338 Lighthouse Ave. (at Richmond Rd.), (718) 987-3500, Cash Only, Admission: $1-$3, Open: W-Su 1-5pm (Dec.-Mar closed weekends) ♿

Garibaldi Meucci Museum

This historic house museum is a great stop if you're on the island. Garibaldi played a major role in Italian Unification and Meucci was the original inventor of the phone. This museum houses artifacts from when they lived there.

420 Tomkins Ave. (at Chesnut Ave.), (718) 442-1608, Cash Only, Admission (suggested): $3, Tu-Su 1pm-5pm ♿

Staten Island Zoo

An alternative to the always crowded Bronx Zoo, take a stroll through Staten Island's smaller counterpart. Wednesdays are free from 2pm-4:45pm.

614 Broadway (bet. Clove Rd., Broadway, and Forest Ave.), (718) 442-3100, Cash Only, Admission: $2-$3, Open: 10am-4:45pm ♿

sites+parks

[cheap *thrills}*

Alice Austen House
Perhaps the most culture for your buck in all of New York City, admission is only $2 at this tribute to one of American's most underappreciated photographers.
(see Sites & Parks)

Ralph's Italian Ices
From the traditional lemon to more exotic flavors like honeydew or peanut butter, these famous ices are the perfect treat to combat New York's grueling summer heat waves.
501 Port Richmond Ave.
(at Catherine St.),
(718) 273-3675

movies & books

Working Girl, 1988
The hair doesn't get much worse than this! Melanie Griffith and Joan Cusack team up in this movie about women working to get to the top. Carly Simon sings the songs as the Staten Island Ferry carts these workers back and forth between the world they live in and where they want to be.

Splendor in the Grass, 1961
This movie catapulted the careers of its two young stars, Natalie Wood and Warren Beatty, not to mention starting their real life romance. The two play high school sweethearts with Wood's character struggling to remain a "good little girl." Wood was nominated for an Academy Award for this fabulous performance.

a saturday
IN STATEN ISLAND

Historic Richmond Town
For a quaint blast from the colonial past, visit the best reenactment north of Virginia. If all-too-convincing reenactments make you want run for the hills this is probably not for you, but otherwise, this portrayal of colonial life will certainly be worth the cheap price of admission.
(see Sites & Parks)

Snug Harbor Cultural Center
Stroll among the flowers and butterflies in the Botanical Gardens, peruse the art in the exhibition space, visit the past in the historical buildings, then eat a picnic brunch on one of the beautiful lawns.
(see Sites & Parks)

Jacques Marchais Museum of Tibetan Art
From the hands-on recreation of Richmond Town, shift gears to something a little more mystical at this center for eastern culture.
(see Sites & Parks)

Basilio Inn
From Tibetan art to Tuscan food, this former 19th Century stable is now an incomparable place for a Staten Island dinner.
(see Restaurants)

shopping

s·h·o·p·p·i·n·g

shopping

Navigating the consumer playground of Manhattan without blowing your wad in the process is an acquired skill. The average new New Yorker is typically so wowed by the selection, the novelties, the truly absurd, that she or he loses all perspective. One wide-eyed newcomer reports purchasing a pair of key-lime platform moon boots just because she mistook them for stylish, not an uncommon mistake among those eager to crash into New York's crazy fashion scene. However, if all you have to go with them is a pair of J. Crew chinos and a couple of lambswool sweaters, such a purchase is premature. Take advantage of street fairs and thrift stores for casual pieces, funky coats, and splurge every once in awhile in a high-end downtown boutique.

SoHo and the stretch up Broadway to 8th St. are dependable first-stops for browsing; you can hit funkier outfitters like **Patricia Field** (10 East 8th St., 254-1699) and **Antique Boutique** (712 Broadway, 460-8830), as well as boutiques like **Cynthia Rowley** (112 Wooster St., 334-1144) and **Todd Oldham** (123 Wooster St., 219-3531). The streets of the East Village, especially those between Second Ave. and Ave. A, yield numerous vintage stores as well as great little shops started by young, trendy designers.

Try the mythical Madison or Fifth Aves. for window-shopping, though uniformed doormen and stifled ambiance may encourage those without high credit lines to remain on the outside looking in. The Upper West Side in the 70s along Columbus Ave. boasts a number of boutiques that cater to the area's gainfully employed, thirtysomething crowd.

On any given weekend, many Manhattan streets are closed off to traffic and empty lots are filled with vendors who create a bazaar-like atmosphere, drawing everyone from neighborhood residents out for a stroll to hardcore hagglers perusing the wares. Offerings vary greatly, with the selection depending largely on the style of the individual market. Nomadic street fairs stop in most neighborhoods and tend to have a wide variety of merchants offering new merchandise such as handmade crafts and clothing as well as inexpensive, commercially produced items, wearable imports, and of course, plenty of food. To find street fairs, be on the lookout for fliers around the neighborhood or check out the "Voice Bulletin Board" on the back of *The Village Voice* where they're often listed.

Flea markets, on the other hand, are more established institutions and operate at the same location every weekend. They tend to fall into one of two categories. The first brings the atmosphere of a cheap and trendy clothing outlet into an open air setting, like at the daily market on the corner of Spring and Wooster Sts. in SoHo, or at the Saturday

and Sunday set-up on Broadway at 4th St. The second more closely approximates a church rummage sale with various tables and racks displaying antiques, some of the best vintage clothing around, and a fair share of plain old junk. Three of the best are found downtown in Chelsea on Sixth Ave. between 25th and 26th Sts., in SoHo on Grand St., and in the East Village on Ave. A at the corner of 11th St. All three are very popular, so try to get there early for the best selection and remember that almost all of the prices are negotiable, so don't be afraid to haggle.

Getting your hands on designer pieces before they sell out can be tough; waiting lists begin immediately after the shows, and fashion fanatics go so far as to bribe salespeople for first dibs on new stock. For the the less-than-gainfully employed, the problem is not how to score that hot new sweater from **Marc Jacobs** (163 Mercer St., 343-1490), it's how to score the sweater for a decent price before it's so shop-worn that it's beyond reasonable hope.

All department stores have end-of-the-year sales; of course, the trick being to gamble on that last markdown. **Barneys New York** (660 Madison Ave., 826-8900) has a semi-annual warehouse sale, but don't believe the hype: Salespeople supposedly hide all the good stuff for their friends!

The real scores are at designer sample sales. New York magazine runs a weekly column called "Sales and Bargains," which often includes showroom sales, and *TimeOut New York* has a similar column called "Shoptalk." True fanatics turn to the S & B Report (683-7612, $59/year), the definitive source of designer showroom information for insider tips. If that's not enough, opt for the preferred subscription ($124/year) which entails weekly fax updates.

The last option for name-brand junkies are the much-vaunted **Century 21** (22 Cortlandt St., 227-9092) and **Loehmann's** (60-66 99th St., 718-271-4000; 101 Seventh Ave., 352-0856). They have somewhat of a circus-like atmosphere, but it's worth sifting through — there are tons of good finds. **Moe Ginsburg** (162 Fifth Ave., 242-3482) in Gramercy is a reasonable outlet for men's dress clothes and shoes that strives for classy ambiance mixed with bargain basement enthusiasm.

A huge rift in the world of secondhand clothing sales exists between vintage stores and thrift stores. Vintage represents the clothes that have been sorted to separate out the junk and is then slapped with hefty price tags; this is the type found in most of the well-traversed shopping areas of Manhattan, and includes notable outposts like the deceptively named **Cheap Jack's** (841 Broadway, 777-9564) and **Andy's Chee-Pees** (691 Broadway, 420-5980). Thrift, on the other hand, encompasses the whole range of castoffs — from garbage to gems — and generally entails sorting through plenty of racks and bins full of the former before discovering any of the latter. But once the great finds come to light, the search process is rendered worthwhile by dirt-cheap prices.

For the willing and bargain-hungry, there's still another stop along the path to thrift store heaven: actually finding thrift stores. Head for the city's fringes — the far reaches of uptown Manhattan and the outer boroughs. Up in Washington Heights lies **Ropa 203** (3775 Tenth Ave., 567-1565), a warehouse that sells piles of clothes by the pound; Harlem secondhand stores can be goldmines, since downtown vintage buyers rarely glean the finest stuff.

Moving beyond Manhattan, a trip out to Queens yields Salvation Army thrift stores that are full of quirky retro that's neither picked-over nor over-priced. Further south, in the Williams-burg and Greenpoint sections of Brooklyn are two local institutions: **Domsey's** (431 Kent Ave., 718-384-6000) has a warehouse overflowing with everything from sweaters to pleather as well as a funky shoe selection; its neighbor to the north, **Pop's Popular Clothing** (7 Franklin St., 718-349-7677), is smaller but contains the best selection of jeans and work-wear around.

While clothing shopping in New York usually entails a trip to some neighborhood as funky and interesting as the product, there are many out-of-the-way areas that house groups of trade stores that belong to one particular industry where you can find amazing bargains. Even if you're not shopping, it's still fun to check out the windows of some of these neighborhood stores, or step in and watch the pros at work.

Antiques:

Wholesale antique dealers are most prevalent on University Pl., but the "wholesale only" signs propped in windows are an arbitrary indication of the actual policies. For flea market antiques, with some vintage vinyl thrown in, try Bond St. off of Broadway. Otherwise, check out Lafayette St. from Bond to Spring Sts. (though beware that not much comes cheaply), or Atlantic Ave. between Smith and Nevins Sts. in Boerum Hill, Brooklyn.

Arcade Games:

Equally impractical for your average dorm room but still fun to browse. Shops selling pinball machines and arcade games line Tenth Ave. north of 42nd St.

Costume Jewelry:

If your budget does not accommodate fine jewelry, check out the costume jewelry district on Broadway between 25th and 30th St. Don't be intimidated by the "wholesale only" signs since the minimum sale may be quite low.

Diamonds:

Still going strong, this legendary strip of 47th St. between Fifth and Sixth Aves. is the prime locale for haggling in the city. Arm yourself with knowledge beforehand to make educated bids.

Electronics:

Guarantees are spotty but the service always enthusiastic at the many storefronts selling electronics along Canal St. near East Broadway; remember to try before you buy.

Flowers and Plants:

Everything from fillers for window boxes to candidates for the roof garden are available cheaply on Sixth Ave. between 26th and 28th Sts. Get there early for the best quality and enjoy that dewy fragrance so absent in New York's dusty dawns.

Garment District:

Running between 30th and 40th Sts. between Seventh Ave. and Broadway is the granddaddy of all of the city's districts, home of New York's famous fashion industry. It's also home to the infamous "sample sales," where designers sell "samples" for cut-rate prices. You can also find great deals on fabric, buttons, and other accouterments. There is an additional strip for fabric sales on Broadway above and below Canal St.

Restaurant Equipment:

Need a large-capacity salad shredder? Formica bar stools? No-frills wholesalers of restaurant equipment line the Bowery just above and just below Houston St., where saloons and flop houses once catered to Skid Row.

Shoes:

Eighth St. between Broadway and Sixth Ave. is the first stop for footwear for savvy New Yorkers. Prices are still competitive across the board, with a selection that favors mid- to high-quality Italian leather and super-trendy platforms in all materials and shapes.

SHOPPING DISTRICTS

clothing

agnès b.
Among the finest in smart, up-to-date women's wear, with the touch that makes you feel like Ingrid Bergman.
SoHo, 116 Prince St. (bet. Wooster and Greene Sts.), 925-4649, MC, V, AmEx, ⓃⓇ to Prince St. ♿

Alice Underground
Behind the hippie-ish exterior is one of Manhattan's biggest and best vintage stores. Skip the bargain bins as there's usually a good reason why the items are being unloaded so cheaply, and shell out a little more for pants and jackets off the racks, where the finds can range from the fabulously unique to solid standards. An excellent selection of winter coats.
SoHo, 481 Broadway (bet. Grand and Broome Sts.), 431-9067, MC, V, AmEx, ⓃⓇ to Prince St. ♿

Andy's Chee-Pees
A good place to find vintage clothing from the '40s, '50s, '60s, '70s, and even '80s. They also carry collectibles from as far back as the '20s, not to mention new clothes as well. This store offers personalized attention and prides itself on being user-friendly.
Greenwich Village, 691 Broadway (bet. 3rd and 4th Sts.), 420-5980, MC, V, AmEx, ❸❻❼❽❾ to Broadway-Lafayette St., ❻ to Bleecker St. ♿

Anna Sui
Rock-n-roll style meets the runway and boutique world in this small designer outpost. Leather pants hang alongside sequined dresses and the atmosphere is relaxed enough to allow for trying it all on without feeling conspicuous. It's expensive, but end-of-season markdowns are often low enough for a reasonable and well-deserved splurge.
SoHo, 113 Greene St. (bet. Spring and Prince Sts.), 941-8406, MC, V, AmEx, Diners, ⓃⓇ to Prince St. ♿

Anthropologie
The grown-up Urban Outfitters. Owned by the same people, with a similar variety of housewares and clothing for women, the bent here is more stylish than trendy, with lots of classic and basic pieces that are of high quality, but prohibitively priced at around $70 and up. The clearance racks generally yield some good finds though, and sometimes paying full price isn't so bad, since the clothes are unlikely to either fall apart or go out of style quickly.
SoHo, 375 West Broadway (bet. Spring and Broome Sts.), 343-7070, MC, V, AmEx, D, ❸❽ to Spring St.

Antique Boutique
This trendy and lively Broadway institution shouts New York at very high prices. Newer, modern, edgy sports wear takes up most of the upstairs, while downstairs is devoted to top-notch vintage coats, shirts, and jeans.
Greenwich Village, 712 Broadway (at Washington Pl.), 460-8830, MC, V, AmEx, Diners, D, ⓃⓇ to 8th St.-NYU

APC
Clothes so simple and perfect that you simultaneously wonder why they cost so much and how you've lived without them for so long. Classics like jeans and button-down shirts hover around the $100 range, so clasp your credit card tightly — it's hard to resist such flawless incarnations of old standards at any price.
SoHo, 131 Mercer St. (bet. Prince and Spring Sts.), 966-9685, MC, V, AmEx, ⓃⓇ to Prince St.

Bally
One of the best-known and best-reputed leather companies in the world, this Swiss tannery sells a vast selection of high-quality leather shoes, bags, belts, and other accessories.
Upper East Side, 628 Madison Ave (at 59th St.), 751-9082, MC, V, AmEx, ❹❺❻ to 59th St., ⓃⓇ to Lexington Ave. ♿

Bang Bang
This is a basic store if you are into the New York club scene. They have the typical club clothing that you don't want to spend a lot of money on because they only cover one-third of your body. The only problem is that you may see someone wearing the same thing on Friday night.
Greenwich Village, 53 East 8th St. (bet. Broadway and University Pl.), 475-8220, MC, V, AmEx, Diners, D, ⓃⓇ to 8th St.-NYU ♿
Also at:
7 other locations in NYC

Beacon's Closet
Many of the hipsters of Williamsburg are avid thrift shoppers and this is the neighborhood outlet for such diversions. A wide assortment of used clothing fills the racks and it doesn't take too much hunting to find something really nice like a suede jacket or a pair of perfectly worn boot-cut Wranglers. The prices tend to be a little expensive for Brooklyn, but are still about one-third what you'd pay in Manhattan. Plus, they'll buy your unwanted clothes or take them in trade.
Williamsburg, Brooklyn, 110 Bedford Ave. (at North 11th St.), (718) 486-0816, MC, V, AmEx, Diners, ❶ to Bedford Ave.

Betsey Johnson

In-your-face girly chic means Betsey's not afraid to flaunt lace alongside faux leather, or pair zebra stripes with fuschia fishnets. Straightforward, sexy slip dresses are surprisingly affordable on sale.
SoHo, 138 Wooster St. (bet. Prince and Houston Sts.), 995-5048, MC, V, AmEx, ⓃⓇ to Prince St. &
Also at:
3 other locations in NYC

Blue

If Cinderella was set in modern-day downtown NYC, then her gown surely would have come from here. This shop offers one-of-a kind fancy dresses that fall somewhere between little girl fairy-tale fantasy and grown up chic. Definitely worth a look if there's an upcoming ball at which you want to be the belle.
East Village, 125 St. Marks Pl. (bet. First Ave. and Avenue A), 228-7744 MC, V, AmEx, ⑥ to Astor Pl.

Built By Wendy & Cake

Two new designers teamed up together to make this store, each with one rack to display their collections. Look for Cake's sophisticated style, while Wendy's tends to be more on the wild side.
SoHo, 7 Centre Market Pl. (bet. Broome and Grand Sts.) 925-6538, MC, V, ⒿⓂⓃⓇⓆⓏⒼ to Canal St. &

Burlington Coat Factory

Why pay more? With six floors of discount coats, suits, shirts and casual sportswear, you're sure to find what you need at the right price.
Lower Manhattan, 45 Park Pl. (bet. Church St. and West Broadway), 571-2630, MC, V, AmEx, D, ②③ to Park Pl.

Also at:
Chelsea, 707 West 23rd St. (at Sixth Ave.), 229-1300, MC, V, AmEx, D, ⑤ to 23rd St. &

Calvin Klein

Pay tribute to the commercial master who made a young American public hunger for androgyny, kiddie-porn, and denim trashiness. Along with its refined, simple men's and women's wear, this flagship megastore boasts roomfuls of classically styled home accessories and a full staff of the predictably trendy, long-limbed photo-session specimens.
Upper East Side, 654 Madison Ave. (at East 60th St.), 292-9000, MC, V, AmEx, Diners, D, ④⑤⑥ to 59th St., ⓃⓇ to Lexington Ave. &

Calypso

Fun and funkily printed fabrics abound in this boutique which successfully attempts to bring an international-island aesthetic to Little Italy. While the inspiration for the clothing styles may be other-wordly, though, the prices all-too-closely mirror those of fashion boutiques only blocks away in SoHo. Paradise doesn't come cheap, after all, for the true fashion elite.
Little Italy, 280 Mott St. (bet. Prince and Houston Sts.), 965-0990, MC, V, AmEx, ⓃⓇ to Prince St.

Canal Jean Co. Inc.

With its well-known checkered flag visible blocks away, this multilevel specialty in discount brand names (such as Levi's) carries more than enough merchandise to satisfy the picky shopper. Calvin Klein underwear, Lip Gloss dresses, and plenty of vintage clothes and jeans crowd the place. Check out the huge, overwhelming downstairs selection of used clothes.

SoHo, 504 Broadway (bet. Spring and Broome Sts.), 226-1130, MC, V, AmEx, Diners, D, ⓃⓇ to Prince St., ⑥ to Spring St. &

Center for the Dull

This dully lit store has great vintage clothing (never used!) and is the place to find vintage Lee's and Wrangler's.
SoHo, 216 Lafayette St. (bet. Spring and Broome Sts.), 925-9699, MC, V, AmEx, D, ⑥ to Spring St.

Century 21

Determined shoppers will find designer items for up to 80 percent off; the other departments attract a slightly less bloodthirsty crowd.
Lower Manhattan, 22 Cortlandt St. (bet. Broadway and Church St.), 227-9092, MC, V, AmEx, D, ⓃⓇ to Cortlandt St. &

Chanel

Coco would be proud. Complete with uniformed doorman, this sparkling shrine to simple elegance with a flair, sells clothing, jewelry, shoes, accessories, and, of course, perfume.
Midtown, 15 East 57th St. (bet. Fifth and Madison Aves.), 355-5050, MC, V, AmEx, Diners, ⑤ to 57th St. &

Cheap Jack's

Don't be fooled by the name of this groovy vintage store; the place is anything but cheap. Browse through the vast selection of plain and Hawaiian shirts, one-of-kind coats, and '40s-, '50s-, '60s- and '70s-style dresses on the first floor; head downstairs where myriad jeans hang. Patience and a keen eye may lead to a heavenly bargain.
Greenwich Village, 841 Broadway (bet. 13th and 14th Sts.), 777-9564, MC, V, AmEx, ⓁⓃⓇ④⑤⑥ to 14th St.-Union Sq. &

Cherry

All the vintage clothing from the '30s to early '80s is "classy," "elegant," "sexy," and "far out." There is a heavy emphasis on '60s and '70s minimalist styles from swimsuits to night-wear, plus designer pieces by Rudi Gernreich (a radical '60s designer), Gucci, and Bob Mackie. You can also find "space-age bio-morphic design" furniture and home accessories such as lamps, phones, speakers, and sculpture. *Lower East Side, 185 Orchard St. (bet. Houston and Stanton Sts.), 358-7131, MC, V, AmEx, D,* ❻ *to Second Ave.*

Club Monaco

This Canadian Company has transformed New York. They have basics with a Trendy kick. Check out their CMX line, which is there, sports line. *Gramercy, 160 5th Ave. (at 21st St.) 352-0936, MC, V, AmEx,* ❻❻ *to 23rd St.* &

Also at:
5 other locations in NYC

Cynthia Rowley

Classic and simple designs, executed in extraordinary fabrics. The prices are relatively low for such an established designer, and much of the clothing comes in mix-and-match pieces, making it easy to achieve the look by integrating a splurge into your existing wardrobe. *SoHo, 112 Wooster St. (bet. Spring and Prince Sts.), 334-1144, MC, V, AmEx,* ❻❻ *to Prince St.* &

D&G

Walking into D&G is a sight for sore eyes. This two floor unisex store features a variety of styles in colors like fushia, lime green, azure blue. For the more tame at heart there is also conservative wear like black pants and Khaki blazers. If you are looking for accessories they also have their own line of belts, bags, and shoes. But be careful — like so many SoHo shops, the prices ain't cheap. *SoHo, 434 West Broadway (bet. Prince and Spring Sts.), 965-8000, MC, V, AmEx,* ❻❻❻❻ *to Broadway-Layayette St.*

Diesel

Two stories worth of youth culture in all its incarnations. Pump your well-toned system full of caffeine with a visit to the cappuccino bar before ravaging the aisles of shoes, underwear, outerwear, and accessories. Afterward,s hit the steel-floored dance floor on the mezzanine. *Upper East Side, 770 Lexington Ave. (at 60th St.), 308-0055, MC, V, AmEx, Diners, D,* ❻❻❻ *to 59th St.,* ❻❻ *to Lexington Ave.*

Domsey's

Four stories of mostly second-hand clothing for women, men, and kids, this store even carries some (new!) housewares. *Williamsburg, Brooklyn, 431 Kent Ave. (at South 9th St.), (718) 384-6000, Cash Only,* ❻❻❻ *to Marcy Ave.* &

Eileen Fisher

A relaxed style of clothing, great for a hot summer day — loose and comfortable, with an always-helpful staff. *SoHo, 395 West Broadway (bet. Spring and Broome Sts.), 431-4567, MC, V, AmEx, D,* ❻❻ *to Spring St.* &

Emporio Armani

Cleanly cut casual suits that are a bit more accessible price-wise than Armani's main line. Just about everything looks classy in the renovated Stanford White building. *Gramercy, 110 Fifth Ave. (at 16th St.), 727-3240, MC, V, AmEx, D,* ❻❻❻❻❻❻ *to 14th St.-Union Sq.* &

Also at:
Upper East Side, 601 Madison Ave. (bet. 67th and 68th Sts.), 317-0800, MC, V, AmEx, D, ❻ *to 68th St.-Hunter College* &

Ermenegildo Zegna

Although less well-known than Armani, his suits are certainly among the finest. *Midtown, 743 Fifth Ave. (bet. 57th and 58th), 421-4488, MC, V, AmEx, Diners,* ❻❻ *to Fifth Ave.* &

Filene's Basement

This bargain staple superstore carries Calvin Klein, Perry Ellis, Kenar, and other designer names, and is worth a look for shoes, lingerie, coats, suits, and evening wear. Check out the occasional clearance sales where many prices are slashed to below $5. *Chelsea, 620 Sixth Ave. (bet. 18th and 19th Sts.), 620-3100, MC, V, AmEx, D,* ❻❻ *to 18th St.* &

Also at:
Upper West Side, 222 Broadway (at 79th St.), 873-8000, MC, V, AmEx, D, ❻❻ *to 79th St.* &

Filth Mart

Would win the award for best place to buy old rock concert t-shirts. In general, there's a great turn over of groovy tees which all seem to fall in the $8-$25 range. Also has a great selection of used jeans and coats, especially those hep vintage leather trenches. *East Village, 531 East 13th St. (between Aves. A and B), 387-0650, MC, V, D,* ❻❻❻❻❻❻ *to 14th St.-Union Sq.* &

555 Soul

Six years ago, designer Camella Ehlke gave the hip-hop crowd something that was finally funky enough for them to wear; Tees and baseball caps jazzed up with some of that downtown vibe.

SoHo, 290 Lafayette St.
(bet. Houston and Prince Sts.),
431-2404, MC, V, AmEx, D,
❻❻❼❿ to Broadway-Lafayette St.,
❷❿ to Prince St. ♿

Givenchy
Audrey Hepburn and Givenchy
helped make each other even
more famous back in their
heyday; designs are still very
French and very chi-chi, though
there's probably no movie star
today that could carry them off
like Hepburn.
*Upper East Side, 954 Madison
Ave. (at 75th St.), 772-1040, MC,
V, AmEx, D,* **❻** *to 77th St.* ♿

Hanae Mori
Vibrantly colorful and irrev-
erently patterned, the shop's
collection of women's fashion
is among the most cutting edge
in contemporary design. Dazzle
the senses even further with
an eyeful of the storefront's
striking stucco front and
off-center chrome cylinder,
designed by Hans Hollein.
*Upper East Side, 27 East 79th St.
(bet. Madison and Fifth Aves.),
472-2352, MC, V, AmEx,*
❻ *to 77th St.* ♿

Hypereality
Formerly an upscale boutique
for those with lots of disposable
income, the new incarnation is
a downtown sample sale. It's a
place to score new garb from
names like Herbie Velez at bargain prices. Join the mailing list
or just stop by and take a gander
at the affordable (yet still hip
and trendy) new look.
*Chelsea, 202 Seventh Ave. (bet.
21st and 22nd Sts.), 620-8180,
MC, V, AmEx,* **❶❾** *to 23rd St.* ♿

INA
This designer consignment store
features a big selection of men's
and women's clothing from

current collections. First-time
shoppers fast become regulars
to the cozy neighborhood store.
Find designer items by Prada,
Helmut Lang, agnès B. and
Joseph at a 1/4 to 1/2 the price.
*SoHo, 21 Prince St. (bet. Mott
and Elizabeth Sts.), 334-9048,
MC, V, AmEx,* **❷❿** *to Prince St.*

Kate Spade Store
Neat and minimalist, the store
matches the bags, each style of
which comes in variety of colors;
she makes basic black to bright
green. A rising star, Spade's
attraction is her simplicity of
design. Simply timeless.
*SoHo, 454 Broome St. (at Mercer
St.), 274-1991, MC, V, AmEx,*
❻❺ *to Spring St.*

Living Doll
Plenty of throwbacks to the
"80s chic" à la Madonna at fair
prices; perfect for young SoHo
migrants on the east side of
Broadway.
*SoHo, 123 Crosby St. (bet. Prince
and Houston Sts.), 625-9410 ,
MC, V, AmEx,* **❻❻❼❿** *to
Broadway-Lafayette St.*

Loehmann's
As legendary as Century 21 in designer junkie circles, this Queens
outpost rewards the shopper
who makes the trek: lots of
big-name labels and high stock
turnover justify frequent trips.
*Rego Park, Queens, 60-66 99th
St. (at the Long Island Expressway), (718) 271-4000, MC, V, D,*
❻❿ *to 63rd Drive-Rego Park* ♿
Also at:
*Chelsea, 101 Seventh Ave. (bet.
16th and 17th Sts.) 352-0856,
MC, V, D,* **❶❾** *to 18th St.* ♿

Lord of the Fleas
So popular that they're
currently operating several
outlets within spitting distance
of each other. This is the place
to go to add a few trendy pieces

to your existing wardrobe or to
find something appropriate for
a night of club-hopping. The
prices and quality are both
generally pretty low which is
ideal for stuff that's in now but
probably won't be next year.
*East Village, 305 East 9th St.
(bet. First and Second Aves.),
260-9130, MC, V, AmEx, D,*
❻ *to Astor Pl.* ♿
Also at:
*East Village, 437 East 12th St.
(bet. 1st Ave. and Ave. A),
533-3554, MC, V, AmEx, D,*
❶ *to First Ave.* ♿
*Upper West Side, 2142 Broadway
(at 75th St.), 875-8815, MC, V,
AmEx, D,* **❶❷❸❾** *to 72nd St.* ♿

Marc Jacobs
This store offers a full selection
of Jacobs' high-end designer
clothing. You're better off buying this hot designer's clothes
here than in department stores
because this store has a wider
selection and more sizes.
*SoHo, 163 Mercer St. (bet. Hous-
ton and Prince Sts.), 343-1490,
MC, V, AmEx, Diners,* **❻❻❼❿** *to
Broadway-Lafayette St.* ♿

Max + Roebling
Showcase for some of New
York's hippest young designers,
including Cake and Living Doll,
with prices that even Williams-
burg's starving artists can swing.
*Williamsburg, Brooklyn, 189
Bedford Ave. (bet. North 6th and
North 7th Sts.), (718) 387-0045,
MC, V, AmEx, Diners, D,*
❶ *to Bedford Ave.*

Meghan Kinney
Just finding this tiny sidestreet
store makes you feel privy to
some sort of secret; while Kinney
has been executing her clean,
just-short-of-being-overly-trendy
designs for years, she's still a
relative unknown. Gunmetal
synthetics and sleek, sexy dresses
are several of her trademarks.

East Village, 312 East 9th St. (bet. First and Second Aves.), 260-6329, MC, V, ❻ to Astor Pl. ♿

Mister Roger

"Italian styles for men" is the only way to view this small boutique. Prices are steep, but the establishment has managed to maintain a beautiful day in the neighborhood for almost 10 yrs.
Washington Heights, 565 West 181st St. (bet. St. Nicholas and Audubon Aves.), 795-1774, MC, V, AmEx, D, ❶❾ to 181st St., ❹ to 181st St. ♿

Miu Miu

Prada's second breakthrough strikes a more contemporary look and is geared toward a younger crowd.
SoHo, 100 Prince St. (bet. Mercer and Greene Sts.), 334-5156, MC, V, AmEx, ❺❻ to Prince St. ♿

Moe Ginsburg

Over 50,000 square feet of suits, overcoats, sportswear, accessories, and shoes, with suppliers from Italy, Canada, and the States. A good option if you just got that internship at Goldman Sachs.
Gramercy, 162 Fifth Ave. (at 21st St.), 242-3482, MC, V, AmEx, D, ❺❻ to 23rd St.

Nicole Miller

This designer is known for her detailed bold silk patterns. They are on everything from eyeglass cases to bow ties to umbrellas. She carries dresses for all occasions with interesting fabrics. While you are there be sure to check out the sale rack.
Upper East Side, 780 Madison Ave. (bet. 66th and 67th Sts.), 288-9779, MC, V, AmEx, D, ❻ to 68th St.-Hunter College
Also at:
SoHo, 134 Prince St. (bet. West Broadway and Wooster St.), 343-1362, MC, V, AmEx, ❻❺ to Spring St. ♿

99X

This boutique sells some of the hippest threads in the city, with the usual high prices; club apparel such as leather pants, itty-bitty skirts, and baby tees.
East Village, 84 East 10th St. (bet. Third and Fourth Aves.), 460-8599, MC, V, AmEx, D, ❻ to Astor Pl.

Oriental Dress Company

Step inside and you'll be greeted by bolt after bolt of colorful silk brocade. The tailor will custom-make you a Chinese dress that fits like a glove for between $100-$250, depending on the type of silk you select. This service is a rarity in the U.S.; custom tailors are usually available only in China and Hong Kong.
Chinatown, 38 Mott St. (at Pell St.), 349-0818, Cash Only, ❻❽❿ to Grand St.

Original Levi's Store

Everything you always wanted to know about denim and more. Much more.
Upper East Side, 750 Lexington Ave. (bet. 59th and 60th Sts.), 826-5957, MC, V, AmEx, D, ❹❺❻ to 59th St., ❺❼ to Lexington ♿

Patricia Fields

The perfect place if you want something really "funky," Patricia Fields has men's and women's clothing, accessories, lingerie, suits, make-up, and a hair salon!?! *Greenwich Village, 10 East 8th St. (bet. University Pl. and Fifth Ave.), 254-1699, MC, V, AmEx, D, ❺❼ to 8th St.-NYU*

Phat Farm

A hip-hop house of style, where XL is the size of choice and clothing's executed well enough to earn the Farm its SoHo digs.
SoHo, 129 Prince St. (bet. West Broadway and Wooster St.), 533-7428, MC, V, AmEx, ❺❼ to Prince St.

Pop's Popular Clothing

This store has been in business for over 50 years. They carry a full line of new and used clothes. You'll find what you're looking for at lower prices than you'd pay at a Manhattan counterpart.
Greenpoint, Brooklyn, 7 Franklin St. (at Mezzoro Ave.), (718) 349-7677, MC, V, AmEx, ❶ to Bedford Ave. ♿

Prada

This sleek, green-walled store is great for window shopping, even if you don't have the bucks to buy. Prada's conservative yet trendy style is on the A list.
Upper East Side, 841 Madison Ave. (at 70th St.), 327-4200, MC, V, AmEx, Diners, ❻ to 68th St.-Hunter College ♿

Ropa 203

Clothes get weighed by the lb. pound at this uptown thrift store that can pull 'em in. "Everybody loves it," says one stylishly dressed Columbia student who shops here regularly. Be prepared for the warehouse setting.
Washington Heights, 3775 Tenth Ave. (at 203rd St.), 567-1565, Cash Only, ❶❾ to Dyckman St.

Screaming Mimi's

One of the sassiest vintage boutiques, fashion here ranges from creative to indulgent; lots of cords, bellbottoms, funky prints, and slinky lingerie. Everything is in excellent shape, having been hand-selected; old shoes and purses help ensure your accessories match your outfit.
Greenwich Village, 382 Lafayette (bet. 4th and Great Jones Sts.), 677-6464, MC, V, AmEx, Diners, D, ❻ to Astor Pl., ♿

Steven Alan

The same coveted labels as his SoHo clothing store, but many items at half the price. Expect

good deals on brands like Tocca. Rebecca Danenberg, and Pixie Yates, etc.
East Village, 330 East 11th St. (bet. First and Second Aves.), 982-2881, MC, V, AmEx, ❻ to Astor Pl. ♿

Sugar Hill Thrift Shop
This excellent option for high-quality vintage clothing, used household merchandise, and jewelry has a purpose: It provides job-training for the formerly homeless. The stock is continually replenished.
Harlem, 409 West 145th St. (bet. Convent and St. Nicholas Aves.), 281-2396, MC, V, ❶❷❸❹ to 145th St.

TG-170
The most sophisticated of the small boutiques on the Ludlow strip features simple dresses, skirts, and tops in subtle but fashionably retro designs, as well as "phat" bags and wallets; gentrification hasn't hit the relatively cheap prices yet.
Lower East Side, 170 Ludlow St. (bet. Houston and Stanton Sts.), 995-8660, MC, V, AmEx, ❻ to Second Ave. ♿

Todd Oldham
One of America's hottest young designers and with good reason: The collections found here key into the young and fresh end of fashion with lots of color, prints, denim and other un-stodgy stuff. Buy if you can afford it!.
SoHo, 123 Wooster St. (bet. Spring and Prince Sts.), 219-3531, MC, V, AmEx, ❶❷ to Prince St. ♿

TSE
With modern styles , this is the best spot for young cashmere-o-philes. Offering blends as well, come for suits, jackets, and other must-haves. Don't miss the goat's-

hair blankets and the soft-as-a-baby's-bottom baby duds.
Upper East Side, 827 Madison Ave. (at 69th St.), 472-7790, MC, V, AmEx, ❻ to 68th St.-Hunter College

Urban Outfitters
This hipster playground for the post-mall generation packs its industrial interior with racks of multicolored, funky kid fashion, suitable for an array of day or evening urban outings. Weave through aisles of vintage clothing, sassy sundresses, and trendy housewares while swaying to the smooth rhythms of ambient music played in the background.
Greenwich Village, 374 Sixth Ave. (at Waverly Pl.), 677-9350, MC, V, AmEx, ❶❷❸❹❺❻❼ to West 4th St.-Washington Sq. ♿

Also at:
3 other locations in NYC

Valentino
Haute couture for those who can afford it. By appointment if necessary.
Upper East Side, 747 Madison Ave. (at 65th St.), 772-6969, MC, V, AmEx, Diners, ❻ to Lexington Ave., ❻ to 68th St.-Hunter College ♿

Von's School of Hard Knocks
Over five years ago a father-and-son sneaker and men's sportswear business spawned the School of Hard Knocks, a men's line with a large hip-hop influence. Everything from jackets and caps, to sneakers and knapsacks can be had for relatively low prices; women's and children's lines recently introduced.
Corona, Queens 106-11 Northern Blvd. (bet. 106th and 107th Sts.), (718) 898-1113, MC, V, AmEx, D, ❼ to 103rd St.-Corona Plaza ♿

World Financial Center
At the center of this mall-like complex of over 40 upscale stores and restaurants, including Ann Taylor and Barneys, is the Winter Garden, which doubles as a performance space.
Lower Manhattan, West St. (bet. Liberty and Vescey Sts.), 945-0505, ❶❾ to Cortlandt St., ❸❹ to World Trade Center ♿

Wu Wear
Wu-tang Clan, the premier rap group of Staten Island, has placed itself on the fashion map with its own offerings of active menswear. View the platinum albums of Ol' Dirty Bastard and Method Man alongside brightly-hued jackets and oversized denim. Prices are moderate, at least for designer labels.
Staten Island, 61A Victory Blvd. (at Montgomery Ave.), (718) 720-9043, MC, V, AmEx, D

Yohji Yamamoto
Definitely one of the up-and-coming designers of the 21st Century, Yamamoto is known for black, but works in many colors and fabrics. Two beautifully poised mannequin's carry evening wear at the entrance, designs that are luxuriously light, as your wallet will be after a purchase here.
SoHo, 103 Grand St. (at Mercer St.), 966-9066, MC, V, AmEx, ❶❷❸❹❺❻ to Canal St.

Yves Saint Laurent
All the latest in YSL designs for both men and women, though the "latest" never deviates much from the signature, tireless elegance. In this case, dress up to shop, or even to window shop.
Upper East Side, 859 Madison Ave. (bet. 70th and 71st Sts.), 517-7400, MC, V, AmEx, D, ❹❺❻ to 68th St.-Hunter College ♿

shoes

Anbar Shoes' Steal

The southeastern corner of TriBeCa is a bargain shoppers paradise, and this is by far the best outlet for shoe deals. Name-brand footwear goes for close-out prices and the selection is remarkably good, especially for those seeking sizes other than a 7 or 8. Perfect for finding cheap and stylish accessories to match an end-of-season clothes purchase in an unusual color.
TriBeCa, 60 Reade St. (bet. Church St. and Broadway), 227-0253, MC, V, AmEx, Diners, D, **AC** *to Chambers St.* &

Cole Haan

Shoes of the very finest materials and nicest design are available in this Upper East Side foot haven. The store utilizes its space so as to display the merchandise (incl. other leather goods) quite well.
Upper East Side, 667 Madison Ave. (at 61st St.), 421-8440, MC, V, AmEx, D, **456** *to 59th St.,* **N R** *to Lexington Ave.* &

Hester Street Shoe Outlet

Carrying women's shoes starting at size 5, this store specializes in platforms and strappy sandals at excellent prices. Accessories and a sundry of random items are also sold.
Lower East Side, 188 Hester St. (at Mulberry St.), 965-0244, MC, V, AmEx, D, **JMNRZ6** *to Canal St.* &

John Fluevog

Possibly the hippest source of shoes in the city, a Fluevog can be spotted a mile away. Chunky platforms, combat-quality boots, and funky, offbeat colors are all well-represented; end-of-the-season sales can yield amazing bargains on the otherwise expensive footwear, usually priced at around $100.

SoHo, 104 Prince St. (at Mercer St.), 431-4484, MC, V, AmEx, D, **N R** *to Prince St.* &

Luichiny

Good for seeing over the downtown crowds, the heels here vary — some of are six inches and spiked, others are five inch platforms flat — but every pair will strike for you a towering image.
Greenwich Village, 21 West 8th St. (bet. Fifth and Sixth Aves.), 477-3445, M, V, AmEx, **ABCDEFO** *to West 4th St.-Washington Sq.*

99X

A staple of punk life in NYC, this is the place to buy creepers and Dr. Martens, with a wide selection of imports from London.
East Village, 84 East 10th St. (bet. 3rd and 4th Aves.) 460-8599, MC, V, AmEx, **LNR456** *to 14th St.-Union Sq.*

Sacco

Trendy, retro, and classic, this chic shop carries it all. Make this store your first stop for well-made, eclectic women's footwear. Shoes tend to be dressy and relatively expensive, but there are always sale selections. Clearances offer an additional 20 percent off the sale price.
Upper West Side, 324 Columbus (bet. 75th and 76th Sts.), 799-5229, MC, V, AmEx, D, **BC** *to 72nd St.* &

Trash and Vaudeville

Once this split-level store defined a look that made New York famous. Now merchandise appears trashy and punkish, but the shoe and boot selection in the back is still one of the best in town.
East Village, 4 St. Marks Pl. (bet. Second and Third Aves.), 982-3590, MC, V, AmEx, D, **6** *to Astor Pl.*

makeup

Face Stockholm

With MAC right up the street, the situation seems too close for comfort, though this Sweden-based company excels at the basics. Personal attention is easy to come by within the airy boutique; the $9 nail polish selection makes you wish you had more fingers. The down-town location is a favored stop for fashionistas and actresses.
SoHo, 110 Prince St. (at Greene St.), 966-9110, MC, V, AmEx, **N R** *to Prince St.* &

Also at:
Upper East Side, 687 Madison Ave. (at 62nd St.), 207-8833, MC, V, AmEx, **N R** *to Lexington Ave.,* **456** *to 59th St.* &

Kiehl's

A must for the famous lip balm, this landmark pharmacy has been in the same location since 1851. Stands out for its friendly service and best of all, it offers generous samples of fabulous skincare products.
East Village, 109 Third Ave. (bet. 13th and 14th Sts.), 677-3171, MC, V, AmEx, Diners, **LNR456** *to 14th St.-Union Sq.* &

L'Occitane

This small French company has all of the essentials plus more — great selections of their own perfumes and candles.
SoHo, 146 Spring St (at Wooster St.), 343-0109, MC, V, AmEx, Diners, **CE** *to Spring St.*

MAC

Makeup straight from Canada and cruelty-free to boot, SoHoites and daytime shoppers are more than willing to pay the price for the name and the creamy and metallic signature look. High quality, too.

SoHo, 113 Spring St. (at Mercer St.), 334-4641, MC, V, AmEx, D, **NR** to Prince St., **6** to Spring St.

Also at:
Greenwich Village, 14 Christopher St. (bet. Sixth and Seventh Aves.), 243-4150, MC, V, AmEx, D, **19** to Christopher St.-Sheridan Sq. &

Sephora

Featuring the new hot way of selling makeup, this self-service store has many established brands to choose from as well as small hard to find companies. Did you ever think shopping for makeup (and perfume, etc.) could be so enjoyable?
SoHo, 555 Broadway (bet. Prince and Spring Sts.), 625-1309, MC, V, AmEx, D, **NR** to Prince St. &

department stores

Barneys New York

Power dressers, and those looking for something more elegant, put dents in their substantial bank accounts at this airy, beautiful legend, which still holds its head high despite the recent Chelsea-branch closure. Head to the top floor for the lowest prices and most casual wear.
Upper East Side, 660 Madison Ave. (at 61st St.), 826-8900, MC, V, AmEx, **NR** to Fifth Ave., **456** to 59th St. &

Bergdorf Goodman

Tour the museum-quality merchandise worthy of its chandelier and marble surroundings in this home of high fashion. To actually purchase something, leave the clientele of wealthy Upper East Siders behind and travel to the fifth floor where less expensive (though still somewhat pricey) sportswear abounds. All monetary trans-

actions occur in a "back room" whose doors blend with the walls. Window displays here are among Fifth Avenue's finest.
Midtown, 754 Fifth Ave. (at 58th St.), 753-7300, MC, V, AmEx, Diners, D, **NR** to Fifth Ave. &

Bloomingdale's

Although the trademark perfume arcade is usually a zoo, the upper floors are open, bright, and filled with helpful salespeople eager to successfully match people with outfits bearing three-digit price tags.
Upper East Side, 1000 Third Ave. (bet. 59th and 60th Sts.), 705-2000, MC, V, AmEx, **456** to 59th St., **NR** Lexington Ave. &

Henri Bendel

One of the plushest shopping experiences around. An elegant staircase winds its way up through the many-storied townhouse, maintaining the splendor of Bendel's original boutiques while incorporating modern accents. Same type of clothing as Bergdorf Goodman or Saks, but somehow classier.
Midtown, 712 Fifth Ave. (bet. 55th and 56th Sts.), 247-1100, MC, V, AmEx, D, **NR** to Fifth Ave.

Macy's

"The Largest Store in the World" often resembles the chaos of the Thanksgiving Day parade they sponsor, especially after work and around Christmas. Most items are lower priced than other department stores, but the service and bathrooms reflect this reduction.
Midtown, 34th St. (at Broadway), 695-4400, MC, V, AmEx, **BDFNQR** to 34th St.

Also at:
Parkchester, The Bronx, 1441 Metropolitan Ave. (bet. Wood Ave. and Metropolitan Oval), (718) 828-7000, MC, AmEx, V, D, **6** to East 177th St.-Parckchester

Downtown Brooklyn, 420 Fulton St. (bet. Hoyt and Elm Sts.), (718) 875-7200, MC, V, AmEx, **23** to Hoyt St.-Fulton Mall

Mart 125

Enclosed, but far too interesting to feel like a mall, this neighborhood staple sells African dress, crafts, cosmetics, and accessories. The food court upstairs offers good, reasonably priced soul food.
Harlem, 260 West 125th St. (bet. Adam Clayton Powell, Jr. and Frederick Douglass Blvds.), 316-3340, **ABCD** to 125th St.

Pearl River Mart

Sort of like a Chinese Woolworth's, this two-floored department store stocks everything its American counterpart does, with a twist: bamboo mats, bedding supplies, electronics, video rentals, a minigrocery section, and traditional cookware.
Chinatown, 277 Canal St. (at Broadway), 431-4770, MC, V, AmEx, **JMNRQ6** to Canal St.

Saks Fifth Avenue

This classy store makes for great, if somewhat dizzying, browsing. Window displays make the Fifth Ave. promenade a bit more exciting; Salvador Dali reputedly crashed his car into one of them after artists didn't execute his design well enough.
Midtown, 611 Fifth Ave. (bet. 49th and 50th Sts.), 753-4000, MC, V, AmEx, Diners, D, **BDFQ** to 47th-50th Sts.-Rockefeller Center &

housewares

ABC Carpet and Home

Expect to find ample mother/daughter pairs ooh-ing and aah-ing their way through six floors of housewares, antiques, and knickknacks. Although fairly expensive, the store is worth a visit for its creative window

displays and extraordinary finds such as a ten-foot tall gilded bird cage. The Parlour Cafe on the ground floor allows weary shoppers to lounge and lunch on the furniture that they can't afford to buy.
Gramercy, 881 and 888 Broadway (at 19th St.), 473-3000, MC, V, AmƐx, ❶❻❼❹❺❻ to 14th St.-Union Sq. ⅃

Depression Modern
Plush, beautiful furniture and retro, refurbished, housewares make for great browsing, test-sitting, and daydreaming of a perfectly decorated home for anyone who longs for the era of their grandparents. It's all very expensive, but the people who run it are amiable and tolerant of browsers.
SoHo, 150 Sullivan St. (bet. Houston and Prince Sts.), 982-5699, Cash Only, ❶❾ to Houston St.

Dom
Need some inflatable furniture for your dorm room? Have a fondness for housewares made of neon-colored plastic? All that and plenty more for the home at this trendy decorator hot spot, as well as other junk, from pens to pillboxes. Most of it is inexpensive and equally suitable for gift-giving or feeding your personal flair for home decorating.
SoHo, 382 West Broadway (bet. Spring and Broome Sts.), 334-5580, MC, V, AmƐx, ❻❺ to Spring St.

Fish's Eddy
This shop sells overstocks of commercial dishes and glasses, often bearing the logos of the restaurants or institutions from whence they came. Prices average about $10 for a dinner plate, but check the stacks along the walls for loose items priced below $5.

Gramercy, 889 Broadway (at 19th St.), 420-9020, MC, V, AmƐx, ❶❻❾❹❺❻ to 14th St.-Union Sq.
Also at:
Upper West Side, 2176 Broadway (at 77th St.), 873-8819, MC, V, AmƐx, ❶❾ to 79th St. ⅃

Jack's 99¢ Stores
Good for the bargain conscious shopper, including items like housewares, groceries, school supplies, toys and shampoo. You know, everything. Upstairs there's Jack's World, featuring more upscale merchandise.
Midtown, 110 West 32nd St. (bet. Sixth and Seventh Aves.), 268-9962, MC, V, D, ❶❷❸❾ to 34th St.-Penn Station ⅃
Also at:
Midtown, 16 East 40th St. (bet. Fifth and Sixth Aves.), 696-5767, MC, V, D, ❽❻❼❻ to 42nd St., ❼ to Fifth Ave.

Just Bulbs
The name really says it all. Find every variety of light bulb imaginable, including those for decoration, gifts, and specific holidays.
Gramercy, 936 Broadway (bet. 21st and 22nd Sts.), 228-7820, MC, V, AmƐx, D, ❻❼ to 23rd St. ⅃

Mood Indigo
This is the first stop on the way to becoming a full-fledged member of cocktail culture. The whole idea is putting some classy retro-style back into drinking, and martinis out of a plastic cup simply will not do. Fortunately, here they offer tons of authentic and unique glasses and accessories from the original cocktail era to choose from. It's all a little expensive, but think of it as investing in some valuable antiques.
SoHo, 181 Prince St. (bet. Thompson and Sullivan Sts.), MC, V, AmƐx, ❻❺ to Spring St.

White Trash
From shiny silver toasters to impressively tacky glassware sets, your own grandmother probably got rid of '50s and '60s junk like this twenty years ago. Nevertheless, it's all hip again and the prices aren't too inflated to be a reasonable and interesting alternative to outfitting your home in Lechters standards.
East Village, 304 East 5th St. (bet. First and Second Aves.), 598-5956, MC, V, ❻ to Second Ave., ❻ to Astor Pl.

gourmet&
specialty

A.L. Bazzini
Primarily nut importers, the shop offers a huge variety of them for sale alongside dried fruits and other specialty items, including gift baskets. For cheap fun, stop by for a look around and treat yourself to an ice cream cone.
TriBeCa, 339 Greenwich St. (at Jay St.), 334-1280, MC, V, AmƐx, ❶❷❸❾ to Chambers St. ⅃

Alleva Dairy, Inc.
Fourth-generation owner, Bob Alleva, serves up hot and cold sandwiches for under $5, authentic enough to keep the idea of Little Italy respectable. Mozzarella is made fresh daily at the oldest Italian cheese store in America.
Little Italy, 188 Grand St. (at Mulberry St.), 226-7990, MC, V, AmƐx, ❻❻❻❻❻❻ to Canal St.

⅃ *While we have made every effort to maintain a high level of accuracy regarding wheelchair accessibility, this designation is based on information provided by each establishment*

Aphrodisia
Herbs, spices, and a variety of teas intended to rejuvenate mind and body.
Greenwich Village, 264 Bleecker St. (bet. Cornelia and Jones Sts.), 989-6440, MC, V, AmEx, ⒶⒷⒸⒹⒺⒻⓄ to West 4th St.-Washington Sq. &

Balducci's
A shrine to the art of fine dining which provides all manner of gourmet foods, from produce to baked goods, to specialized deli entrées, dinners, and sandwiches. Join the downtown elite and indulge in one of the delicacies.
Greenwich Village, 424 Sixth Ave. (at 9th St.), 673-2600, MC, V, AmEx, ⒶⒷⒸⒹⒺⒻⓄ to West 4th St.-Washington Sq. &

Brooklyn Brewery
New York's closest approximation to a hometown beer is brewed here, and on weekends they open the place up. That means free brewery tours, beer tastings, and merchandise for sale. The hats and T-shirts make excellent gifts for any beer lover on your list. They've recently begun using the space as a gallery and performance space as well, making this a perfect day of cheap fun for a variety of different tastes.
Williamsburg, Brooklyn, North 11th St. (bet. Berry St. and Wythe Ave.), (718) 486-7422, MC, V, AmEx, ⓛ to Bedford Ave. &

The Damascus Breads & Pastries Shop
Hands-down the best pita bread in Brooklyn, and it has recently caught on in Manhattan supermarkets. But why not buy it fresh here, where a six-pack goes for 55¢, and other staff-of-life items are equally cheap.

Cobble Hill, Brooklyn, 195 Atlantic Ave. (bet. Court and Clinton Sts.), (718) 625-7070, Cash Only, ❷❸❹❺ to Borough Hall, ⓂⓃⓇ to Court St.

Dean & DeLuca
One of New York's most revered specialty food stores, it's the Zabar's of downtown. Stop by for a caffeine break at the stand-up espresso bar, pick up some paté for your next dinner party, and ogle the produce section, full of fruits and vegetables suitable for a still-life masterpiece. They also offer specialty breads, meats, cheeses, desserts, and quality packaged foods. If you have to bring a special addition to a dinner or an impressionable host a gift, come here.
SoHo, 560 Broadway (at Prince St.), 226-6800, MC, V, AmEx, D, ⓃⓇ to Prince St. &

Di Palo Fine Foods
Has everything you'll need when you're planning an Italian feast. The guys who work here are charming and will help you choose the ingredients: fresh mozzarella, sun-dried tomatoes, sausages, bread, etc. for what is sure to be a memorable meal.
Little Italy, 206 Grand St. (at Mott St.) 226-1033, MC, V, AmEx, ⒿⓂⓃⓇⓆ to Canal St. &

Dynasty Supermarket
One of Chinatown's largest supermarkets, boasting a full herb and medicine counter, an in-house butcher and fishmonger, a beef-jerky bar, and best of all, weekly sales.
Chinatown, 68 Elizabeth St. (at Hester St.), 966-4943, MC, V, ⒿⓂⓃⓇⒺⓆ to Canal St., ⓃⓇ to Prince St.

Ecce Panis
A bread store with an extra (and expensive!) flair, they most definitely have bragging rights

to the best chocolate bread in NYC. Go for the free samples.
Upper East Side, 1120 Third Ave. (at 66th St.), 535 2099, MC, V, AmEx, Diners, ❹❺❻ to 68th St.-Hunter College &
Also at:
Four other locations in NYC

Economy Candy
Calling itself a "nosher's" paradise on the Lower East Side, this is the best discount store in the city for penny candy, imported chocolates, nuts, sweets, and gourmet savories like mustards, chutney, tea, and spices. Try their dense, chewy, pistachio-laden Turkish delight, the most authentic this side of Byzantium.
Lower East Side, 108 Rivington St. (bet. Essex and Ludlow Sts.), 254-1832, MC, V, AmEx, ⒿⓂⓏ to Essex St., Ⓕ to Delancey St. &

Eli's Vinegar Factory
An ex-mustard and vinegar factory converted into a gourmet food warehouse with retail prices, including the best deals on imported caviar in the city. Exotic imports beckon from between stacks of fresh produce and gourmet delights.
Upper East Side, 431 East 91st St. (bet. First and York Aves.), 987-0885, MC, V, AmEx, D, ❹❺❻ to 86th St.

Elk Candy
Resist, if possible, the urge not to eat the cute, stylized confectioners, renowned for more than sixty years for its marvelous marzipan.
Upper East Side, 1628 Second Ave. (bet. 84th and 85th Sts.), 650-1177, V, MC, AmEx, ❹❺❻ to 86th St. &

Fairway
"Like no other market" reads the awning, and this is indeed the most popular, largest, and lowest-priced produce and gourmet

market on the West Side. A full deli counter offers prepared hot and cold dishes, the cheese department stocks an array of imports, and the bakery sells over a million bagels every year. *Morningside Heights, 2328 12th Ave. (at 133rd St.), 234-3883, MC, V, AmEx, ❶❾ to 125th St.*

Also at:

Upper West Side, 2127 Broadway (at 74th St.), 595-1888, MC, V, AmEx, ❶❷❸❾ to 72nd St. ⟁

Kam Wo Herb and Tea Co., Inc.
Drawers of medicine line the walls in this apothecary shop, smelling thickly of herbs. Specialty medicinal cookware and a library of health books written by the boss himself, Dr. Leung. Herbs, weighed out on hand-scales and wrapped in white rice-paper envelopes, will cure any ailment. *Chinatown, 211 Grand St. (near Elizabeth St.), 966-6370, MC, V, ❻❼❽❾❿❽ to Canal St. ⟁*

La Maison du Chocolat
As one might guess, chocolate is this store's specialty, and it comes in many shapes and sizes, none of which even approach being healthy or veer far from being absolutely divine. *Upper East Side, 1018 Madison Ave. (bet. 78th and 79th Sts.), 744-7117, MC, V, AmEx, ❻ to 77th St. ⟁*

M. Rohrs House of Fine Teas & Coffee
Satiating the ever-fluctuating caffeine addictions of locals for over 100 years with its wide selection of refined tea leaves and coffee beans. Wooden counters and aged tea canisters with beveled mirrors retain the shops original, old-world charm, an anomaly among slick coffee bars. *Upper East Side, 303 East 85th St. (at Second Ave.), 396-4456, MC, V, AmEx, ❹❺❻ to 86th St. ⟁*

McNulty's Tea & Coffee
Hear the soothing staccato of coffee beans cascading into brass scales in this dark, woodsy specialty shop, which boasts over 250 varieties of tea and coffee. Prices are competitive, ranging from $9 to $30/lb. Mail order is available for far-flung java lovers. *Greenwich Village, 109 Christopher St. (bet. Bleecker and Hudson Sts.), 242-5351, MC, V, AmEx, Diners, D, ❶❾ to Christopher St.-Sheridan Sq.*

Mondel Chocolates
Florence Mondel has been catering to Morningside Heights chocoholics for more than 50 years. Her modest store is filled with homemade fudge and marzipan, as well as a dozen different kinds of truffles. *Morningside Heights, 2913 Broadway (at 114th St.), 864-2111, V, MC, AmEx, ❶❾ to 116th St.-Columbia University*

Veniero Pasticceria
This legendary Italian bakery is murder on the waistline — spectacular deserts, sensational pastries by the pound, and legendary wedding cakes. *East Village, 342 East 11th St. (between 1st and 2nd Aves.), 674-7264, MC, V, AmEx, D, ❶ to 1st Ave. ⟁*

Zabar's
A name with impressive caché in uptown circles, this longtime Upper West Side institution is the prime source for gourmet meats, cheese, breads, and produce. Upstairs is an equally well-stocked kitchenware department featuring at least 30 kinds of whisks. The store can get shoulder-to-shoulder crowded on the weekends and holidays. *Upper West Side, 2245 Broadway (at 80th St.), 787-2000, MC, V, AmEx, ❶❾ to 79th St.*

shopping in new york city

arts

visual arts

v·i·s·u·a·l·a·r·t·s

New York has fostered the cutting edge of the art world for decades, from the stark minimalism of Jacob Kline to Alfred Stieglitz' clean urban angles, and the sprawling graffiti of counterculture phenomenon Jean-Michel Basquiat. Although artists like multimedia pioneer Bill Viola and celestial abstractionist Ross Bleckner may enjoy one-man shows at the Whitney and in swank 57th Street galleries like Mary Boone's, the proverbial struggling artist begins more modestly: Many emerging artists get their breaks in galleries like the Lower East Side's Esso, where Parsons, School of Visual Arts, and Pratt grads explore the aftermath of pop art; at burgeoning BoHo paradise Pierogi 2000; and on the walls and sidewalks of the East Village and SoHo, where street-level graffiti artists turn pocked cement into canvas.

Like struggling actors, most struggling artists have day jobs; they are likely to work in spaces which betray their pursuits, like at Limbo, a perennially popular Ave. A coffeehouse whose rotating installations come across as either pretentious or promising. The Anchorage, a space which opens up beneath the Brooklyn Bridge in the summer, displays intriguing and provocative pieces on its sweeping brick walls and archways. Neophytes should begin with a copy of *Gallery Guide*, free in most showrooms, to become familiar with what the city has to offer.

Rising rents have caused many galleries to flee SoHo for Chelsea, the Lower East Side, and Williamsburg, Brooklyn, although devoted daytrippers still flock to the cast-iron buildings that are central to the art world. Don't be intimidated by stodgy guards or uppity desk clerks; if you can't get up the nerve, try starting at low-key spots like The Drawing Center or Exit Art, or get your feet wet at one of the city's excellent museums, which consistently launch forward-thinking, provocative exhibits that keep abreast of national and international trends. The ambitious and defiant curators of the Whitney's Biennial, a show occurring in summers of odd-numbered years, never fail to provoke critical and public outcry with their unveilings. Once you've raised your confidence level, try crashing a well-attended white wine reception (on 57th St. in Midtown, or along West Broadway or Prince St. in SoHo) for some insight into the gossip,

intrigue, and sordid details of the city's art world.

New York's influence on the course of 20th Century art reflects the same rhythm of modulation and progress that characterizes most of the city's history. Beginning with the Ashcan School shortly after the turn of the 20th Century, New York has emerged as an artistic laboratory in which experimentation is the norm and deviation is embraced.

Exchanging the 19th Century's "art-for-art's-sake" sensibilities for what one leader of the movement called "art for life," members of the Ashcan School grew dissatisfied with the academic elitism of contemporary artists. They painted what they saw around them, favoring a Bowery street urchin as a subject over a nude in a studio. Celebrating the vitality that the city provided them, Ashcan artists Maurice Prendergast and George Lukes helped unmoor 20th Century art from its neoclassical foundations.

Working concurrently, the Photo-Secession group was determined to firmly establish photography, an upstart among the fine arts. Alfred Stieglitz and his cohorts also embraced other experimental artists looking for "legitimacy." Opening the seminal 291 Gallery in 1905, he organized exhibitions responsible for introducing

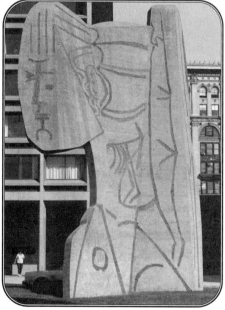

America to the works of many of Europe's avant-garde, with shows featuring Picasso, Braque, and Picabia: the United States' first encounter with Cubism.

The onset of World War I brought many European artists to New York. Picabia and Marcel Duchamp met Man Ray and launched the city's historic Dada movement. Commenting obliquely on the nonsense of "the human condition," New York's Dadaists mocked both the establishment and the avant-garde. When the United States entered the war, the group disbanded temporarily as its expatriate constituents fled to different parts of the world. The group reconvened in Paris in 1921.

As New York established itself as a "vertical city," skyscrapers and other urban novelties became subjects for a new group of urban artists. Inspired by the grid street-plan and the sea of rectangular forms, Dutch painter Piet Mondrian perfected his aesthetic of right angles. The Precisionists emerged in the 1920s, enchanted with the city's buildings, bridges, waterfronts, and warehouses, and aimed for a new, objective portrayal.

After Paris fell to Germany in 1940, New York hosted an influx of European avant-guard artists making the city the world's undisputed artistic capital. The influence of émigré artists, such as Mondrian, Fernand Leger, and Max Ernst, precipitated an infusion of freedom and expressionism in American art, though their work had been foreshadowed in the homegrown organization, American Abstract Artists, which formed in 1936.

Abandoning most things mimetic, the aptly dubbed Abstract Expressionists appended Freud's notion of the subconscious to Surrealism's notion of human-as-automaton, adding concepts prevalent in mythology and American Indian traditions as well. This amalgam, a kind of automatic art analogous to stream-of-consciousness writing, is one popular rationale explaining the work of such artists as Jackson Pollack, Willem de Kooning, and Mark Rothko. The movement's first significant museum recognition was not until an immensely popular 1958 exhibit, which eventually traveled to Europe. Other important members of what came to be known as the New York School included Clyfford Still, Robert Motherwell, Lee Krasner, Franz Kline, Elaine de Kooning, and Arshile Gorky. America's artistic dominance following the New York School's success led to the founding of an unprecedented number of galleries.

In the '60s, Abstraction gave way to pop art. Presaged by Jasper Johns and Robert Rauschenberg in the '50s, who tampered with images from popular culture, this new wave of artists attempted to elevate the residue of American life to a fine aesthetic, blurring the distinction between high art and kitsch. Andy Warhol, Roy Lichtenstein, and Claes Oldenburg, among others, distilled Abstract Expressionism's esoteric, cerebral qualities into popular, visceral derivatives.

Supplemented in the late '60s by the subtlety of conceptual art and minimalism, New York became the art world's hotbed of innovation, variety, and nontraditional aesthetics. Whereas, for instance, Warhol's concept of American life focused on its predominantly wild consumer culture, artists like Robert Morris contested that vision with more elemental works. Meanwhile, other artists were developing their own styles; Helen Frankenthaler used broad strokes of thin paint to create ethereal, haunting canvases; Frank Stella and Robert Ryman used geometry to produce stark works in the shape of protractors; May Stevens and Nancy Spero took their cues from the liberalism of the '70s to critique sexism, racism, and imperialism.

Performance art, popular in the '70s, added a more immediate sense of interaction between viewer and artist. To better suit these "dialogues," large exhibitions slowly gave way to more intimate galleries and performance spaces.

Many contemporary city artists continue to challenge mainstream culture with works infused with

Just one example of an artist, model, and studio in New York City.

a political consciousness. A student at the Pratt Institute in the late '60s, Robert Mapplethorpe exhibited his photographs largely in the more conservative mid-West. His work later became known for its explicit homoeroticism, inciting a furor when included in a federally funded exhibit. Painter Keith Haring, who studied at the School of Visual Arts in the '80s, adopted a decidedly more self-conscious political voice, which, even after his death, continues to promote federal support for the arts and AIDS research.

The same energy that has allowed New York's art scene to re-energize areas once considered "uninteresting" and "industrial" — words used to describe SoHo of the late '60s and early '70s, and TriBeCa in the mid-'70s — continues to inspire progress, thought, and change. New York's catalog of 20th-century art is uniquely dynamic, earning the city a seminal role in the current direction of Western art.

in the *p*ublic eye

Often obscured, overlooked, or dismissed with mild bewilderment, are the pieces of public sculpture that pepper the city. With a little research, it's even possible to make sense of these abstract pieces!

The artistic trends of the 1950s and '60s are evident in Isamu Noguchi's "Sunken Garden" sculpture, constructed with granite, glass, and basalt stones imported from Kyoto in 1961. Completed in 1964, Nogushi's glass-enclosed sculpture garden reflects sunlight aimed at the forecourt of One Chase Manhattan Plaza. Lying adjacent to the ground floor's banking area and visible from the street-level plaza above, the sculpture was inspired by the raked patterns of Japanese rock gardens from the Uji River in Kyoto. In the '70s, Jean Dubuffet's whimsical "Group of Four Trees" was added to the plaza, pairing its synthetic aluminum and fiberglass frame with the natural stones of Noguchi's piece.

In the mid-1960s at Lincoln Center, sculptures were chosen to represent the urban redevelopment programs which were reshaping the city, and city beautification through sculpture placement was also taking place around the same time downtown. In 1961, an ordinance known as the "Plaza Law" required building developers to provide an open forecourt at street level — an ideal space for new sculpture. In an ambitious exhibition staged by the Parks Department, twenty-nine contemporary sculptures were placed throughout Manhattan, including Astor Place's familiar tilted steel black box. Formally entitled "Alamo," but more commonly referred to as The Cube, this piece, designed by Bernard Rosenthal in 1967, was one of the first abstract sculptures on city property and has since served as a hangout for pre-pubescent skateboarders.

A few blocks to the southwest, in the court among three prongs of the residential complex at New York University Towers, Picasso's 1968 "Bust of Sylvette" towers between Mercer St. and LaGuardia Pl. Critics complain that the piece exemplifies the problems inherent in enlarging a small piece to monumental scale, but that doesn't mitigate local resident's pride in having the 20th Century master's work grace their otherwise empty courtyard.

Central Park - It is by far one of New York City's most artistic places. From oversized concerts by artists such as Garth Brooks and Paul Simon to movies á la Disney, it has proven itself a time-honored stomping ground for artists of all kinds. Shakespeare in the Park, the Metropolitan Opera, SummerStage, etc., have all made their mark on the park, if you will. In addition to all the aural excitement, there is an abundance of visual art all over the park - just keep your eyes wide open!

how to MUSEUM *a* GOER

There are two reasons why New Yorkers visit museums: to have an art experience or to have a people experience, and never the two shall meet! In either scenario, a blockbuster show on a Saturday afternoon is to be avoided at peril of insanity. There are far more relaxing ways to enjoy New York City museums, whether your motivation is artistic or sociological.

New York museums offer more programs and visitor services than any other city's, and their combined collections boast a broader range and greater depth of quality. Most have permanent exhibitions, as well as temporary ones; since the latter of these is more likely to draw bigger crowds, permanent installations offer the best opportunities to look in relative peace and solitude. Because the number of people you'll have to elbow in order to see a picture will impact your overall experience, remember that early mornings and weekdays are best for quiet times, whereas visitor traffic peaks on weekends and afternoons.

Regardless of when you decide to visit, a few tips to remember will help you navigate through the basics. Most museums have baggage checks, which can be a blessing or a curse, depending on your schedule. Often guards in larger museums won't let you enter the galleries if you're sporting a backpack, so be prepared to spend time winding through drop-off and pick-up lines. When you've made your way to the ticket counter, ask the clerk whether the admission is fixed, or if it is suggested donation. If it's fixed, you might get a discount with student identification, senior citizen card, or membership at another major museum. If the admission is suggested, then avoid dark looks and a guilty conscience by coughing up as much as you can afford, congratulating yourself on supporting a worthy cause.

Once in the galleries, try to maximize your experience by spending time with particular works that you find interesting, perhaps trying to understand the relationships between a group of works. Reading wall labels and exhibition brochures can

*Museum art is indoors **and** out*

Andrée Marie Hymel is Assistant Director of the Contemporary Art Center, Cincinnati, and the contributor of this article. A recent graduate of the Arts Administration program at Columbia University, Ms. Hymel is the author of Museum Directorship: A Digest of Contemporary Opinion.

help clarify the logic of a particular installation, as well as informing you of a particular artist's chronology. While you may feel that you get more out of a show with a headset, try looking through an exhibition first without it. You may discover things with a fresh eye that are otherwise overwhelmed by too many didactics.

If the museum's galleries are crowded, you may have to fall in line, waiting until people move away so you can have dibs on looking. In the way that it is rude to stand in front of someone who is watching television, remember that it is sacrilege to interrupt a person engaged with a work of art by walking in front of him or her. Just take a detour behind the viewers to move around the gallery and you'll eschew sharp looks. Also, avoid remonstrance from high-strung guards by putting your hands behind your back whenever you get close to a picture or sculpture. Your nose might end up touching the work, Pinocchio, but the guard won't utter a peep if you're hands are out of the way!

To decide which museum to visit, make two decisions: the type of art you'd like to see and the type of atmosphere you'd like to see it in. Most art museums can be classified as traditional (Greek to Impressionists), Modern (from the past century), or Contemporary (from approximately the past decade); and as mastadonically large, manageably medium, or intimately small with varying degrees of traffic. To learn the current programs and events in any New York museum, check out *The Village Voice*, *Gallery Guide*, or visit Citysearch. com, where you'll find links to each museum Website and details on exhibitions, lectures, symposia, workshops and concerts.

Beyond the endless flow of available museum programs, New Yorkers rely on several staples for an art fix. The tranquil Fort Tryon Park is a picturesque setting for **The Cloisters** (923-3700), which offers reliable sanctity with medieval collections; although the better known museums in New York are reliable, sometimes less celebrated venues provide the most special experiences. For example, **The Metropolitan Museum of Art** (Fifth Avenue at 82nd St., 535-7710) is encyclopedic and can be counted on to provide the finest examples from antiquity to modernity, but for an interesting caveat, check out its Gubbio Studiolo from the Palace of Duke Federico da Montefeltro, where meticulously inlaid wood panels never fail to awe. Meanwhile, the **Museum of Modern Art**, a.k.a. MoMA, proudly displays its postcard-perfect modern masterpieces from van Gogh to Warhol, but the tucked-away Dia Center for the Arts quietly produces exhibitions of contemporary preciousness, consistently celebrated by the New York art world.

For a memorable experience that will always bring a smile, **P.S.1** in Queens offers an enlightened, contemporary program in a renovated public school. Be sure to learn when the breathtaking James Turrell room will be open before you go, and don't forget to ask the front desk to show you the Pipiotti Rist installation, which is so delightfully subtle that only the initiated can locate it.

If architecture is your passion, two New York museums to visit are the **Solomon R. Guggenheim Museum** and the **Morgan Library**. Although the former's admission prices for exhibitions can be steep, you can enjoy the interior view of Frank Lloyd Wright's spiraling building without paying to see a show. Similarly, Mr. Morgan's library, designed by the lavish McKim, Mead, and White, only requests donations for admittance.

Unlike most city's museums, New York's attract every conceivable type of person — local and foreigner, old and young, highbrow and lowbrow. With approximately 5.4 million people visiting the Metropolitan Museum annually, socializing can be just as much fun as seeing exhibitions. The Met proudly offers two of the best venues for just that: the Iris B. Gerald Cantor Roof Garden during summer days, and the elegant entrance hall balcony every Friday evening, where you can enjoy a glass of wine to live chamber music. Jazz evenings at the Guggenheim are also a growing attraction.

New Yorkers also like to rejuvenate with a good meal or by relaxing in a museum café. The Sette MoMA has an enticing menu and Sarabeth's, downstairs from **The Whitney Museum of American Art**, will not disappoint. While the cavernous cafeteria at the Met may make you feel herded like cattle, it's a welcome respite from roaming the galleries. As for cafés, the undisputed champs are the Morgan Library and P.S.1. Enjoy a cappuccino in the elegant glass canopy of the Morgan's tasteful canteen, The Garden Court, or interact with contemporary art installations at P.S.1, where artists have been commissioned to transform the space, create chairs, couches and more to enliven the experience.

Before leaving, make sure you reserve time for browsing through the museum's gift shops. The Metropolitan's, like the rest of the museum, is expansive and suspiciously reminiscent of a department store. If The Met shop is a bit too frumpy, consider the amazing merchandise at The MoMA Design Store, which is located across the street from the museum. And for a cozy read, sink into one of the couches at **The New Museum of Contemporary Art's bookstore**, where you'll find a variety of provocative contemporary subjects.

art supplies

The Art Store

This brand new retailer with a downtown vibe has all of the supplies you need as well as some extras.
East Village, 1-5 Bond St (bet. Broadway and Lafayette St.), 533-2444, MC, V, AmEx, ⑥ to Bleecker St. ♿

Lee's Art Shop

Paints and brushes are just the beginning at this valuable resource for artists who work in all media. Drafting supplies, silk screens, a good selection of pens and stationary, and a framing service.
Midtown, 220 West 57th St. (bet. Seventh Ave. and Broadway), 247-0110, MC, V, AmEx, ⓃⓇ to 57th St.

Pearl Paint

Located at the crossroads of SoHo, TriBeCa, Little Italy, and Chinatown this is the world's largest discount art supplier. In addition to the veritable superstore of art supplies, it offers custom framing, furniture, and home decorating.
TriBeCa, 308 Canal St. (bet. Church St. and Broadway), 431-7932, MC, V, AmEx, D, ⒿⓂⓃⓇⓏ⑥ to Canal St. ♿

Sam Flax

Whether in search of gouache, canvas, or some stylish wrapping paper, shoppers will find it all at this well-staffed store. Check out the sale section in back for some good furniture bargains as well.
Gramercy, 12 West 20th St. (bet. Fifth and Sixth Aves.), 620-3038, MC, V, AmEx, ⑤ to 23rd Street, ⓃⓇ to 23rd St.

Utrecht

Supply closet for many Parsons School of Design students, Utrecht has all of basic art supplies. Unlike other art stores in the area, however it carries its own line of products, usually less expensive than equivalent brand names.
East Village, 111 Fourth Ave. (bet. 11th and 12th Sts.), 777-5353, MC, V, AmEx, D, ④ⓁⓃⓇ④⑤⑥ to 14th St.-Union Sq. ♿

cultural institutions

Alliance Française

Brush up on the language of love at Tuesday's $7 screenings of French flicks ($5.50 for members;, dance classes and more than 200 language courses are also available. Members enjoy free films, culinary and wine tastings, travel seminars, art excursions, discounts on French performances around the city, and the use of the multimedia library.
Upper East Side, 22 East 60th Street (bet. Madison and Park Aves.), 355-6100, ④⑤⑥ to 59th St., ⓃⓇ to Lexington Ave. ♿

The American Academy of Arts and Letters

Recent initiates, Oliver Sacks and Elie Wiesel included, attest to the prestige of this exclusive society created to honor American artists, writers, and composers. Check out samples of honorees' works inside the gallery. For a good look at the neighboring Trinity Church Cemetery, stop by the South Gallery, but call ahead — the Academy is only open to the public three times a year.
Washington Heights, 633 West 155th St. (bet. Broadway and Riverside Dr.), 368-5900, ① to 157th St. ♿

American Ballet Theatre

Drop-in classes to the tune of $12 a pop ($110 buys ten classes) for aspiring prima donnas at one of the country's premier studios. Alaine Haubert and Diana Cartier teach regularly, though guest instructors from the ABT Artistic Staff occasionally fill in. Advanced dancers should stop by at 10am Monday, Wednesday, or Friday, while intermediates will be best served by the 6pm weekday classes.
Gramercy, 890 Broadway (at 19th St.), 3rd Floor, 477-3030, ④ⓁⓃⓇ④⑤⑥ to 14th St.-Union Sq. ♿

American Folk Art Institute

Classes and workshops are offered in all manners of media. Lectures and other panels are also held here.
Upper West Side, 2 Lincoln Sq. (Columbus Ave. bet. 65th and 66th Sts.), 977-7170, ①⑨ to 66th St.-Lincoln Center ♿

The American Numismatic Society

If you had one of those penny books as a kid, this is your chance to see what you may have had if you'd only stuck with it. Numismatics has been practiced in these hallowed halls since 1858, and their library maintains over 70 thousand volumes. Other pursuits include a fellowship program for grad students and museum professionals, publishing monographs and journals, and running the annual conference on coinage in America.
Washington Heights, Audubon Terrace, 155th St. at Broadway, 234-3130, ① to 157th St. ♿

Americas Society

Inter-American policy issues come up for debate at the conferences and study groups organized by the Society's Western Hemisphere Department; the Cultural Affairs department offers an extensive arts library, lectures in conjunction with special exhibits, and concerts with receptions for the white wine crowd.
Upper East Side, 680 Park Ave. (at 68th St.), 249-8950, ⑥ to 68th St.-Hunter College ⑤

Asia Society

Celebrate Asian cultural awareness with notable film series, lectures, and an art collection featuring sculpture, paintings, ceramics, prints and bronzes from across Asia. Prominent authors and public leaders speak regularly here; other programs for the public include dance performances, well-attended art exhibits usually gathered from private collections, and receptions involving community and professional organizations.
Upper East Side, 725 Park Ave. (at 70th St.), 288-6400, MC, V, AmEx, ⑥ to 68th St.-Hunter College ⑤

Bronfman Center for Jewish Student Life

In a townhouse built for Lockwood De Forest, a wealthy exporter, the center presents free lectures focusing on Jewish religious concerns and Israeli politics for an almost exclusively NYU audience. De Forest founded workshops in India to revive the art of woodworking, so the center is replete with the fruits of his labor — intricately-carved teak wood imported from India.
Greenwich Village, 7 East 10th St. (bet. University Pl. & Fifth Ave.), 998-4114, ⑩⑬ to 8th St.-NYU ⑤

Brooklyn Academy of Music

Offering contemporary performing arts and cinema, this glorious building, erected in 1908, attracts audiences from all over the metropolitan area. The Brooklyn Philharmonic is the resident orchestra and The New Wave Festival, an avant-garde series, takes place here.
Fort Greene, Brooklyn, 30 Lafayette Ave. (at Ashland St.), (718) 636-4111, ⑩⑬②③④⑤ to Atlantic Ave., ⑬⑩⑩⑬ to Pacific St. ⑤

China Institute

America's oldest bicultural organization focusing on China promotes awareness of that country's culture, history, language, and arts through semester-long classes in Mandarin, Cantonese, Tai Chi, calligraphy, cooking, & painting. Seminars, lecture series, and film screenings with Chinese and Chinese-American themes are also regularly scheduled.
Upper East Side, 125 East 65th St. (bet. Lexington and Park Aves.), 744-8181, ⑥ to 68th St.-Hunter College

The Hispanic Society of America

Described by a delighted visitor as "one of the city's hidden gems," the museum focuses on the art, literature, and cultural history of Spain; it also offers a reference library which is open to the public.
Washington Heights, 613 West 155th St. (at Broadway), 690-0743, ① to 157th St.

Istituto Italiano di Cultura

The Italian consulate operates this center for the dissemination of the country's culture; attend concerts, exhibits and lectures occurring frequently, or just swing by to flip through Italian mags for some insight into the Pope or haute couture.

Upper East Side, 686 Park Ave. (bet. 68th and 69th Sts.), 879-4242, ⑥ to 68th St.-Hunter College ⑤

Japan Society

An all-purpose center of Japanese art and culture, located appropriately enough in Japan House, with exhibitions on the second floor and a stone-lined pool garden on the first floor, complete with bamboo shafts.
Midtown, 333 East 47th St. (bet. First and Second Aves.), 832-1155, ⑥ to 51st St., ⑥⑥ to Lexington-3rd Aves. ⑤

La Maison Française

The epicenter of Francophone and Francophilic life at New York University. Call for information about free lectures, usually in French, along with conferences and exhibitions which are presented in the center's historic 19th Century carriage house.
Greenwich Village, 16 Washington Mews (at University Pl.), 998-8750, ⑩⑬ to 8th St.-NYU ⑤

New York Historical Society

An imposing building across from the Park houses both a library and a museum with a wealth of information and images of New York up to the turn-of-the-century. The museum also features a permanent installation of 19th century paintings.
Upper West Side, 2 West 77th St. (at Central Park West), 873-3400, ⑬⑥ to 81st St. - Museum of Natural History ⑤

New York Public Library

The main facility of the city's extensive library system sits at 42nd St. and Fifth Ave. It was designed by Carrere and Hastings, and is considered one of the five greatest libraries in the world. The library issues

borrowers' cards to anyone who lives, works, or attends school in New York State, so make sure to drop by any local branch and get yourself one.
Midtown, 455 Fifth Ave. (at 40th St.), 42nd St., 930-0830, B D F Q to 42nd St., 7 to Fifth Ave. &

New York Society Library
George Washington, James Fenimore Cooper, Henry Thoreau, and Herman Melville all frequented the oldest circulating library in New York, founded in 1754. Nowadays you'll have to fork over 90 bucks ($135 for non-students) for the privilege of perusing literature in the luxurious reading rooms. Non-members are accommodated in the ground floor's reference room.
Upper East Side, 53 East 79th St. (bet. Madison and Park Aves.), 288-6900, 6 to 77th St.

New York Zendo Shobo-ji
New Yorkers looking to escape urban chaos seek out this serene temple, complete with rock gardens, instructions on correct breathing, meditation, posture, etiquette, and Oriental floor cushions. Hard-core enthusiasts can partake of a purer experience on one of the weekend retreats held at an affiliated monastery in the Catskills.
Upper East Side, 223 East 67th St. (bet. Second and Third Aves.), 861-3333, 6 to 68th St.-Hunter College &

92nd Street Y
One of New York's most valuable cultural resources serves as a source for a multitude of workshops, classes, and speaking and reading series. The Unterberg Poetry Series is by far the city's most star-studded, consistently drawing the finest poets and authors — national and international, established and emerging.

Upper East Side, 1395 Lexington Avenue (at 92nd St.), 996-1100, 6 to 96th St. &

Schomburg Center for Research in Black Culture
World-famous for its extensive research facilities, this branch of the New York Public Library is an invaluable resource for scholars of black history and culture.
Harlem, 515 Malcolm X Blvd. (at 135th St.), 491-2200, 2 3 to 135th St. &

The Spanish Institute
Exhibitions, events, and lectures acquaint visitors with Spanish culture. Semester-long language classes include the perks of access to both the reference collection and reading room with current publications. Go, Iberia, go!
Upper East Side, 684 Park Ave. (bet. 68th and 69th Sts.), 628-0420, 6 to 68th St. - Hunter College &

galleries

Acquavella
Uptown gallery hoppers never overlook this mother lode of 19th and 20th Century European masters and postwar European and American pieces.
Upper East Side, 18 East 79th St. (bet. Fifth and Madison Aves.), 734-6300, 6 to 77th St. &

Annina Nosei Gallery
As an artist who brilliantly features works from one end of the globe to the other, Nosei has recently focused particularly on contemporary work from many Latin American countries.
Chelsea, 530 West 22nd St., 2nd Fl. (bet. Tenth & Eleventh Aves.), 741-8695, C E to 23rd St. &

Apex Art C.P.
Off the beaten path of art with a fresh perspective, this is one of the best places to find innovative work; appreciating it comes easily also, since the staffers are far less aloof than most of their SoHo counterparts. Shows tend to feature a combination of efforts by a few different artists and include both painting and sculpture.
TriBeCa, 291 Church St. (bet. Walker and White Sts.), 431-5270, 1 9 to Franklin St. &

Artist's Space
A testing ground where new artists get the chance to cut their teeth, pay their dues, and show their stuff to the gallery world. Shows generally focus on a central theme and contain several new artists with work that fits in. Check out up-and-coming talent in its larval stages.
SoHo, 38 Greene Street (bet. Grand and Broome Sts.), 226-3970, J M N R Z 6 to Canal St. &

Barbara Gladstone
This enormous space has tall ceilings and two levels displaying contemporary and modern art in various media, including rotating painting, sculpture, video installations, and photography.
Chelsea, 515 West 24th St. (bet. Tenth and Eleventh Aves.), 206-9300, C E to 23rd St. &

Basilico Fine Arts
One-person shows are the standard at this sprawling showroom where promising newcomers attempt to prove themselves. Pieces are displayed in an unusually manageable fashion.
SoHo, 26 Wooster St. (bet. Grand and Canal Sts.), 966-1831, A C E Canal St.

Bullet Space

This "Urban Artist Collaborative" in a deteriorating building showcases city artists known for political and challenging works. The stark gallery also has a musical space, community center, and residence for artists. Open weekends 2pm-5pm, by appointment only.
East Village, 292 East 3rd St. (bet. Aves. C and D), 982-3580, ⑥ *to Second Ave.*

Christie's

Scope out the goods at the free public viewing five days before an auction at this New York branch of the London legend; 19th and 20th Century European art, traditionally favored here, is still a strong suit.
Upper East Side, 502 Park Ave. (at 59th St.), 546-1007, ❹❺❻ *to 59th St.,* ❻❼ *to Lexington Ave.*

David Zwirner

Whatever the well-known featured artist displays, it's done to near perfection, to the delight of critics and other viewers. Even if the style isn't something you find particularly inspiring, the high level of technique demonstrated is easy to admire.
SoHo, 43 Greene St. (bet. Grand and Broome Sts.), 966-9074, ❶❼❼❼❼❼ *to Canal St.*

Dia Center for the Arts

Dia opened its main exhibition facility in a four-story renovated warehouse in 1987, dedicating it to large-scale, long-term exhibitions, offering artists the opportunity to develop new work or a focused presentation of work on a full floor.
Chelsea, 548 West 22nd St. (bet. Tenth and Eleventh Aves.), 989-5566, ❻❼ *to 23rd St.*

Esso

If there is a mien that suggests I-just-became-legal at a drinking establishment, then the artistic counterpart that suggests I-just-finished-art-school reigns at this funky downtown space, where pop art is reworked for a generation that grew up on the Smurfs and Atari.
Lower East Side, 191 Chrystie St., 6th Fl. (bet. Rivington and Stanton Sts.) 714-8192, ⑥ *to Second Ave.*

Exit Art — The First World

A huge upstairs loft space, complete with a café made for lingering when gallery hopping becomes tiresome, and a shop filled with art trinkets. Never stodgy, themed group shows are favored. Past innovations include having the artists move their studios into the gallery and an exhibit of art/paraphernalia from social protest movements. Openings here should not be missed.
SoHo, 548 Broadway, 2nd Fl. (bet. Prince and Spring Sts.), 966-7745, ❼❼ *to Prince St.*

Gagosian

A vast gallery filled by established artists who are often eager to take advantage of the space. As such, large paintings, three-dimensional pieces, and sculpture often come into play, and the results can be more absorbing than a similar show executed in a smaller area. Even when this physical potential isn't realized, the art is usually worth checking out.
SoHo, 136 Wooster St. (bet. Prince and Houston Sts.), 228-2828, ❼❼ *to Prince St.*

Also at:
Upper East Side, 980 Madison Ave. (bet. 76th and 77th Sts.), 744-2313, ⑥ *to 77th St.*

Greene Naftali Gallery

A western exposure bathes the space in natural light. Works are contemporary and tend to be experimental; genres range from sculpture and painting to multimedia exhibits.
Chelsea, 526 est. 26th St., 8th Fl. (bet. Tenth and Eleventh Aves.), 463-7770, ❻❼ *to 23rd St.*

Grey Art Gallery

Both foreign and domestic contemporary artists display their work at this offbeat gallery on New York University's main campus.
Greenwich Village, 100 Washington Sq. East (at Waverly Pl.), 998-6780, ❼❼ *to 8th St.-NYU*

Jack Tilton Gallery

The artists shown here are respected, but not necessarily for producing conventional pieces. Often, the stuff on display requires a second look to see what's really going on.
SoHo, 49 Greene St. (bet. Broome and Grand Sts.), 941-1775, ❶❼❼ *to Canal St.*

Jeffrey Deitch Projects

The small entryway here gives way to big-time modern art inside. Don't pass up the chance to experience anything from relatively tame non-traditional sculpture installations to a Russian performance artist living inside a doghouse within the gallery and getting confrontational with visitors (just two of the recent offerings).
SoHo, 76 Grand St. (bet. Wooster and Greene Sts.), 343-7300, ❶❼❼❼❼❼ *to Canal St.*

Jessica Fredericks Gallery

Housed in a brownstone building, this smallish space consists of one main viewing room showcasing established and emerging artists.

*Chelsea, 504 West 22nd St.
(bet. Tenth and Eleventh Aves.),
633-6555,* **CE** to 23rd St.

Knoedler Gallery

Not to be missed by art
historians or art historians
in-the-making, the oldest New
York-based art gallery, established in 1846, exhibits such
modern greats as Nancy Graves,
Robert Motherwell, Frank Stella,
and Robert Rauschenberg.
*Upper East Side, 19 East 70th St.
(bet. Madison and Fifth Aves.),
794-0550,* **6** to 68th St.-Hunter
College

Linda Kirkland Gallery

Modest in size, but not in vision,
the gallery's focus is to "exhibit
art that combines a conceptual
bent with a sensual visual form."
*Chelsea, 504 West 22nd St., 2nd
Fl. (bet. Tenth and Eleventh
Aves.), 627-3930,* **CE** to 23rd St.

Mary Boone Gallery

This longtime SoHo staple
recently headed for greener
grass up north — an elegant
address on Fifth Ave. Many
artists, among them Ross
Bleckner, who had a show at the
Guggenheim a few years back,
came along for the ride.
*Midtown, 745 Fifth Ave., 4th Fl.
(bet. 57th and 58th Sts.),
752-2929,* **NR** to Fifth Ave. &

Matthew Marks

Both outposts of his extinct
Madison Avenue gallery, Marks
fills his two downtown spaces
with contemporary big names,
including Nan Goldin, Brice
Marden and Willem de Kooning.
*Chelsea, 523 West 24th St.
(bet. Tenth and Eleventh Aves.),
243-0200,* **CE** to 23rd St. &
Also at:
*522 West 22nd St. (bet. 10th and
11th Aves.), 243-0200,* **CE** to
23rd St. &

Metro Pictures

A slick 3 room gallery featuring
up to three artists at a time,
Metro represents hot U.S. talent,
and notable imports, such as the
German Martin Kippenberger.
*Chelsea, 519 West 24th St.
(bet. Tenth and Eleventh Aves.),
206-7100,* **CE** to 23rd St. &

Miriam and Ira D. Wallach Art Gallery

Located on the eighth floor of
Schermerhorn Hall, Columbia
University's gallery presents
traveling exhibitions throughout
the year, curated by professors
and students who ensure an
academic tilt to the line-up.
Lectures and receptions are
often sponsored in conjunction
with exhibits.
*Morningside Heights,
2960 Broadway (at 116th St.),
854-7288,* **19** to 116th St.-
Columbia University &

Momenta Art

The neighborhood's most grown-
up gallery, yet still beyond the
orbit of the conventional. The
focus is on group shows featuring works by many artists
reflecting a central, provocative
theme, and the execution ranges
from competent to brilliant. Well
worth the trip for anyone looking for something beyond the
SoHo scene.
*Williamsburg, Brooklyn, 72 Berry
Street (bet. 9th and 10th Sts.),
(718) 218-8058,* **L** to Bedford Ave.

New World Art Center

This "New Renaissance" gallery
has an ambitious agenda, as it
seeks to unite fine, graphic, literary, film, video, photographic,
designing, and performing artists
under one roof. The splintered
focus keeps exhibits changing
monthly.
*SoHo, 250 Lafayette St.
(bet. Prince and Spring Sts.),
941-9296,* **6** to Spring St. &

Pace Wildenstein Gallery, Midtown

An old hand at this art thing, this
multilevel space hosts somewhat
famous names, like Alexander
Calder and Chuck Close.
*Midtown, 32 E. 57th St. (at Mad-
ison Ave.), 421-3292,* **456** to
59th St., **NR** to Lexington Ave. &

Pace Wildenstein Gallery, SoHo

A Manhattan art world standard
with several outlets throughout
the city, the SoHo branch is a
testament to the quality that
sustains its popularity. Housed
in a large and accessible
street level space, they offer
solo shows by some fine
established artists not yet
past their prime, such as
Elizabeth Murray.
*SoHo, 142 Greene St. (bet.
Houston and Prince Sts.),
431-9224,* **NR** to Prince St. &

Pat Hearn

Formerly part of the East Village
and SoHo scenes, Hearn's
Chelsea gallery presents off-beat
work by emerging to mid-career
Contemporary American and
European artists. A veteran of
the art scene, she has propelled
numerous artists' careers, among
them George Condo, Philip
Taaffe, and Peter Schuyff.
*Chelsea, 530 West 22nd St.
(bet. Tenth and Eleventh Aves.),
727-7366,* **CE** to 23rd St. &

Paul Morris Gallery

Formerly Morris Healy, Chelsea
pioneers Paul Morris and
Thomas Healy have gone their
seperate ways. Healy's space
displays contemporary art.
*Chelsea, 465 West 23rd St.
(bet. Tenth and Eleventh Aves.),
727-2752,* **CE** to 23rd St. &

Paula Cooper Gallery

You'll have to squint to read the lettering at this gallery's entrance on the south side of the street. Woodwork in the two rooms resembles a cross between a barn and a church; tall ceilings in the back room allow for massive installments. Natural light filters through fogged windows.
Chelsea, 534 West 21st St. (bet. Tenth and Eleventh Aves.), 255-1105, **CE** to 23rd St. &

Peter Blum

Frequently swerving to the odd and often obscure, this snazzy space — a former fire station — features paintings and sculpture by known artists, as well as architectural sketches, non-Western archeological artifacts.
SoHo, 99 Wooster St. (bet. Prince and Spring Sts.), 343-0441, **NR** to Prince St., &

Phyllis Kind

Since the work of established white male artists still constitutes the majority of what makes it into serious galleries, this deceptively large space often contains shows that challenge this order. Artists like Alison Saar – who are from African-American, female or other underrepresented groups — regularly produce some of the most thought-provoking installations you're likely to see.
SoHo, 136 Greene St. (bet. Prince and Houston Sts.), 925-1200, **NR** to Prince St. &

Pierogi 2000

The name reflects the way the traditional Polish flavor of the community melds with the influx of forward-focused artists and others, and like most Williamsburg galleries, the art here is as far outside of the mainstream as the location. The gallery serves as everything from an outlet for resurrections of art treasures unseen for years to a center for many of the area's resident artists, many of whom can be found hanging out on its stoop.
Williamsburg, Brooklyn, 177 North 9th St. (bet. Bedford and Driggs Aves.), (718) 599-2144, **L** to Bedford Ave.

PPOW

Started in the '80s in the East Village by two women, this gallery moved here after developing an excellent reputation. The two rooms generally each contain work by a different artist. Women artists are well represented here, as are others with perspectives that don't fit into the old standards so well, like those of the late well-known AIDS-chronicler David Wojnarowicz, whose estate the gallery owns.
SoHo, 476 Broome St., 3rd Fl. (bet. Wooster and Greene Sts.), 941-8642, **NR** to Prince St. &

Salander-O'Reilly Galleries

Twentieth century Modernist American painters of the Stieglitz group are exhibited alongside a new generation of similarly daring, young artists.
Upper East Side, 20 East 79th St. (bet. Madison and Fifth Aves.), 879-6606, **6** to 77th St.

SoHo Photo Gallery

One of the most well-established photography galleries in town, with shows highlighting many different styles. Additionally, they offer classes on the history and work of various photographers, and to help people learn and improve artistic skills. Call for schedule information.
TriBeCa, 15 White St. (bet. Sixth Ave. and West Broadway), 226-8571, **19** to Franklin St. &

Staley-Wise

Love photography? Sorting through the array of different styles that get thrown together based on the fact that they all somehow involve using a camera and film as media can be daunting. This is the place for those who love the glamour aspect of photography, featuring work ranging from old classic *Life* magazine-style celeb photos to work by today's most prominent fashion photographers. The attitude that commercial success is validation rather than a sign of selling out is prominent here.
SoHo, 560 Broadway, Suite 305 (at Prince St.), 966-6223, **NR** to Prince St. &

Storefront for Art and Architecture

Only open from March to November, this unique international gallery favors abstract works, and often organizes shows along geographical themes. The name is derived from the gallery's unique facade.
Lower East Side, 97 Kenmare St. (bet. Mulberry and Lafayette Sts.) 431-5795, **6** to Spring St.

303 Gallery

An intimate gallery on a single floor exhibits contemporary work in many different media.
Chelsea, 525 West 22nd St. (bet. Tenth and Eleventh Aves.), 255-1121, **CE** to 23rd St.

William Secord Gallery

While the occasional feline or barnyard theme sneaks in, this anomalous uptown gallery is known for its carefully (and very seriously) curated and meticulously selected dog art. True canine addicts not fully satiated by this gallery alone need not distress: a similar showcase, the Dog Museum, once directed by Secord as well, exists in St. Louis.

Upper East Side, 52 East 76th Street, 3rd Floor (bet. Park and Madison Aves.), 249-0075, ❻ to 77th St.

𝔪𝔲𝔰𝔢𝔲𝔪𝔰

Abigail Adams Smith Museum

John Adams' daughter wanted to replicate Mount Vernon here, but ended up with this 1799 carriage house. Formerly a hotel, it later became offices for Standard Oil. Now the museum displays classic American memorabilia from the 1820s-40s in reconstructed rooms — a tavern, kitchen, bedroom, and several parlors. There are lectures regularly, along with live music and an outdoor café open during the summer months.

Upper East Side, 421 East 61st St. (bet. First and York Aves.), 838-6878, MC, V, AmEx, Admission: $2-$3, Open: Tu-Su 11am-4pm, ❹❺❻ to 59th St., ❻❼ to Lexington Ave.

African American Wax Museum and History Museum of Harlem

Nelson Mandela and Magic Johnson, together at last in life-size wax sculpture. Opened in 1989 by fashion designer and innovative artist Raven Chanticleer, the museum allows tours daily, by appointment only.

Harlem, 316 West 115th St. (bet. Manhattan and Frederick Douglass Aves.), 678-7818, Cash Only, Admission (suggested): $5-$10, Open: by appointment only, ❻❼ to 116th St.

Alternative Museum

Founded and operated by artists, this strikingly introspective nonprofit organization features a range of works that compel viewers to examine the relationship between society and art.

SoHo, 594 Broadway, Suite 402 (bet. Houston and Prince Sts.), 966-4444, Cash Only, Admission (suggested): $3, Open: Tu-Sa 11am-6pm, ❻❼❽ to Broadway-Lafayette St., ❻❼ to Prince St. ♿

American Craft Museum

Utilitarian, 20th-century American art, from chairs to teapots, finds a home in this magnificent space. Exhibits in the past have included textiles and intricate weavings.

Midtown, 40 West 53rd St. (bet. Fifth and Sixth Aves.), 956-3535, Cash Only, Admission: $2.50-$5, Open: Tu 10am-8pm, W-Su 10am-5pm, ❻❼ to Fifth Ave. ♿

American Museum of the Moving Image

"One has the sense of being transported from the everyday world straight to the set of a modern-day Oz," wrote Stephen Holden in *The New York Times*, referring to "Behind the Screen," one of the permanent exhibits at this museum devoted to the art, history, technique, and technology of the visual media and its influence on culture and society. Housed in the old Paramount Studios at the heart of Queens' old movie district, the museum is a treasure trove of movie memorabilia from the '30s through the '60s. Regular film series at the Riklis Theater screen over 500 movies a year, shown on weekends, free with admission.

Long Island City, Queens, 35th Ave. (at 36th St.), (718) 784-4520, Cash Only, Admission: $4.50-$8.50, Open: Tu-F 12pm-5pm, weekends 11pm-6pm, ❻ to 36th Ave. (Washington Ave.) ♿

American Museum of Natural History

A taxidermist's paradise and proud owner of a fantastic floor of dinosaurs. The museum also houses a Hall of Human Evolution and Biology, chronicling human development from ape to homo sapiens. Eat lunch under the big blue whale.

Upper West Side, 79th St. and Central Park West, 769-5100, MC, V, AmEx, Admission (suggested): $4.50-$8, Open: Su-Th 10am-5:45pm, F-Sa 10am-8:45pm, ❻❼ to 81st St.-Museum of Natural History ♿

Asian American Arts Center

As the name suggests, Asian-American artists have top-billing at this thriving community arts center, which supports activities ranging from traditional dance performances to the journal on contemporary Asian-American artists, *Arts Spiral*. Around Chinese New Year, the Asia Folk Arts Festival brings traditional arts produced both here and abroad for display.

Lower Manhattan, 28 Bowery (bet. Bayard and Pell Sts.), 233-2154, Admission: free, Open: Tu-F noon-6pm, Sa 4pm-6pm, ❻❼❽❾❻ to Canal St.

Bronx Museum of the Arts

True to its slogan,"It's more than just a museum," the space serves not only as a site for visual arts exhibitions, but also as a performance space, an artists' forum, and a center for "art making workshops." Its commitment to multicultural programming is evident in its diverse array of shows and weekly events.

Fordham, The Bronx, 1040 Grand Concourse (at 165th St.), (718) 681-6000, Admission (suggested): $1-$3, W 3pm-9pm, Th-F 10am-5pm, weekends noon-6pm, ❻❼❹ to 161st St.-Yankee Stadium ♿

The Brooklyn Museum of Art

A world-class museum with strong permanent collections and impressive special exhibitions. The American paintings are excellent, the Egyptian Collection is outstanding, and there's a lovely sculpture garden as well. Located next to the botanical garden, it's a great way to get away from it all while remaining in the City.
Prospect Heights, Brooklyn, 200 Eastern Parkway (at Washington Ave.), (718) 638-5000, MC, V, AmEx, Admission (suggested): $1.50-$4, Open: W-F 10am-5pm, weekends 11am-6pm, ❷❸ to Eastern Parkway-Brooklyn Museum ♿

Casa Italiana Zerilli-Marimò

The former home of General Winfield Scott, hero of the Mexican-American War and Chief-of-Staff of the U.S. Army in the 1850s. Call for information about free lectures, films, and art exhibits that focus on Italian culture.
Greenwich Village, 24 West 12th St. (bet. Fifth and Sixth Aves.), 998-8730, Admission: free, Open: Tu-F 10am-6pm, Sa 11am-5pm, ❻ to 14th St., ❶ to Sixth Ave.

Children's Museum of Manhattan

Apartment-bred kids get a taste of nature in the Urban Tree House, see what makes TV tick at the Time Warner Media Center, and read about the life and works of Dr. Seuss at this creative, interactive museum for children of all ages. Lots of wild water fun when it gets hot.
Upper West Side, 212 West 83rd St. (bet. Broadway and Amsterdam Aves.), 721-1234, MC, V, AmEx, Admission: $6, Open: W-Sa 10am-5pm, summers Tu-Su 10am-5pm, ❶❾ to 86th St. ♿

The Cloisters

A smorgasbord of old-style European glories, not to mention the finest picnicking in the city. The Met has their famed medieval collection here, including the breathtaking Unicorn tapestries, and medieval-themed readings and concerts keep hobbyists and scholars busy. The Cloisters themselves are a collection of European chapels and buildings in the Gothic and Romantic styles that were disassembled and shipped overseas stone by stone by John D. Rockefeller, Jr. and George Barnard, then reassembled way uptown.
Washington Heights, Fort Tryon Park, 923-3700, Cash Only, Admission (suggested): $5-$10, Open: Tu-Su 9:30am-5:30pm ❹ to 190th St.

The Cooper-Hewitt Museum

The Smithsonian's National Museum of Design utilizes its 11,000 square feet to present landmark historic pieces as well as pioneering contemporary designs. Attention is paid to both the one-of-a-kind and the mass-produced. The building itself, once the Carnegie Mansion, boasts an eye-catching ceiling and an intricate staircase. Come free from 5pm-9pm, Tuesdays.
Upper East Side, 2 East 91st St. (at Fifth Ave.), 849-8400, MC, V, AmEx, Admission: $3-$5, Open: Tu 10am-9pm, W-Sa 10am-5pm, Su 12pm-5pm, ❹❺❻ to 86th St.

Czech Center

Exhibits on Czech culture and contemporary art; one recent show included photographs taken by blind children.
Upper East Side, 1109 Madison Ave. (at 83rd St.), 288-0830, Cash Only, Admission (suggested): $3, Open: Tu, W, F 9am-5pm, Th 9am-7pm, ❹❺❻ to 86th St. ♿

Deutsches Haus

Lecture series by scholars and cultural emissaries, readings by visiting German language authors, and a beautiful gallery space and library with an extensive periodical section are all open to the public. The NYU community enjoys a free film series showcasing everything from Weimar cinema to the contemporary work of artists like Wim Wenders. A ten week German language programs costs $430.
Greenwich Village, 42 Washington Pl. (bet. University Pl. and Fifth Ave.), 998-8660, Admission: free, Open: M-F 11am-8pm, Sa 10am-4pm, ❶❷ to 8th St.-NYU

The Drawing Center

This nonprofit organization has an extensive collection of works on paper, including lots of drawings by a variety of new and established artists. The operation has been so successful that a second space recently opened across the street.
SoHo, 35 Wooster St. (bet. Grand and Broome Sts.), 219-2166, Admission: free, Open: Tu-F 10am-6pm, Sa 11am-5pm, ❶❷❸ to Canal St. ♿

Dyckman Farmhouse Museum

A museum of 18th Century farmhouse life, located in one of Manhattan's oldest residences, reminds urbanites that the city did not simply spring from the soil full-grown. Period furnishings and quiet gardens maintain the mood. Benches out front are ideal for catching rays or hanging out with the area's elderly population (and no, none of them actually lived here).
Washington Heights, 4881 Broadway (at 204th St.), 304-9422, Admission: free, Open: Tu-Su 11am-4pm, ❹ to 207th St.

El Museo del Barrio

Located at the tippy top of Museum Mile, this museum establishes a forum that perserves and projects the cultural heritage of Puerto Ricans and all Latin Americans in the U.S. The museum hosts bilingual public programs, educational activities, and festivals.
1230 Fifth Ave. (at 104th St.), 831-7272, MC, V, AmEx, Admission (suggested): $2-$4 Open: W-Su 11am-5pm, ⑥ to 103rd St. &

Fashion Institute of Technology

Exhibits feature famously fabulous designers, as well as work by talented FIT students.
Chelsea, 227 West 27th St. (at Seventh Ave.), 217-7999, Admission: free, Open: Tu-F noon-8pm, Sa 10am-5pm, ①⑨ to 28th St. &

FIRE Museum

If a field trip to the fire station is a favorite childhood memory, don't miss this chance to relive it. The collection, housed in a renovated Beaux-Arts style firehouse from 1904, is the country's largest; it's full of all the standard firehouse trappings, old engines and pump cars, and plenty of intriguing NYC fire history.
SoHo, 278 Spring St. (bet. Houston and Varick Sts.), 691-1303, MC, V, AmEx, Admission: $1-$4, Open: Tu-Su, 10am-4pm, ⒸⒺ to Spring St. &

Fraunces Tavern Museum

George Washington gave his farewell address to his officers after the Revolution at this Georgian mansion, which was home to the Departments of Foreign Affairs, Treasury, and War during New York's brief spell as capital city. Now the museum specializes in the American history and culture of the 18th and 19th Centuries, with plenty of period rooms in which to play pretend.
Lower Manhattan, 54 Pearl St. (at Broad St.), 425-1778, Cash Only, Admission: $1-$2.50, Open: M-F 10am-4:45pm, weekends 12pm-4pm, ④⑤ to Broad St., ⓃⓇ to Whitehall St.-South Ferry

Frick Collection

Steel kingpin Henry Clay Frick built this mansion with his fine art collection and a future museum in mind. The museum's been realized and now offers a rare chance to view masterpieces displayed in a residential setting. Highlights include portraits by El Greco, Rembrandt, and Renoir, and waterscapes by Turner. One of the most soothing spots in the city is the sun-lit, virtually sound-proof indoor courtyard with marble benches and a drizzling fountain. The mail-in procedure for free tickets to Sunday concerts is an ordeal, but no tickets are required to listen in from the courtyard. Children under ten are not admitted.
Upper East Side, 1 East 70th St. (at Fifth Ave.), 288-0700, MC, V, AmEx, Admission: $5-$7, Open: Tu-Sa 10am-6pm, Su 1pm-6pm, ⑥ to 68th St.-Hunter College &

Garibaldi Meucci Museum

This historic house museum is a great stop if you're on the island. Garibaldi played a major role in Italian Unification and Meucci was the original inventor of the phone. This museum houses artifacts from when they lived there.
Staten Island, 420 Tomkins Ave. (at Chesnut Ave.), (718)442-1608, Cash Only, Admission (suggested): $3, Open: Tu-Su 1pm-5pm &

Guggenheim SoHo

Opened in 1992, an ENEL virtual reality gallery and an electronic reading room with CD-ROMs are several of the ultramodern highlights of this downtown counterpart to its Museum Mile heavyweight, which opened in 1992. Though the architecture is hardly Frank Lloyd Wright, the SoHo building, designed by Arata Isozaki, is airy and conducive to the curators' ambitious programs, which re-examine 20th Century innovators like Max Beckmann and showcase contemporary stars like media artist Bill Viola.
SoHo, 575 Broadway (at Prince St.), 423-3500, Cash Only, Admission: $5-$8, Open: Su, W-F 11am-6pm, Sa 11am-8pm, ⓃⓇ to Prince St. &

The International Center for Photography

Founded in 1974, one of the youngest members of Museum Mile showcases over 45,000 photographs and serves as a learning center for budding photographers of all levels of expertise.
Upper East Side, 1130 Fifth Ave. (at 94th St.), 860-1777, Cash Only, Admission: $4-$6, Open: Tu 11am-8pm, W-Su 11am-6pm, ⑥ to 96th St. &

The Isamu Noguchi Garden Museum

More than 300 works in granite, steel and marble, including the famous Akari paper light sculptures by Isamu Noguchi, who also designed the twelve galleries and the outdoor sculpture garden. Open April to October. A shuttle runs from 70th St. and Park Ave. on weekends.
Long Island City, 32-37 Vernon Blvd. (at 33rd Rd.), (718)204-7088, Cash Only, Admission: $2-$4, Open: W-F 10am-5pm, Sa-Su 11am-6pm, Ⓝ to Broadway &

Jacques Marchais Museum of Tibetan Art

Housed in a two-story stone building resembling a Himalayan Budhist monastery and set in a terraced garden overlooking New York Bay, the museum features a permanent collection of Tibetan and other Buddhist art and ethnography. Notable past visitors include the Dalai Lama, who came in 1991.
Staten Island, 338 Lighthouse Ave. (at Richmond Rd.), (718) 987-3500, Cash Only, Admission: $1-$3, Open: W-Su 1-5pm (Dec.-Mar closed weekends) ♿

Jewish Museum

The largest collection of Judaica in the world outside of Israel, housed in an imperious French Renaissance structure, boasts over 27,000 works in its permanent collection. Works detail the Jewish experience throughout history and feature archeological pieces, ceremonial objects, modern masterpieces by Marc Chagall and Frank Stella, and even an interactive computer program based on the Talmud. The first two floors host temporary installations and exhibits. Admission is free for children under 12 and for everyone Tuesdays 5pm-8pm.
Upper East Side, 1109 Fifth Ave. (at 92nd St.), 423-3200, MC, V, AmEx, Admission: $5.50-8, Open: M, W, Th 11am-5:45pm, Tu 11am-8pm, ❻ *to 96th St.* ♿

King Juan Carlos I of Spain Center

King Juan Carlos I himself showed up along with Queen Sophia and Hillary Clinton to inaugurate the new hub of Spanish culture in the city. Housed in architect Stanford White's historic 19th Century Renaissance-style Judson Hall, the center encourages the study of Spain and the rest of the Spanish-speaking world via lectures, colloquia, and conferences with scholars and dignitaries.
Greenwich Village, 53 Washington Square South (bet. Thompson St. and 6th Ave.), 998-3650, Admission: free, Open: M-F 7pm-9pm, ❶❷❸❹❺❻❼❽ *to West 4th St.-Washington Sq.* ♿

King Manor Museum

Home of Rufus King, delegate to the Constitutional Convention. The oldest house in southeast Queens has been restored to reflect the King family's tenancy in the early 19th century. Visitors can tour King's library and read pages from his diary, account books, and letters; guided tours are available in English and Spanish. Exhibit galleries are devoted to local history and to village life in Jamaica during the early 1800s.
King Park/Jamaica, Queens, inside King Park, Jamaica Ave. (bet. 150th and 153rd Sts.), (718) 206-0547, Cash Only, Admission: $2, Open: March-Dec. weekends noon-4pm, ❻❿❷ *to Jamaica Center/Parsons-Archer*

Lower East Side Tenement Museum

Chronicling an era when these streets were the most densely packed in the world, the building that houses this unique museum, built in 1863, predates existing housing laws. It exhibits bedrooms, typically eight square feet, common rooms of twelve by eleven feet, and apartments with no windows, running water or electric lights.
Lower East Side, 90 Orchard St. (bet. Broome and Delancey Sts.), 431-0233, MC, V, AmEx, Admission: $6-$8, Open: Tu-F 1pm-4pm, weekends 11am-4:30pm, ❶❿❷ *to Essex St.* ❻ *to Delancey St.*

The Metropolitan Museum of Art

Where to begin? The Met seems to be as big and sprawling as the city itself, and similarly the trick is finding the hidden (or not so hidden) treasures. Favorites include the spectacular Temple of Dendur, the American Wing Garden Court, the Medieval section, and in the summer, the Roof Garden where an older crowd sips white wine and ponders the sculptures (out loud). Don't do too much or follow a strict plan — this is the best place to get lost in the City.
Upper East Side, Fifth Ave. (at 82nd St.), 535-7710, MC, V, AmEx, Admission (suggested): $5-$10, Open: Tu-Th, 9:15am-5:45pm, F-Sa 9:15am-8:45pm, Su 9:30am-5pm, ❹❺❻ *to 86th St.* ♿

The Morgan Library

The country's largest collection of Mesopotamian cylinder seals now rests where J.P. Morgan used to pad about in slippers, though the appeal of this library and museum is much broader. The library's renowned collection of rare books, manuscripts, and drawings have, as their principal focus, the history, art, and literature of Western civilization.
Midtown, 29 East 36th St. (bet. Madison and Park Aves.), 685-0610, Cash Only, Admission: $5-7, Open: Tu-Th 10:30am-5pm, F 10:30am-8pm, Sa 10:30am-6pm, Su noon-6pm, ❻ *to 33rd St.* ♿

Morris-Jumel Mansion

Down from the remaining farmhouse is the area's extant Georgian mansion, where Washington kept his headquarters during the Revolution.
Washington Heights, 65 Jumel Terrace (at 160th St.), 923-8008, Cash Only, Admission: $3, Open: W-Su 10am-4pm, ❶❷❸ *to 163rd St.-Amsterdam Ave.*

The Museum for African Art

Exhibits seeking to facilitate a greater understanding of African art change twice a year at this two-floor showcase, one of two of its kind in the country. Complex exhibits often incorporate elements of folk art, sculpture, and more conventional media to examine pervasive concepts in the tradition. Film and video presentations, performance art, and interactive, hands-on workshops take place in the newly opened Educational Department.
SoHo, 593 Broadway (bet. Houston and Prince Sts.), 966-1313, MC, V, AmEx, Admission: $2.50-$5, Open: Tu-F 10:30am-5:30pm, weekends noon-6pm, **NR** *to Prince St.* &

Museum of American Folk Art

A compact venue which shatters the stereotypes of folk art with exhibits ranging from portraits to weathervanes to pottery. Some displays are thematic, while others are based around the personal holdings of prominent collectors.
Upper West Side, 2 Lincoln Sq. (at Columbus Ave. and 66th St.), 977-7298, Cash Only, Admission (suggested): $3, Open: Tu-Su 11:30am-7:30pm, **19** *to 66th St.-Lincoln Center* &

Museum of American Illustration

View the work of key illustrators like Norman Rockwell and N.C. Wyeth at the home of the elite Society of Illustrators, which claims a long history of service to none other than the United States Army. Educational opportunities include sketch classes and lectures.
Upper East Side, 128 East 63rd St. (bet. Park and Lexington Aves.), 838-2560, Admission: free, Open: Tu 10am-8pm, W-F 10am-5pm, Sa noon-4pm, **456** *to 59th St.,* **NR** *to Lexington Ave.*

Museum of Chinese in the Americas

No Chinatown experience is complete without a visit to this community-oriented museum, the first ever dedicated to the history of Chinese Americans. The award-winning permanent exhibition entitled "Where Is Home?" features a moving collection of memorabilia, photographs, and commentary exploring the diverse identities and experiences of Chinese Americans.
Chinatown, 70 Mulberry St., 2nd fl. (at Bayard St.), 619-4785, Cash Only, Admission: $1, Open: Tu-Sa noon-5pm, **JMNRZ6** *to Canal St.*

Museum of Modern Art

Toeing a precarious line between avant-garde and establishment, this New York institution holds the world's most comprehensive collection of 19th and 20th Century art, ranging from paintings to sculpture to photographs and beyond. Take a break amidst the Rodin sculptures in the outdoor garden. Admission is free on Friday 5:30pm-8pm, along with free jazz in the café. Entry is always free with Columbia University ID.
Midtown, 11 West 53rd St. (bet. Fifth and Sixth Aves.), 708-9400, MC, V, AmEx, Admission: $5.50-$9.50, Open: M, Tu, Th, Sa, Su 10:30am-5:45pm, F 10:30am-8:15pm, **EF** *to Fifth Ave.* &

Museum of Television and Radio

Watch TV all day and still feel cultured. Computer consoles and viewing cubicles access tens of thousands of programs (and you thought cable was overwhelming), though if your tastes are way obscure, you should order ahead of time. A nostalgic display of Kermit the Frog and friends alone is worth the trip.
Midtown, 25 West 52nd St. (bet. Fifth and Sixth Aves.), 621-6800, MC, V, AmEx, Admission: $3-$6 (students), Open: Tu, W, F-Su noon-6pm, Th noon-8pm, **EF** *to Fifth Ave.* &

Museum of the City of New York

In light of its ego, it's fitting that New York was the first city to get its own museum. Exhibits glorify New York's vast history, and include photographs, furniture, costumes, and toys. The Sunday concert series and the Big Apple Film make the trip worthwhile.
Upper East Side, 1220 Fifth Ave. (bet. 103rd and 104th Sts.), 534-1672, Cash Only, Admission (suggested): $4-$5, Open: W-Sat 10am-5pm, Su noon-5pm, **6** *to 103rd St.* &

National Academy of Design

Founded in 1825 to promote the art of design in America through painting, sculpture, architecture, and engraving, the academy still strives to meet its same purpose through training young artists and serving as a fraternal organization for other distinguished American artists. Its permanent exhibit features works by such 19th Century masters as Winslow Homer, John Singer Sargent, and Thomas Eakins, and such contemporary artists as Robert Rauschenberg, Isabel Bishop, and Phillip Johnson.
Upper East Side, 1083 Fifth Ave. (bet. 89th and 90th Sts.), 369-4880, MC, V, AmEx, Admission: $4.50-8, Open: W, Th, Sa, Su noon-5pm, F 10am-8pm, **456** *to 86th St.* &

The National Museum of the American Indian

The Old Custom House contains this extensive, well-curated museum, one of the few Smithsonian Institutions outside of Washington. The exhibits are fascinating, though the federal architecture and the beautiful rotunda alone merit the trip.
1 Bowling Green (in Battery Park), 668-6624, Open: F-W 10am-5pm, Th 10am-8pm, **④⑤** *to Bowling Green,* **①⑨** *to South Ferry* ♿

The New Museum of Contemporary Art

Founded by Maciaa Tucker in 1977, this unique museum takes contemporary to a whole new level: Its semi-permanent collection contains works created in the past decade; once the age of a piece reaches double digits, it is exchanged for something new, which is in turn retained for ten years.
583 Broadway (between Houston and Prince Sts.), 219-1222, Admission: $3-$5 (18 and under free), Open: W, Su noon-6 p.m., Th-Sa noon-8 p.m. **⑥⑧⓪** *to Broadway-Lafayette St.,* **⑩⓷** *to Prince St.*

New York Hall of Science

While designed primarily for kids, this playground of hands-on exhibits appeals to the science nut in everyone. The newly expanded exhibition hall boasts a Technology Gallery, with access to the Internet and a wide range of CD-ROMs. Thursday and Friday are free 2pm-5pm.
Corona, Queens, 47-01 111th Street (in Flushing Meadows Corona Park), (718) 699-0005, MC, V, Amex, Admission: $4-$6, M-W 9:30am-2pm, Th-F Open: 9:30am-5pm, **⓻** *to 111th St.* ♿

The New York Transit Museum

While you may consider the turnstiles in working stations antique, the originals are really housed in this authentic 1930s subway station. Vintage subway maps and mosaics comprise the permanent collection, along with exhibitions chronicling the development of rapid transit. Tag along with a school group for a field trip to somewhere great like the Metro-North car-repair facility.
Downtown Brooklyn, Corner of Boerum Pl. and Schermerhorn St., (718) 243-3060, Cash Only, Admission: $1.50-$3, Open: Tu-F 10am-4pm, weekends 12pm-5pm, **②③④⑤** *to Borough Hall* ♿

New York Unearthed

Archeology and New York may seem like strange bedfellows, but this smallish museum does the juxtaposition justice; artifacts along the lines of cannon balls and bones, as well as excavation finds, are on display. The Lower Gallery offers the chance to watch conservationists working busily behind glass. And you thought this city was just built on top of a bunch of garbage.
Lower Manhattan, 17 State St. (at Water St.), 748-8628, Admission: Free, M-F noon-6pm **①⑨** *to South Ferry* ♿

Nicholas Roerich Museum

Discreetly hidden among a row of brownstones, this museum honors Nicholas Roerich, the artist who designed an international peace symbol during World War II.
Upper West Side, 319 West 107th St. (bet. Broadway and Riverside Dr.), 864-7752, Admission: Free, Tu-Su 10am-5pm, **①⑨** *to 110th St.*

P.S. 1

If the name didn't give you a clue P.S.1. is housed in an old school building, three stories high. The museum has plenty of nooks and crannies, all of which are filled with interesting and enlightening contemporary art exhibits. All of the museum's exhibits are temporary — so you can visit P.S.1. again and again!
Long Island City, Queens, 22-25 Jackson Ave. (at 46th Ave.), (718) 784-2084, Admission (suggested): $2-$5, Open: W-S 12pm-6pm, **⑤⑥** *to 23rd St. (Ely Ave.),* **⑥** *Court Sq.* ♿

The Queen's Country Farm Museum

Dating back to 1772, this farm covers 52 acres of land and is the only working farm of its era that has been restored and reopened to the public. Open year-round.
Kew Gardens, Queens, 73-50 Little Neck Pkwy (bet. 74th Ave. and 73rd Rd.), (718) 347-3276, Admission: free, Open: M-F 9am-5pm, Sa-Su 10am-5pm, **⑤⑥** *to Union Turnpike-Kew Gardens* ♿

Queens Museum of Art

The must-see exhibit of this small museum, which is located right opposite the Unisphere and housed in the original U.N., is the scale model of New York City, the largest of its kind. 1/2 price admission for students.
Flushing, Queens, Flushing Meadows Corona Park (at Grand Central Pkwy.), (718) 592-9700, Cash Only, Admission (suggested): $2-$4, W-F, 10am-5pm, weekends 12pm-5pm, **⓻** *to Willets Point-Shea Stadium* ♿

Solomon R. Guggenheim Museum

It's now hard to imagine upper Fifth Ave. without Frank Lloyd

Wright's famous spiral of a building, home to one of the most remarkable 20th Century art collections in the world. Special exhibits wind their way down interior ramps.
Upper East Side, 1071 Fifth Ave. (at 89th St.), 360-3500, MC, V, AmEx, Admission: $7-$12, Su-W 10am-6pm, F-Sa 10am-8pm, ❹❺❻ *to 86th St.* ⅟

Sotheby's
Don your most expensive dress and pretend you're an heiress at Manhattan's other leading auction house; collectibles sold here range from rare coins, jewels, and vintage wine to decorative and fine arts. Admission here is free, but the glossy catalog will set you back about $20 bucks.
Upper East Side, 1334 York Ave. (at 72nd St.), 606-7000, MC, V, Admission: free, Open: M-F 9am-5pm, ❻ *to 68th St.-Hunter College.* ⅟

Studio Museum in Harlem
From its origins as a rented loft back in 1967, this intriguing museum has burgeoned into one of the most innovative, focusing on arts from Africa and Black America. The artists-in-residence program gives emerging artists gallery space, and the Cooperative School Program puts professional artists in Harlem schools.
Harlem, 144 West 125th St. (bet. Adam Clayton Powell, Jr. and Malcolm X Blvds.), 864-4500, Cash Only, Admission: $3-$5, Open: W-F 10am-5pm, weekends 1pm-6pm, ❷❸❻❹ *to 125th St.* ⅟

Ukrainian Museum
This small museum features exhibits of contemporary Ukrainian culture and history. Recent exhibitions have included folk art and Easter eggs.
East Village, 203 Second Ave. (bet. 12th and 13th Sts.), 228-0110, Cash Only, Admission: $2-$3, Open: W-Su 1pm-5pm, ❹❻❻ *to 14th St.-Union Sq.* ⅟

The Whitney Museum of American Art
A motherlode of American avant-garde and post-modern art. Provocative shows are the rule: the ever-controversial Biennial, an exhibit of contemporary works held in odd-numbered years, never fails to rile critics.
Upper East Side, 945 Madison Ave. (at 75th St.), 570-3676, MC, V, AmEx, Admission: $7-$9, Open: W, F, Sa-Su 11am6pm, Th 1-8pm, ❻ *to 77th St.* ⅟

Yeshiva University Museum
The country's oldest Jewish institution of higher learning regularly holds exhibits on historical and contemporary Jewish themes, such as "Sacred Realm: The Emergence of the Synagogue in the Ancient World."
Washington Heights, 2520 Amsterdam Ave. (bet. 185th and 186th Sts.), 960-5390, Cash Only, Admission: $2-$3, Open: Tu-Th 10:30-5pm, Su noon-6pm, ❶❾ *to 181st St.* ⅟

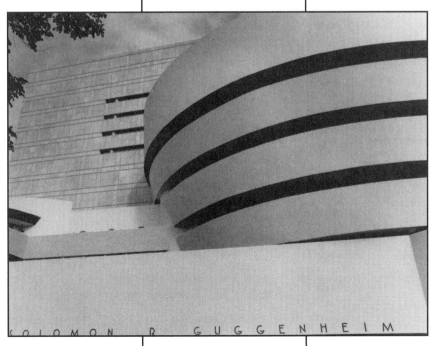

SOLOMON R GUGGENHEIM

performing arts

p·e·r·f·o·r·m·i·n·g·a·r·t·s

At the heart of New York's performance industry lies the Broadway Theater District, the area from 42nd to 53rd Sts. and between 6th and 9th Aves., whose glittering lights and glamour draw visitors from all over the world. But despite the enormous amount of revenue generated by successful shows and high ticket prices, launching a production is among the most costly and risky of business propositions. As a result of the prohibitive fiscal pressures which new productions must face, a thriving community has also developed away from Midtown's main drag, particularly in the downtown area which originally housed many of the major theaters. The result is three categories of production: Broadway, Off-Broadway, and Off-Off-Broadway.

While the city's professional theater debuted in 1750 with an imported production of Richard III (the first in a succession of exchanges between the British and American stages), the New York theater scene really got its start around the turn of the century. High society frequented productions by stage luminaries like Lunt and Fontanne, the Barrymores, and the Booths. Meanwhile, the less endowed packed the vaudeville, variety, and minstrel theaters along the Bowery. Vaudeville often fed Broadway during the teens and the '20s: Before launching their movie careers, performers such as the Marx Brothers graced Broadway stages with their Vaudeville circuit reviews.

Edna St. Vincent Millay and her literary friends helped to launch the Provincetown Players and similar avant-garde theaters in Greenwich Village, like the Group Theater, which staged works by playwrights such as Eugene O'Neill and Clifford Odets. O'Neill called the city home during this pre-World War I period. "Anna Christie," his Pulitzer Prize-winning drama, was based on the seedy Lower East Side nightlife and was set in Jimmy the Priest's, the boarding house frequented by the playwright himself.

The Broadway scene hit its height in the late '20s, with literally hundreds of shows opening each year. In a time of such bounty, there were certainly a few bad apples. The critics of the time, such as Robert Benchley, Dorothy Parker, and Alexander Woollcott, were never out of work. Several New York writers, playwrights, actors, and critics — including the dignitaries previously mentioned — lunched together regularly at Midtown's Algonquin Hotel. These gatherings were vicious and productive and served as an artistic think-tank in a time of tremendous theatrical activity. George S. Kaufman (along with writing partners Moss Hart and Marc Connelly) was very active during this period, penning scores of incredible comedies, sev-

eral of which were based on the exploits of this group of wits and intellectuals. The World War II and post-war periods were also quite fruitful for New York drama, as two brilliant young playwrights came to make their mark on American theater. Tennessee Williams set new standards with works such as "A Streetcar Named Desire," "The Glass Menagerie," "Cat on a Hot Tin Roof," and "Camino Real." Brooklyn-based Arthur Miller gave us the American classics "Death of a Salesman," "The Crucible," and "A View from the Bridge."

Impresario Joseph Papp founded the Public Theater, producing works such as "Hair" and "A Chorus Line." In addition, Papp started the New York Shakespeare Festival, now a New York institution. Off-Broadway and Off-Off-Broadway theaters boomed with the works of innovative artists and new groups, such as the Open Theater and the Wooster Group (which spawned monologist Spalding Gray). In the late '70s and moving into the '80s, playwrights such as August Wilson and Wendy Wasserstein brought minority voices to Broadway.

The mid-eighties saw the introduction of a genre of AIDS-related plays, such as "The Normal Heart" by Larry Kramer, and Tony Kushner's "Angels in America." The '80s also ushered in the era of the uber-musical: costly theatrical monsters such as "Cats," "The Phantom of the Opera," and "Les Miserables," which crushed all in their path. Sometimes the uber-musical is an electrifying experience, occasionally because the production is exciting and important, but usually because it stimulates the same part of the brain that experiences a jolt at the sight of a car crash.

Musicals have taken on a different quality from the brassy productions of the eighties. "Rent," a '90s version of "La Bohème," snuck up to Broadway from downtown's esteemed New York Theater Workshop and went on to take the 1996 Tony award for best musical as well as a Pulitzer Prize the same year, is still filling seats. In 1998, Disney's "The Lion King," directed by Julie Taymor and hailed by critics and audiences alike, was also awarded the Tony for best musical. Last year saw a comeback of grittier drama, with stunning revivals of "Death of a Salesman" and O'Neill's "The Iceman Cometh."

Off off broadway

It's pretty clear what someone's talking about if they mention a Broadway show. But what exactly does the phrase "Off-Off" signify? Here's a simple guide:

• "*On Broadway*" means the district of theaters clustered around Times Sq., between 41st and 54th Sts. Tickets easily cost as much as $80 a pop, and there is the chance of shelling out that much to end up witnessing the kind of empty spectacle that films provide more inexpensively. Lately, however, Broadway has been providing the kind of entertainment that these ticket prices require, and over the last few years shows like "Rent," "Cabaret," and "The Lion King" have been drawing huge crowds and enlivening the strip.

• *Off-Broadway* originally meant theaters in Greenwich Village, the majority of which have a seating capacity of 500 or less. Lately, however, this term has come to refer to smaller theaters anywhere throughout the city. Off-Broadway shows tend to have greater literary and social importance, a wider variety in quality of the productions, and cheaper ticket prices (up to $40). Resident theaters, like the Manhattan Theatre Club, Roundabout Theatre, Playwrights Horizons, and Vineyard Theatre are all examples of such venues.

• *Off-Off Broadway* is a term used to refer to productions featuring actors who are often non-equity, typically working in theaters of less than 200 seats. Here you can find exciting, daring, brilliant performances at shoestring pricing. Conversely, of course, there are the occasional painful freak-shows. Conservative theatergoers should perhaps avoid Off-Off Broadway; the more adventurous who take the risk will find interesting experimental theater in abundance.

t*icchke eatps

Shakespeare in the Park

Productions can be uneven and the star-studded casts underwhelming and overblown, but what better way to spend a balmy summer evening than sitting under the night sky in this intimate theater-in-the-round watching the best dramas by the best writer in the Western world? Tickets are free, but working folks will have to take a personal day to line up at sunrise to obtain seats to the more popular shows. (The bigger the stars, the longer the queue.) Tickets are distributed the day of the performance beginning at 1pm at the Delacorte and Public Theaters.

Central Park (at West 79th St.),
539-8500,Open: Tu-Su, June-September,
B C to 81st St.-Museum of Natural History

Standing Room and Rush Tickets

Many shows offer discounts at the box office of the theater a few hours before curtain; generally balcony seats or standing room. Ushers often turn a blind eye while you sneak down to the orchestra or mezzanine and find empty seats.
Various theaters

Theatre Development Fund

TDF is the best program for college students. A $15 annual fee pays for a spot on the mailing list for Broadway tickets for $13-$22, and TDF's "4-for-$28" voucher program gains admittance to Off-Off Broadway shows. Send a legal-size, SASE for an application and allow six to eight weeks for processing.
Midtown, 1501 Broadway. Suite 2110 (bet. 43rd and 44th Sts.) 221-0013 (recorded information), 221-0885 (live operator)

TKTS

This booth sells same-day tickets to Broadway shows and Off-Broadway dance and opera at 25-50% discounts. Even the best seats are available, but come early or you'll wind up with a "partial view" spot. The wait can be long — up to an hour or so, but is usually enlivened by the delicious chaos of the surroundings.

Midtown, West 47th St. (at Broadway), 221-0013, Cash Only, Open: W-Sa (for matinees) 10am-2pm, M-Sa (for evening shows: 3pm-8pm, Su 11am-closing), **1 2 3 7 9 N R S** to 42nd St.-Times Sq.

Also at:

Lower Manhattan, 2 World Trade Center (at the mezzanine), 221-0013,Cash Only, M-F 11am-5:30pm, Sa 11am-3:30pm, **1 9** to Cortlandt St.

Two for Ones

Many universities are part of a theater promotion program that offers students coupons known as "twofers": Two tickets to big-budget productions for the price of one. Visit a school's Student Activities office for information about the program.

Actor's Playhouse

Gay-and-lesbian-themed shows often command the stage at this Off-Broadway space. Though the seats may be dingy and worn, and the floor may retain a stickiness from a soda that was spilled long ago, it's still the best cutting-edge queer theater. *Greenwich Village, 100 Seventh Ave. South (bet. Grove and Bleecker Sts.), 307-4100, MC, V, AmEx, D,* ❶❾ to Christopher St.-Sheridan Sq.

The African Poetry Theater, Inc.

Fledgling poets, playwrights, directors, and actors all do shows regularly. For those in need of more structured training, various dance, drum and Shakespeare classes are available. *Jamaica, Queens, 176-03 Jamaica Ave. (at 176th St.), (718)523-3312, Cash Only,* ❶ to 179th St.-Jamaica &

Alvin Ailey American Dance Theater

"The dance came from the people. It should be given back to the people," said the choreographer for whom this theatre, located in City Center, was named. Ailey developed the repertoire here with the uniqueness of black cultural expression in mind. Pieces are often set to music by jazz greats such as Duke Ellington and Wynton Marsalis. Works performed include both those choreographed by the late Ailey himself and choreographers who shared his vision. *Midtown, 131 West 55th St. (bet. Sixth and Seventh Aves.), 581-1212, MC, V, AmEx,* ❶❸ to 57th St., ❷ to 57th St. &

Amato Opera House

Head downtown to see the divas of tomorrow paying their dues in an intimate setting. An alternative for opera lovers who lack the funds for nosebleed seats at the Met. One of Amato's goals is to foster opera appreciation by making it more accessible, so many performances are English translations of Italian operas. *East Village, 319 Bowery St. (at 2nd St.), 228-8200, Cash Only,* ❶❶❸❾ to Broadway-Lafayette St., ❻ to Bleecker St.

American Ballet Theater

This dance giant, once led by legends like Lucia Chase, Oliver Smith, and Mikhail Baryshnikov, and now headed by former Principal Dancer Kevin McKenzie, continues to stage staggering performances at its home in Lincoln Center. Classical ballet had its first renaissance here, and new works have been commissioned specifically for the ballet by key composers such as Balanchine, Antony Tudor, and Agnes de Mille. Call for schedules. *Upper West Side, West 66th St. (at Broadway, 362-6000, MC, V, AmEx,* ❶❾ to 66th-Lincoln Center &

American Jewish Theatre

A performance space for plays directly related to the American Jewish experience. *Chelsea, 307 West 26th St. (bet. Eighth and Ninth Aves.), 633-9797, MC, V, AmEx,* ❸❸ to 23rd St.

Apollo Theater

Fostering such performers as Josephine Baker, the Supremes, and Bill Cosby, since it started integrating black audiences and performers in 1935, this multi-use theater is in full swing thanks to a revival effort in the '80. The televised "Amateur Night" rages on Wednesdays, and both comedians and children's flicks find space here; the stage even hosted James Brown's post-prison comeback concert. *Harlem, 253 West 125th St. (bet. Adam Clayton Powell, Jr. and Frederick Douglass Blvds.), 744-5838, MC, V, AmEx, D,* ❶❸❸❸ to 125th St.

Avery Fisher Hall

Over a hundred virtuosos led by Kurt Masur play Western classics, with an emphasis on European standards and American innovations. Home to the New York Philharmonic. *Upper West Side, 10 Lincoln Center Plaza (at 64th St. and Broadway), 875-5030,* ❶❾ to 66th St.-Lincoln Center &

Bargemusic

Excellent chamber music on the water in the moonlight; bring a date and get all mushy on this cozy converted coffee barge. *Fulton Ferry Landing, Brooklyn, Water St. (at River Sts.), (718) 624-4061, Cash Only,* ❷❸ to High St.-Brooklyn Bridge

Bessie Schonberg Theater

Home to the Dance Theater Workshop, a non-profit organization dedicated to assisting and promoting independent artists in the community, this intimate space seats 100 people and stages cutting-edge dance and musical performances. *Chelsea, 219 West 19th St. (bet. Seventh and Eighth Aves.), 924-0077, MC, V,* ❶❾ to 18th St.

Black Spectrum Theater Company, Inc.

Three to five large-scale productions a year, with directors favoring socially conscious works by both emerging and established writers. Kids and teens get in on the action with their own productions at this Roy Wilkins park-based company.

Jamaica, Queens, 119-07 Merrick Blvd. (at 177th St. and Baisley Blvd.), (718) 723-1800, Cash Only, ❸❶❷ *to Jamaica Center-Parsons/Archer* ♿

Bouwerie Lane Theatre

Founded in 1973 by Eve Adamson, this old-fashioned, European-style, one-stage theater is home to the Jean Cocteau Repertory which performs modern updates of theatrical classics. *Greenwich Village, 330 Bowery (at Bond St.), 677-0060, MC, V, AmΣx,* ❻❶❻❻ *to Broadway-Lafayette St.,* ❻ *to Bleecker St.*

The Brooklyn Academy of Music (BAM)

Although the Brooklyn Philharmonic has distinguished itself with its range and a repertoire that runs the gamut from European classics to selections from African-American traditions, its pet projects are clearly those rooted in the avant garde, which are best realized in BAM's provocative yearly "Next Wave" festival that consistently pushes the boundaries of classical music. *Fort Greene, Brooklyn, 30 Lafayette Ave. (at Ashland Pl.), (718) 636-4100, MC, V,* ❷❶❷❷❸❹❺ *to Atlantic Ave.* ♿

Carnegie Hall

A century has passed since Tchaikovsky conducted at the inauguration, but this stage keeps abreast of musical trends in their many variations: The Beastie Boys and the Tibetan Freedom Fighters have appeared on the same stage as today's classical giants like Emanuel Ax. Jazz performers are also frequent guests. *Midtown, 881 Seventh Ave. (at 57th St.), 247-7800, MC, V, AmΣx,* ❶❶ *to 57th St.* ♿

Castillo Theater

For the last decade, this space has served as a "cultural laboratory" for Artistic Director Fred Newman to practice Developmental Theater, a genre which is predicated on a number of postmodern philosophies but boils down to the idea of psychotherapy for performer and audience members alike. The focus is on black, Latino, gay, and the international avant-garde — which means you can expect anything. *Greenwich Village, 500 Greenwich St. (bet. Spring and Canal Sts.), 941-1234, MC, V, AmΣx, D,* ❶❷❸ *to Canal St.* ♿

Centerfold Coffeehouse at Church of St. Paul and St. Andrew

Poetry readings are free but hit or miss, so prepare to indulge some neophyte bards; evening jams with folk and jazz bands provide dependable, cheap weekend entertainment. *Upper West Side, 263 West 86th St. (bet. Broadway and West End Ave.), 362-3179, Cash Only,* ❶❷ *to 86th St.*

Cherry Lane Theatre

Founded in the 1920s by a literary circle headed by the poet Edna St. Vincent Millay, Cherry Lane's productions are led by the best of the century's avant-garde and adventurous new pieces. *Greenwich Village, 38 Commerce St. (bet. Seventh Ave. South and Barrow St.), 989-2020, MC, V, AmΣx,* ❶❷ *to Christopher St-Sheridan Sq.* ♿

Chicago City Limits

No alcohol is served at New York's best improv theater, but you may get a buzz from the audience participation. *Upper East Side, 1105 First Ave. (at 61st St.), 888-5233, MC, V, AmΣx,* ❶❷❸ *to 59th St.,* ❶❷ *to Lexington Ave.*

Colden Center For the Performing Arts at Queens College

The oldest, largest arts presenter in Queens, with over 300,000 visitors annually. Features classical, pop, jazz, theater, opera, and children's events weekly. *Flushing, Queens, 65-30 Kissena Blvd. (at the Long Island Expressway), (718) 793-8080, MC, V, AmΣx, D,* ❼ *to Main St.-Flushing*

Collective Unconscious

Every possible configuration of campy art and anti-art event takes place at this downtown performance space. The hip, tongue-in-cheek crowd takes nothing seriously — especially not the art world. Popular open mike at Reverend Jen's Anti-Slam, Wednesday nights. *Lower East Side, 145 Ludlow St. (bet. Stanton and Rivington Sts.), 254-5277, Cash Only,* ❻ *to Second Ave.*

The Comic Strip Live

New York's most famous comedy theater regularly plays host to mainstream big-name performers and other crowd-pleasers. No cover Mondays. *Upper East Side, 1568 Second Ave. (bet. 81st and 82nd Sts.), 861-9386, MC, V, AmΣx, D,* ❹❺❻ *to 86th St.* ♿

Context

"Like a kitchen with lots of different vegetation," is the somewhat convoluted definition for this multi-media performing arts space, showing dance theater, experimental musical performances, and opera regularly. Shows can go on for up to two weeks by popular demand. *East Village, 28 Ave. A (bet. Second and Third Aves.), 505-2702, MC, V, AmΣx,* ❻ *to Second Ave.*

Dance Theater of Harlem

This world-renowned, neo-classical company, founded in 1969 as a school and now one of the country's most competitive, dabbles in a bit of everything: jazz, tap dance, modern ballet, and ethnic genres. Students of all ages and at all levels perform in a monthly open house, usually with accompanying performances by guest artists.
Harlem, 466 West 152nd St. (bet. St. Nicholas and Amsterdam Aves.), 690-2800, MC, V, AmEx, D, **ABCD** *to 155th St.*

Harkness Dance Center at the 92nd St. Y

The Upper East Side's cultural mecca hosts professional performances as well informal shows of works-in-progress or new works. The dance workshops are a good reason for visiting, with programs like Argentine Tango Party, boasting Madonna's Evita coaches as instructors, and Israeli Folk Dancing classes occurring regularly.
Upper East Side, 1395 Lexington Ave. (bet. 91st and 92nd Sts.), MC, V, AmEx, 996-1100, **456** *to 86th St.* &

HERE

The western end of SoHo is as underdeveloped as TriBeCa but with a funkier feel, creating the perfect atmosphere for this unconventional arts venue. Attractions include gallery shows of fine art and theater productions of new plays by younger playwrights with great stories to tell.
SoHo, 145 Sixth Ave. (bet. Spring and Broome Sts.), 647-0202, MC, V, AmEx, **CE** *to Spring St.* &

The Irish Repertory Theatre

An intimate performance space for a variety of Irish and Irish-American plays.

Chelsea, 132 West 22nd St. (bet. Sixth and Seventh Aves.), 727-2737, MC, V, AmEx, **F** *to 23rd St.,* **1 9** *to 23rd St.* &

Jamaica Center for Arts & Learning

A neo-Italian Renaissance structure built in 1898, houses a non-profit community cultural center dedicated to making all genres of the performing arts accessible to the Jamaica community.
Jamaica, Queens, 161-04 Jamaica Ave. (at 161st St.), (718) 658-7400, Cash Only, **EJZ** *to Jamaica Center-Parsons/Archer* &

Joyce SoHo

All professional and aspiring dancers are familiar with this branch of the Joyce, the venue of choice for seeing all genres in a setting that's not stiflingly formal. Performances are Thursday-Sunday nights, with tickets available 30 minutes before curtain.
SoHo, 155 Mercer St. (bet. Houston and Prince Sts.), 334-7479, Cash Only, **NR** *to Prince St.* &

Joyce Theater

The unlikely successor to a former porno palace, this hotbed of talent inherited a large stage and virtually clear sightlines, which create an ideal setting for performances by top touring companies from around the world. The "Altogether Different" series promotes promising up-and-coming companies yearly.
Chelsea, 175 Eighth Ave. (at 19th St.), 242-0800, MC, V, AmEx, **1 9** *to 18th St.* &

The Kitchen

Located among dismal warehouses, this raw space thrives on experimental music and dance performed in a black box theater with bleachers seating about 150 and a multi-media lab with visual arts exhibitions. Past performers include Laurie

Anderson, David Byrne, and Eric Bogosian. Check out the café theater on the second floor.
Chelsea, 512 West 19th St. (bet. Tenth and Eleventh Aves.), 255-5793, MC, V, AmEx, **1 9** *to 18th St.* **CE** *to 23rd St.* &

La MaMa etc.

Four small theaters offer new and experimental dance and theater, as well as off-beat performance. The avant-garde nature of the place means shows are hit or miss, but cheap tickets make it worthwhile to test the odds.
East Village, 74A East 4th St. (bet. Second Ave. and Bowery), 475-7710, MC, V, AmEx, **F** *to Second Ave.*

Langston Hughes Community Library and Cultural Center

Year-round readings and performances, as well as a wealth of reference materials in the on-site library.
Corona, Queens, 102-09 Northern Blvd. (at 102nd St.), (718) 651-1100, Cash Only, **7** *to 103rd St.-Corona Plaza*

Lincoln Center Theater

A bastion of New York theater, its dramatic offerings make up the largest non-profit theater in the country. Artistic director Andre Bishop consistently presents high-profile premieres and revivals with top-name actors and directors. Consisting of two theaters — the Broadway-sized Vivian Beaumont and the smaller Mitzi Newhouse — recent seasons at Lincoln Center Theater have seen Helen Hunt and Paul Rudd in "Twelfth Night" and Kevin Kline in Chekhov's "Ivanov." In addition, international theatrical works of all kinds are presented every summer as part of Lincoln Center's annual festival.

Upper West Side, 150 West 65th St. (bet. Columbus and Amsterdam Aves.), 362-7600, MC, V, AmEx, **❶❾** to 66th St.-Lincoln Center &

Lucille Lortel Theater
Cramped between the music-pumping, glittered, merchandise-selling shops of Christopher St. is this premier Off-Broadway space, site of the first American production of Brecht and Weill's "Threepenny Opera." Recent successes have included "Collected Stories" and "As Bees in Honey Drown."
Greenwich Village, 121 Christopher St. (bet. Bleecker and Hudson Sts.), 924-2817, MC, V, AmEx, **❶❾** to Christopher St.-Sheridan Sq. &

Manhattan School of Music
Prodigies at one of the country's most prestigious conservatories perform, usually for free.
Morningside Heights, 120 Claremont Ave. (at 122nd St.), 749-2802, Cash Only, **❶❾** to 125th St.

Manhattan Theatre Club
Terence McNally, A.R. Gurney, and Richard Greenberg are just a few of the playwrights whose work has been featured at MTC, one of the oldest subscription-based theater companies in the city. The company presents a broad range of work, mixing audience-pleasers and more challenging pieces on its two stages. MTC received a great deal of media attention in 1998 as the site of McNally's controversial Corpus Christi.
Midtown, 131 West 55th St. (bet. Sixth and Seventh Aves.), 399-3000, MC, V, AmEx, **❶❾** to 57th St, **❶** to 57th St. &

Metropolitan Opera
When the Carnegies were the nouveau riche, Old Money's monopoly on the city's theater boxes frustrated the family so much that they went and built their own opera house. Though the original Met was further downtown, its current location retains a historic stodginess. A safely classical though consistently outstanding repertory. Check out the Chagall tapestries in the lobby.
Upper West Side, Lincoln Center (at 66th St. and Broadway), 362-6000, MC, V, AmEx, **❶❾** to 66th St.-Lincoln Center &

Miller Theater
The student price of five bucks buys a consistently impressive line-up, from readings by poet demigods such as Pulitzer prize winners Richard Howard and Louise Glück to performances by established professionals like Yo Yo Ma and Ann Bogart's SITI troupe. The theater's curators also present film retrospectives featuring hard-to-find directors and actors.
Morningside Heights, 2960 Broadway (at 116th St.), 854-7799, MC, V, AmEx, D, **❶❾** to 116th St.-Columbia University &

Minetta Lane Theater
Revues and new plays in a notably comfortable seating. Recent shows include the acclaimed docudrama "Gross Indecency — The Three Trials of Oscar Wilde," recounting the legal ordeals that made the artist one of homosexuality's most prominent martyrs.
Greenwich Village, 18 Minetta Lane (bet. MacDougal St. and Sixth Ave.), 420-8000, MC, V, **❶❷❸❹❺❻❼** to West 4th St.-Washington Sq. &

Nada
A storefront theater that in a few short years has acquired a wide-ranging reputation, including an Obie award. Catch a show almost every night.

Lower East Side, 167 Ludlow St. (bet. Houston and Stanton Sts.), 420-1466, Cash Only, **❻** to Second Ave &

New York State Theater
Home to two of the city's artistic treasures. First, the New York City Ballet, a top-notch company which produces a particularly breathtaking Nutcracker, with champagne galore and lots of six-year olds made up like dolls. In addition, the theater houses the New York City Opera, which renews and redefines the soul of the genre through stellar, innovative performances of both forgotten and familiar works. (Since the theater is smaller than the nearby Metropolitan Opera House, better seats are more attainable here, while costing less.)
Upper West Side, 20 Lincoln Center Plaza (at 64th St. and Broadway), 870-5570, MC, V, AmEx, **❶❾** to 66th St.-Lincoln Center &

New York Theatre Workshop
This downtown theater staple caters to a hip crowd and often presents work from the farther corners of the mainstream. It's the original home of Broadway sensation "Rent," as well as the rock musical "Bright Lights, Big City" and "The Most Fabulous Story Ever Told." Annual "Just Add Water" festival presents work in development for future seasons. Rush tickets are available for most performances.
East Village, 79 East 4th St. (bet. Second Ave. and Bowery), 460-5475, MC, V, AmEx, **❻** to 2nd Ave. &

P.S. 122
This small performance space in a converted school serves as a showplace for cutting-edge dance, theater and performance

art. Artists range from obscure but talented newcomers to established members of the downtown scene.
East Village, 150 First Ave. (at 9th St.), 477-5288, MC, V, AmEx, ⑥ to Astor Pl. ♿

Pearl Theater
This classic repertoire/resident company sticks to a strict pre-WWI itinerary, with productions of Shakespeare, Moliere, Sophocles, and others of their ilk, as well as revived relics. Shows generally run seven weeks.
East Village, 80 St. Marks Pl. (at First Ave.), 598-9802, MC, V, D, ⑥ to Astor Pl. ♿

Playwrights Horizons
Long the anchor of Theater Row, this theater company has been premiering innovative and new American plays for the past twenty-five years. The work of Christopher Durang and Wendy Wasserstein was first presented here, as was Stephen Sondheim and James Lapine's Pulitzer Prize-winning musical "Sunday In The Park With George." The upstairs Studio Theater presents work by up-and-coming writers.
Midtown, 416 West 42nd St. (bet. Ninth and Tenth Aves.), 564-1235, MC, V, AmEx, ⒶⒸⒺ to 42nd St.

Public Theater
Founded by the legendary Joseph Papp, "A Chorus Line" started here. The beautiful red brick Italian Renaissance style building was once the Astor Library and became the permanent home of the New York Shakespeare Festival in 1967. Along with the Bard and other classics, the five stages here also host an eclectic mix of European imports, established, and up and-coming American playwrights. New York's most venerable avant-garde theater, now

featuring Joe's Pub, a performance space/bar featuring live music, dance, and spoken word.
East Village, 425 Lafayette St. (bet. Astor Pl. and 4th St.), 539-8500, MC, V, AmEx, D, ⑥ to Astor Pl. ♿

Roundabout Theatre
The most consistently intelligent indigenous productions and European imports on Broadway proper, including the recent Tony-winning hit, "Cabaret."
Midtown, 1530 Broadway (bet. 44th and 45th Sts.), 869-8400, MC, V, AmEx, ⓃⓇⓈ①②③⑦⑨ to 42nd St.-Times Sq. ♿

SoHo Repertory Theatre
Home for anything new and compelling, from freshly adapted literary works to personal dramas. Well known for excellent casting choices, the theater generally offers several overlapping runs from which to choose.
TriBeca, 46 Walker St. (bet. Church and Broadway Sts.), 334-0962, MC, V, AmEx, ⒶⒸⒺ to Canal St. ♿

St. Clement's Theatre
A working theater for thirty-five years, this charming little church has hosted some of the best Off-Broadway theater in the city. Episcopal services are still held here regularly. Conveniently located on Restaurant Row and around the corner from the greatest concentration of ethnic restaurants in the city.
Midtown, 423 West 46th St. (bet. Ninth and Tenth Aves.), 246-7277, MC, V, AmEx, ⒶⒸⒺ to 42nd St. ♿

St. Mark's Church-in-the-Bowery
A quiet and beautiful cultural oasis in the bustling East Village, this century-old church is home to three excellent arts "projects,"

including Danspace and the Ontological Theater. Most notable is the Poetry Project, one of the only programs of its kind, offering special literary events and workshops for budding poets, a forum for both well-known and up-and-coming poets to read their work.
East Village, 131 East 10th St. (at Second Ave.), 674-6377, Cash Only, ⑥ to Astor Pl.

Signature Theatre Company
Under the leadership of visionary artistic director James Houghton, the Signature has carved out a unique mission: highlighting the work of one major playwright each season. Past seasons have included retrospectives and world premieres from Arthur Miller, John Guare, Adrienne Kennedy, and Sam Shepard. The 1999-2000 season will feature the work of Maria Irene Fornes; the 2000-2001 season, the theater's tenth, will feature premiere works from past season's subjects.
Midtown, 555 West 42nd St. (bet. Tenth and Eleventh Aves.), 244-7529, MC, V, AmEx, ⒶⒸⒺ to 42nd St. ♿

Stand-Up NY
Brett Butler and Dennis Leary cut their teeth here years ago and still swing by to pay their respects when in the neighborhood.
Upper West Side, 236 West 78th St. (bet. Amsterdam Ave. and Broadway), 595-0850, MC, V, AmEx, D, ①⑨ to 79th St. ♿

Sullivan St. Playhouse
Home since 1960 to "The Fantasticks," the longest running show in U.S. history. Don't miss the art gallery upstairs, which boasts a varied collection of "Fantasticks" memorabilia from around the world so extensive that it shares space with the ladies' room.

Greenwich Village, 181 Sullivan St. (bet. Houston and Bleecker Sts.), 674-3838, AmEx, ❶❾ to Houston St. &

Surf Reality

"Anything can happen here," boasts one of the regulars at this zany alternative comedy space. The tiny, makeshift stage hosts acts too silly or outrageous for the mainstream comedy circuit. New York's most bizarre performers turn out for Faceboyz Open Mike, Wednesdays, 8pm-3am; $3 to sign up and perform. Once a woman pulled an onion out of her vagina.
Lower East Side, 172 Allen St., 2nd Fl. (bet. Stanton and Rivington Sts.), 673-4182, Cash Only, ❺ to Second Ave.

Symphony Space

Playing host to an incredible range of talent, this spacious theater consistently offers up unique programs, often incorporating disparate genres into a unifying theme. Home to such ongoing favorites as "Selected Shorts," where actors and authors read short stories; an annual Bloomsday celebration; "Wall to Wall" music festivals, devoted to individual artists; and World Music Institute shows of international performers.
Upper West Side, 2537 Broadway (at 95th St.), 864-5400, MC, V, AmEx, ❶❷❸❾ to 96th St. &

Thalia Spanish Theater

One of New York's hottest stages for established and new Hispanic playwrights, actors, and directors. Three productions yearly, as well as three ongoing showcases in music, dance, and special events.
Sunnyside, Queens, 41-17 Greenpoint Ave. (bet. 41st and 42nd Sts.), (718) 729-3880, Cash Only, ❼ to 40th St. (Lowery St.) &

Theatre for a New Audience

Some of the most innovative, provocative, thoughtful, and coherent productions of Shakespeare and other classics. Call for venue locations.
Greenwich Village, 154 Christopher St., Suite 3D (bet. Greenwich and Washington Sts.) 229-2819, MC, V, AmEx, D, ❶❾ to Christopher St.-Sheridan Sq. &

TriBeCa Performing Arts Center

Inconspicuously housed in the main building of the Borough of Manhattan Community College, this large venue is easy to miss. That would be a shame since the programming is excellent, offering multicultural music, dance, theater from around the world, and urban youth-themed performances consistent with the diverse student population. The college connection means cheap student-rate tickets.
TriBeCa, 199 Chambers St. (bet. Greenwich St. and the West Side Hghwy.), 346-8510, MC, V, AmEx, ❶❷❸❾ to Chambers St. &

Trinity Church

Functional, historic, and aesthetic qualities make this the ideal venue for chamber music and organ recitals. Lunchtime performances are still free.
Lower Manhattan, 74 Trinity Pl. (at Broadway and Wall St.), 602-0873, Cash Only, ❷❸ to Wall St. &

Variety Arts Theater

Campy theater and a distorted dose of pop culture. Recent productions have included a new work by writer/drag queen Charles Busch and a musical based on the life of Patsy Cline. Proof that theater doesn't have to be dull or squeaky-clean.
East Village, 110 Third Ave. (bet. 13th and 14th Sts.), 239-6200, MC, V, AmEx, D, ❶❽❺❹❺❻ to 14th St.-Union Sq. &

Vineyard Theatre

In recent years this Union Sq. favorite has emerged as a major source of excellent new plays and musicals. Nicky Silver, Tina Landau, Craig Lucas, and Polly Pen have all presented new work here in the past few seasons. The Vineyard's 120-seat theater was also the site of the New York premieres of Pulitzer Prize winners "Three Tall Women" and "How I Learned to Drive." Special discount passes available for students under 30.
Gramercy, 108 East 15th St. (bet. Union Sq. and Irving Pl.) 353-3366, MC, V, AmEx, ❶❽❾ ❹❺❻ to 14th St.-Union Sq.

Worth St. Theater

Begun as a small-time theater company on its namesake Worth St., it's since grown into bigger digs on Laight St. and remains a testing ground for new productions that larger companies lack the freedom to attempt. A fine place to catch several one-acts that all fit into a grander theme, satisfying the urge for consistency without putting all your eggs in one basket.
TriBeCa, 13-17 Laight St. (at Varick St.), 604-4195, Cash Only, ❶❾ to Canal St.

& While we have made every effort to maintain a high level of accuracy regarding wheelchair accessibility, this designation is based on information provided by each establishment

literature

li•t•e•r•a•t•u•r•e

From the restrictive elegance of Edith Wharton's New York, to the grim realism of Nathanael West's *Miss Lonelyhearts*; from Tama Janowitz's *Slaves of New York*, through to Oscar Hijuelos' *Mr. Ives' Christmas* — New York is depicted in literature as the city where your dreams can come brilliantly true and, often, how tragic that brilliance can be. Manhattan seems to increase human appetites for money, love, and success — and writers, who work in isolation and reflection, view it all with an inquisitive eye.

The uneasy relationship between writers and New York City is over a century old. Wharton and Henry James had to leave their restricted society backgrounds in order to develop as artists; but invariably, their best stories came from their New York experiences. By the turn of the 20th Century, many styles of writing had come into vogue, the most prominent of which was the naturalistic style represented by Dreiser's *Sister Carrie*, and later by H. L. Mencken, among others. In Greenwich Village, literary journals began flourishing between 1910 and 1920. Nineteen twenty-five marked the inception of the *New Yorker* magazine representing a new major voice: witty, urbane, and utterly lacking in Victorian complacency. Meanwhile, the Harlem Renaissance gathered black artists from all corners of the nation at various clubs and salons in the 1920s and '30s; Langston Hughes, Countee Cullen, Zora Neale Hurston, and Ralph Ellison are only a few of the writers who sang Harlem's praises. F. Scott Fitzgerald — whose forays into society ended tragically, both in fiction and life — was renowned in the early '20s for his drunken exploits at the Biltmore Hotel with his talented, beautiful, unbalanced wife, Zelda. Dorothy Parker engaged in similar excesses, viewing the world with an acerbity which distanced her from those who would admire her quick wit. (Once, when challenged to make a joke using the word "horticulture," she is rumored to have quipped, "You can lead a whore to culture, but you can't make her think.")

In post-World War II New York, a growing Bohemia, led by Anaïs Nin and James Agee, established itself in the Village, and beckoned college students John Berryman, Allen Ginsberg, and Jack Kerouac from Columbia University into downtown's gritty world of heavy drinking and sexual liberalism. Kerouac, Ginsberg, and William S. Burroughs developed what would become the Beat aesthetic. Soon after, Ginsberg moved to the then-seedy East Village, renting an apartment on East 7th St.; Burroughs followed. The subculture of the decidedly rough-around-the-edges area played a major role in Burroughs' *Junkie*, Ginsberg's famous poem, "Howl," and Kerouac's *The Subterraneans*, all published in the mid-1950s.

An air of heavy pretension hung over the uptown literary scene in the late '60s and early '70s, as self-conscious intellectual journals flourished, stimulated by the double impact of Marxism and feminism on the academic world. *The Paris Review* moved to the city in the late '60s and began publishing a series of interesting interviews with writers. A return to the patrician salons became fashionable amongst intellectuals. Although a great number of literary luminaries lived in New York during this time, they did not constitute a community per se and many of them had left the city by the end of the '70s.

In the '80s, the most prominent novels reflected the materialist feeding frenzy which took hold of the city during the economic boom of the Reagan Era: Tom Wolfe's *The Bonfire of the Vanities* and Bret Easton Ellis' *American Psycho* scathingly represent Wall Street ethics run amuck. Meanwhile, Brooklyn-based author Paul Auster marked the quieter pace of life in "The New York Trilogy" of *City of Glass, Ghosts,* and *The Locked Room,* although he too grasped the runaway nature of urban decay in *In the Country of Last Things.*

At the turn of the twenty-first century, the literary scene in the city is fully reinvigorated, many using the city itself as a prominent character. And

AbcdEfgHijk

if contemporary New York is a subject fit for ambitious writers, it is also a city of ambitious readers and thinkers. The revival of the spoken word is perhaps an exciting outcome of the blending of Beat narrative and Latino immigrants' cultural history. The Unterberg Poetry Series at the 92nd Street Y offers a variety of readings and a lecture series with the most fascinating writers working today. At Symphony Space, accomplished actors and authors read published short stories. Tiny coffee shops and bars throughout the city feature weekly readings where the next generation of writers raise their voices, hoping to be heard above the hiss of an espresso maker. The Strand Bookstore and other great independent bookstores are shrines to the written word. On any day you can go in them and see New Yorkers, their heads bent over a new — or long-beloved — title, silent for once.

Writers' Resources

The Fountain Pen Hospital
Whether you want a Bic or a Mont Blanc, the knowledgeable staff will find a match.
The sale and repair of antique and limited-edition pens are also specialties.
TriBeCa, 10 Warren St. (bet. Broadway and Church St.), 964-0580,
AmEx, MC, V, Diners, D, ❶❷❸❾ to Chambers St. ♿

Kate's Paperie
The city's deluxe source for paper products, Kate's features one of a kind handmade stationary, cards, albums, and wrapping paper, as well as an outstanding collection of rubber stamps, pens, and notebooks. A peerless paradise for diarists and letter writers.
SoHo, 561 Broadway (bet. Prince and Spring Sts.), 941-9816, MC, V, AmEx, ❶❾ to Prince St. ♿
Greenwich Village, 8 West 13th St. (bet. Fifth and Sixth Aves.), 633-0570,
❶❸❼❹❺❻ to 14th St.-Union Sq. ♿
Upper East Side, 1282 Third Ave. (bet. 73rd and 74th Sts.), 396-3970, MC, V, AmEx, ❻ to 77th St. ♿

Museum of American Folk Art Book and Gift Shop
A museum gift shop with an extra artsy flare; Things tend to be pricey but charming.
Midtown, 2 Lincoln Sq., (bet. 65th and 66th Sts. on Columbus Ave.), 496-2966,
MC, V, AmEx, D, ❶❾ to 66th St.-Lincoln Center ♿

New York Public Library Shop
All manner of trinkets and souvenirs for bibliophiles as well as the merely literate.
Midtown, 455 Fifth Ave. (bet. 40th and 42nd Sts.), 930-0641, MC, V, AmEx,
❸❶❻❷ to 42nd St., ❼ to Fifth Ave. ♿

Progressive Unlimited
This tiny but well-stocked spot near Harlem's primary artery maintains an Afro-centric twist
Harlem, 14 East 125th St. (bet. Madison and Fifth Aves.), 427-7084, Cash Only, ❹❺❻ to 125th St.

LmnoPqrSt

I n few venues is the "mall-ation" of New York more evident than book stores, where impersonal, homogeneous monoliths seem to be the wave of the future, destroying the unique flavors which help to make a neighborhood what it is. However, two stores in the heart of Park Slope, Brooklyn — **Nkiru** (in-kee-roo) **Books** (76 St. Marks Ave.) and **Community Book Store and Cafe of Park Slope** (143 Seventh Ave.) — continue to stand strong in spite of the grave presence of a nearby Death Star, Barnes & Noble.

Nkiru means 'the best is yet to come,' in the Nigerian language of Ibo and as you enter, the best is laid out for the buying. Packed into the small store is an amazing array of wares: posters, post cards, Polaroid pictures, calendars, cassette tapes, CDs, buttons, blues and jazz photographs, jarred cosmic ocean salts, vegetable soap, dermatology creams, African shampoos, fertility dolls and a great collection of afro-centric grown-up and children's books, urban magazines, and community newsletters.

Located on the edge of Park Slope, off commercial Flatbush Ave., Nkiru was founded in 1974 by Adelaide Miller and her daughter, Leothy, and was bought by actors/musicians, Mos Def and Talib Kweli on January 1, 1999. Each has had the same goal of disseminating accurate information, positive images, and quality books on African Americans, Native Americans, Caribbean Americans, Eskimos, indigenous cultures and subjects concerning the Diaspora. Nkiru also holds book signings, music events, and a spoken word series called Foundations where heavy poets and up-and-coming local MCs, musicians, and novelists perform once a month in hopes of creating a gathering place to stimulate creativity and imaginations

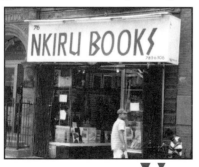

through listening. Celebs like Maya Angelou have also put in appearances. It's a bold vision but, as Assistant manager Rubix says, "There's 8 million stories in the city. Every one of them is told differently but all are happening in the same exact place. We just want to make sure our community maintains a voice amidst all that noise."

Up the Slope, Community Book Store and Cafe of Park Slope has been a cozy, familial, literary hub ever since its doors were opened in 1971. Though in the big city, manager Catherine Bohne says, "It has a small town feel. Everyone knows everyone else." Most of the staff aspires to be writers; all are well read and happy to chat about current books, to or help you find that something you've been looking for by that author you heard about from somewhere you just can't remember. While the store stocks well over 17 thousand titles, it is the personality and intimacy of the place that stands out. Back in the outdoor garden, a frog and cat lounge by the small Feng Shui waterfall — what the two animals have come to call home. An indoor café has fresh sandwiches, coffee, wine, beer, and enough tables for sitting, reading, and thinking for as long as one chooses.

During the summer, sit outside with a glass of wine and a friend or a book until ten in the evening. The store also holds readings twice a week in the spring and fall with such noted authors as Mary Gordon and Paul Auster, along with local unpublished authors, too. Philosophy groups, travel lectures, book clubs and a flautist round out the amenities.

Bohne says they were initially alarmed when the Barnes & Noble opened up the street but, after an initial lag, business is back up. As an independent bookstore, she continues, they are very lucky to be in the Park Slope community because they receive a lot of local support. According to her patrons, the biggest difference between her shop and the chain, beyond the obvious size, is when folks ask about a book at Community Bookstore, they'll get an answer of real substance instead of blank stares.

Academy Bookstore

Find used or otherwise discounted books on every subject, especially art, architecture, photography, history, and philosophy.
Chelsea, 10 West 18th St. (bet. Fifth and Sixth Aves.), 242-4848, MC, V, AmEx, D, ❶❷ to Sixth Ave., ❶❷❸❹ to 14th St.

Applause Theatre and Cinema Books

Scripts, books, and screenplays. Perfect for the cinephile who has time to browse.
Upper West Side, 211 West 71st St. (bet. Broadway and West End Ave.), 496-7511, MC, V, AmEx, D, ❶❷❸❹ to 72nd St.

Argosy Bookstore

Rare books, old maps, and lithographs fill this time warp of towering bookshelves and cluttered desks. The bargains here are on the outside table.
Upper East Side, 116 East 59th St. (bet. Park and Lexington Aves.), 753-4455, MC, V, AmEx, ❶❷ to Lexington Ave., ❹❺❻ to 59th St.

Bank St. Bookstore

Serving the fledgling schoolteachers of the nearby Bank St. College with an extensive selection of children's books, educational theory, and planning guides. Flip through old faves like *Madeleine* and *Where the Wild Things Are*.
Morningside Heights, 2879 Broadway (at 112th St.), 678-1654, MC, V, AmEx, ❶❷ to Cathedral Parkway (110th St.) ♿

Biography Bookshop

Muckrakers, voyeurs, and fan club presidents come to this high-ceilinged and brick-walled store for the latest on their respective celebs. Boasts an impressive gay & lesbian section.

Greenwich Village, 400 Bleecker St. (at 11th St.), 807-8655, MC, V, AmEx, D, ❶❷ to Christopher St.-Sheridan Sq.

Black Books Plus

African and African-American issues are the top priority at this rare find which stocks a selection spanning a number of genres exclusively by and about African-American.
Upper West Side, 702 Amsterdam Ave. (at 94th St.), 749-9632, MC, V, AmEx, ❶❷❸❹ to 96th St. ♿

Blackout Books

The radical writings available here are required reading for any potential East Village resident. Browsers can educate themselves on political uprisings, sexual liberation, or just have a good laugh with the books, newspapers, magazines, and alternative comic books. For the civic-minded, there's a board in back noting local meetings.
East Village, 50 Ave. B (bet. 3rd and 4th Sts.), 777-1967, Cash Only, ❻ to Second Ave.

Book Ark

Relief for those weary of superstores. Fiction offerings are solid, as is the foreign language and rare book selections.
Upper West Side, 173 West 81st St. (bet. Amsterdam and Columbus Aves.), 787-3914, MC, V, AmEx, ❶❷ to 79th St, ❸❹ to 81st St.

Bookberries

Coffee table books are the specialty of this store — huge volumes loaded with pictures, especially of travel and food. In the rear is a children's section.
Upper East Side, 983 Lexington Ave. (at 71st St.), 794-9400, MC, V, AmEx, ❻ to 68th St.-Hunter College

Booklink

Come for quality fiction and children's books; also a sampling of intellectual and academic periodicals. Specializes in Scottish and Middle Eastern Literature.
Park Slope, Brooklyn, 99 Seventh Ave. (bet. President and Union Sts.), (718) 783-6067, MC, V, AmEx, ❷❸ to Seventh Ave. ♿

Community Book Store and Cafe

This integral part of Park Slope's social life carries a mixture of current best-sellers and classic fiction, with a wonderful café and garden in the back. The owners also coax well-known authors out for readings, most recently Mary Gordon and Pete Hamill.
Park Slope, Brooklyn, 143 Seventh Ave. (bet. Garfield and Carroll Sts.), (718) 783-3075, MC, V, AmEx, D, ❷❸ to Seventh Ave.

Complete Traveller

The best store for new and out-of-print books providing information for real trips and fuel for the imagination; the prices reflect the quality and the selection. The staff is amiable, erudite, and willing to discuss anything from city politics to traveling in the sub-Sahara.
Midtown, 199 Madison Ave. (at 35th St.), 685-9007, MC, V, AmEx, D, Diners, ❻ to 33rd St. ♿

A Different Light

The East Coast branch of the largest gay and lesbian specialty book vendor in the country feels refined but homey. A mellow crowd browses through great selections from kitsch to academia and partakes of the small cafe's coffee and sandwiches. The store regularly hosts lectures, musicians, and poets, and offers free movies (with popcorn!) on Sundays.

Chelsea, 151 West 19th St. (bet. Sixth and Seventh Aves.), 989-4850, MC, V, AmƐx, ❶❾ *to 18th St.*

Dina News

Though the staff tends to frown upon browsing, try to sneak a peek at this impressive selection of periodicals, including a number of foreign magazines and newspapers.
Upper West Side, 2077 Broadway (bet. 71st and 72nd Sts.), 875-8824, MC, V, AmƐx, D, ❶❷❸❾ *to 72nd St.*

The Drama Bookshop

Plays, biographies, acting/directing and writing manuals, and much more.
Midtown, 723 Seventh Ave. (bet. 48th and 49th Sts.), 2nd fl., 944-0595, MC, V, AmƐx, D, ❶❾ *to 50th St.,* ❾❿ *to 49th St.* ⚊

East-West Books

As the name suggests, the emphasis here is on introducing Western readers to the literature of the East, specializing in religious and philosophical traditions from Mahayana Buddhism to neo-Confucianism. The staff will make special orders.
Greenwich Village, 78 Fifth Ave. (bet. 13th and 14th Sts.), 243-5994, MC, V, AmƐx, ❶❿❹❹❺❻ *to 14th St.-Union Sq.,* ❼ *to 14th St.* ⚊

Fashion Design Books

Located at the heart of FIT's urban campus, this unique take on the university bookstore stocks a plethora of fashion mags, from the popular to the obscure, and art and design books. In lieu of office accessories, you'll find art and sewing supplies.
Chelsea, 234 West 27th St. (bet. Seventh and Eighth Aves.), 633-9646, MC, V, AmƐx, D, ❶❾ *to 28rd St.*

Forbidden Planet

Comics fans seeking everything from superheroes to the latest Eightball cruise the racks to weed out the best of the new and used selection.
Greenwich Village, 840 Broadway (at 13th St.), 473-1576, MC, V, AmƐx, D, ❶❿❹❹❺❻ *to 14th St.-Union Sq.* ⚊

Gotham Book Mart

This average-sized bookstore may not be the greatest place to pick up the latest best seller, but with a generous selection of new and used books and with helpful salespeople, this is an ideal place to find some great literature.
Midtown, 41 West 47th St. (bet. Fifth and Sixth Aves.), 719-4448, MC, V, AmƐx, ❷❹❼❻ *to 47-50 Sts.-Rockefeller Center.*

Gryphon

Crowded shelves of used books climbing almost to the ceiling and piled on the floor. "I'd like it more if I could actually turn around in the aisles," complains one regular. There are books here which can be found nowhere else in Manhattan; you just have to look, real hard.
Upper West Side, 2246 Broadway (bet. 80th and 81 Sts.), 362-0706, V, MC, ❶❾ *to 79th St.* ⚊

Hacker Art Books, Inc.

An eager, knowledgeable staff headed by Pierre, the Parisian manager and conversationalist extraordinaire, can help browsers wade through the initially intimidating selection. The clientele are true art-lovers, not just collectors.
Midtown, 45 West 57th St. (bet. Fifth and Sixth Aves.), 688-7600, MC, V, ❾❿ *to Fifth Avenue,* ❺❻ *to 5th Ave.* ⚊

Hotalings

Walls of magazines, including one of the city's finest selections of foreign-language periodicals.
Midtown, 142 West 42nd St. (bet. Sixth and Seventh Aves.), 840-1868, MC, V, AmƐx, ❾❿❸ ❶❷❸❾❼ *to 42nd St.-Times Sq.*

Housing Works Used Bookstore Cafe

Used books SoHo style. No dingy paperbacks with tattered covers and peculiar odors here. Instead, browse through nearly pristine coffee table art books and hardcover fiction with jackets fully intact, all at low used-book prices. There's also a coffee bar for refueling while settling on what to take home.
SoHo, 126 Crosby St. (bet. Houston and Prince Sts.), 334-3324, MC, V, AmƐx, ❻❿❼❻ *to Broadway-Lafayette St.,* ❾❿ *to Prince Street* ⚊

Just Jake

TriBeCa is full of pampered children, so it only makes sense that the stores catering to their needs are rather extraordinary. Here, find an "A" selection of children's books nearly as large as a small grown-up bookstore with choices for various age groups, along with lots of well-made and interesting educational toys. Fun enough to intrigue children and responsible enough to impress their parents.
TriBeCa, 40 Hudson St. (at Duane St.), 267-1716, MC, V, AmƐx, D, ❶❷❸❾ *to Chambers St.* ⚊

K & W Books and Stationary

One of the biggest Chinese bookstores, K & W carries Hello Kitty toys and a large selection of books in Chinese and in English on topics like martial arts, bonsai care, Buddhism, and knife throwing.

Chinatown, 131 Bowery St. (bet. Grand and Broome Sts.), 343-0780, Cash Only, ❿❽❶❻❷❻ to Canal St.

Kinokuniya Bookstore

Japanese books, some in English translation, with a diverse selection of stationary and gifts. *Midtown, 10 West 49th St. (bet Fifth and Sixth Aves.), 765-7766, MC, V, AmEx,* ❶❸❶❻❶ to 47th-50th Sts.-Rockefeller Center

Kitchen Arts & Letters

With a fabulous selection of over 10,000 cookbooks, the definitive answer to "what's cooking?" for either the novice or the gourmet. *Upper East Side, 1435 Lexington Ave. (bet. 93rd and 94th Sts.), 876-5550, MC, V,* ❻ to 96th St.

Labyrinth Books

Professors and students alike applaud this recent addition to Morningside's healthy population of bookstores, made possible in part by the rare generosity of its landlord (Columbia). Relying on a strong selection of academic titles rather than coffee and comfy furniture, Labyrinth is a welcome retreat for hard-core bibliophiles. *Morningside Heights, 536 112th St. (bet. Broadway and Amsterdam Ave.), 865-1588, MC, V, AmEx, D,* ❶❾ to Cathedral Parkway (110th St.) ⅃

Lectorum Book Store

Spanish and Latin American authors whose native-language tomes are dispersed throughout the store comprise the bulk of the selection. Translations of popular titles by the likes of Stephen King and James Cavell, bibles, dictionaries, and a host of other reference books round

out the offerings. Check at the desk for information on lectures and readings. *Chelsea, 137 West 14th St. (bet. Sixth and Seventh Aves.), 741-0220, MC, V, AmEx,* ❶❷❸❾ to 14th St., ❶❶ to Sixth Ave.

Liberation Book Store

One of the country's largest and best selections of books about black history and culture. Posters, calendars, and greeting cards are also available. *Harlem, 421 Lenox Ave. (at 131st St.), 281-4615, Cash Only,* ❷❸ to 135th St. ⅃

Librairie de France

One-stop shopping for French émigrés and Francophiles. New York's largest French-language bookstore sells magazines upstairs and a vast assortment of literature, history, and biographies available downstairs. *Midtown, 610 Fifth Ave. on the Rockefeller Center Promenade (bet. 49th and 50th Sts.), 581-8810, MC, V, AmEx,* ❸❶❻❶ to 47th-50th Sts.-Rockefeller Center

Macondo Books, Inc.

Pick up an import from either Spain or South America here. The store caters to native speakers with an excellent selection of literature, plays, and poetry. *Chelsea, 221 West 14th St. (bet. Seventh and Eighth Aves.), 741-3108, MC, V, AmEx,* ❶❷❸❾ to 14th St.

Manhattan Comics and Cards

Action figures gaze down at customers navigating the stacks of comic books; mags run the gamut of old, new, latest, and greatest. Scavenge through the half-price bins. *Chelsea, 228 West 23rd St. (bet. Seventh and Eighth Aves.), 243-9349, MC, V,* ❶❾ to 23rd St., ❻❶ to 23rd St.

Murder Ink

This specialty bookstore featuring new and used mystery fiction is every aspiring sleuth's dream. Their stock includes many classic whodunits as well as novels featuring elements of espionage and suspense. A mecca for the city's true mystery buffs, this shop has frequent book-signings. *Upper West Side, 2486 Broadway (bet. 92nd and 93rd Sts.), 362-8905, MC, V, AmEx,* ❶❷❸❾ to 96th St. ⅃

The Mysterious Bookshop

Serving the city's voracious mystery readers, this store stocks both current and out-of-print books as well as a healthy number of imports from Britain. *Midtown, 129 West 56th St. (bet. Sixth and Seventh Aves.), 765-0900, MC, V, AmEx,* ❶❷❶❻❶❶❾ to 59th St.-Columbus Circle

Oscar Wilde Memorial Bookstore

For over twenty-five years, New York City's flagship gay bookstore has been offering books for and by gays and lesbians, as well as videotapes, music, T-shirts, and jewelry. Occasional readings by established authors are scheduled. *Greenwich Village, 15 Christopher St. (at Sixth Ave.), 255-8097, MC, V, AmEx, D,* ❶❾ to Christopher St.-Sheridan Sq.

Papyrus

Though its hegemony was slightly infringed upon with the introduction of Labyrinth bookstore, this smallish store stocks a little bit of everything. The literature and travel sections are excellent, as is the selection of textbooks, which often run cheaper than at Columbia University's bookstore. *Morningside Heights, 2915 Broadway (at 114th St.), 222-3350, MC, V, AmEx, D,* ❶❾ to 116th St.-Columbia University ⅃

Partners & Crime

Serving West Village mystery aficionados, P&C carries a lot of current mysteries and a shelf of out-of-print books; the staff will special order books not in stock. Call for a schedule of readings and radio plays.
Greenwich Village, 44 Greenwich Ave. (bet. Sixth and Seventh Aves.) 243-0440, MC, V, AmEx, ⒶⒷⒸⒹⒺⒻⓄ *to West 4th St.-Washington Sq.*

A Photographer's Place

New and used books from camera manuals to texts on fashion photography line the intimate wood-paneled walls of this photographer's pit stop.
SoHo, 133 Mercer St. (bet. Prince and Spring Sts.), 966-2356, MC, V, AmEx, D, ⓃⓇ *to Prince St.*

Posman's

Avoid coming during the beginning-of-the-semester madness in January or September, as the lines to buy school books are endless. Off-season, browse through new and used academic titles at your leisure.
Greenwich Village, 1 University Pl. (bet. Waverly Pl. and 8th St.), 533-2665, MC, V, AmEx, D, ⓃⓇ *to 8th St.-NYU* &

Rizzoli

Pop in to escape the chaos of Midtown and get lost in this dark, warm store which, like its downtown counterpart, specializes in beautiful architecture, art, design, and coffee table books. Literature and non-fiction selections are not inspiring.
Midtown, 31 West 57th St. (bet. Fifth and Sixth Aves.), 759-2424, MC, V, AmEx, D, ⓃⓇ *to 57th St.* &
Also at:
SoHo, 454 West Broadway (bet. Houston and Prince Sts.), 674-1616, MC, V, AmEx, D, ⓃⓇ *to Prince St.*

St. Marks Books

Why go to a chain when everything you'd ever want can be found in the tall racks of this favorite excursion? Literature, sci-fi, and mystery are all strong suits. Plus, it's just cooler to shop here.
East Village, 31 Third Ave. (at 9th St.), 260-7853, MC, V, AmEx, D, ⑥ *to Astor Pl.* &

St. Mark's Comics

From "The X-Men" to less conventional titles like "Sexy Sushi," there's enough here for any comic book connoisseur.
East Village, 11 St. Marks Pl. (bet. Second and Third Aves.), 598-9439, MC, V, AmEx, ⑥ *to Astor Pl.*

See Hear

Want to buy a 'zine without getting stared down and scoffed at by the ultra-cool record store guy? Check out the largest array of homemade publications around, with lots of stuff for hardcore and indie-rock fans as well as those who just appreciate irreverent writing that doesn't answer to advertisers.
East Village, 59 East 7th St. (bet. First and Second Aves.), 505-9781, MC, V, ⑥ *to Astor Pl.*

Shakespeare & Co.

One of four locations left after the recent demise of the Upper West Side store, offering a diverse selection of books, and the soul of an actual bookstore, too.
Upper East Side, 939 Lexington Ave. (bet. 68th and 69th Sts.), 570-0201 MC, V, AmEx, D, ⑥ *to 68th St.-Hunter College*
Also at:
Greenwich Village, 716 Broadway (at Washington Pl.), 529-1330, MC, V, AmEx, ⓃⓇ *to 8th St.-NYU*
Gramercy, 137 E. 23rd St. (at Lexington Ave.), 220-5199, MC, V, AmEx, ⑥ *to 23rd St.*

Lower Manhattan, 1 Whitehall St. (bet. Stone and Bridge Sts.), 742-7025, MC, V, AmEx, ⓃⓇ *to Whitehall St.-South Ferry* &

SoHo Books

The best sale tables around await outside this bargain book cavern, which offers everything from slightly outdated editions of *Let's Go* guides to slick Generation X novels for $1.98 each, or three for five dollars. (Where on earth is Donna Tartt these days?)
SoHo, 351 West Broadway (bet. Broome and Grand Sts.), MC, AmEx, V, 226-3395, ⒶⒸⒺ *to Canal St.*

South St. Seaport Museum Shop

Any wannabe sailors who pride themselves on knowing how to tie knots can learn the rest from one of the many books about ships, port histories, and New York City from the colonial period to the 19th Century.
Lower Manhattan, 12-14 Fulton St. (bet. South and Front Sts.), 748-8663, MC, V, AmEx, ⒿⓂⓏ ②③④⑤ *to Fulton St.* &

The Strand Bookstore

Advertising "eight miles of books," The Strand is a heavenly sight for New York's many bibliophiles: three cavernous floors of bookshelves, stuffed solid, and tables crammed into the few remaining spaces in between. The right strategy is key — browse slowly, and, with the proper investment of time, you'll turn up books you never even dreamed existed.
Greenwich Village, 828 Broadway (at 12th St.), 473-1452, MC, V, AmEx, D, ⒧ⓃⓇ④⑤⑥ *to 14th St.-Union Sq.*

The Strand Book Annex

As if "eight miles of books" wasn't enough, here's another 15,000 square feet (2-3 miles) of Strand, with wider aisles, more windows, and a generally less cluttered feel.

Lower Manhattan, 95 Fulton St. (at William St.), 732-6070, MC, V, AmEx, D, **🅐🅜②③④⑤** to Fulton St.

Sufi Books

If there's such a thing as a typical neighborhood spiritual book shop, this is TriBeCa's. The quiet atmosphere with a soft-spoken staff to match contains a wealth of Eastern religion resources and smaller sections on Judaism, Christianity, Islam, and Suffism to feed spiritual quests of any ilk.

TriBeCa, 227 West Broadway (bet. Franklin and White Sts.), 334-5212, MC, V, AmEx, **①⑨** to Franklin St.

Unity Book Center

"You say you want a revolution?" If reading about one suffices, this smallish shop chock-full of radical leftist writings is the place to go.

Check out the great Marxist, African-American, and women authors who most likely didn't make your high school government class reading list.

Chelsea, 237 West 23rd St. (bet. Seventh and Eighth Aves.), 242-2934, Cash Only, **🅒🅔** *to 23rd St.,* **①⑨** *to 23rd St.*

Urban Center Books

Books on every architectural topic, from urban design to Freudian interpretations of city planning, line the walls of this cozy nook, complete with a fireplace and library ladders. Enjoy your purchase in the courtyard outside.

Midtown, 457 Madison Ave. (at 51st St.), 935-3592, MC, V, **🅔🅕** *to Fifth Ave.*

West Side Judaica

This haven of Judaica supplies music, art, decorations, and children's educational tools as well as a number of books dealing with Jewish issues. Closes at 3pm on Fridays for Shabbat and doesn't reopen until Sunday.

Upper West Side, 2412 Broadway (bet. 88th and 89th Sts.), 362-7846, MC, V, **①⑨** *to 86th St.* ♿

Wow Comics

Those who can't always make it to Manhattan's larger comic stores take heart in this comfortable mainstay — remember, even Peter Parker lived in an outer borough at first, commuting into town to do his crime-fighting as Spiderman! New and old releases from a variety of both mainstream and independent companies are sold alongside baseball cards, action figurines, and other memorabilia.

Parkchester, The Bronx, 2395 Westchester Ave. (at Zerega Ave.), (718) 829-0461, MC, V, AmEx, D, **⑥** *to Zerega Ave.*

Zakka

Insight into the world of the Japanese adolescent. Bookstore, boutique and video palace focusing on Japanese pop culture.

Chinatown, 147 Grand St. (at Lafayette St.), 431-3961, MC, V, AmEx, **🅙🅜🅝🅠②⑥** *to Canal St.*

f i l m & t v

New Yorker Mae West once said to a Hollywood studio executive, "I'm a big girl, from a big town — so don't blow smoke at me, little man." After decades of losing ground to Los Angeles as the film production capital of the country, New York is hot again in the '90s, both as a location and a production site. New Yorkers acknowledge this with a "but-of-course" attitude and a warning to filmmakers using their city: Don't get Hollywood on us, and don't expect any more respect than the next schmuck on the street. After all, the birthplace of film on this side of the Atlantic doesn't owe anyone anything.

New York's early motion picture powerhouses included Carl Laemmle, Adolph Zukor, and Cecil B. DeMille, all of whom helped to form local film companies. In 1920, Zukor's Famous Players-Lasky company (soon to become Paramount) opened a new studio in Astoria which would soon be converted to combine motion picture with sound.

While the perpetual sunshine drew most of New York's studios to California in the '20s and '30s, agents and executives still scanned New York stages for talent, realizing, with the advent of "talkies," that many of the stunningly beautiful silent-screen stars had unappealing voices and needed to be replaced with stage actors from Broadway. In the '40s, neo-realism, film noir, and avant-garde filmmaking deepened the power and complexity of image on film. New York, with its combination of grit and glamour, was the perfect setting for the noir sub-genre. In the '50s when Hollywood was focusing on teenyboppers and Technicolor, New York television and filmmakers found increasing meaning in social realism, as seen in the films of Andy Warhol. On The Waterfront (1954) was a revolutionary combination of method acting and on-location shooting (Brooklyn and Hoboken, NJ) whose stark simplicity stood out from the over-elaborate films by producer David O. Selznick and other proponents of the dying studio system. In 1966, Mayor John V. Lindsey established the Mayor's Office of Film, Theater and Broadcasting to encourage and assist productions in NYC.

Realism merged with pageantry in the 1972 production of The Godfather, shot in a converted garage (used for, among other films, Woody Allen's Annie Hall in 1977). This marked the beginning of a decade of great American films, many reflections on the American Dream, New York style. With hindsight, it seems clear that in 1986, when Spike Lee scraped together funding for his second feature-length film, Do the Right Thing, he set the stage for the surge of independent films which would revolutionize the business in the '90s. Spike's newest venture, Summer of Sam (1999), shot in The Bronx, is a look back on the summer of 1977, notorious for a serial killing spree.

On any given day in Manhattan (and the four outer boroughs), there are hundreds of films in production, from the simplest student short to a Meg Ryan/Tom Hanks film which shuts down an eight-block stretch of Columbus Ave. While the West Coast may have the studio market cornered, this town's got the grips and gaffers to beat the pants off those phonies in La-La land.

film festivals

There are festivals in New York to celebrate every type of film and filmmaker. To keep up with it all it's important to keep an eye on The New York Times, and on what's going on at Lincoln Center and the Museum of Modern Art (MoMA), which host prestigious, big-name festivals. The New York Film Festival, held annually in September and October, has been celebrating American and foreign films for several decades. Tickets for this event, particularly opening and closing nights, are snapped up weeks in advance. Another hot festival, particularly as the trend for indies continues to heat up, is the New Directors/New Films series produced by the Film Society of Lincoln Center and held at MoMA in March and April. Here, industry bigwigs and idealistic film students eye one another with wary hunger. (For both of these big festivals call the Film Society of Lincoln Center at 875-5610 for more information.)

Films looking for distribution are also featured at

Ever wanted to find out if Letterman's jokes about the fifty-degree temperature in the Ed Sullivan Theater are well-founded? Luckily, the practice of packing theaters full of eager beavers (usually out-of-towners, who tend to be more excitable than New Yorkers) will allow you to see for yourself. If you request tickets by mail, send in your postcard well in advance of the date you want to see the show, since many tapings have six-to-twelve month waiting lists. Locals tend to get last dibs, so try to have an out-of-town friend make the request on your behalf. Stand-by seats are available for most shows for those who are willing to arrive very early and wait in line.

Late Night with Conan O'Brien — Send a postcard requesting tickets 4-5 months in advance, or drop by before 9am the day of the show to try to get one of the limited same-day tickets. Taping takes place Tuesday through Friday at 5:30pm.
30 Rockefeller Plaza (bet. Fifth and Sixth Aves.), 664-4000

Late Show with David Letterman — Drop a postcard to Dave in the mail for advanced tickets (two tickets per mailing address). For standby tickets call 247-6497 at 11am on taping days; none are issued in person. Taping takes place on Monday through Thursday at 5:30pm.
Ed Sullivan Theater, 1697 Broadway (at 54th St.), 975-5853

TELEVISION
screenings

Live with Regis and Kathy Lee — If you can bear the saccharine content, request tickets in advance via postcard or arrive prior to 8am for standby tickets. The show is taped on weekdays at 9am.
7 Lincoln Sq. (at 67th St. and Columbus Ave.), 465-1000

Montel Williams — Phone or write for tickets for tapings at 10am, 1:30pm, and 3:30pm each Thursday and Friday.
356 West 58th St. (bet. Eighth and Ninth Aves.), 989-8880

Rosie O'Donnell — Send a postcard (March-June only) requesting tickets in advance — there's a twelve month wait so don't hold your breath! Day-of tickets are distributed at 8am. Taping takes place Monday-Thursday at 10am.
30 Rockefeller Plaza (bet. Fifth and Sixth Aves.), 664-4000

Sally Jesse Raphael — Tickets are available by sending a postcard in advance or showing up at least two hours before taping, which is from 1-3pm, Monday thru Wednesday.
515 West 57th St. (bet. Tenth and Eleventh Aves.), 582-1722

Saturday Night Live — Postcards requesting tickets are only accepted in August, when the annual ticket lottery is held. Standby tickets are distributed Saturdays at 9:45am for same-night tapings at 11:30pm. Call in advance for production schedule.
30 Rockefeller Plaza (bet. Fifth and Sixth Aves.), 664-4000

the Independent Feature Film Market in September at the Angelika Film Center, sponsored by the Independent Feature Project. The IFP has been a godsend to filmmakers in New York — but the tickets at the Film Market are priced to cater to serious filmmakers, and are expensive, even with the membership discount. (Call the Angelika Film Center for info at 995-2000).

Once summer arrives, films are screened for free at The HBO/Bryant Park Film Festival (Sixth Ave. at 42nd St.) on Mondays at sunset. For a really authentic New York City experience, bring a picnic dinner, a blanket, and a friend — sit back and watch *King Kong* or *Vertigo* under the stars. (Call the hotline at 512-5700 for more information, and be aware that Tuesdays serves as rain dates.)

During the first two weeks of every August, enjoy air-conditioned splendor and affordable ticket prices at the Harlem Week Black Film Festival at the Adam Clayton Powell Jr. State Office Building (749-5298). Also, keep an eye out for independent arts theaters like the Film Forum (727-8110) which has festivals of its own, year-round.

cinemas

Angelika Film Center

Recently taken over by City Cinemas, this film multiplex remains largely unchanged from its independent days. The films aren't as great as they used to be and they come and go a lot more quickly, but enjoying cappuccino and gelato from the well-stocked café in the lobby is still an option as is the possibility of running into celebrities like Bono or Brad Pitt. Just be careful not to mess with the sassy staff.
Greenwich Village, 18 West Houston St. (at Mercer St.), 995-2000, ❻❿❺❻ *to Broadway-Lafayette St.* ♿

Anthology Film Archives

Started in 1970 as a museum devoted to avant garde cinema, this institution has since become a mecca for established and aspiring artists seeking inspiration and hardened film buffs seeking things even they've never heard of. With a vast library and programming designed to showcase it, an excellent opportunity is provided to see rare foreign films, early works by now-established directors, and legendary but rarely seen Warhol flicks, etc.
East Village, 32 Second Ave. (at 2nd St.), 505-5181, ❻ *to Second Ave.*

Cinema Village

This duplex has a reputation for hosting questionable flicks of the adult persuasion, but it actually accommodates a far wider array of independent films, with themes ranging from homosexuality to kung fu action to African Diaspora.
Greenwich Village, 22 East 12th St. (bet. University Pl. and Fifth Ave.), 924-3363, ❹❿❺❹❺❻ *to 14th St.-Union Sq.*

City Cinemas Village East

By all indications this seems to be just another many-screened showplace for big-budget Hollywood productions, but within the nondescript exterior lies the preserved interior of the old Yiddish Theater complete with its original adornments and multitiered theater-style seating. So for a real treat, buy a ticket for whatever is showing in Theater Number One and get there early to check out this historical landmark.
East Village, 181-189 Second Ave. (at 12th St.), 529-6799, ❹❿❹ ❹❺❻ *to 14th St.-Union Sq.* ♿

Film Forum

Two programs run in this classic setting. Program One has first-run independent and foreign feature films as well as some excellent documentaries. Program Two screens revivals including reissues of individual classics as well as film series featuring everything from the complete works of great, if sometimes obscure, directors to genre films, making this the place to go when nothing at the Sony megaplex seems particularly appealing.
Greenwich Village, 209 West Houston St. (bet. Sixth Ave. and Varick St.), 727-8110, ❶❾ *to Houston St.* ♿

Lincoln Plaza Cinemas

Down the street but still in the shadow of its titan neighbor Sony, this smallish theater doesn't want to do the big-budget Hollywood schtick anyway, preferring foreign and independent film festival standouts and a few surprises.
Upper West Side, 1886 Broadway (at 62nd St.), 757-2280, ❹❿❹❹❿❶❾ *to 59th St.-Columbus Circle* ♿

NYU's Program Board

By the students, for the students, and offered at the oh-so-student-friendly rate of $2 a pop. The theater's screen spans a minimal width and metallic fold-up chairs do little to keep viewers comfortable, but the cash saved can readily be shoved into a back pocket for extra padding.
Greenwich Village, 566 LaGuardia Pl. (bet. 3rd and 4th Sts.), 998-4999, ❹❿❹❹❿❺❻ *to West 4th St.-Washington Sq.*

Ocularis

On Sunday evenings, this arts and performance space in a converted mayonnaise factory, screens non-commercial independent films, foreign films and classics together with short and medium length works by independent film makers. Though the folding chairs may leave you with a stiff back, the quality of the productions and the price ($5) are worth it. At Galapagos Art Performance Space.
Williamsburg, Brooklyn, 70 North 6th St. (bet. Wythe and Kent Aves.), (718) 388-8713, ❶ *to Bedford Ave.* ♿

The Paris

Highbrow European first runs and revivals show at this tiny midtown movie house behind the Plaza Hotel. Very civilized.
Midtown, 4 West 58th St. (bet. Fifth and Sixth Aves.), 688-3800, ❿❿ *to Fifth Ave.* ♿

Quad Cinema

As can be expected with most theaters which run primarily independent flicks, the screens here are smaller than in first-run theaters. But the films, which include many foreign and revival series, are so choice that screen size is the last thing considered. Tucked away from heavy street traffic on 13th St., and with only 4 screens hosting its wares,

there's little chance the intimate, neighborhood appeal of this movie house will be mainstreamed any time soon.
Greenwich Village, 34 West 13th St. (bet. Fifth and Sixth Aves.), 225-8800, ❶❻❼❹❺❻ *to 14th St.-Union Sq.* ♿

The Screening Room
A place to catch independent and foreign film hits or classics like *Breakfast at Tiffany's* (shown every Sunday). The unique seating makes it feel as comfy as a Blockbuster night, without the Bud Light and the remote. Diners at the restaurant next door get seated first for shows, so take a dinner-and-movie date.
TriBeCa, 54 Varick St. (at Canal St.), 334-2100, ❶❾ *to Canal St.* ♿

Sony IMAX at Lincoln Center
By far the multiplex's coolest attraction: Nature films, which were always amusing for their magnificent underwater action shots and close-ups of snouts and bug eyes, have given way a bit to plot-oriented pieces (the idea of plot is used very liberally). The show on New York City's history draws a crowd.
Upper West Side, 1992 Broadway (at 68th St.), 336-5000, ❶❾ *to 66th St.-Lincoln Center* ♿

Walter Reade Theater/Film Society of Lincoln Center
Since 1985, this luxurious theater has been the home of NYC's elite film club, which screens everything from Jim Carrey to Jean-Luc Godard, with an emphasis on the latter end of the spectrum. NewDirectors/New Films, in conjunction with MoMA, has premiered work by such directors as Pedro Almodóvar and Peter Greenaway, while film festivals sport titles like "Rendez-Vous with French Cinema Today." Overall, rich in retro and avant-

garde classics, just avoid the post-film talk if you fear pretension.
Upper West Side, 70 Lincoln Center Plaza (at Columbus Ave.), 875-5600, ❶❾ *to 66th St.-Lincoln Center* ♿

Worldwide Cinemas
Inflation recently pushed the price per movie from two bucks to three, but it's still a great deal for slightly older films. Groups of teenagers sometimes talk back to the screen.
Midtown, 340 West 50th St. (bet. Eighth and Ninth Aves.), 246-1583, ❻❺ *50th St.* ♿

The Ziegfeld Theater
This namesake of the old show palace that housed the Ziegfeld Follies restores some of the glamour and sense of occasion to the typical movie-dinner date. The biggest and best screen in town on which to see blockbuster new releases and re-mastered old ones like *Vertigo*, *Lawrence of Arabia*, and the *Star Wars* Trilogy.
Midtown, 141 West 54th St. (bet. Sixth and Seventh Aves.), 765-7600, ❶❶❻ *to Seventh Ave.*

video & film stores

Anime Crash
Mecca of Asian pop culture, specializing in Japanimation and Hong Kong Action videos, books, magazines, and general kitsch, with Sanrio merchandise and Japanese model kits.
Greenwich Village, 13 East 4th St. (bet. Broadway and Lafayette St.), 254-4670, MC, V, AmEx, Diners, D, ❻❻❻ *to Broadway-Lafayette St.,* ❻ *to Bleecker St.*

Jerry Ohlinger's Movie Material Store, Inc.
Shoeboxes of old publicity shots, movie stills, and posters crowd this treasure trove of memora-

bilia for avid film buffs; color stills go for around $5.50. Don't miss the autographed pics of Orson Welles and Montgomery Clift by the door.
Chelsea, 242 West 14th St. (bet. Seventh and Eighth Aves.), 989-0869, MC, V, AmEx, D, ❶❻❻ *to 14th St.,* ❶ *to Eighth Ave.*

Kim's Video
The most interesting selection of videos in town; everything from the typical new releases to the most esoteric arthouse, foreign and genre flicks. Be forewarned, most everything is arranged by director or some odd category — come with something in mind or deal with the staff, which is knowledgeable, but eager to prove it.
East Village, 85 Ave. A (bet. 5th and 6th Sts.), 529-3410, MC, V, AmEx, ❻ *to Second Ave.* ♿

Kim's Video and Music
Less pedantic than their East Village counterparts, the staff here still knows what's up and has no qualms about either helping you sift though a gaggle of out-there directors, or matching your trivia on obscure Weimar actresses. Better foreign film selection at this location.
Greenwich Village, 350 Bleecker St. (at West 10th St.), 675-8996, MC, V, AmEx, ❶❾ *to Christopher St.-Sheridan Sq.*

UEE
Find out who's hot in Hong Kong cinema or pick up on the craze of renting the most recent soaps, beauty pageants and live concerts you didn't catch the first time around. $100 rents you 60 videos (75 if you take advantage of "rent 4 get 1 free"), which translates to 25 at Blockbuster.
Chinatown, 118 Mott St., 219-0327, Cash Only, ❻❿❻❻❷❻ *to Canal St.* ♿

music

m·u·s·i·c

To paraphrase John Phillip Sousa, music will endure "as long as people hear it through their feet instead of their brains." This is especially pertinent to live music, the stuff that gets us out there on the streets and in the clubs rather than sitting at home listening to the radio or watching that cultural placebo, MTV.

New York's small-club music scene has been at the heart of many of the movements that have defined American culture over the last century, and as more venues have sprung up over the last decade, like weeds pushing through the largest sidewalk in the world, music has taken on an increasingly central role in a New York evening.

"Eclectic" is one of everyone's favorite buzz words, and it's probably the best word to describe the current New York City music scene. If you've heard it on the radio, seen it in the record store, or hummed it to yourself and have no idea where you got it, chances are you'll find it in New York, alongside several dozen imitations, variations, and interpretations of it. The city that never sleeps — or as Ani DiFranco more aptly put it, "the city that never shuts up" — is restless for a reason.

Because of New York's status as the nation's cultural center, music exists here on both a national and a local level. Almost every night visitors can catch large touring acts playing close by. A typical week might see Willie Nelson at Tramps on Sunday, Vanilla Ice at CBGB on Monday, Bonnie Raitt at nearby Long Island's Jones Beach on Tuesday, Joan Baez at Carnegie Hall on Wednesday, an intimate Thursday evening with Tori Amos, at Irving Plaza followed by a packed-house encore at Madison Square Garden on Friday, and Saturday night is anybody's guess — from Aerosmith to ZZ Top, you'll find it here!

For those seeking local fare, the menu is extensive and varied. Garage acts blare out of every open door in the East Village, while Lincoln Center hosts star-studded shows, like one with David Bowie conducting. Cover bands rule the night at Wetlands, while singer-songwriters ply their acoustic trade at The Bitter End. Jazz riffs waft through the streets surrounding Blue Note, unaware of the lounge acts derived from them across town at the Fez under Time Cafe (themselves in the dark that, just up the street at the Nuyorican Poet's Café, they are being experimented with and transformed into a new musical form by a young unknown). Meanwhile, on every street corner and subway platform in Manhattan, it seems that someone has taken up the guitar, keyboard, klezmer, or tabla, and is dying to entertain you.

If "going out to see some bands" sounds like something you could have just done in your hometown, treat yourself to some of New York's best-kept secrets: Woody Allen indulges his third passion, the clarinet, Mondays at The Hotel Carlyle, though at $50 the tickets are a little high, even by New York standards; The Mingus Big Band's regularly sold-out shows have become an institution at Fez under Time Cafe on Thursday nights for a more reasonable $18; or, for, about the same price, you can catch a special program series at the Bottom Line such as "Nightbirds" or "Required Listening," where four or five top artists share the stage and swap songs and stories in round-robin fashion. High quality versions on a smaller and cheaper scale abound, such as the artist tribute series at The Living Room.

As in almost any major city, there are plenty of places to hang with friends and hear some good music. New York, though, stands out in this way particularly: At a high proportion of its clubs, music is the primary attraction, rather than being a buzz in the background. In other words, many New York City venues are considered listening rooms, and that's what you're expected to do. A number of clubs even have the bar in a separate room to keep the socializing and the clinking of glasses isolated from the music, a rare treat for artists who often have to struggle to be the center of attention at their own gig. Keep this in mind when you're sampling the venue menu, and open yourself up to the variety and caliber of music this town has to offer.

acoustic music
u•n•p•l•u•g•g•e•d

The best musicians in the world are in New York City, and those on the acoustic scene are no exception. Whether it's Eddie from Ohio, Dave's True Story, or Jim's Big Ego, you can find your choice act, and you can practically sit in their laps while they play; happily, small clubs are where it's at these days.

The acoustic scene is thriving. Singer-songwriters play not only their own sets, but often share stages with each other, jamming together, sharing audiences, lending support. Songwriter circles abound from smaller rooms like **The Bitter End** (147 Bleecker St., 673-7030) and **Dark Star Lounge** (158 West 72nd St., 362-2590) to the larger stages, such as at **Bottom Line** (15 West 4th St., 228-7880).

This resurgence may be due to the turn towards acoustic-driven music in the pop charts, with artists such as Shawn Colvin, Elliot Smith, and Duncan Sheik pushing things along. And it is not surprising that many of these artists have a home base in New York City. The activity and romance of the world's most crowded, lively, and idiosyncratic town is a constant source of inspiration for songwriters and musicians alike.

In the past few years, many new clubs have sprung up to house acoustic music, among them **Eureka Joe** (168 Fifth Ave., 741-7500), **The Baggot Inn** (82 West 3rd St., 477-0622), and, for the ultra-hip, **The Living Room** (84 Stanton St., 533-7237). Industry showcases happen all over the place, downtown from **Mercury Lounge** (217 E. Houston St., 260-1214) and **CB's 313 Gallery** (313 Bowery, 677-

0455), on up to **Le Bar Bat** (311 West 57th St., 307-7228). And recent large-scale productions, such as the CMJ Music Festival and the popular New York-based television program Sessions at West 54th (PBS) have been proof that NYC is seen as a crucial hub for new music.

The greatest thing about seeing live acoustic music in New York is how close the audience can get to the performers. At **The Bitter End**, a performer might borrow a corner of your table for his or her glass of water. At Columbia University's **Postcrypt Coffeehouse** (Broadway and 116th St., 854-1953), the room is so well-suited for acoustics that there is no sound system at all, just the natural resonance of guitar and vocals playing off 200-year-old brick walls. You can be as close to Lou Reed at **Knitting Factory** (74 Leonard St., 219-3006) as you were to your taxi driver earlier that day. If this sort of intensity and intimacy is important to you when you go out to hear live music, New York's acoustic scene is made for you.

Suzanne Vega played some of her first shows "unplugged" in Morningside Heights

---

country time

Country music is hard to come by in New York City, even harder than most people would believe. Although WKCR out of Columbia University has some fine country, western, and honky tonk programming — everything from Hank Williams, Sr. to Jimmy Rodgers to Patsy Cline — there is not one commercial radio station that plays country music in Manhattan on a regular basis. And if you think finding music on the dial is tough, you should try finding it live.

The Rodeo Bar & Grill (375 Third Ave., 683-6500)

is an establishment that has, along with other music types, great country. Get there early for one of the few tables up front or be prepared to stand. Another hidden secret is the **Cowgirl Hall of Fame** (519 Hudson St., 633-1133). Curator Sherry Holmes has created a unique blend of southern food and cowgirl attire that covers the walls, and you can expect to hear Patsy Montana or any one of the cowgirl stars crooning in the background.

For a scene right out of a movie, be sure to drop by **Hogs & Heifers** (859 Washington St., 929-0655). This joint has one heck of a jukebox and frequently a strange mix of cowboys and bikers. For live music every Monday night, **9C** (700 East 9th St.,

Holding a music festival in New York City is kind of like having "Ocean Day" at Sea World, or having "Birthday Day" at, well, a place where they have birthdays every day. On the slowest weeknight there are over one hundred acts playing in Manhattan alone, and it would take a city that just doesn't know when to quit to try and hold music festivals in the middle of all that.

Fortunately, New York is just such a place. Not only are there festivals right in the middle of the action, but they tend to bring new and innovative elements to the scene. Take for instance the **Digital Club Festival** (www.digitalclubfest.com), only a few years old and already a major summer event. Produced by Knitting Factory's Michael Dorf and Irving Plaza's Andrew Rasiej, the Festival involves four nights of music spread out over twenty New York clubs. Local participants purchase a pass that entitles them to general admission for all of the shows for the entire period. But the big audience is the one watching the 24-hour a day internet broadcasts and rebroadcasts of shows, participating in on-line discussions about the bands, purchasing their CDs, and voting on the best acts. More than 20,000 viewers physically attend the festival, while several hundred thousand around the world attend via computer, making the New York club scene the biggest musical event on-line as well as off.

For national acts, though, the it-festival is the immensely popular (and mostly free) **SummerStage** (www.summerstage.org) held in Central Park throughout June, July, and August. Sponsored by the city and private donors, SummerStage features popular headliners as well as world beat artists, classical music, electronica, DJs, lectures, work-shops, dance classes, drum circles, and more. Central Park is an adventure any day, but the first show of SummerStage signals the true beginning of summer for any concert-going New Yorker.

New York has always been famous as the country's primary source of jazz; this is no less true in the festival arena. **The Bell Atlantic Jazz Festival** (www.jazzfest.com), held in early June, and the **JVC Jazz Festival New York** (www.jvc.com), held immediately after, are showcases for upcoming talent as well as gatherings for extant heroes.

The festival list goes on in size and variety. The **CMJ MusicFest** (www.cmj.com), held in the New York Hilton over four days in September, is the world's largest music industry gathering, and claims to have launched the careers of bands ranging from R.E.M. to Hole. The recent upstart **Guinness Fleadh**, held in June on Randall's Island between Manhattan and Queens, is already the largest Irish festival going, featuring more superstar acts than you can raise a pint to.

Although there's no dearth of culture in leaner months, almost all of New York's festivals take place in the summer ones. Perhaps this is because warmer weather attracts the crowds, but it has been suggested — and this is just a rumor, mind you — that with the healthy summer music scene, it just takes nine months to recuperate.

ani difranco
festival queen

358-0048) hosts some of the best musicians in the city. The cozy atmosphere allows you to interact with the musicians, so don't be afraid to say howdy and support the artists.

For big country acts like Willie Nelson, Merle Haggard, and more contemporary stars, be sure to follow the listings at **Tramps** (51 West 21st St., 544-1666). These artists sell out fast, so be sure to purchase your tickets ahead of time. Tramps has become the city's leader in bringing the best national musicians into the city to play at the club level. **Bottom Line** (15 West 4th St., 228-7880), though it doesn't bring in as much country as Tramps, maintains a roster of musicians of the highest caliber: Lyle Lovett, Ramblin' Jack Elliot, and June Carter Cash have all appeared there recently. The tables are small and tight, but the sound system is excellent and the audience is church-mouse quiet during the shows.

So being a country music fan in New York City is not so bad if you know where to look. Don't expect Garth to play the Park again in the near future, but keep up on the country scene by listening to the Rowdy Redneck — last heard working Sunday afternoons on WKCR — and follow the listings for Tramps, Bottom Line, and Rodeo Bar & Grill. Otherwise, keep your boots shined, and don't be afraid to be country in the city.

dave's true story

~ *interview*

*After more than seven years as New York's most clever jazz combo, **Dave's True Story** singer Kelly Flint and songwriter/guitarist Dave Cantor have built up a loyal audience who follow them from club to club for Dave's brilliantly funny lyrics delivered by Kelly's heartbreaking voice. You can see where they're playing next by pointing your mouse to www.davestruestory.com.*

How does NYC compare to other cities where you've performed?
Dave: Aside from the money aspect, New York has good venues. Audiences are with few exceptions a lot of fun. San Francisco and its environs is another great place for venues and audiences.

Kelly: Well, in Amsterdam they wanted me to bite, instead of autograph, our CD booklet. I've never had a request like that in NY.

What is the NYC music scene's best-kept secret?
D: Hell, if I knew, it wouldn't be much of a secret.
K: Dave's True Story.

What's the strangest experience you've ever had at a NYC gig?
D: As a solo performer, I once played on the same night as a guy who stabbed a pot roast with a butcher knife while singing along to a tape of one of Charles Manson's songs.
K: God, how can I beat that? I dreamed we were playing the Bottom Line and I looked down and I was naked. Does that count?

Describe the perfect audience.
D: Listens attentively, laughs at the right places, applauds wildly while throwing panties and twenty dollar bills onto the stage.
K: Perfectly silent and adoring while I'm singing, laughing uncontrollably at all my jokes while throwing fifty dollar bills onto the stage.

Where do you go to listen to live music?
D&K: Arlene Grocery, Fez under Time Cafe, Bottom Line, The Living Room, CB's 313 Gallery, and Den of Cin, to name a few.

What do you love about New York?
D: Years ago I saw the Scorsese movie *After Hours* and wished my life were more like that. Then I moved back to New York and for the first few years, my life was a lot like that.
K: It's home.

What do you hate about New York?
D: Crowded streets, idiots on bikes, Giuliani, and not enough Starbucks.
K: It's home.

How has New York shaped you as an artist?
D: It has crushed my spirit and robbed me of the will to live.
K: I no longer take %$#! from anybody, anywhere because I'm right most of the time.

*Michael Dorf became a fixture on the New York music scene when he emigrated from Wisconsin in 1987 to found the **Knitting Factory** — originally a small performance space on Houston St., now New York's alternative darling, known for its avant-garde jazz shows and the recordings it releases through Knitting Factory Records. In 1994, Dorf founded the Digital Club Festival, bringing international attention to local artists and securing himself as a cornerstone of the city's music scene.*

What is the mission of the Knitting Factory?
We pay attention to being a conduit between the artist and the fan. As a performance venue, we try to pay as much attention to the artist['s] experience as well as the customer[s']...

How do you decide what gets played at the Knitting Factory?
Well, now that we have more stages we can look for different things. I used to say, "Let's look for the most left of center, most cutting edge performers." But now that we have so many mouths to feed, we've taken a more balanced approached in our programming.

How did Knitting Factory Records get started?
I came to New York to get involved in the record business, and I failed trying to run a small record label before starting the club. So very quickly after [the Knitting Factory] opened, I started Knitting Factory Records, and to me that was even more of an opportunity to be a conduit between the people and the artist. Because if maybe fifty people came to a show, and I recorded it live, we might be able to sell five hundred or two thousand discs of that show and we are now able to reach more people on a larger scale. And that led to festival production, getting more people to pay attention to what we're trying to do with the artistic community.

Is that how the Digital Club Music Festival came about?
Yes. The festival also happened at the right time and the right place. When the Knitting Factory moved from Houston St. to TriBeCa in 1994, that was the year that the New Music Seminar went out of business. So I called all the club owners and we created the festival, mostly me and Andrew Rasiej from Irving Plaza. We got Apple to sponsor it originally, then it was the Intel Music Festival, and now Andrew and I are partners on the Digital Club Festival.

What is your goal with the festival?
Our goal is to reach as many people around the world as we can and try to let them go club hopping in New York for four days.

How does New York compare with other cities?
New York is the greatest music scene in the world. No question about it. There are certainly a lot of other great music scenes, but there's nothing like New York, period. The local community is extremely vivacious right now, and it is a very, very strong community.

Who are your favorite New York artists?
It's an impossible question for anyone who's familiar with this scene to answer. My favorite artists are the ones who are not mad at me right now.

Where else would you encourage visitors to see live music?
You've got to check out classic places like The Village Vanguard, CBGB, Irving Plaza, and Tramps, but you've also got to check out cool event happenings, whether it's DJ Spooky doing something in a loft, or something at the AlterKnit Theatre (the Knitting Factory's alternative stage). There are always those things going on, it's just looking in *The Village Voice* and finding them.

~ interview

*Jake Stigers and Keith Cotton form the core of the piano-driven New York pop group **Doublewide**, which has been performing in NYC for the past 3½ years. Doublewide can be regularly seen at the hippest clubs in the East Village.*

What makes New York stand out in an artist's mind?
New York can be a tough place to play, while other cities can be easier because they don't have as much live music as New York does. The New York audience can get overloaded.

What are your favorite things to do in New York?
Drink Robitussin and ride the Staten Island Ferry.

Besides yourselves, who are your favorite New York bands and artists?
It depends if you're talking old school, like Willie Nile, or new school, which can be most anything you might stumble upon on a night out down on Ludlow Street.

Where do you go to listen to live music?
Den of Cin, Arlene Grocery, and Mercury Lounge.

Describe the worst show you've ever had.
The worst night was when we had three people in the audience, two of which were heckling us. The best part is that one of the hecklers was Keith's girlfriend.

Describe your best show.
The best was a night that we opened for a band named Mini-King at Mercury Lounge. We felt bad for the headline act that night after we got done with the room.

What's your dream gig?
Opening for Supertramp during the first live music telecast from the moon.

What's the best New York has to offer?
We love the drag queens.

What's the worst?
We hate Mayor Guiliani and the subway system. We really miss the porn industry and the way Times Square used to be.

~ *interview*

d o u b l e w i d e

*Matt Winters books the **Postcrypt Coffeehouse** at Columbia University, the nation's oldest collegiate venue, famous for its acoustic-only policy and its role in the careers of artists like Ani DiFranco and Suzanne Vega. He is also the director of the American department and host of "The Moonshine Show" for WKCR 89.9FM, the nation's first regularly broadcasting FM station.*

~ interview

What sets the Postcrypt apart from other venues?
The space and the atmosphere. The Postcrypt is completely acoustic; there are no microphones and no P.A. The room carries the sound completely, and both the performers and the audience receive a very clear, very natural sound. We light the room with candles and minimal stage lamps and that creates a relaxed, gothic atmosphere. People like to play with the wax.

How do you pick artists for the Postcrypt?
Any way we can. Lots of artists send us their press kits, and we review those and book based on their demo tapes and CDs. We book performers who play at our open stages, which we hold about once per month. We take recommendations of other venues and people in the know. We also stumble across artists at other venues & festivals.

How strong is the New York music scene in terms of local artists?
It's so strong that one can go for years without hearing about some of the best artists. New York is such a great place to be a songwriter, in my opinion, because there are so many things to write songs about that one can't find elsewhere. Whatever type of music one is interested in, there are people playing it, and more importantly, there is a venue for that type of music.

What is the value of the small musician in New York, a place that offers so many larger, national-scale distractions?
I think that small musicians have an edge up in many ways on a lot of national acts. The biggest

reason for that is the fact that they will work for cheaper. I love to get "big name" acts into the Postcrypt, but when I can get three very talented but lesser known people for the same amount of money or less, I'm going to opt for that. I also think that smaller musicians are a lot more genuine and a lot more fun to go and hear. There's a very different feeling at the Postcrypt, where I can ask Howard Emerson what the heck he just did on his guitar to make that noise versus seeing Corey Harris at Irving Plaza. The fact that our audience can approach any of our performers after a show is a terrific, terrific asset.

Why do you think so many small venues have sprung up over the last ten years?
Because there's an audience for it. One also has to note that half of the venues that have sprung up have changed their format or closed completely. But I think people look for a casual atmosphere, where they can hear a lot of good music (and probably some not-so-good music) at a cheap price. It's a thing to do in New York: go out with some friends and hear some acts that you've never even heard of before and see what you get.

How friendly is radio to local artists?
I think that radio is very unfriendly, truth be told. The largest station in New York that broadcasts acoustic and folk music has a tendency to ignore the local scene in favor of national artists. I don't find that there's enough folk and acoustic music on the air in New York, compared to a scene like Boston's where it's all over the place.

What would you like to see in New York radio?
I'd like to see more folk and acoustic music, and I'd like to see more visibility for all of the different radio stations in the print media. I think that they really under-report what is going on in New York, with the exception of David Hinckley's excellent column in the *Daily News*.

What are your favorite New York acts?
I have way too many to name.

What are your favorite venues?
The Postcrypt is obviously my favorite for many reasons. But I might also be found at The Fort at Sidewalk Cafe, The Bitter End, Wetlands, or even Mercury Lounge when I'm digging a rock 'n' roll show.

Acme Underground

All cleaned up and ready to rock and roll: This low-frills basement stage got a makeover and a brand new sound system last year for its spruced-up lineups. Have legitimate ID ready; the doorman is not taking any sorry excuses.

alternative rock
Greenwich Village, 9 Great Jones St. (bet. Broadway and Lafayette St.), 420-1934, Cash Only, Cover: $5-$10, Open: 7pm-4am, **N R** *to 8th St.-NYU,* **6** *to Astor Pl.* ⮐

Arlene Grocery

Only in existence for a couple of years now, Arlene has quickly established itself as one of the premiere showcasing venues for many of the New York record labels. The bands play for free here to build up a fan base and get their names out. Square room, elevated stage, great sound system. Food next door, full bar.

acoustic, pop, rock, ska
Lower East Side, 95 Stanton St. (bet. Ludlow and Orchard Sts.), 358-1633, www.arlenegrocery. com, Cash Only, Cover: Free, Open: 6pm-4am, **F** *to Second Ave.* ♿ ⮐ **21+**

The Baggot Inn

A darkly lit music venue in the heart of the Village. A great place to see some of your favorite acoustic singer/ songwriters, with plenty of table seating and dollar draft happy hours. No food, full bar.

acoustic, pop, rock
Greenwich Village, 82 West 3rd St. (bet. Thompson and Sullivan Sts.), 477-0622, www.thebaggot inn.com, MC, V, AmEx, Cover: free-$5, Open: 11am-4am, **A B C D E F Q** *to West 4th St.- Washington Sq.* ⮐ **21+**

The Bitter End

Opened 40 years ago, The Bitter End has seen countless performers rise from its stage to stardom, including Bob Dylan, Joni Mitchell, Tracy Chapman, and Jackson Browne. Boasting a friendly atmosphere and great live music, The Bitter End is perhaps the most famous small club in New York. No food, full bar.

blues, folk, funk, R&B, rock
Greenwich Village, 147 Bleecker St. (bet. Thompson St. and La-Guardia Pl.), 673-7030, www. bitterend.com, MC, V, AmEx, Cover: $5-$10, Open: M-F 7pm-2am, Sa-Su 7pm-4am, **A B C D E F Q** *West 4th St.-Washington Sq.* ♿ ⮐ **21+**

Blue Note

Though the regular features are a bit of an assault on the pocketbook, the five dollar after-hours shows on Fridays and Saturdays are a real bargain. Don't miss B.B. King's annual visit, and if you have the money to spend, see some of the national jazz acts that come through that you won't see anywhere else. Full continental menu, full bar.

jazz
Greenwich Village, 131 West 3rd St. (bet. MacDougal St. and 6th Ave.), 475-8592, www.bluenote. net, MC, V, AmEx, Cover: $25 and up, Open: Su noon-6pm and 7pm-2am, M-Th 7pm-2am, F-Sa 7pm-4am, **A B C D E F Q** *to West 4th St.-Washington Sq.* ⮐

Bottom Line

One of New York's oldest and most celebrated venues, beloved by performers and audiences alike. Welcomes local and national acts ranging from '70s artists Jimmy Webb, John Hiatt, and Paul Simon to contemporary faves Dan Bern, Jill Sobule, and David Wilcox. A true "listening room." Shows are at 7:30pm and 10:30pm. Full kitchen, full bar.

all genres and periods
Greenwich Village, 15 West 4th St. (at Mercer St.), 228-7880, Cash Only, Cover: $15-$25, Open: 10am-11pm (box office), **N R** *to 8th St.-NYU,* **6** *to Bleecker St.* ♿ **18+**

Bowery Ballroom

Less than two years old, the Bowery Ballroom is quickly earning a reputation as one of the best-kept secrets in New York. A gothic-decorated candlelit balcony overlooking a large main room gives guests the feeling that they've stepped into a Transylvanian nightclub. The Bowery is run by another of New York's premiere venues, the Mercury Lounge, and somehow manages to be more spacious and more intimate at the same time. Shows run about five nights a week. No food, full bar.

acoustic, country, eclectic, hip-hop, latin, pop
East Village, 6 Delancey St. (bet. Bowery and Chrystie St.), 533-2111, MC, V, Cover: $10-$20, Open: 8pm-1am, **B D Q** *to Grand St.* ♿ ⮐

Brownies

One of New York's premiere venues for showcasing bands not quite on the full-blown commercial radio scene; many play here regularly just before they begin the climb up the charts. Sunday shows all ages. No food, full bar.

blues, rock
East Village, 169 Ave. A (bet. 10th and 11th Sts.), 420-8392, MC, V, AmEx, Cover: $6-$10, Open: 7pm-3am, **6** *to Astor Pl.,* **L** *to 1st Ave.* ♿ ⮐ **21+**

♿	= wheelchair accessible
⮐	= smoking permitted
21+	= must be 21 years old
18+	= must be 18 years old

Carnegie Hall

Still the reigning champ of bourgeois nightlife, this legendary institution is the artist's Valhalla. Concerts usually take place every night of the week except July-August, when the Hall is closed for the season. The majority of acts are classical, but you still may catch the occasional Joan Baez or David Bowie if you're lucky. Adjoining restaurant and bar serves American cuisine.

classical, pop, special events
Midtown, 881 Seventh Ave. (at 57th St.), 247-7800, www.carnegiehall.org, MC, V, AmEx, Cover: $16-$150, Open: 2pm-4pm, 8pm-10pm, **NR** *to 57th St.* ⅼ

CBGB

One of the most famous and longstanding venues in New York, CBGB has been a mecca for artists since the 1970s, launching acts like Blondie, Ramones, Talking Heads, Live, Helmet, and Living Colour. You can still catch local and national acts every night of the week as CBGB celebrates its 25th anniversary. No food, full bar.

alternative, pop, rock
East Village, 315 Bowery (at Bleecker St.), 982-4052, www.cbgb.com, Cash Only, Cover: $3-$12, Open: 7pm-4am, **G** *to Bleecker St.* ⅼ ↩

CB's 313 Gallery

The acoustic sibling of the renowned CBGB's rock club next door. Its high ceiling, wood floor, and provocative artwork give it a unique urban atmosphere. The club is outfitted with a superior sound system and staff, and offers some of the best acoustic-based music in town. A downstairs lounge, with DJ, serves brick oven pizza. No food, full bar.

acoustic, electronica, folk, rock

East Village, 313 Bowery (at Bleecker St.), 677-0455, www.cbgb.com, MC, V, AmEx, Diners, D, Cover: $5-$6, Open: 12pm-2am, **F** *to Second Ave.,* **G** *to Bleecker St.* ⅼ ↩ *21+*

Coney Island High

It's not a high school and it's not on Coney Island, but with a different theme every night of the week, this carnival-motif venue offers a sideshow of the city's more rockin' acts. Check out established and national performers downstairs and breaking bands upstairs, or even pick up some Manic Panic hair dye at the new Coney Island High Commissary. No food, full bar.

hardcore, metal, punk, rock, ska
East Village, 15 St. Marks Pl. (bet. 2nd and 3rd Aves.), 674-7959, www.coneyhigh.com, AmEx, Cover: $5-$15, Open: 7pm-4am, **G** *to Astor Pl.* ⅼ ↩

Connolly's

You can't be Irish in New York if you haven't heard of Black 47, the Dublin rock band, a musical hero to the local Irish community. Black 47 plays at Connolly's every Saturday, with other acts occasionally playing the odd night. Connolly's is one of the few venues in New York centered around a single band. Full menu, full bar (of course).

Irish rock
Midtown, 14 East 47th St. (bet. Fifth and Madison Aves.), 867-3767, www.connollysnyc.com, MC, V, AmEx, Cover: $10, Open: 11am-4am, **BDFQ** *to 47-50th Sts.-Rockefeller Center* ⅼ ↩

Continental

Everybody from Patti Smith to The Ramones have played this famous East Village club. Even Guns n' Roses could be seen here before they hit it big. There's an indoor ATM for the cash-strapped. No food, full bar.

hard rock, ska
East Village, 25 Third Ave. (at St. Marks Pl.), 529-6924, www.nytrash.com/continental, Cash Only, Cover: Free-$5, Open: 4pm-4am, **G** *to Bleecker St.* ⅼ ↩ *21+*

Cotton Club

A Harlem legend since before you were born, the Cotton Club is still kicking for the ongoing Harlem renaissance and will probably be around for a few more. Show times vary widely and you must call for reservations. The "don't miss": $25 gospel brunches every weekend. Full southern menu and full bar.

gospel, jazz, swing
Harlem, 656 West 125th St. (bet. Broadway and Riverside Dr.), 663-7980, MC, V, Cover: $15-$30, Open: varies by show, **10** *to 125th St.* *21+*

Dark Star Lounge

Clean and cozy, with a grand piano and an even grander menu. Its setting, uptown and away from the trendiness of the East and West Villages, has made it attractive to neighborhood musicians of some stature, such as Jeff Gollub, Holly Palmer, and drummer for Shawn Colvin, Shawn Pelton. Sunday nights host the popular Michael Raye's Soul Gathering. Full menu, full bar.

acoustic, blues, country, jazz, R&B
Upper West Side, 158 West 72nd St. (bet. Broadway and Columbus Ave.), 362-2590, www.thetriad.com, MC, V, AmEx, D, Cover: $5-$10, Open: 5pm-4am, **1239** *to 72nd St.* ⅼ ↩

Den of Cin

One of the East Village's newest clubs. A small listening room underneath the famous Two Boots Video. A comfortable space to hear up-and-coming local and touring artists. Many performers play solo here because of the small space, which only adds to the intimacy of the show. Beer and wine available.

acoustic, pop, solo artists
East Village, 44 Ave. A (at 3rd St.), 613-1670, Cash Only, No cover, Open: 8pm-1am, **F** *to Second Ave.* ⌐ **21+**

Don't Tell Mama

Wrest control of the microphone away from fellow exhibitionists at this extrovert's paradise where patrons are invited to sing along with the waitstaff, the pianist, and the mixed gay/straight clientele.

piano bar, pop
Midtown, 343 West 46th St. (bet. Eighth and Ninth Aves.), 757-0788, MC, V, AmEx, Diners, Cover: $10-$20, Open: 4pm-4am, **C E** *to 50th St.* ⌐

Downtime

A large room with high ceilings, an upper level with a pool table, pinball, and plenty of seating at the bar and at tables makes this a comfortable room to listen to emergent New York bands. One of the best open mic nights in town (Thurs.). No food, full bar.

hiphop, pop, rock
Midtown, 251 West 30th St. (bet. 7th and 8th Aves.), 695-2747, MC, V, AmEx, Cover: $5-$10, Open: W-Sa 5pm-4am, **1 9** *to 28th St.* ⌐ **21+**

The Duplex

This piano bar right off Sheridan Sq. has been providing live show tunes for years. A mature contingent lingers here, so tweed is more prevalent than muscle-tees. Large and elegantly decorated, the legendary space offers cabaret upstairs; shows are varied and frequent, so make reservations. Younger men may find the paternalistic attitude grating.

cabaret

Greenwich Village, 61 Christopher St. (at Seventh Ave. South), 255-5438, Cash Only, Cover: Free, Open: 4pm-4am, **1 9** *to Christopher St.-Sheridan Sq.* ⌐

Elbow Room

A long, spacious room with comfy couches along the wall. Very hip and retro vibe, often presenting national touring acts along with New York's hardest rockin' bands. You can often catch some favorite radio bands here before they are headlining at Irving Plaza.

pop, rock
Greenwich Village, 144 Bleecker St. (bet. Thompson St. and La-Guardia Pl.), 979-8434, www. elbowroom.com, MC, V, AmEx, Cover: $5-$15, Open: 6pm-4am, **A B C D E F Q** *to West 4th St.-Washington Sq.* ⌐ **21+**

Fez under Time Cafe

Originally the sight of Sticky Mike's, a Warhol hangout, now housing hip singer-songwriters like Ellis Paul, Peter Mulvey, and Jennifer Kimball. Features the occasional big name appearance, like Sheryl Crow or Joni Mitchell. This unique room has mirrored columns and sparkly vinyl booths, and every so often the room vibrates from the subway train passing by underneath. Hidden treasure: the Mingus Big Band every Thursday night. Full menu, full bar.

acoustic, comedy, jazz, rock, singer-songwritter
East Village, 380 Lafayette St. (at Great Jones St.), 533-3000, MC, V, AmEx, Cover: $8-$15, Open: Su-Th 6pm-2am, F-Sa 6pm-4am, **6** *to Bleecker St.,* ⌐ **21+** *(on weekends)*

The Fort at Sidewalk Cafe

Before moving to the backroom of the Sidewalk Cafe, the Fort was an after-hours club on the Lower East Side. It still retains

its underground appeal, centered around manager Lach's Anti-Folk Anti-Hoot on Mondays, which is an open mic unlike others in the Bleecker St. folk scene. Sidewalk Cafe features one of the cheapest breakfast specials in NYC, as well as a full menu and bar.

folk, anti-folk, rock
East Village, 94 Ave. A (at 6th St.), 473-7373, MC, V, AmEx, Cover: $3, Open: M-Th 8pm-4am, F-Sa 24hrs, **F** *to Second Ave.* ♿ ⌐

Hammerstein Ballroom

Opened in 1906 by the famous theater personality Oscar Hammerstein, the ballroom is the setting for a number of national touring acts as well as television broadcasts and corporate events. Music may be seen anywhere from zero to five nights a week, an eclectic roster ranging from Hanson to Manson. No food, several bars.

ethnic, hip-hop, metal, pop, punk, rhythm, rock
Midtown, 311 West 34th St. (bet. Eighth & Ninth Aves.), 279-7740, www.mcstudios.com, Cash Only, Cover: $20-$60, Open: various hrs., **A C E** *to 34th St.-Penn Sta.* ♿ ⌐

Irving PLaza

Not the place to see local bands, more of a venue for national touring acts such as the Indigo Girls and Ben Folds Five. Most performers have major record label backing and a fair amount of radio play. While the Plaza is a large, comfortable club with high ceilings and several levels, it's a place to come for its choice acts, not for its setting. Check out the swing dancing on Sunday nights for $13. No food, full bar.

most genres of music (radio-friendly)
East Village, 17 Irving Pl. (at 15th St.), 777-6800, www.irvingplaza. com, Cash Only, Cover: varies, Open: M-Sa noon-6pm, **L N R** *4 5 6 to 14th St.-Union Sq.* ♿ ⌐

Kenny's Castaways

One of the landmark bars in the West Village. A good place to have a beer and see some up-and-coming local bands. You can listen to the music from the cozy upper level if you want to get away from the crowd. No food, full bar.

blues, rock
Greenwich Village, 157 Bleecker St. (bet. Thopson and Sullivan Sts.), 473-9870, MC, V, AmEx, Cover: $5-$10, Open: 12am-4am, ➊➋➌➍➎➏➐ *to West 4th St.-Washington Sq.* ♿ ↩ *21+*

Knitting Factory

One would be hard pressed to find a more original, more eclectic, or more New York venue than the Knitting Factory. With four performance spaces, a record label, and a reputation knowing what's good versus what's popular, this is probably the only venue in town where a visitor could justify spending the entire night. No food, full bar.

alternative, avant-garde, blues, cowpunk, jazz, klezmer, rock, world
TriBeCa, 74 Leonard St. (bet. Broadway and Church St.), 219-3006, www.knittingfactory.com, MC, V, AmEx, Cover: $6-$30, Open: M-F 5pm-3am, Sa-Su 6pm-3am, ➊➒ *to Franklin St.* ↩

The Living Room

Currently reigning as one of the hippest songwriter venues in New York, even though (or maybe because) it's been around for years. A small room with a relaxed atmosphere and some of the top names in innovative music playing for tips only, like local faves Trina Hamlin and Dayna Kurtz. Not a place to sit and chat, but your silence will be well-rewarded. Food is excellent and cheap, and there is a full bar.

acoustic, experimental, folk, jazz
East Village, 84 Staton St. (at Allen St.), 533-7237, www. livingroomny.com, Cash Only, Cover: free, Open: 8:30pm-2am, ➍ *to Second Ave.* ♿ ↩

Mercury Lounge

Just five years ago a headstone shop, the Mercury Lounge has established itself as a premiere venues for "just-breaking" bands. High stage, excellent sound system, and standing room only for three to five acts per night. No food, bar in the front room.

acoustic, alternative, rock
East Village, 217 East Houston St. (bet. Essex and Norfolk Sts.), 260-1214, www.mercurylounge nyc.com, MC, V, Cover: $7-$12, Open: 8pm-12am, ➍ *to Second Ave.* ↩ *21+*

Nightingale Bar

Home of bands like Blues Traveler, the Nightingale has a reputation as the favorite late night jam spot for many now-famous acts. Chris Barrow from the Spin Doctors can still be seen solo on Wednesday nights. You can see local acts here seven nights a week. No food, full bar with happy hour from 1pm-8pm daily!

pop and rock bands with the occasional soloist
East Village, 213 Second Ave. (at 13th St.), 473-9398, Cash Only, Cover: free-$10, Open: M-Sa 1pm-4am, Su 7pm-4am, ➏➍➊➎➏ *to 14th St.-Union Sq.,* ➌ *to Third Ave.* ♿ ↩ *18+*

Nuyorican Poets Cafe

The Nuyorican has made a name for itself as a center for experimental music and spoken word art in New York City. Besides its performances, visitors can see visual art exhibits and film retrospectives. Best value: Friday night poetry slam, from which is fielded NYC's nationally competitive team. No food, but wine & beer available.

acoustic, experimental, hip-hop, latin, jazz, salsa, spoken word
East Village, 236 East 3rd St. (bet. Aves. B and C), 505-8183, www.nuyorican.org, Cash Only, Cover: $6-$25, Open: 7:30pm-2am, ➍ *to 2nd Ave.* ♿ ↩

OHM Nightclub

Latin music and live bands on Wednesdays as well as savory Spanish cooking draws a crowd that is young, mixed and attractive. Free admission for ladies before 9pm.

dance, hip hop, house, funk, R&B
Gramercy, 16 West 22nd St. (at Fifth Ave.), 229-2000, MC, V, Am Ex, Cover: $5-$15, Open: Th-Sa 8pm-4am, ➏➑ *to 23rd St.* ♿↩

Orange Bear

A good after-work bar if you're hanging out in the City Hall/World Trade Center area. Most performers are unknown locals working on their acts. Sundays, the space is used intermittently as an art gallery and for poetry readings. No food, full bar.

acoustic, blues
Lower Manhattan, 47 Murray St. (bet. Church St. and Broadway), 566-3705, MC, V, AmEx, Cover: free-$5, Open: 11am-4am, ➊➋➌➒ *to Chambers St.,* ➏➑ *to City Hall* ♿ ↩ *21+*

Postcrypt Coffeehouse

Located in the basement of a chapel on the Columbia University campus and seating only fifty, the Postcrypt is one of the most unique rooms in the city. No electronic equipment is allowed on the stage and the only lighting is from candles stuck in wine bottles and chandeliers. Suzanne Vega played her first gig here when she was a student at Barnard College across the street. Snacks and bottled beer available.

acoustic, country, folk, jazz
Morningside Heights, Columbia University (at 116th St. and Broadway), 854-1953, www. columbia.edu/-crypt/, Cash Only, Cover: free, Open: F-Sa 9pm-12 am (during school year only), ❶❾ to 116th St.-Columbia University

Rodeo Bar and Grill

As the name implies, the Rodeo Bar is a Texas-style put-your-boots-up kinda place, complete with a stuffed buffalo dangling precariously above the bar.
Remember the Blues Brothers? "We play both kinds of music: country AND western." Well, it's not that bad, but it can make a lost Lone Star soul feel a little more at home. Full Tex-Mex menu, full bar.
country, rock, rockabilly, western
Gramercy, 375 3rd Ave. (bet. 27th and 28th Sts.), 683-6500, www.rodeobar.com, MC, V, AmEx, Cover: free, Open: Su-Th 11:30am-2am, F-Sa 11:30am-4am, ❻ *to 28th St.* & ⌐

Roseland

With its start as a popular ball-room in the 1930s, the newly renovated Roseland is still one of the more frequented venues in town. Large enough to draw a sizable crowd but small enough to retain some of that club charm, these days expect to find the bigger names in alternative acts like Radiohead and Beck stopping by for a gig. No food, full bar.
alternative rock, dance, pop
Midtown, 239 West 52nd St. (bet. Broadway and Eighth Ave.), 777-6800,www.roselandballroom. com, Cash Only, Cover: $15-$20, open: M-Sa noon-6pm (box office), ❶❾ *to 50th St.* & ⌐

Shine

It would be tough to tell someone which night to show up to this eclectic venue. The Tuesday night drum and bass party? The Wednesday night DJ cook-off? The weekly Friday and Saturday late night freakouts, with, for example, fire jugglers, trapeze artists, burlesque, and cabaret? Maybe you should just catch an early band and go from there. No food, full bar.
alternative, hip-hop, percussion, rock, R&B
TriBeCa, 285 West Broadway (at Canal St.), 941-0900, MC, V, AmEx, Cover: $8-$15, Open: T-Sa 9:30pm-4am, ❶❷❸ *to Canal St.* & ⌐ *21+*

SOB's

Though the name stands for "Sounds Of Brazil," that doesn't even begin to cover the scope of the first world beat club in New York. As a foundation of world rhythm and groove in the United States, it's like stepping into a different country every night as African, Middle Eastern, Celtic, Caribbean, and Latin American artists use this club as a home base for national tours.
Tropical food, full bar.
world beat
Greenwich Village, 204 Varick St. (at Houston St.), 243-4940, www. sobs.com, MC, V, AmEx, Cover: $10-$25, Open: M-Sa 6:30pm-4am, ❶❾ *to Houston* & ⌐ *21+*

SoHa

Though featuring music only on Sundays, Mondays, and Wednes-days, SoHa is one of the few places north of the Upper West Side and south of Harlem (hence the name "SoHa") to see live bands. Other nights of the week you can enjoy the cozy lounge atmosphere and bring in food from several of the ethnic eateries on the block.
Adjoining restaurants, full bar.

avant-garde, bebop, big band, brazilian, jazz, swing
Morningside Heights, 988 Amsterdam Ave. (bet. 108th and 109th Sts.), 678-0098, MC, V, AmEx, Cover: None, Open: 4pm-4am, ❶❾ *to 110th St.* & ⌐ *21+*

Smoke

Move over SoHa - there's a new kid in town and let it be known that this kid came to play! Smoke came on the scene in early 1999 and quickly made a name for itself with live jazz acts such as George Coleman, Slide Hampton, Cecil Payne, Leon Parker, and Eric Alexander, just to name a few. Don't miss the Wednesday Blues night and Sunday evening theatre, too. Some food, full bar.
jazz, blues
Morningside Heights, 2751 Broadway (bet. 105th and 106th Sts), 864-6662, MC, V, Cover: M-Th none, F-Su varies, Open: 5pm-4am, ❶❾ *to 110th St.* ⌐

The Sun Music Company

A new version of the famous but recently-defunct Fast Folk Cafe, The Sun Music Company is more of a place for the performer than the audience. Weekend shows regularly feature touring artists and indie-label acts, and Mondays host a workshop series on things such as guitar playing, songwriting, vocal technique, and music business issues. Wine, beer, and snacks are available.
contemporary acoustic
Upper East Side, 340 East 71st St. (at First Ave.), 396-9521, Cash Only, Cover: $10, Open: 8:30pm-12am, ❻ *to 68th St.-Hunter College* &

The Supper Club

As one of New York's more ele-gant venues, be prepared to dress up for a night of dinner and dancing on the town. Historically a ballroom, The Supper Club is at the center of

New York's popular swing scene every Friday and Saturday night. During the rest of the week, catch a live band under the sparkling chandelier and painted gold stars. French and American Continental served from 5:30pm-12:30am, music from 8:00pm-4:00am, full bar is always open.

1940s lindyhop, jump, swing, occasional private rock/pop concerts

Midtown, 240 West 47th St. (bet. Broadway and Eighth Ave.), 921-1940, www.citysearch.com/nyc/supperclub, MC, V, AmEx, Cover: $15-$20, Open: 5:30pm-4am, ❶❾ *to 50th St.,* ❶❻ *to 49th St.* ♿ ✉ *18+*

Sweet Basil

This homey jazz restaurant hasn't changed since it opened twenty-five years ago, demonstrated by the '70s-style lamp shades still dotting the room. Saturday/Sunday brunch with no cover from 2pm-6pm features Chuck Folds & Friends; other days, Cho the bartender is reason enough to stop by.

jazz

Greenwich Village, 88 Seventh Avenue South (bet. Grove and Bleecker Sts.), 242-1785, MC, V, AmEx, Cover: $17.50-$20, Open: 12:30pm-3:00am, ❶❾ *to Christopher St.-Sheridan Sq.* ♿ ✉

Tramps

Though Tramps books national touring acts of all style and genre, it's an especially good place to catch the larger Texas legends like Joe Ely and Robert Earl Keen on their way through town. Appropriately, the large room has a massive bar, great acoustics, and a bit of an Old West feel. For smaller acts there's Tramps Cafe next door, serving food for both venues. Full cajun menu, full bar.

alternative, blues, country, jazz, rap, rock

Gramercy, 51 West 21st St. (bet. Fifth and Sixth Aves.), 544-1666, Cash Only, Cover: $10-$35, Open: 7pm-12:30am, ❻ *to 23rd St.* ♿ ✉

The Village Vanguard

With regulars like Woody Guthrie, Lenny Bruce, and Pete Seeger, this 64-year-old club was already a legendary center for folk music and social commentary before it became a legend as a jazz club in the fifties. Some of the most important jazz recordings in the world, from Coltrane to Davis to Rollins to Evans, were created within these hallowed walls. You can still catch the top quality mainstream and avant-garde jazz acts each night. No food, full bar.

jazz

Greenwich Village, 178 Seventh Ave. South (bet. 11th St. and Waverly Pl.), 255-4037, www.villagevanguard.net, Cash Only, Cover: $15-$20, Open: 8:30pm-2am, ❶❷❸❾ *to 14th St.*

West Bank Café's Laurie Beachman Theatre

West Bank Café's cabaret room is just below the restaurant and bar. A place for a nice dinner followed by a relaxing evening downstairs. Great for entertaining out-of-town business clients. Full American menu upstairs and full bar on both levels.

cabaret

Midtown, 407 West 42nd St. (bet. Ninth and Tenth Aves.), 695-6909, MC, V, AmEx, Cover: $15-$30, Open: 12pm-1am, ❶❻❼ *to 42nd St.* ♿

Wetlands

Not a stop-off in a series of bar-hops, but a place to go for the entire evening. Bands play upstairs and downstairs at the same time, usually spacing their breaks so there is always music happening somewhere. There is often a "jam feel" to the place, like at a Grateful Dead or Blues

Traveler show. Worth the trip just to see the VW bus parked inside the lobby, out of which are sold t-shirts, bumper stickers, and CDs of the evening's acts. No food, full bar.

acoustic-rock, jam-bands, reggae, rock

TriBeCa, 161 Hudson St. (at Laight St.), 386-3600, Cash Only, Cover: $5-$20, Open: 8pm-4am, ❶❾ *to Canal St.* ♿ ✉ *18+*

music stores

Asian Music and Gift

What's the Chinese pop equivalent of Mariah Carey? Huge selections of the most current popular music of Asia, Chinese oldies, LP's for karaoke diehards and American/Chinese blockbuster smashes, Japanimation, ceramic toys, and oversized cloth posters of Asian teen idols that sell out in the blink of an eye.

Chinatown, 151 Canal St. (at Bowery), 226-6696, Cash Only, ❻❻❼ *to Grand St.*

Bleecker Bob's

Enough old school, punk, New York hard-core, and new wave records and CDs to find an old pressing of Stranglers or Television records. This refreshingly ugly music store is a prime locale for trashy rock-n-roll.

Greenwich, 118 West 3rd St. (bet. Sixth Ave. and Mac-Dougal St.), 475-9677, MC, V, AmEx, ❶❷❸❻❾❻❼ *to West 4th St.-Washington Sq.*

Bleecker Street Records

A hearty selection of CDs and vinyl specializing in Rock 'n' Roll, current pop hits, Reggae, Blues, and lots of oldies.

Greenwich Village, 239 Bleecker St. (at Sixth Ave.), 255-7899, MC, V, AmEx, ❶❷❸❻❾ ❻❼ *to West 4th St.-Washington Sq.* ♿

Chelsea Second Hand Guitars

Just window shopping is enough to make Eddie Van Halen drool. "Anything you're looking for, we can find through our network," boasts the dude at the counter. Go in and try one on for size: Strats, Les Pauls, Fenders, etc. Vintage guitars for the finger-picking connoisseur.
Chelsea, 220 West 23rd St. (bet. Seventh and Eighth Aves.), 675-4993, MC ,V, AmEx, ❶❾ to 23rd St., ❻❿ to 23rd. St. ♿

Dance Tracks

Domestic house and acid jazz, as well as remarkably cheap Euro imports. Classic dance cuts for collectors to catch up on.
East Village, 91 East 3rd St. (at First Ave.), 260-8729, MC, V, AmEx, D, ❻ to Second Ave.

Fat Beats

Indispensable for hip-hop fans, this well-stocked shop also doesn't do too badly in the reggae department either.
Greenwich Village, 406 Sixth Ave. (bet. 8th and 9th Sts.), 673-3883, MC, V, AmEx, ❶❷❸❹❺❻❾ to West 4th St.-Washington Sq.

Matt Umanov Guitars

Anyone in a band knows this long-time Village institution. Acoustic and electric instruments at reasonable prices; knowledge-able staff to boot.
Greenwich Village, 273 Bleecker St. (at Morton St.), 675-2157, MC, V, AmEx, D, ❶❷❸❹❺❻❾ to West 4th St.-Washington Sq., ❶❾ to Christopher St.-Sheridan Sq. ♿

Midnight Records

Calling all spinners, DJs, and jazz heads. Remember those large round disks with deep grooves in them? This dealer of vinyl, with both old and new collectibles, is living proof that albums have not comple-tely gone the way of the dino-saur. Check out their virtual site at www.midnightrecords.com.
Chelsea, 263 West 23rd St. (bet. Seventh and Eighth Aves.), 675-2768, MC, V, AmEx, D, ❶❾ to 23rd St., ❻❿ to 23rd St. ♿

Mondo Kim's

The sheer size and breadth of the selection, that goes far beyond the world of big name pop stars, is namely what recom-mends this alternative and indie megastore. The used selection is equally good, and their used CD policy a steal — they'll exchange your old stuff, as long as it's not damaged, straight across for any other used CD.
East Village, 6 St. Marks Pl. (at Third Ave.), 505-0311, MC, V, AmEx, ❻ to Astor Pl. ♿

The Music Factory

The latest in contemporary music including hip-hop, gospel, jazz, reggae and soul. Cassettes, vinyl, CD's, and even videotapes are available at very affordable prices at this local DJ hang-out.
Jamaica, Queens, 162-01 Jamaica Ave. (at 162nd St.), (718) 291-3135, MC, V, AmEx, D, ❻❿❷ to Jamaica Center.-Parsons/Archer ♿

Other Music

Well-deserved haven for indie-rock lovers which also offers a full selection of ambient, kraut rock, psychedelia, and noise. Keep an eye out for special in-store performances (arranged by owners Chris Vanderloo, Josh Madell, and Jeff Gibson), which have already featured Yo La Tengo and Jowe Head.
Greenwich Village, 15 East 4th St. (bet. Broadway and Lafa-yette St.), 477-8150, MC, V, AmEx, ❻❿ to 8th St.-NYU, ❻ to Astor Pl. ♿

Rocks In Your Head

Around since 1978 this store offers an eclectic selection; music from the past 40 years, both indie and major rock titles, with a great techno section and lots of box-sets. Best of all, the staff is very friendly and always willing to help.
SoHo, 157 Prince St. (bet. Broadway and Thompson St.), 475-6729, MC, V, AmEx, ❻❿ to Spring St.

Sam Ash

Ever want to DJ? Sprawling along 48th St., these four music shops fulfill almost every music-making need, selling acoustic instru-ments, recording equipment, MIDI systems, computers and software, DJ equipment, lighting, sheet music, and other items. The staff knows its stuff, and most locations rent and repair instruments and equipment.
Greenwich Village, 160 West 48th St. (bet. Sixth and Seventh Aves.), 719-2299, MC, V, AmEx, D, ❻❿ to 49th St., ❻❼❽❾ to 47-50 St.-Rockefeller Center ♿

Venus Records

There's lots of strange stuff you might have been unable to find new elsewhere, already on the rack at used prices. Also some imports and other rarities for megafans, and a downstairs full of old vinyl where the hard-core record buffs hang out.
East Village, 13 St. Marks Pl. (bet. Second and Third Aves.), 598-4459, MC, V, AmEx, D, ❻ to Astor Pl.

Vinylmania

Specializing in house music and imports. You can listen before you buy.
Greenwich Village, 60 Carmine St. (bet. Seventh Ave. and Bedford St.), 924-7223, MC, V, AmEx, ❶❾ to Houston St.

restaurants & cafes

restaurants
r·e·s·t·a·u·r·a·n·t·s

Restaurant trends in New York City change as quickly as traffic lights. Gone are the '80s, when the approach to entrées was to make them too small and beautiful to eat. A new dining era has dawned and chefs who have traditionally been preoccupied with presentation are also making sure that their customers don't leave hungry. By utilizing an ever-widening assortment of exotic ingredients like foie gras, truffles (the mushroom not the chocolate), langoustes, and sweetbreads, chefs are pushing the envelope, encouraging New Yorkers to be more adventurous with their taste buds than ever before.

But this doesn't mean that you can't still get a good steak — they've been opening fast as a cattle stampede in the late '90s. Because NYC is so diverse ethnically, it's possible to immerse yourself in different cultures simply by choosing the right neighborhood restaurant to dine in. And Chinatown is a lot closer than Hong Kong if you're looking for a traditional Sunday brunch of dim sum.

There's no need to travel to Katmandu when you can go to 6th St. between First and Second Aves. and dine in what is known as Little India. The Ukrainian diners of the East Village still serve a mean borscht and pierogi combo, and the intersection of Ninth Ave. and 14th St. is quickly becoming known as Little Belgium.

In spite of all this exoticism, you can still find a down-home American meal of meatloaf and mashed potatoes. And while the local diner is sure to offer reasonably priced familiar fare like hamburgers, milkshakes, pork chops and apple sauce, there is an increasing number of moderately priced bistros serving new twists on these old standbys under the heading of "New American" cuisine.

With nearly two thousand restaurants to choose from, deciding what and where to eat in New York can be a harrowing task. We hope our restaurant recommendations will make it easier for you to enjoy the New York's dynamic dining scene in all its incarnations.

how to be a RESTAURANT-GOER

Never before has the restaurant scene in New York City offered so many good choices for a memorable dining experience.

Fifteen years ago, there was a select list of about ten restaurants (including The Quilted Giraffe) which were the only places to go for a seduction — whether business or romance. If you took your guest elsewhere, it was a slight to his or her importance. As recently as eight years ago, there were twenty-five or so restaurants providing all the ingredients for a perfect night out. Some were less expensive and less formal, but this had become perfectly acceptable.

Today there are probably a hundred restaurants in the Big Apple whose selection would flatter your guest and impress him or her with good food. This broad selection is the result of food critics bestowing their stamp of approval on less extravagant places (almost everybody wanted to spend less, and now we have it) and of two other important influences: better domestic food products and a vast increase in the number of talented chefs who have worked in good restaurants and have followed their dream to open their own establishments.

As choices have expanded for diners, restaurateurs have played with the factors of decor, menu ethnicity, and menu price to stand out and attract customers. At one point, it was French for high quality and extravagance, Italian for fun, casual and ethnic, and Chinese or Indian for a cheap night out. Today there are expensive and casual ethnic restaurants — Danny Meyer's Indian-inspired Tabla on Madison Square Park and the new Ruby Foo's are examples of ethnic restaurants going up the scale in ambiance and design.

Luckily, the Zagat Survey has emerged to help figure out if a particular restaurant will make you

Barry Wine, contributor of this article, was the restauranteur behind The Quilted Giraffe, one of New York's hottest restaurants of the 1980s.

happy. It is reliable because the comments come from customers and, in New York City, these ratings are updated every year. Zagat provides insights on a restaurant's popularity, price, and food quality. Beware of the assumption that the most popular restaurants always have the best food! Reality is, on the other hand, that overall high quality is consistently expensive — it costs money to use the best ingredients, have talented people in both the kitchen and the front of the house, and maintain comfortable and clean premises.

You can tell a lot about a restaurant, though, simply from the way they answer the phone and take reservations. The more care and welcoming that aspect, the better the whole experience will be. Check out whether the sidewalk in front of the place has been cleaned, another mark of attention to presentation.

For restaurants that don't take reservations, those with the longest lines might be the best! While strolling in any of the interesting neighborhoods in New York, restaurants that look good from the street — clean windows, nice lighting, a menu board outside that is well cared for — are the kinds of places to walk into. Word gets around quickly in New York and it is unlikely that a good restaurant will be empty.

Reservations are sometimes difficult to arrange in the hottest restaurants, whether you are a visitor or a native New Yorker. All restaurants, though, have cancellations at the last minute, and the best way to get a table at a place that seems to be always booked is to show up at the door, offer to have a drink at the bar and ask to be seated if something opens up. If you are well mannered and not pushy, this works more than you would expect. Being polite and flexible will give you one up.

A large group, on the other hand, should plan ahead and select the type of restaurant that can best accommodate bigger parties. Big places, like some of the Chinese restaurants and many steakhouses that have opened up recently, can seat big parties and get the food out fine. A fine dining restaurant, with lots of cooks in the kitchen, could also do it. However, large groups shouldn't expect to be seated unannounced at smaller restaurants, which may have as few as two cooks preparing meals in sauce pans. Woks work for large quantities; sauté pans don't!

There are great restaurants in New York for every occasion. Here are some of my current favorites — some which have been around for many years, and some newcomers:

Sparks Steak House for the best steak.
Great for business dinners with guests who would rather not be in a formal, possibly intimidating, environment.

Harry Cipriani for rubbing shoulders with the cream of the jet-set. (I once sat next to a king!)

Jean Georges for a cutting edge, expensive experience. (Also, in the expensive category: **Daniel** for classical elegance; for intimacy, **Chanterelle**, the model of the French restaurant run by a husband and wife team.)

Milos for perfect seafood ingredients, cooked simply with olive oil and herbs in a chic setting.

The Downtown Brooklyn Diner when my guests want great chicken soup, brisket and fabulous rice pudding in a casual setting.

Osteria del Circo for first class Italian food with a very warm welcome from one of the omnipresent, charming owners.

The Mercer Kitchen when I want to eat the wasabi and tuna pizza I patented at the Quilted Giraffe with a very downtown crowd.

Blue Water Grill for fairly priced seafood, the best oysters, and live jazz.

Bond Street for quality, inventive sushi and cooked Japanese food in a very trendy setting — if I am wearing black and with youngish friends! (**Nobu** for the same when I am with guests who aren't wearing black but want to see movie stars.)

Ruby Foo's for a fun Pan-Asian experience in a really happening place, attracts a very pretty crowd — same owner as **Blue Water Grill**.

Tavern on the Green when I want Christmas decorations in the summer or when I want to sit in a beautiful garden with romantic lighting.

Eleven Madison Park and **Gramercy Tavern** when I want my guests to be really taken care of and have great food and service in a really comfortable setting.

A𝒶

ACME

Comfort food with cleaned-up southern style. Choose from entrées like catfish and fried chicken, and be sure to accompany them with a side of heavenly skin-on mashed potatoes. By night, the place becomes packed both at the tables and around the bar with downtown twenty- and thirtysomethings making up the scene.
East Village, 9 Great Jones St. (bet. Broadway and Lafayette St.), 420-1334, MC, V, Diners, D, *Entrées: $6-$15*, ❻ to Astor Pl., ❿❽ to 8th St.-NYU ⛓ ⬑ ♿

Alley's End

Literally at the end of an alley on a vaguely unsavory block of Chelsea, finding this restaurant is half the fun. But only half. Prim and relaxed, this hide-away is a hidden jewel, with an interior garden and a banquet room, complete with fireplace, for larger parties. No longer undiscovered, there tends to be a crowd weekend nights, but the cute quarters and quality food make it worthwhile.
Chelsea, 311 West 17th St. (bet. Eighth and Ninth Aves.), 627-8899, MC, V, D, *Entrées: $12-$22*, ❶❸❼ to 14th St., ❶ to Eighth Ave., ❶❾ to 18th St. ⬑

Alison on Dominick

Small, intimate, and appropriately nestled away in the relatively barren western edge of SoHo, this place is truly unique. The food is flawlessly prepared upscale French Bistro fare and perfectly matched ambiance. Ideal for a romantic dinner.
SoHo, 38 Dominick St. (bet. Varick and Hudson Sts.), 727-1188, MC, V, AmEx, Diners, *Entrées: $28-$38*, ❸❺ to Spring St. ⬑

Alouette

This intimate bi-level French bistro serves up savory and inventive cuisine in a rich, warm atmosphere — an anomaly for the Upper West Side. Donning red velvet drapery and lace-curtained windows, Alouette is a romantic option in West Side dining. The prices are great in exchange for this culinary and atmospheric decadence.
Upper West Side, 2588 Broadway (bet. 97th and 98th Sts.), 222-6808, MC, V, AmEx, Diners, *Entrées: $16-$22*, ❶❾ to 96th St.

Amin Indian Cuisine

Dinner here avoids the circus-like pitfalls of Sixth Street's outfits. Curries, kebabs, and kormas are spicy enough to satisfy natives, and will only set you back about $10. Combo platters allow for both gluttony and variety.
Chelsea, 155 Eighth Ave. (bet. 17th and 18th Sts.), 929-7020, MC, V, AmEx, *Entrées: $7-$19*, ❶❸❼ to 14th St., ❶ to Eighth Ave. ♿

Amsterdam Café

Friendly neighborhood feel with a good menu of classic bar items and pastas. Their weekend brunch for $4.95 is the best deal in the area, the cute bartenders another plus!
Morningside Heights, 1207 Amsterdam Ave. (bet. 119th and 120th Sts.), 662-6330, MC, V, AmEx, Diners, D, *Entrées: $7-$10*, ❶❾ to 116th St.-Columbia University ⬑ ♿

Andalousia

A relatively yuppie-free zone for quality Moroccan fare; $20 buys the three-course prix fixe that offers plenty of options, though it's just as easy to subsist on dips and light lamb dishes.

Dark and understated, no liquor license means its BYOB.
Greenwich Village, 28 Cornelia St. (bet. Bleecker and West 4th Sts.), 929-3693, MC, V, *Entrées: $12-$20*, ❶❷❸❹❺❻❼❾ to West 4th St.-Washington Sq. ⛓ ♿

Angelica Kitchen

A vegetarian's paradise as well as an introductory course forvegan-phobic carnivores, offering tangy soups, tofu and pesto sandwiches, and tofu-lemon "cheesecake." Portions are generous and very moderately priced.
East Village, 300 East 12th St. (bet. First and Second Aves.), 228-2909, Cash Only, Entrées: $6-$12, ❻ to First Ave., ❿❽ ❹❺❻ to Union Sq.-14th St. ⛓ ♿

Anglers and Writers

No longer home to the *Paris Review* crowd, but the soups and stews are probably better now than they were in the good old days. There will often be a wait for Sunday brunch.
Greenwich Village, 420 Hudson St. (at St. Lukes Pl.), 675-0810, Cash Only, Entrées: $8-$14, ❶❾ to Christopher St.-Sheridan Sq. ⛓

Annam Brahma Restaurant

The eclectic menu's only unifying thread is that everything is prepared sans meat, meaning everything from Indian ratia to tofu omelets to chapatti roll-ups may grace your table. Thursdays the cooks rally around pasta for Italian day; Tuesdays put Chinese vegetarian mainstays center stage. Check out the books, tapes, and other items for sale in the back of the restaurant.
Jamaica, Queens, 84-43 164th St. (at 85th Ave.), (718) 523-2600, Cash Only, Entrées: $4-$8, ❻ to Parsons Blvd. ⛓ ♿

Around the Clock

There's not much to recommend during the day, but the late-late-night crowd qualifies as a revealing cross-section of the East Village's maladjusted. Depending on how far the hands are past midnight when you swing by, either bleary-eyed club kids with the munchies are killing time or else the harried waitstaff is halfheartedly trying to oblige the grumpy, idiosyncratic, early-morning regulars.
East Village, 8 Stuyvesant St. (at Third Ave.), 598-0402, MC, V, AmEx, Diners, D, Entrées: $5-$10, ❻ *to Astor Pl.* ↩

Atlantis

This fish market not only supplies Morningside Heights with fish flown in daily, but also, to Columbia students' delight, has an in-house sushi chef who prepares orders directly for take out, eliminating the middle man.
Morningside Heights, 588 West 110th St. (bet. Broadway and Amsterdam Aves.), 749-6073, MC, V, AmEx, Entrées: $3-$9, ❶❾ *to 110th St.*

Audubon Bar and Grill

Gourmet Caribbean/French fusion cuisine is right at home at this Washington Heights newcomer. Its barbecue and pasta dishes are also delicious and worth the trip uptown. On a historical note, the restaurant is located on the site where Malcolm X was assassinated.
Washington Heights, 3956 Broadway (at 166th St.), 928-5200, MC, V, AmEx, Entrées: $8-$12, ❶❾ *to 168th St.* ↩ 🚲

B b

Babylon

Even on a slow day, expect to wait a bit while owner Damon Gordon prepares your Mediterranean style veggie meal in his one-man kitchen set-up. No worries though: The sunny '70s vibe is conducive to chilling for hours with pen and paper in hand, and Gordon will kindly refill your mug a bunch of times, before your crepe emerges from the steamer, fluffy, with a flaky, buttery crust.
Lower East Side, 237 Eldridge St. (bet. Houston and Stanton Sts.), 505-7546, Cash Only, Entrées: $4-$7, ❺ *to Second Ave.* ♿ ↩

Bachue

This vegan breakfast, lunch, and dinner place has one large store-front window which ensures most of the tables are well-lit. The restaurant is a rare treat: one of the few places in the city where you can order delicious (egg-less) pancakes and waffles, as well as a fine selection of bean, pasta, seitan, tempeh, tofu, and vegetable dishes.
Gramercy, 36 West 21st St. (bet. Fifth and Sixth Aves.), 229-0870, MC, V, AmEx, D, Entrées: $5-$13, ❻ *to 23rd St.,* ❺❻ *to 23rd St.* ♿ 🚲

Balthazar

This SoHo gem already has a reservation line and a ten minute wait. Onlookers rave about the lofty bistro decor and surprisingly arrogant-free staff. The authentic French brasserie "looks just like Paris", sounds it, too.
SoHo, 80 Spring St. (bet. Broadway and Lafayette St.), 965-1414, MC, V, AmEx, Entrées: $20, ❻ *to Spring St.* ♿ ↩

Baluchi's

Named after Pakistan's Balochistan, this bonafide Indian restaurant does justice to the sultry opulence for which the region is known. Numerous options will satisfy vegetarians, including pallak paneer and Basmati rice.
SoHo, 193 Spring St. (bet. Thompson and Sullivan Sts.), 226-2828, MC, V, AmEx, Diners, Entrées: $10-$14, ❻❺ *to Spring St.* ♿ 🚲

Basilio Inn

Housed in a 19th Century stable imbued with a Tuscan rustic flavor, the Inn serves up incredible Italian — the red snapper Livornese is divine — the likes of which Manhattanites have never seen. Prices reflect the Island's low rent and low pretension.
Staten Island, 2-6 Galesville Court, (718) 447-9292, AmEx, Entrées: $12-$14 ♿

BBQ

An eden for budget-constrained carnivores. The decor is trite and the breadth of the menu is confined to the obvious, but where do fall-off-the-bone tender meat with satisfyingly greasy fries sell for less than the price of a couple of Happy Meals? The only things missing from the Southern cookout ambiance are the horseflies.
Greenwich Village, 21 University Pl. (at 8th St.), 674-4450, MC, V, AmEx, Entrées: $5-$10, ❺❻ *to 8th St.-NYU* ♿ 🚲

Bell Cafe

It's rare that a place can be cool without lapsing into obnoxiousness; that's precisely what makes this place so special. The scene is definitely late-night, serving up huge portions of mostly vegetarian fare from around the globe until the wee hours of the morning, and it's equally accom-

modating for beverages and long conversation. There's excellent free live music every night. Great alternative to the bar scene.
SoHo, 310 Spring St. (bet. Hudson and Greenwich Sts.), 334-2355, MC, V, AmEx, D, Entrées: $5-$10, **❶❾** *to Houston St.* ⌐

Bendix Diner

Whether it's because of the motto's invitation to "get fat" or because of the subsequent surprise of a health-conscious menu, patrons have been congregating at this casual hot-spot in such numbers that owners have been forced to expand. Greasy spoon prices mean the American-Thai fusion dishes leave no room for guilt.
Chelsea, 219 Eighth Ave. (at 21st St.), 366-0560, MC, V, AmEx, D, Entrées: $6-$8, **❶❻** *to 23rd St.* ⌐♿

Also at:
East Village, 167 First Ave. (bet. 10th and 11th Sts.), 260-4220, MC, V, AmEx, Entrées: $6-$18, **❻** *to Astor Place*

The Bistro at Candy Bar

Currently on the A-list for stylish, late-night dining, this vibrant bar and restaurant, famous for its mile-long cocktail menu, attracts a boisterous and amiable, largely gay crowd for sizable helpings of tasty basics, as well as eclectic ethnic entrées: Mom's meatloaf with red bliss mashed potatoes tops the American portion of the menu, followed by the more exotic braised lamb shank with creamy polenta and fall vegetables. For starters or smaller appetites, try the ginger-chicken satay or the grilled portabello mushrooms with the sun dried tomato coulis.

Chelsea, 131 Eighth Ave. (bet. 16th and 17th Sts.), 229-9702, MC, V, Diners, D, Entrées: $8-$16, **❶❸❿** *to 14th St.,* **❶** *to Eighth Ave.* ⌐ ⌐

Bistro Margot

A French treasure hidden in Little Italy, gourmet enough to satisfy the upper-crust, older patrons who don't mind the bloated pricing. The preponderance of two-person tables and the seductive lighting emphasize its viability as a date restaurant.
Soho, 26 Prince St. (at Mott St.), 274-1027, Cash Only, Entrées: $5-$13, **❻** *to Spring St.,* **❽❻❶❶** *to Broadway-Lafayette St.* ⌐ ⌐

Blue Ribbon Sushi

Let the simple yet elegant modern Japanese decor draw you into this fashionable SoHo sushi haven and you shall be rewarded with yellowtail and tuna of melt-in-your-mouth freshness. Closed Mondays, the restaurant is open for dinner until 2am but accepts no reservations, so weekend waits can be long, especially taking into consideration the space's diminutive dimensions.
SoHo, 119 Sullivan St. (bet. Prince and Spring Sts.), 343-0404, MC, V, AmEx, Diners, Entrées: $20-$30, **❸❻** *to Spring St.* ⌐

Blue Water Grill

With everything from live jazz to an oyster bar, this delightful seafood café will keep you happy whether you're looking to eat or simply people-watch.
Gramercy, 31 Union Square West (at 16th St.), 675-9500, MC, V, AmEx, Entrées: $25-$35, **❶❿❻** **❹❺❻** *to 14th St.-Union Sq.* ⌐ ⌐

Bo Ky

Seafood variations served over rice and noodles are the staples of the Chinese menu. The central location attracts both tourists and locals on lunch break; efficient service moves patrons in and out in a hurry.
Chinatown, 80 Bayard St. (at Mott St.), 406-2292, Cash Only, Entrées: $5, **❽❿❻❻❷❻** *to Canal St.* ⌐

Boca Chica

Great for anyone who likes to have fun when paying to eat out. The atmosphere is decidedly festive and colorful, a perfect match to the South American and Caribbean food they serve. Best bets are the menu choices with pork or seafood, staples of the cuisine that you've probably never tasted like this before, which should be accompanied by one of their exotic margaritas.
East Village, 13 First Ave. (at 1st St.), 473-0108, MC, V, AmEx, Entrées: $8-$14, **❻** *to Second Ave.*

Bodega

An upscale diner that caters equally to neighborhood dwellers and to office types on days when there's no business lunching to be done. The atmosphere is clean, colorful and efficient, well-suited to the eclectic menu which has all sorts of quick and interesting choices like the Santa Fe wrap that's great topped with almost anything.
TriBeCa, 136 West Broadway (bet. Duane and Thomas Sts.), 285-1155, MC, V, AmEx, Entrées: $7-$13, **❶❷❸❾** *to Chambers St.* ⌐♿

Bolivar

Walk through the door and it's practically Sedona, by way of Third Ave. The rustic floors, cozy tables, and stucco alcoves

all make for nice atmosphere, though dining can get cramped. Prices are fine for retired condo denizens, but students may want to wait until the parents come to town.
Upper East Side, 206 East 60th St. (at Third Ave.), 838-0440, MC, V, AmEx, Diners, Entrées: $20-$35, ❹❺❻ *to 59th St.,* ❍❡ *Lexington Ave.* ♿ ⌐

Bolo
Food Network favorite Bobby Flay's version of "Fantasy Spanish" cuisine doesn't miss a beat at this relaxed Flatiron restaurant. Sangria, rabbit on roasted pea risotto, and sautéed wild mushrooms with chile oil are only a few of Mr. Flay's playful gastronomic creations. A comprehensive selection of fine wines and ports are perfect complements to a meal that is the stuff dreams are made of.
Gramercy, 23 East 22nd St. (bet. Broadway and Park Ave. South), 228-2200, MC, V, AmEx, Entrées: $25-$30, ❍❡ *to 23rd St.* ♿ ⌐

Bond Street
This Japanese-inspired three tier restaurant is sophisticated but casual with room for private parties and good Japanese food all in a historic brownstone.
East Village, 6 Bond St. (bet. Lafayette St. and Broadway), 777-2500, MC, V, AmEx, Entrées: $20-$30, ❻ *to Bleecker St.*

Boulevard
A fun family restaurant with Sesame Street-style murals and all-you-can-eat specials on Monday nights; screaming babies covered in mashed potatoes, platefuls of enormous dinosaur ribs, and the Maryland crabcakes are all part of the charm. You'll have to request the aptly named "Liquid Hell" barbecue sauce, which is kept hidden in back.

Upper West Side, 2398 Broadway (at 88th St.), 874-7400, MC, V, AmEx, Entrées: $7-$18, ❶❾ *to 86th St.* ⌐ ✂

Bouley Bakery
Reserve well in advance for what many consider to be "the perfect meal." The white walls, curved ceiling, and green stone floors all work to create an ambiance that is both elegant and casual. Bouley Bakery maintains the Bouley reputation for excellence by using the finest regional ingredients, and taking great care with each meal served. The waitstaff will help you order, so sit back and relax.
TriBeCa, 120 West Broadway (bet. Duane and Reade Sts.), 964-2525, MC, V, AmEx, Entrées: $20-$25, ❶❾ *to Franklin St.* ♿

Bridge Cafe
Even if you're not a part of the city's political machine, the attentive staff will provide you with reliable standards at this adorable eatery just south of City Hall, one of former mayor Ed Koch's favorite haunts. Mostly a middle-aged crowd with spin doctors and other politicos.
Lower Manhattan, 279 Water St. (at Dover St.), 227-3344, MC, V, AmEx, Entrées: $12-$22, ❹❺❻ *to Brooklyn Bridge-City Hall* ♿ ⌐

Broadway's Jerusalem II Kosher Pizza
The most popular Kosher Pizza joint in Manhattan. Lots of students from the nearby Stern College for Women drop by for a slice, as do Jewish office workers or tourists heading outo a Broadway show. Delivery is available to almost anyone anywhere in the world.
Midtown, 1375 Broadway (bet. 37th and 38th Sts.), 398-1475, Cash Only, Entrées: $5-$15, ❶❷❸❾ *to 34th St.* ♿ ✂

Bruculino
Sicilian seafood cooked to perfection is served in the soothing wood and wave interior of this West Side culinary treasure. Dishes are inventive and colorful. Outdoor seating is available on the terrace. Try the specials of the evening and leave room for coffee and dessert!
Upper West Side, 225 Columbus Ave. (at 70th St.), 579-3966, MC, V, AmEx, Entrées: $10-$20, ❶❾ *to 72nd St.* ✂

Bryant Park Grill
Nestled up against the backside of the main branch of the Public Library, a restaurant would be hard-pressed to be more picturesque, especially in spring, when Bryant Park assumes its full majesty. The American-Continental food is tasty, if pricey, and the after-work bar and dinner scene at the Grill and its outdoor cafe buzzes with "suits" letting loose. Brunch is excellent.
Midtown, 25 West 40th St. (bet. Fifth and Sixth Aves.), 840-6500, MC, V, AmEx, Entrées: $14-$24, ❶❷❸❾ *to 42nd St.,* ❼ *to Fifth Ave.* ♿ ⌐

Bubby's
Forego the fancily named sandwiches, which don't merit their prices, in favor of the sturdier main fare, like quesadillas served with great salsa. Gorgeous ceiling-high windows afford people-watching and the wooden floor and benches evoke the comfort level of an unpretentious, rather rustic, cafe. Great brunch.
TriBeCa, 120 Hudson St. (at North Moore St.), 219-0666, MC, V, AmEx, Entrées: $7-$15, ❶❾ *to Franklin St.* ♿ ⌐ ✂

C𝕔

Cafe Des Artistés

You'll feel glamorous at this classic New York restaurant. Don't get addicted to that feeling though, because visiting this romantic rendezvous too often will clean out your wallet as seductively as it filled you up. *Upper West Side, 1 West 67th St. (bet. Columbus Ave. and Central Park West), 877-3500, MC, V, AmEx, Diners, Entrées: $30-$40,* **①⑨** to 66th St.-Lincoln Center ♿🚻

Café Fès

Reliable Moroccan fare in the heart of Greenwich Village. The cushioned stools in this intimate setting inspire you to lean toward your companion and share a bottle from the impressive selection of Moroccan wines. Try the traditional couscous or a more daring duck dish wrapped in a filo shell and sprinkled with cinnamon and sugar. Don't overlook the sumptuous desserts including the croustillant, a date and almond pastry drizzled with chocolate. *Greenwich Village, 246 West 4th St. (at Charles St.), 924-7653, MC, V, Amex, Diners, D, Entrées:$15,* **①⑨** to Christopher St.-Sheridan Sq. ♿🚻

Cafe Gitane

A bastion of France on the edge of Little Italy, authentic from the menu offerings to the aloof waitstaff. Perfect ambiance for flipping through fashion rags, drinking cappuccino, and the standard downtown sports of posing and people-watching. *Little Italy, 242 Mott St. (bet. Houston and Prince Sts.), 334-9552, Cash Only, Entrées: $7-$10,* **⑥⑧** to Prince St. 🚻

Café Noir

A trendy spot for late-night dining, the bar is generally inundated with well-dressed air-kissing types looking for fun. The atmosphere is Spanish-Moroccan, as is the food. Eschew the more expensive entrées in favor of lighter fare like sandwiches and tapas which combine simple ingredients to perfection. Use the difference in price to splurge on a good bottle of wine from their extensive list of French vintages. *TriBeCa, 32 Grand St. (at Thompson St.), 431-7910, AmEx, Entrées: $12-$18,* **ⒶⒸⒺ** to Canal St. 🚻

Café Un Deux Trois

Though a little strenuous on the wallet, this busy, touristy spot is perfect for a bowl of savory French onion soup or a delectable dish of crème brulée. Avoid the high prices by sitting at the bar. If you're up for a full meal, sit table-side for a plate of steak and pomme frittes and let your imagination run wild as you design your own table cloth with a cup full of crayons. *Midtown, 123 West 44th St. (bet. Sixth Ave. and Broadway), 354-4148, MC, V, AmEx, Diners, Entrees: $15-24,* **ⓃⓇⒸⒶ①②③⑦⑨** to 42nd St.-Times Sq. ♿

Cafe Yola

On a warm night, step through the cozy asymmetrical dining room into the back garden. Tucked in between apartment buildings, the outdoor space achieves a European atmosphere. Candlelight, ivy, and good wine make this the ideal place for a romantic dinner and quiet conversation. *East Village, 337 East 10th St. (bet. Aves. A and B), 677-1913, Cash Only, Entrées: $8-17,* **Ⓛ** to First Ave. 🚻

Caffé Pertutti

Bright and breezy, with a hard-tiled floor and marble-topped tables, this neighborhood café hosts intellectual tête-à-têtes while serving up Italian standards which hardly merit their above-average prices. The salads, however, are enormous and tasty, and the desserts usually taste as good as they look. *Morningside Heights, 2888 Broadway (bet. 112th and 113th Sts.), 864-1143, Cash Only, Entrées: $7-$12,* **①⑨** to Cathedral Parkway (110th St.) ♿

Caffé Taci

Crowds of Columbia students eat adequately prepared Italian basics in the mock-ruin interior of this popular, dimly-lit eatery. Manhattan School of Music students sing live opera on Friday and Saturday nights; due to slow service, diners can theoretically hear one in its entirety. *Morningside Heights, 2841 Broadway (at 110th St.), 678-5345, Cash Only, Entrées: $5-$14,* **①⑨** to Cathedral Pkwy. (110th St.) ♿🚻

Cal's

A striking open loft space gives you ample elbow room and surprising privacy while dining, yielding an unusually relaxed atmosphere for this trendy neighborhood. The food is quite good, and the risotto is a standout, as is the waitstaff. *Gramercy, 55 West 21st St. (bet. Fifth and Sixth Aves.), 929-0740, MC, V, AmEx, Diners, Entrées: $16-$20,* **Ⓕ** to 23rd St., **ⓃⓇ** to 23rd St. ♿🚻

Camille's

Named after the owner's mother, this cozy Columbia magnet is reliably good. Pizzas are a bargain at $4.25, and the hearty pasta dishes are topped with light and flavorful sauces. It's difficult to eat this well for less money; breakfast is a particularly cheap alternative to bacon 'n egg grease-balls at area diners. *Morningside Heights, 1135 Amsterdam Ave. (at 116th St.), 749-2428, MC, V, AmEx, Entrées: $3-$9,* ❶❾ *to 116th St.-Columbia University* ⚭

Cargo Cafe

Just a stone's throw from the Staten Island Ferry terminal, this modern, trendy spot is hard to miss. A youngish local crowd congregates on the terrace in summer for delectable fresh fish specials like pan-seared tuna. Sandwiches, burgers, and salads make appearances as well. Local artists often showcase their work and live jazz cooks up Thursdays. *Staten Island, 120 Bay St. (at Flosson Terrace), (718) 876- 0539, MC, V, AmEx, D, Entrées: $10-$15,* ♿ ⬅ ⚭

Carmichael's

Wizened locals fill up on soul food after Sunday's sermon at this slightly derelict, though cozy, neighborhood favorite. The fried chicken is amazing. *Jamaica, Queens, 117-08 Guy R. Brewer Blvd. (at 118th Ave.), (718) 723-6908, Cash Only, Entrées: $6- $10,* ❺ *to Jamaica Center-Parsons/Archer* ♿

Carmine's

Come with a group of friends and order up a storm of family-style Italian. Seating is slow, so a visit to this enormous darkwood institution happily mandates a stop at the lovely bar, characteristic of New York's old-school haunts. *Upper West Side, 2450 Broadway (bet. 90th and 91st Sts.), 362-2200, MC, V, AmEx, Entrées: $15-$25,* ❶❷❸❾ *to 96th St.* ♿ ⬅ ⚭
Also at:

Midtown, 200 West 44th St. (bet. Broadway and Eighth Ave.), 221-3800, MC, V, AmEx, Entrées: $15-$25, ❶❷❸❼❾❶❷❸❼❾ *to 42nd St.-Times Sq.*

Castillo de Jagua

A homely but decent Dominican dive in the heart of Loisaida, this place pleases with rice & beans, fried plantains, cafe con leche, and fresh squeezed O.J. to the beat of loud salsa music. *Lower East Side, 113 Rivington St. (bet. Ludlow and Essex Sts.), 982-6412, Cash Only,* ❺ *to Delancey St.,* ❶❷❸ *to Essex St.* ♿ ⬅ ⚭

Chanterelle

One of the city's most high-brow restaurants, serving elegant cuisine in a lovely high-ceilinged dining room. The prix fixe lunch is superb, and the most affordable option. *TriBeCa, 2 Harrison St. (at Hudson St.), 966-6960, MC, V, AmEx, Diners, D, Entrées: $20-$30,* ❶❾ *to Franklin St.* ♿

Chi-Chi Steak

Featuring a 4pm-8pm happy hour with extensive cocktail menu, this trendy spot serves American fare to a largely gay clientele. *Greenwich Village, 135 Christopher St. (bet. Hudson and Greenwich Sts.), 462-0027, Cash Only, Entrées: $5-$10,* ❶❾ *to Christopher St.-Sheridan Sq.* ⬅

City Crab and Seafood Co.

Big, brash, and bustling, this urbane seafood house just steps from Union Sq. is a mainstay for the area's white-collar crowd. The giant oyster bar is quite a scene after work; it's trendy and gimmicky, but it certainly works. *Gramercy, 235 Park Ave. South (at 19th St.), 529-3800, MC, V, AmEx, D, Entrées: $15-$28,* ❶❷❸ ❹❺❻ *to 14th St.-Union Sq.* ♿ ⚭

Coogan's Restaurant

Latinos and Irish congregate at this upscale pub to partake of classics such as shell steak, shrimp scampi, French onion soup, and roast beef au jus. Karaoke nights on Tuesdays and Thursdays enhance the eclecticism of this popular local hangout, just down the street from the Columbia Presbyterian Medical Center. *Washington Heights, 4015 Broadway (at 168th and 169th Sts.), 928-1234, MC, V, AmEx, Entrées: $9-$17,* ❶❷❸❶❾ *to 168th St.-Washington Heights* ♿ ⬅ ⚭

Copeland's

A rich and varied menu offers everything from braised oxtails and gumbo to grain-fed catfish and shrimp Creole. The atmosphere is for serious eating; Sunday's gospel brunch is among the neighborhood's finest. *Harlem, 547 West 145th St. (bet. Broadway and Amsterdam Ave.), 234-2357, MC, V, AmEx, D, Entrées: $9-$25,* ❶❾ *to 145th St.* ♿ ⬅ ⚭

Cornelia Street Cafe

The leisurely ambiance of soothing lights coupled with a background jazz and blues blend complements the similarly unforced take on simple New American cuisine. Venture downstairs after dinner to catch nightly theater, jazz, and poetry performances in the cabaret. *Greenwich Village, 29 Cornelia St. (bet. Bleecker and West 4th Sts.), 989-9318, MC, V, AmEx, Diners, Entrées: $12-$15,* ❶❷❸❶❷❸❼❾ *to West 4th St.-Washington Sq.* ⬅

Corner Bistro

Locals lament the marathon waits at this immensely popular burger-and-beer joint, but they still throng despite the slow service. It's the prime territory to see and be seen: the basic, effortlessly funky version of the neighborhood haunt made palatable to yuppie Villagers by virtue of its enduring cachet and steady stream of televised college basketball games. Tables long ago marked by penknives crowd the middle, though intimate space may be free in back. *Greenwich Village, 331 West 4th St. (bet. 12th and Jane Sts.), 242-9502, Cash Only, Entrées: $4-$6,* **ⒶⒸⒺ** *to 14th St.,* **Ⓛ** *to Eighth Ave.* ♿ ⟼

Cotton Club
During the legendary gospel brunches, diners in their Sunday best chow on basics like fried chicken, yams, and corn bread at this slightly dried-up but still entertaining granddaddy of Harlem glamour. Call for seating times or to make reservations. *Morningside Heights, 656 West 125th St. (bet. Broadway and Riverside Ave.), 663-7980, MC, V, Entrées: $25,* **Ⓛ⑨** *to 125th St.*

Cowgirl Hall of Fame
Before riot-girls there were cowgirls and at this Greenwich Village fave owner Sherry Delamarter won't let gringos forget. Come for the history lesson and eclectic Chuckwagon dishes like eggplant fritters and Frito pie. Yeehaw! *Greenwich Village, 519 Hudson St. (at 10th St.), 633-1133, MC, V, AmEx, Entrées: $8-$15,* **Ⓛ⑨** *to Christopher St.-Sheridan Sq.* ♿ ⟼ ♿

Cucina
One of the best restaurants in New York and it's not even in Manhattan. Everything's great here, but the risotto is what people rave about. The antipasto is the best this side of Tuscany and the wine and dessert menus

are superb. Plus there's valet parking on weekends! In a word: perfect. *Park Slope, Brooklyn, 256 Fifth Ave. (bet. Garfield Pl. and Carroll St.), (718) 230-0711, MC, V, AmEx, Diners, D, Entrées: $15-$28,* **ⓂⓃⓇ** *to Union St.* ♿ ♿

The Cupping Room Cafe
A wonderful spot with an ambitious, if slightly pricey, brunch. Even at peak hours, there's plenty of space in the large, airy, main room, so the wait is never too long. Portions are generous; try the delicious eggs Florentine and the many types of pancakes. *SoHo, 359 West Broadway (at Broome St.), 925-2898, MC, V, AmEx, Entrées: $7-$15,* **ⒶⒸⒺ** *to Canal St.*

Cyclo
You can't miss this East Village eatery, what with the cyclo parked out front. Though the noise volume is high and the tables a bit cramped, the light and fresh Vietnamese cuisine more than compensates. The jellyfish and shrimp salad in a chili lime dressing is one of the more unusual appetizers, and the oxtail broth with noodles, sliced beef, scallions, and fresh herbs with fill you up without bogging you down. *East Village, 203 First Ave. (bet. 12th and 13th Sts.), 673-3957, MC, V, AmEx, Entrees: $9-$14,* **Ⓛ** *to 1st Ave.* ♿

D𝒹

Daniel
Another one of New York's finest: amazing food, beautiful setting, and, of course, prices to match. *Upper East Side, 60 East 65th St. (bet Park and Madison Aves.), 288-0033, MC, V, AmEx, Diners, Entrées: $40-$60,* **④⑥⑥** *to 68th St.-Hunter College* ♿

Dante Restaurant
Mature crowds of businessmen and nearby St. John's University professors and athletes visit this dimly lit Italian bistro and bar. *Kew Gardens, Queens, 168-12 Union Turnpike, (718) 380-3340, Entrées: $7-$13.25, MC, V, AmEx,* **ⒺⒻ** *to Union Turnpike-Kew Gardens* ♿

Deli Kasbah
Orthodox patrons fill the dining room, while take-out satisfies folks of all faiths with amazingly fresh meats and stellar entrées, like the jumbo pastrami burger. The menu has a Middle Eastern slant, with lots of hummus, babaganoush, and falafel; sample all three of them in the Kasbah Combination. *Upper West Side, 251 West 85th St. (bet. Broadway and West End Ave.), 496-1500, MC, V, D, Entrées: $8-$20,* **①⑨** *to 86th St.* ♿

Dish of Salt
Giant wooden parrots and colorful banners cater to the exotica stereotype, but the greasy and decidedly Americanized Chinese food is safe enough for the after work and pre-theater crowds. *Midtown, 133 West 47th St. (bet. Sixth and Seventh Aves.), 921-4242, MC, V, AmEx, Entrées: $18-$27,* **ⓃⓇ** *to 49th St.*

Dojo
The American and Japanese influenced dishes really only please fans of macrobiotic fare. The dirt-cheap prices and a frisky social scene are enough to lure NYU undergrads away from their meal-plan fare. *Greenwich Village, 14 West 4th St. (bet. Mercer St. and Broadway), 505-8934, Cash Only, Entrées:$3-$7,* **ⓃⓇ** *to 8th St.-NYU,* **Ⓖ** *to Bleecker St.* ♿

Also at:
East Village, 24 St. Marks Pl. (bet. Second and Third Aves.), 674-9821, Cash Only, Entrées: $3-$7, **6** *to Astor Pl.* 🚇

Dominick's
Good Italian, one of the better restaurants in The Bronx.
Be wary of the wait.
East Tremont, The Bronx, 2335 Arthur Ave. (at 187th St.), (718) 733-2807, Cash Only, Entrées: $23-$30, **BD** *to 182-183 Sts.* ♿

Don Giovanni
For a slice of the neighborhood, sit outside at a table and enjoy a pie at Don Giovanni. Made in a brick oven, with thin crust, fresh mozzarella, and a sweet tomato sauce, this pizza is bound to please. Be forewarned: delivery takes at least an hour.
Midtown, 358 West 44th St. (bet. Eighth and Ninth Aves.), 581-4939, MC, V, AmEx, Entrées: $7 -$22, **ACE** *to 42nd St.* ♿ 🚇

The Downtown Brooklyn Diner
A great standby. This diner is open 24 hours and serves breakfast, lunch, and dinner.
Downtown Brooklyn, 515 Atlantic Ave. (at Third Ave.), (718) 243-9172, MC, V, D, Entrées: $6-$8, **DDNR2345** *to Atlantic Ave.* 🚲

Ee

El Cid Tapas
Fit for Picasso, this tiny secret features the most authentic tapas this side of Barcelona. Go with a group and split a pitcher of white or red sangria, and fight over the last bite of marinated quail, seafood salad, or, their specialty, braised sweetbreads in garlic sauce. Come early on weekends.

Chelsea, 322 West 15th St. (bet. Eighth and Ninth Aves.), 929-9332, AmEx, Diners, Entrées: $10-$18, **ACE** *to 14th St.,* **L** *to Eighth Ave.* ♿

El Nuevo Sambuca Restaurant
Mirrored pillars and a loomingly dark piano room serve as an appropriately classy backdrop to an "international" culinary selection. Daytime and evening hours strongly differ in mood and cuisine.
Washington Heights, 4199 Broadway (at 178st St.), 795-4744, MC, V, AmEx, D, Entrées: $7-$17, **19** *to 181st St.* ♿ 🚲

El Pollo
All hail Peru's favorite bird — the chicken — at one of the city's very few Peruvian kitchens. Order the "pollo" in whole, half, or quarter portions and expect it to be spicy and succulent. Don't pass up the Andean peasant staples — the "mote" (Peruvian corn) and the "papas rellenas" (stuffed potatoes) are two of the country's crowning culinary achievements.
Upper East Side, 1746 First Ave. (bet. 90th and 91st Sts.), 996-7810, MC, V, AmEx, Entrées: $5-$10, **456** *to 86th St.* ♿

El Sitio de Astoria
Set the mood for truck-stop romance with your table's jukebox, although deals like the bandejas completas — a massive serving of meat, rice, beans, plantains, and croquettes — aren't among the wisest first-date choices, but getting a little tipsy on the sangria is all part of the fun.
Long Island City, Queens, 35-55 31st St., (718) 278-7694, MC, V, AmEx, Entrées: $7-$13, **N** *to 36th Ave. (Washington Ave)* ♿

El Teddy's
Known for its crazy, amusement-park facade, this TriBeCa favorite specializes in Tex-Mex cuisine and legendary margaritas. Bar scene is mostly Wall Streeters and neighborhood types during the week, though it definitely picks up with a rather chi-chi crowd later in the night.
TriBeCa, 219 West Broadway (bet. White and Franklin Sts.), 941-7070, MC, V, AmEx, Diners, D, Entrées: $15-$19, **19** *to Franklin St.,* **ACE** *to Canal St.*

Elaine's
A magnet for A-list hometown celebs often-featured in gossip columns. This popular hangout serves up standard American fare; quality blows hot and cold (mostly cold), but coming here for the food is like living in New York for the weather: it just shouldn't be a priority. Regulars include Woody Allen, Barbara Walters, and George Plimpton; Pat Riley also frequented this chic dining room.
Upper East Side, 1703 Second Ave. (bet. 88th and 89th Sts.), 534-8103, MC, V, AmEx, Diners, D, Entrées: $15-$25, **456** *to 86th St.* ♿

Eleven Madison Park
This upscale hotspot serves New York seasonal cuisine with a French influence. Along with the regular menu they have a fine à la carte. Go just for the grandeur of the space, which it shares with another creation by the same restauranteur — Tabla.
Gramercy, 11 Madison Ave. (at 24th St.), 889-0905, MC, V, AmEx, Diners, D, Entrées: $30-$45, **6** *to 23rd St.* ♿

Elias Corner
You'll have to read the reviews on the wall or point at fish in

the glass case — there are no menus — but either way Elias Corner will stuff you silly. Across the street from its old location, this seafood pleasure house features rough charm and primitive décor, but no matter: Delicious red snapper, octopus, and squid, along with bottles of cheap but effective wine make this completely worth the trip to Astoria.
Astoria, Queens, 24-02 31st St. (at 24th Ave.), (718) 932-1510, Cash Only, $8-$16, ⑩ to Astoria Blvd. (Hoyt Ave.) ♿

Empire Diner
Featured in Woody Allen's opening montage of *Manhattan*, this almost-24-hour eatery (it's closed 4am-8:30am) boasts an upscale diner menu, complemented by a jazz pianist. It's a great club-hopping pit stop; staying up for prix-fixe brunch is well worth the sleep deprivation. Don't go à la carte, as the prices soar.
Chelsea, 210 Tenth Ave. (at 22nd St.), 243-2736, MC, V, AmEx, Entrées: $5-$18, ⓒⒺ to 23rd St.

F̷

Famous Famiglia's
Come for the photos of celebrities on the wall, the jocular service, and the delicious and greasy pizza. The 'hood's finest garlic twists and the pizza's garlicky tomato sauce will keep the vampires away.
Morningside Heights, 2859 Broadway (at 111th St.), 865-1234, Cash Only, Entrées: $14.50, ①⑨ to Cathedral Pkwy. (110th St.) ♿

♿ = wheelchair access
🚬 = smoking section
🚲 = delivery available

Fanelli's
One of the last remnants of pre-gentrification SoHo. Everything about this place is unpretentious, from the spare decor to the sturdy pub-style food, which is what keeps it going strong as an alternative all the other too chic and trendy restaurants in the neighborhood. Be prepared to wait; on weekends they're often packed for hours.
SoHo, 94 Prince St. (at Mercer St.), 226-9412, MC, V, AmEx, Entrées: $5-$10, ⓃⓇ to Prince St.

First
Show a date you're hip by eating at this swanky, late night crowd-pleaser. Martinis come in several sizes, shapes, and flavors while the seasonal menu offers an unusual mix of incredible dinners. The candle lit tables and low lighting may make you feel like you have entered a black & white movie — put on your Humphrey Bogart accent and grab a cigar!
East Village, 87 1st Ave. (bet. 5th and 6th Sts.), 674-3823, MC, V, AmEx, Entrées: $15-20, Ⓕ to 2nd Ave., ⑥ to Astor Pl. 🚬

The Flame
Better known as a neighborhood icon than for its food, The Flame nonetheless ably serves up the expected diner menu, from omelets to burgers to gyros. The business crowd converges around 1pm for lunch, but otherwise there is ample seating and rarely (if ever) a wait. A good place to chat without having to fork over lots of dough.
Midtown, 893 Ninth Ave. (at 58th St.), 765-7962, MC, V, AmEx, D, Entrées: $4-$12, ⒶⒷⒸⒹ①⑨ to 59th St.-Columbus Circle ♿ 🚲

Florent
Fanciful bistro fare is available at all hours on weekends for a sophisticated and slightly affected mixed gay and straight

crowd in the hip Meat-Packing District. Housed in an old diner, the space is cool and understated; dishes are a mix of French and American classics.
Greenwich Village, 69 Gansevoort St. (bet. Greenwich and Washington Sts.) 989-5779, Cash Only, Entrées: $6-$16, ⒶⒸⒺ to 14th St., Ⓛ to Eighth Ave. ♿

14 Wall St. Restaurant
Join stockbrokers and investment bankers carrying on the legacy of J.P. Morgan by puffing cigars and sipping scotch in his old library, the closest thing to a private dining room in the city. The breakfast room overlooks the Harbor.
Lower Manhattan, 14 Wall St. (bet. Broadway and Broad St.), 233-2780, MC, V, AmEx, D, Entrées: $20-$25, ②③ to Wall St. ♿ 🚬

Fraunces Tavern
If you're a history buff, head here. Marvel at the spot where George Washington bid farewell to his troops in 1783 before feasting on cornish hen and crab cakes. The effect of the dark-wood paneling and enormous leather chairs can be either cozy or enervating, depending on how busy the place is.
Lower Manhattan, 54 Pearl St. (at Broad St.), 269-0144, MC, V, AmEx, Diners, D, Entrées: $12-$21, ①②④ to Broad St. ♿

Friend of a Farmer
Only in Gramercy could you find a Vermont snugness more convincing than anything in the Green Mountain State itself. While dinner is hearty and well-prepared, featuring stick-to-your-ribs specialties like shepherd's and chicken pot pies, the crowded brunch is the best feature. Another plus is that you've possibly seen similar prices in Montpelier.

Gramercy, 77 Irving Pl. (bet. 17th and 18th Sts.), 477-2188, MC, V, AmEx, Entrées: $8-$22, ❶❹❻ ❹❺❻ to 14th St.-Union Sq. ♿ 🚇

G g

Gabriel's

Among the crème de la crème of the bevy of restaurants around Lincoln Center, the combination of casual and class here is just about perfect. Beautiful decor, an astonishing, seasonal menu (order the delectable butternut squash ravioli if on the menu!), and a refined yet informal staff all account for why this is one of New York's hottest spots for dinner. Come after 7:45 pm to avoid the pre-concert crowd. *Upper West Side, 11 West 60th St. (bet. Broadway and Columbus Ave.), 956-4600, MC ,V, AmEx, Entrées: $17-$25,* ❶❷❸❶❾ to 59th St.-Columbus Circle.

Galaxy

This dark, cozy, Irving Plaza neighbor has a ceiling spattered with twinkling stars and swirling blue planets. After sampling hemp-infused dishes like soba noodles, tiger shrimp, and garden burger, you might feel like you're dining on cloud nine. For your non-culinary needs, they also sell a complete line of hemp products, from lip balm to textiles. *Gramercy, 15 Irving Place (at 15th St.), 777-3631, MC, V, Entrées: $8-10,* ❶❺❻❹❺❻ to 14th St.-Union Sq. ♿

Garage Restaurant & Café

Suburban steak house meets Greenwich Village panache at this sprawling multi-leveled village favorite. Its famous weekend jazz brunch offers both top-notch music and a mean eggs benedict. During the week, come for the music but stay for the unforgettable mussels, or their hearty sandwiches and raw bar. *Greenwich Village, 99 Seventh Ave. South (at Grove St.), 645-0600, MC, V, AmEx, Entrées: $8-$20,* ❶❾ to Christopher St.-Sheridan Sq. ♿

Gascogne

Feast on sumptuously prepared food, sip cognac, and surreptitiously loosen your belt a notch. Creative fowl like quail, wild boar, and rabbit all grace the menu. If the weather proves as good as the food, take a seat in the exquisite back garden, though indoors is atmospheric as well. As close to royalty as the bourgeoisie can get. *Chelsea, 158 Eighth Ave. (bet. 17th and 18th Sts.), 675-6564, MC, V, AmEx, Entrées: $18-$21,* ❹❾❺ to 14th St., ❶ to Eighth Ave. ♿

Gennaro

Native Italian chef Gennaro Picone graced several upscale Manhattan establishments before opening his own place where he serves unpretentious, truly Italian (not Italian-American) dishes in a tiny, unassuming space. The decor may seem a little rough around the edges, but the food is most definitely not (try the gnocchi), and the prices are so reasonable that they impose a $20 minimum. But be warned, the waits are long and the space is cramped. *Upper West Side, 665 Amsterdam Ave. (bet. 92nd and 93rd Sts.), 665-5348, Cash Only, Entrées: $9-14,* ❶❷❸❾ to 96th St. ♿

Global 33

This low-lit lounge/restaurant remains true to its name with a menu of international tapas-style dishes and an interior reminiscent of a '60s airport lounge. The petite dishes are artfully presented and delicious: Tart ceviche is heaped into a martini glass, cool roasted beets are served with warm goat cheese. Global also has a full menu of swanky cocktails, highlighted by some of the best Cosmopolitans around. Rotating DJs add to the festive feel (and the noise level). Open 6pm-2:30am, Sat. until 4am. *East Village, 93 Second Ave. (bet. 5th and 6th Sts.), 477-8427, MC, V, AmEx, Entrées: $4-$12,* ❻ to Second Ave. 🚇

Golden Unicorn

More sanitized and polished than most Chinatown dim sum houses, this chandeliered restaurant has become especially popular among tourists and local businessmen hosting lunch meeting. Delicious dim sum is served Hong-Kong style, stacked on metal carts piloted by vigorous employees. *Chinatown, 18 East Broadway (at Catherine St.), 941-0911, MC, V, AmEx, Diners, D, Entrées: $8-$11,* ❸❹❻ to Grand St.

Good Enough to Eat

The line to get into this popular brunch spot can often be seen from a few blocks away (no reservations accepted). Those who stick it out choose from ample portions of old-fashioned favorites and enjoy the warm, cozy atmosphere. "Just like Mom used to make" specialties include Cinnamon Swirl French Toast ($8.50) and Lumberjack breakfast ($8.00). Dinner is served nightly. *Upper West Side, 483 Amsterdam Ave. (between 83rd and 84th St.), 496-0163, MC, V, AmEx, Entrées: $7-$16,* ❶❾ to 86th St. ♿

Gotham Bar and Grill

Architecturally brilliant entrées like Atlantic salmon with ramps, morels, sweet peas, and chervil, betray the hand of one of the city's finest gourmets, Alfred Portale, and his kitchen team of all-star chefs, who've made Gotham's New American cuisine a staple for New York connoisseurs. Entrées bypass typical meats for rabbit, pheasant, and a couple so rare they're probably endangered. Sample it all with a $19.99 prix fixe lunch in the spacious, angular dining room. Don't pass up the most divine warm chocolate cake in all of NYC.
Greenwich Village, 12 East 12th St. (bet. Fifth Ave. and University Pl.), 620-4020, MC, V, AmEx, Diners, Entrées: $25-$40, ❶❶❶ ❹❺❻ *to 14th St.-Union Sq.* ♿

Gramercy Tavern

Don't be fooled by the rustic decor: Prices reflect the all-star clientele at this hot-spot for hobnobbing and networking. Stargazers may be willing to pay the price for a chance at sharing lunch with Johnny Depp.
Gramercy, 42 East 20th St. (bet. Park Ave. South and Broadway), 477-0777, MC, V, AmEx, Diners, Entrées: $18-$25, ❻❻ *to 23rd St.*

The Grange Hall

The coziest corner in the Village is home to one of its very finest restaurants. One of Uma Thurman's known haunts, this classy outpost of European refinement and American-style roasts and chicken dishes displays excellent taste without being ostentatious. Great for cocktails, the Hall is also famed for brunch.
Greenwich Village, 50 Commerce St. (bet. Bedford and Hudson Sts.), 924-5246, AmEx, Entrées: $12-$25, ❶❾ *to Christopher St.-Sheridan Sq.* ♿

Granville Restaurant/Lounge

Depending on the hour, the scene at this dark wood and leather-laden newcomer is set either by professionals or beautiful people. Dress accordingly and practice some posing in the upstairs cigar lounge.
Gramercy, 40 East 20th St. (bet. Broadway and Park Ave. South), 253-9088, MC, V, AmEx, Diners, Entrées: $18-$25, ❻❻ *to 23rd St.* ♿

Greenwich Cafe

Skip the entrées for the stylish array of appetizers at this spacious 24-hour cafe, staffed by waitpeople with the best cheekbones and most chic wardrobes in the West Village. Weekend night-hawks might encounter a chic party for slinky models and their agents; brunch guests are serenaded with soothing jazz. Outdoor seating is available in the summer.
Greenwich Village, 75 Greenwich Ave. (at Seventh Ave. South), 255-5450, MC, V, AmEx, Diners, D, Entrées: $10-$12, ❶❷❸❹ *to 14th St.* ♿

Grimaldi's

Every New Yorker claims to know the best pizzeria in the city, but Grimaldi's may be the real thing. Old Brooklyn ambiance is en-hanced by Sinatra and Bennett crooning as you savor crisp, thin-crust pizza that will satisfy even the most discriminating pizza lovers.
Fulton Ferry Landing, Brooklyn, 19 Old Fulton St. (bet. Water and Front Sts.), (718) 858-4300, Cash Only, Entrées: $12-$20, ❹❻ *to High St.-Brooklyn Bridge* ♿

Hh

Harry Cipriani

If you can stand the attitude, come to look for celebrities and feel like one yourself.
Upper East Side, 781 Fifth Ave. (bet. 59th and 60th Sts.), 753-5566, MC,V, AmEx, Diners, D, Entrées: $40, ❹❺❻ *to 59th St.,* ❻❻ *to Lexington Ave.* ♿

Harry's at Hanover Square

If you're in the mood for suits, cigars, and meat, this Wall St. hangout is the place. Order a martini and scan the great wine list as you enjoy one of Harry's excellent steaks. Not known for its feminine touches, it's not the place for "ladies who lunch." Like the stock market, it's closed on weekends.
Lower Manhattan, 1 Hanover Sq. (bet. Pearl and Stone Sts.), 425-3412, MC, V, AmEx, Diners, D, Entrées: $14-$30, ❻❻ *to Whitehall St.-South Ferry* ♿

Healthy Henrietta's

Bulky macrobiotic burritos recommend this charming BoHo outpost, where the living is oh-so-simple. Food comes straight from the earth and the slight twang of an acoustic guitar sounds as Manhattan's urbanity is just a twinkle on the horizon.
Brooklyn Heights, Brooklyn, 60 Henry St. (bet. Orange and Cranberry Sts.), (718) 858-8478, AmEx, Entrées: $6-$12, ❷❸ *to Clark St.* ♿

Also at:
Park Slope, Brooklyn, 787 Union St. (bet. Fifth and Sixth Aves.), (718) 622-2924, AmEx, Entrées: $6-$12, ❶❶❻ *to Union St.* ♿

The Heights

This slick restaurant-bar now has a rooftop garden which is heated in the cooler months. Potent margaritas, fresh salsa with tricolored chips, and an eager waitstaff make this a favorite among Columbia students. Start early by slurping $2.50 margaritas during happy hour between 5pm and 7pm.

Morningside Heights, 2867 Broadway (at 111th St.), 866-7035, MC, V, Entrées: $8-$15, ❶❾ to 110th St. ⌐

Home

The name conjures up the American iconography of mom and apple pie, but despite the low pretension and familiar line-up of pork chops and chocolate pudding, this refined Village eatery is a bit too urbane to qualify as a suburban transplant. Chefs may not infuse the catfish with mom's love, but they are committed to resisting the strong French trends in New American cuisine, instead steering culinary attention toward hometown faves. Homes' homemade ketchup proves again why classics never go out of style.
Greenwich Village, 20 Cornelia St. (bet. Bleecker and West 4th Sts.), 243-9579, AmEx, Entrées: $13-$17, ❶❷❸❹❺❻❼ *to West 4th St.-Washington Sq.* ⌐

Hudson River Club

Advertising that this Wall Street professional haven "specializes in food from the Hudson" might not seem too smart, but the seasonal seafood masterpieces are delectable. Gorge on artfully prepared shellfish while Lady Liberty gazes stolidly in the distance.
Lower Manhattan, 4 World Financial Center, 250 Vesey St. (at West St.), 786-1500, MC, V, AmEx, Diners, D, Entrées: $28-$36, ❶❾ *to Cortlandt St.,* ❷❸ *to World Trade Center* ⌐

I i

Il Boschetto

Reliable, if not cheap, Bronx Italian. Large ortions make it worth the trip.
Baychester, The Bronx, 1660 East Gun Hill Rd. (at Tiemann Ave.),

(718) 379-9335, MC, V, AmEx, Diners, D, Entrées: $25-$35, ❺ to Gun Hill Rd. ⌐

Indigo

Creative cuisine and impeccable presentation make this tucked-away gem a find. With chef Scott Bryan from Siena (the restaurant, not the city), this excellent but unpretentious French-American bistro also has reasonable prices. Votive candles set a subtle indigo mood and the coat check gives everyone a little more room. Try the sorbet for dessert and understand why the next table called it 'orgasmic.'
Greenwich Village, 142 West 10th St. (bet. Greenwich Ave. and Waverly Pl.), 691-7757, AmEx, Entrées: $14-$16, ❶❾ *to Christopher St.-Sheridan Sq.* ⌐

Ithaka

The authentic Greek fare and unpretentious atmosphere attracts locals interested in food, not hype. Preparing the food before you in an open kitchen, the portly chef expertly unfolds filo dough as he greets the regulars and offers recommendations. You may be tempted to stuff yourself on the abundant entrées, such as the striped bass baked with feta cheese, but leave room for the baklava and other homemade desserts.
Greenwich Village, 48 Barrow St. (bet. Bedford and Bleecker Sts.), 727-8886, MC, V, Amex, Diners, Entrées: $16-$19, ❶❾ *to Christopher St.-Sheridan Sq.* ⌐

J j

Jean Georges

Undoubtedly one of the best in New York; be warned, it's hard to get in despite the three dining areas.

Upper West Side, 1 Central Park West (bet. 60th and 61st Sts.), 299-3900, MC, V, AmEx, Diners, Entrées: $40-$50, ❶❷❸❹❾ to 59th St.-Columbus Circle ⌐

Jerry's

A longtime crowd pleaser, Jerry's still has a line out the door for weekend brunch. Try a plate of stellar tuna salad or citrus-marinated chicken — they're all the rage. This hot lunch spot draws a huge art crowd and plenty of celebrities. Jerry's has maintained a down-to-earth atmosphere, despite its popularity.
SoHo, 101 Prince St. (bet. Greene and Mercer Sts.), 966-9464, MC, V, AmEx, Entrees: $9-$13, ❶❷ *to Prince St.* ⌐

Jimmy's Bronx Café

After just four years in the Bronx, this "Latin Restaurant and Entertainment Complex" has become the nucleus for nightlife in the borough's Latino community. Upstairs, seafood is served into the wee hours as patrons watch boxing and baseball on the large TVs. Downstairs, the dance floor resembles a hotel ballroom, built for high capacity. As at other Latin clubs, there's no such thing as overdressing, though casual seems prevalent. Salsa dancing on Tuesday nights.
Fordham, The Bronx, 281 West Fordham Rd. (at Major Deegan Expressway), (718) 329-2000, MC, V, AmEx, Entrées: $8-$18, ❶❾ *to 207th St.* ⌐

Joe Allen

Upscale thespians, including bonafide Broadway celebs in search of some post-performance relaxation, come to this dark and elegant but unpretentious eatery to fill up on gourmet meatloaf and hot fudge pudding cake. On

Sunday nights 8pm to closing, fifteen percent of every check goes to Broadway Cares/Equity Fights AIDS.
Midtown, 326 West 46th St. (bet. Eighth and Ninth Aves.), 581-6464, MC, V, Entrées: $10-$20, **A** **C** **E** *to 42nd St.* &

Joe's Shanghai
Tourists, locals, and suburban Chinese flock here for the juicy crabmeat buns for which Joe's is deservedly famous. Friendly service and the savory quality of the rest of the fare keeps customers coming back for more.
Chinatown, 9 Pell St. (bet. Bowery and Mott St.), 233-8888, Cash Only, Entrées: $9-$20, **J** **M** **N** **R** **Z** **6** *to Canal St.*

John's of Bleecker Street
This thin, coal-oven-baked pizza is preceded by its well-deserved reputation. A good place for groups to hang out. No slices, only whole pies — the mark of an excellent pizzeria.
Greenwich VIllage, 278 Bleecker St. (bet. Sixth and Seventh Aves.), 243-1680, Cash Only, Entrées: $12, **A** **B** **C** **D** **E** **F** **Q** *toWest 4th St.-Washington Sq.* &

Junior's
Sample "New York's Best Cheesecake" (don't confuse it with the cheese pie!) or just about anything else you can imagine at this monster diner/ bar, open till 2am on weekends. Busy bar, with eclectic group of patrons. Speedy service, but sometimes a wait for a table on weekends.
Downtown Brooklyn, 386 Flatbush Ave. (at DeKalb Ave.), (718) 852-5257, MC, V, AmEx, D, Entrées: $6-$15, **D** **M** **N** **Q** **R** *to DeKalb Ave.* & ↰

K k

Katz's Delicatessen
Steaming pastrami and corned beef sandwiches and other artery-clogging delicacies await at this cavernous, superior (non-Kosher) delicatessen, where yellowing paint and curling posters exhorting patrons to "Send a salami to your boy in the army" prove that nothing much has changed here in about 50 years. A dollar tip to one of the gruff, portly attendants behind the counter will beget a sandwich big enough to feed a family of 5.
Lower East Side, 205 East Houston St. (at Ludlow St.), 254-2246, MC, V, AmEx, Entrées: $5-$15, **F** *to Second Ave.* & ⚲

Kin Khao
Don't be surprised to see a budding supermodel sitting down the bench from you here; this place is *very* trendy. However, the atmosphere isn't prohibitive to normal people and once you get inside, the waitstaff is unpretentious and the decor is beautiful and comfortable. The food is Thai, and the quality isn't all that consistent; to be safe stick to one of the noodle dishes that are almost always delectable.
SoHo, 171 Spring St. (bet. West Broadway and Thompson St.), 966-3939, MC, V, AmEx, Entrées: $11-$18, **C** **E** *to Spring St.* &

Kitchen Club
Serving up Continental cuisine with a Japanese twist, this "friendly little place" has an eccentric feel to it. The turquoise curtains, huge checkered tile floor, and French doors which open out onto the street may have something to do with the unique atmosphere.
SoHo, 30 Prince St. (at Mott St.) 274-0025, MC, V, AmEx, Entrées: $16-$24, **N** **R** *to Prince St.,* **6** *to Spring St.* &

L l

La Poème
Inside the antique-laden dining room of chef Martine Abitbol's daytime home, aging poets and artists chatter while seated around a taffeta-covered table crowded with platters of steaming seafood. The Abitbol family's husky pads his way across the floor toward the kitchen while Martine leaves her stove momentarily to ask customers how they are enjoying the hearty Tunisian and Corsican influenced dishes.
SoHo, 14 Prince St. (at Elizabeth St.), 941-1106, Cash Only, Entrées: $10-$15, **N** **R** *to Prince St.*

Lanza's
Authentic Italian food *sans* gimmicks or fancy perversions. The clientele is large and loyal, filling the restaurant nightly for both the classy old-style ambiance and superior food at bargain prices. Thankfully it's neither trendy nor cutting-edge.
East Village, 168 First Ave. (bet. 10th and 11th Sts.), 674-7014, MC, V, AmEx, Diners, Entrées: $11-$17, **N** **R** **4** **5** **6** *to 14th St.-Union Sq.,* **L** *to First Ave.* & ⚲

Layla
For authentic food from a trendy restaurant with beautiful decor, this is as good as it gets. The menu is a mix of standards like tabouleh and new creations centered around fish and lamb. Even when the food isn't incredible, the beautiful setting is enough to compensate.
TriBeCa, 211 West Broadway (at Franklin St.), 431-0700, MC, V, AmEx, Entrées: $19-$27, **1** **9** *to Franklin St.* &

Le Bilboquet

Chain-smoking Eurotrash trail crowds of beautiful people into this diminutive French bistro, currently boasting some of the hippest new lounging turf. Models can't appreciate the menu, but don't let that stop you from taking advantage of the well-executed bistro fare. *Upper East Side, 25 East 63rd St. (bet. Madison and Park Aves.), 751-3036, MC, V, AmEx, Entrés: $17-$24, 456 to 59th St., NR to Lexington Ave.* ⌐

Le Café Bruxelles

One of a number of Belgian joints now open on the West Side, this is perhaps the most consistent. The staff is authentically ethnic, the setting cozy, and the food — mussels, fabulous frites, and beers brewed at monasteries — is très, très bon. *Greenwich Village, 118 Greenwich Ave. (at 13th St.), 206-1830, MC, V, AmEx, Diners, Entrées: $12-$18, A CE to 14th St., L to Eighth Ave.* ⌐

Le Cirque 2000

Set in the historic Villard Houses, attached to the New York Palace Hotel, Le Cirque combines the refinement of the past with giddy designs of the future. Longtime chef Sottha Khunn's French classic creations add civility to Adam Tihany's pleasantly outrageous decor, and Jacques Torres' perfect desserts will leave you reeling. *Midtown, 455 Madison Ave. (bet. 50th and 51st Sts.), 303-7788, MC, V, AmEx, Diners, Entrées: $28-$38, 6 to 51st St., EF to Lexington-3rd Aves.* ⅋

Le Gamin

A more successful stab than most at replicating a Parisian café, this neighborhood joint serves crepes, croque monsieur, quiche, and salads to a laid-back, lingering crowd. Family types mix with the downtown chic; the lack of a liquor license encourages people to bring their own beer or wine. A great stopover for a cappuccino while club-hopping or a good setting for more lengthy leisure and a latte. The French menu has English subtitles. *Chelsea, 183 Ninth Ave. (at 21st St.), 243-8864, Cash Only, Entrées: $7-$10, CE to 23rd St.* ⅋

Also at:

SoHo, 51 MacDougal St. (bet. Houston and Prince Sts.), Cash Only, Entrées: $10-$15 254-4678, CE to Spring St. ⅋ ⌐

Le Grenier

The cuisine at this popular neighborhood spot is straight from the Ivory Coast, to which the locals in African garb and the outbursts in French attest. Indeed, although patrons are assured of authentic West African dishes like jolof rice and suppu kavjan, anyone outside of the community may feel a bit uncomfortable. *Harlem, 2264 Frederick Douglass Blvd. (bet. 121st and 122nd Sts.), 666-0653, Cash Only, Entrées: $7-$10, ABCD to 125th St.*

Le Madri

Le Madri blends homey and chic in a spacious restaurant featuring modern dishes rooted in Italian tradition. Conventional creations, like French fries and fried calamari, come off surprisingly well, but best are the house-made pastas, anything from the wood-burning oven, the seafood, and the popular osso buco. Desserts deserve special mention, truly Italian in their subtlety and simplicity. (Try a *real* tiramisu.) There's also the extra perk of a possible celebrity spotting, and valet parking. *Chelsea, 168 West 18th St. (at 7th Ave.), 727-8022, MC, V, AmEx, Diners, D, Entrées: $18-$26, 19 to 18th St.* ⅋ ⌐ ⚙

Le Pain Quotidien

The smell of freshly baked bread welcomes you to this cozy Belgian bakery/café featuring a giant communal wooden table and some of the flakiest croissants this side of the Atlantic. Everything from rustic baguettes to country loaves, for which European flour is specially imported, is masterfully prepared and baked on the premises in batches throughout the day. A delicious array of breakfast and lunch dishes are also served. *Upper East Side, 1311 Madison Ave. (bet. 84th and 85th Sts.), 327-4900, Cash Only, Entrées: $8-$12, 456 to 86th St.*

Also at:

SoHo, 100 Grand St. (at Mercer St.), 625-9009, Cash Only, ACE to Canal St.

Le Refuge Inn

Good French food at a bed and breakfast; be careful, you'll be tempted to stay the night. *City Island, The Bronx, 620 City Island Ave. (at Sutherland St.), (718) 885-2478, AmEx, Entrées: $45-$55* ⌐

Le Tableau

An unusual reprieve from typical East Village flamboyance, this adorable French restaurant offers high quality food and wonderful service to a casual mix of clientele. The daily rotating specials menu should encourage you to make repeat visits, but be sure you make a reservation Friday or Saturday nights for parties of five and up to enjoy the live jazz band (and remember, a full band in a popular restaurant makes for cozy dining!). *East Village, 511 East 5th St. (bet. Aves. A and B), 260-1333, Cash Only, Entrées: $12-16, F to 2nd Ave., 6 to Astor Pl.* ⅋

Les Deux Gamins

French-inspired omelets, salads, and rich entrées consistently attract crowds at this endearing, perennially popular bistro. Brunch goes down perfectly with cafe au lait or cocoa in warmed bowls on a lazy Sunday morning. Service can be harried, though the crowd of low-key locals in their late 20s is tolerant.
Greenwich Village, 170 Waverly Pl. (at Grove St.), 807-7357, AmEx, Entrées: $14-$23, ①⑨ to Christopher St. ⌐

Les Halles

Authentically Parisian, down to the boucherie by the front door, this bustling brasserie is well-known for its memorable steak frites and onion soup. Cramped tables mean people-watching and eavesdropping are favored diversions.
Gramercy, 411 Park Ave. South (bet. 28th and 29th Sts.), 679-4111, MC, V, AmEx, D, Entrées: $12-$22, ⑥ to 28th St. ⌐ &

Lexington Candy Shoppe

Its antique malt-mix dispenser and shake machine have been churning since 1925, making a meal at this old-fashioned soda fountain and diner a historical event. Pay homage by ordering one of the burgers sizzling on a small griddle and a complicated dairy concoction.
Upper East Side, 1226 Lexington Ave. (at 83rd St.), 288-0057, MC, V, AmEx, Entrées: $6-$8, ④⑤⑥ to 86th St. & ⌐

⌐ = WHEELCHAIR ACCESS
⌐ = SMOKING SECTION
⌐ = DELIVERY AVAILABLE

Life Cafe

Featured in the Broadway play *Rent*, this eclectic source of nutritious Cal-Mex is an East Village landmark of laid-back creativity. Check out the rotating exhibits by local artists, preferably during the weekday happy hour (5pm-9pm).
East Village, 343 East 10th St. (at Ave. B), 477-8791, MC, V, D, Entrées: $7-$12, ❶ to First Ave. & ⌐

Lobster Box

Pretty views and good lobster, but it's not as memorable as it used to be.
City Island, The Bronx, 34 City Island Ave. (bet. Belden and Rochelle Sts.), (718) 885-1952, MC, V, AmEx, Entrées: $25-$35 &

The Lobster Club

Chef/owner Anne Rosenzweig made headlines years ago when she stormed the citadel of all-male chefs at the city's top-rated restaurants. Indulge in one of her signature dishes like corn cakes with crème fraîche and caviar, or chocolate-bread pudding swimming in brandy-custard sauce; in all her cooking, Rosenzweig wonderfully combines French technique and American heartiness.
Upper East Side, 24 East 80th St. (bet. Madison and Fifth Aves.), 249-6500, MC, V, AmEx, Diners, Entrées: $18-$28, ⑥ to 77th St.

Londel's

Owner Londel Davis greets customers at the door of his sophisticated new Strivers Row supperclub, a harbinger of gentrification in this quickly changing neighborhood. Harlem's hottest restaurant serves delicious, painstakingly prepared Southern food like smothered pork chops and pan-seared red snapper to the neighborhood's most upwardly mobile. Sunday brunch draws a crowd, as do the live jazz and blues acts Friday and Saturday nights.
Harlem, 2620 Frederick Douglass Blvd. (bet. 139th and 140th Sts.), 234-6114, MC, V, AmEx, D, Entrées: $9-$16, ❶❷❸❹ to 145th St. ⌐

Luna

Show up early or plan to spend time waiting in line for this favorite neighborhood haunt. The Plaza it's not, but expect hearty, down-home Italian cooking. The sagging floorboards might even remind you of grandma's house.
Little Italy, 112 Mulberry St. (at Canal St.) 226-8657, MC, V, AmEx, Entrées: $9-$17, ❶❶❶❷❷❸ to Canal St. ⌐

Mabat

Like any ethnic neighborhood restaurant in the outer boroughs, this place may not be as fancy as its Manhattan counterparts, but it makes up for it in authenticity and price. Nearly everything here is very good.
Midwood, Brooklyn, 1809 East 7th St. (bet. Quentin Rd. and Kings Highway), (718) 339-3300, Cash Only, Entrées: $14-$16, ❶❷ to King's Highway ⌐

Madras Mahal

Vegetarian Kosher Indian food attracts an eclectic crowd, ranging from vegetarian Indians to Orthodox Jews. The atmosphere is friendly and service staff is dedicated.
Gramercy, 104 Lexington Ave. (bet. 27th and 28th Sts.), 684-4010, AmEx, D, MC, V, Entrées: $7-$12, ⑥ to 28th St. ⌐

Mama Joy's

In the front window a handwritten copy of a Zagat review sings the praises of this cramped deli's mind-boggling list of cheeses. Sandwiches here are great, but go elsewhere for standard grocery items. Columbia students come for the vast beer selection just before the 1am closing time.
Morningside Heights, 2892 Broadway (at 113th St.), 662-0716, MC, V, AmEx, Entrées: $5, ❶❾ to 110th St. 👟

Mamas Food Shop

Mama is, in fact, a man who cooked so much food for his friends that his space evolved into a restaurant. All the food is homestyle excellence, and the portions are huge. Try the grilled salmon, don't miss the awesome mac-and-cheese. Across the street, get soup and sandwiches at Stepmamas, a spin-off.
East Village, 200 East 3rd St. (bet. Aves. A and B), 777-4425, Cash Only, Entrées: $6-$8, ❻ to Second Ave. 👟

Mangia

Gourmet Mediterranean cuisine and friendly waitstaff at this lunch restaurant make it a culinary hot-spot for the surrounding working worlds of businesses, galleries and museums. Mangia's diverse array of pastas, sandwiches, and entrées — including an "antipasto table," with a wonderful selection of foods ranging from paella to rare tuna — is sure to quench anyone's desire for a gastro-nomic thrill. In a rush? Stop at the café downstairs for equally delicious take-out dining.
Midtown, 50 West 57th St. (bet. Fifth and Sixth Aves.), 582-5554, MC, V, AmEx, Diners, D, Entrées: $11-15, ❻ to 57th St. 👟

Mario's

Good pizza and pasta, but beware of tourists.
East Tremont, The Bronx, 2342 Arthur Ave. (bet. 184th and 186th Sts.), (718) 584-1188, MC, V, AmEx, Entrées: $25-$30, ❻❼ to 182-183 Sts.

Marylou's

Elegant restaurant and bar sunken into the basement level of a fashionable townhouse. Entrées tend towards expensive seafood, but the bar is cozy and the crowd is mostly regulars.
Greenwich Village, 21 West 9th St. (bet. Fifth and Sixth Aves.), 533-0012, MC, V, AmEx, Diners, D, Entrées: $14-$22, ❶❷❸❹❺❻❼ to West 4th St.-Washington Sq. 📞

Match Uptown

A dose of uptown swank and sophistication with a dash of pretension flavor this hip New American menu with its own in-house sushi bar, sit-in bar, and caviar service. Mood lighting, an older crowd, and comfortable seating make for a pleasant dining experience. Food is colorful, artfully prepared, and fabulous. Dessert is a must!
Upper East Side, 33 East 60th St. (bet. Madison and Park Aves.), 906-9177, MC, V, AmEx, Entrées: $25-30, ❹❺❻ to 59th St., ❹❻ to Lexington Ave. 📞

Maya

Excellent cuisine, excellent service, and a comfortable atmosphere make dining at this "Gourmet Mexican" truly a euphoric experience. The food is that good. Colorful and flavorful, the dishes are inventive with surprising combinations. Try the mango margaritas and the guacamole with fresh chips.
Upper East Side, 1191 First Ave. (at 64th St.), 585-1818, MC, V, AmEx, Entrées: $17-$25, ❹❺❻ to 59th St., ❹❻ to Lexington Ave. 📞

Mekka

People of all types are drawn to the excellent Southern and Caribbean food at this urban, hip-hop restaurant. Difficult as it is to resist, don't devour too much of the complementary cornbread, or you may find yourself incapable of walking at the end of the night, or worse yet, you won't have room for the peach cobbler, which is a must.
East Village, 14 Ave. A (bet. Houston and 2nd Sts.), 475-8500, MC, V, AmEx, D, Entrées: $14, ❻ to Second Ave.

The Mercer Kitchen

Specializing in American provincial food, you can sit under the sidewalk on SoHo streets in a glass-encased dining room and see the people walking above.
SoHo, 99 Prince St. (at Mercer St.), 966-5454, MC, V, AmEx, Diners, Entrées: $25-$30, ❶❼ to Prince St.

Merchants, NY

The downtown branch of a trio of sleek establishments of the same name, some actually order food here to go with their martini or cosmopolitan; check out the downstairs sofa scene for ultimate cushiness. The appetizer and dessert menus are excellent.
Chelsea, 112 Seventh Ave. (bet. 16th and 17th Sts.), 366-7267, MC, V, AmEx, D, Entrées: $10-$18, ❶❾ to 18th St. 📞

Also at:
Upper West Side, 521 Columbus Ave. (bet. 85th and 86th Sts.), 721-3689, MC, V, AmEx, Diners, Entrées: $10-$18, ❶❸ to 86th St. 📞

Upper East Side, 1125 First Ave. (at 62nd St.), 832-1551, MC, V, AmEx, Diners, Entrées: $13-$19, ❹❺❻ to 59th St., ❻❼ to Lexington Ave. 🚬

Mesa Grill
Bobby Flay's limitless imagination has bestowed upon the city a masterful array of Southwestern flavors served in a light, airy space that pulses with festivity. A New York favorite, this restaurant is an eye-opener for those yet unacquainted with the exuberance of Flay's cuisine. *Gramercy, 102 Fifth Ave. (bet. 15th and 16th Sts.), 807-7400, MC, V, AmEx, D, Entrées: $18-$29,* ❻❼❹❺❻ to 14th St-Union Sq. ♿ 🚬

Metisse
Ooh la la! With this rich, delicious, reasonably priced food, you might blink and think you've found Paris in New York. *Upper West Side, 239 West 105th St. (at Broadway), 666-8825, MC, V, AmEx, Entrées: $10-$14,* ❶❾ to 103rd St. ♿

Metro Diner
Unique to the world of diners, this veggie-friendly establishment offers all the standard diner fare — only fresh! — with a splash of Mediterranean dishes including a variety of salads and vegetarian plates. Grab a booth and soak in its streamlined train car decor. A great post-movie hangout. *Upper West Side, 2641 Broadway (at 100th St.), 866-0800, MC, V, AmEx, Entrées: $10-$14,* ❶❷❸❾ to 96th St. ♿ 🚲

Mi Cocina
Mexican cuisine, West Village-style: haute, pricey, and with a generous supply of liquor. The most savory south-of-the-border

dishes here may not be authentic, but the place is chic. *Greenwich Village, 57 Jane St. (at Hudson St.), 627-8273, MC, V, AmEx, Diners, Entrées: $13-$22,* ❶❷❸ to 14th St., ❶ to Eighth Ave. 🚲

Michael Jordan's Steakhouse
This upscale steakhouse is part of Grand Central's make-over. Stop by for dinner before grabbing the Metro-North up-state, or make the trip to this gorgeous station just to enjoy a martini at the end of the day. *Grand Central Station (on the west balcony), 23 Vanderbuilt Ave. (bet. Park and Lexington Aves.), 655-2300, MC, V, AmEx, Entrées: $35-$55,* ❹❺❻❼ to 42nd St.-Grand Central Station ♿

Milos
Greek Mediterranean food including a market place to see the fish you'll eat and have it weighed by the pound. *Midtown, 125 West 55th St. (bet. Sixth and Seventh Aves.), 245-7400, MC, V, AmEx, Diners, Entrées: $40-$60,* ❻❼ to 57th St. ♿

Mocca Hungarian
Throw your doctor's caveats regarding cholesterol to the wind and dig into peasant staples like goulash and stuffed cabbage. The decor takes its cues from communist functionalism. *Upper East Side, 1588 Second Ave. (bet. 82nd and 83rd Sts.), 734-6470, Cash Only, Entrées: $7-$14,* ❹❺❻ to 86th St. ♿

Monte's
Extant since 1918, the charm of this amicable basement trattoria will remain long after the taste has slipped away. The menu spares no calorie, so go all the way and try the zabaglione served cold with strawberries.

Greenwich Village, 97 MacDougal St. (at 3rd St.), 228-9194, MC, V, AmEx, Diners, D, Entrées: $7-$13, ❶❷❸❹❺❻❼ to West 4th Street-Washington Sq. 🚲

N*n*

New Prospect Café
A diminutive cutie, the light menu here features some excellent seafood vegetable dishes and nice, reasonably priced wine. Not for New York's night owls, the kitchen closes by 10pm; on the other hand, brunch is excellent and always crowded. *Prospect Heights, Brooklyn, 393 Flatbush Ave. (bet. Plaza St. and Sterling Pl.), (718) 638-2148, MC, V, AmEx, Entrées $9-$16,* ❷❸ to Grand Army Plaza, ❼❼ to Seventh Ave. ♿

New York Noodletown
While its uniquely savory crab dishes best explain the mobs of people, any of the roasted meat entrées are a good bet for quick, cheap eats; this spot carries cachet with those who know the ins and outs of Chinatown eats. *Chinatown, 28 Bowery (at Pell St.), 349-0923, Cash Only, Entrées: $4-$10,* ❻❼❼ to Grand St.

Niko's
Nearly always crammed to capacity, this tavern offers a range of delicacies that take cues from all over the Mediterranean, particularly Greece and Lebanon. Noteworthy are the stuffed grape leaves and the rodos yuvetsi, a lamb stew. Afterwards, choose from among the array of authentic honey-drenched desserts. *Upper West Side, 2161 Broadway (at 76th St.), 873-7000, MC, V, AmEx, D, Entrées: $10-$18,* ❶❷❸❾ to 72nd St. ♿ 🚲

Nino's Pizza

There must be a thousand different slice joints in this city, but this is without a doubt one of the very best. In addition to making great pizza, the place looks out on Tompkins Square Park and keeps hours as late as any bar. A plain slice is always a safe bet, but the more adventuresome shouldn't miss the white pizza with fresh tomatoes. Mmmmmm.

East Village, 131 St. Marks Pl. (at Ave. A), 979-8688, Cash Only, Entrées: $10, ❻ *to Astor Pl.* ⑁

Nobu

One of the hottest and best restaurants in the city, offering exquisite L.A.-style Japanese cuisine served in a pristinely decorated, lofty, and uncluttered space for the rich, famous, and gourmands. Reservations must be made 30 days in advance, leaving you plenty of time to eagerly anticipate the meal.

TriBeCa, 105 Hudson St. (at Franklin St.), 219-0500, MC, V, AmEx, Diners, Entrées: $20-$30, ❶❾ *to Franklin St.* ♿

O

O Padeiro

This Portuguese bakery-cum-restaurant cum bar accomplishes noteworthy feats with egg and garlic, but its most tasteful feature is the decor: elevated breads, baked on the premises, and stylish fans accent the lofty ceilings. A café by day, it successfully converts itself into a casual dinner spot. Try the wine tasting menu to sample delicious, but under-appreciated, Portuguese wines.

Chelsea, 641 Sixth Ave. (bet. 19th and 20th Sts.), 414-9661, MC, V, Amex, Entrées: $16, ❻ *to 23rd St.,* ❶❾ *to 18th St.* ♿ ⑁

The Odeon

After many years, this place remains one of the most stylish eateries around. Its secret seems to be maintaining atmosphere and decor that are classically stylish, rather than trendy, and serving excellent brasserie food for the late-night dining crowd. More suitable for making the scene with a group than an intimate dinner for two.

TriBeCa, 145 West Broadway (bet. Duane and Thomas Sts.), 233-0507, MC, V, AmEx, Diners, D, Entrées: $15, ❶❷❸❾ *to Chambers St.* ♿ ⬅

Odessa

The hippest of the East Village's Eastern European diners, open 24 hours. Everything from standard diner food to potato pancakes and other regional fare finds its way onto the menu. The location makes it perfect for a food break while cruising the Ave. A bar scene, and to continue drinking you need only walk next door to their lounge, recently opened in the restaurant's pre-expansion and remodeling digs.

East Village, 119 Ave. A (bet. 7th and 8th Sts.), 253-1470, MC, V, AmEx, Entrées: $6-$12, ❻ *to Second Ave.* ♿ ⬅ ⑁

Old Devil Moon

East Village restaurant specializing in southern food with a cool and funky atmosphere and big portions.

East Village, 511 East 12th St. (bet. Aves. A and B), 475-4357, MC, V, AmEx, Diners, Entrées: $12, ❻ *to First Ave.* ♿ ⬅

147

Known as much for its fashionable clientele as for its delicious menu, the decor here is subtle yet elegant, the food simple yet scrumptious. You can't go wrong

ordering, but we especially recommend the chilled vegetable rolls as an appetizer. After your meal, hang out until the wee hours at the stylish bar.

Chelsea, 147 West 15th St. (bet. Sixth and Seventh Aves.), 929-5000, MC, V, AmEx, Entrées: $15-$25, ❶❷❸❾ *to 14th St.* ♿ ⬅

Onieal's Grand Street

This turn-of-the-century tavern, rumored to have been frequented by Teddy Roosevelt during his tenure as police commissioner. Onieal's retains its old world charm for the bankers, architects, models and celebrities who come for the flavorful dishes and grown-up surroundings. New American with Italian overtures, it also features a traditional Irish breakfast, while at night it transforms into a popular late night lounge.

Chinatown, 174 Grand Street (bet. Baxter and Mulberry Sts.), 941-9119, MC, V, AmEx, Entrées: $15-$18, ❻❻❻ *to Grand St.,* ❻❻❻❻❷❻ *to Canal St.* ⬅

Osteria del Circo

Everyone should be able to find something at this Midtown Northern Italian, with fish, pasta, pizza, and meat.

Midtown, 120 West 55th St. (bet. Sixth and Seventh Aves.), 265-3636, MC, V, AmEx, Diners, Entrées: $30-$40, ❶❻ *to 57th St.* ♿ ⬅

Oznot's Dish

This quirky restaurant has become a premiere site for nouveau ethnic cuisine, combining Mediterranean flavors and French presentation. With bright mosaics covering the walls and a year-round sunroom, Oznot's is elegantly hip: the waitstaff is

down-to-earth but knowledge-able, the ambience laid back but classy, and the food superior but moderately priced. The expansive menu, offering outrageous meat dishes as well as vegetarian delights, boasts a selection of 300 wines.
Williamsburg, Brooklyn, 79 Berry St., (at North 9th St.), (718) 599-6596, MC, V, Entrées: $15-$17, ❶ *to Bedford Ave.*

Ozu

Though prompt seating can be a problem, this small, Japanese macrobiotic, near-organic restaurant wins points for its creative tofu, grain, noodle, tempura, and vegetable dishes. The ambitious side orders will transport you to new levels of sensual awareness, especially the three-root sesame salad with carrot, burdock root, and daikon radish.
Upper West Side, 566 Amsterdam Ave. (at 87th St.), 787-8316, MC, V, Entrées: $7-$12, ❶❾ *to 86th St.*

P℗

Palacinka

"It's anything you want it to be," according to co-owner Tariq, but in particular this BYOB café serves tired and trendy SoHo shoppers delicious French-style crepes as a light meal or for dessert. It's worth a visit just to appreciate the unusual, but obviously trendy decor: a smattering of random antiques amidst metal tables and chairs that can be easily positioned for a romantic meeting over a cup of coffee. Be prepared to sit a while —crepes are made to order.
SoHo, 28 Grand St. (bet. 6th Ave. and Thompson St.), 625-0362, Cash Only, Entrees: $6-$8, ❶❸❺ *to Canal St.* ♿ ⌐

Pamir

Savory pilaf complements the well-executed lamb and chicken dishes, from kebabs to quabilli palaw, at this cozy uptown enclave of Afghan cuisine adorned with hand-tooled metalwork and bright Afghan rugs. Denim-clad patrons will feel self-conscious in the upscale atmosphere.
Upper East Side, 1437 Second Ave. (bet. 74th and 75th Sts.), 734-3791, MC, V, Entrées: $11-$16, ❻ *to 77th St.* ♿ ᪲

Pão!

When dinning at Pão! watch motorcycles zoom by and taxis clatter up the street. Huge framed menus feature delicious Portuguese seafood dishes, but the steak, topped with garlic and spicy cream sauce is their specialty. A small bar inside.
Greenwich Village, 322 Spring St. (at Greenwich St.), 334-5464, MC, V, AmEx, Entrées: $13-$16, ❻❶ *to Spring St.* ♿ ⌐

Park Avalon

Elegant and stylish, sink back and soak up the self-esteem of this crowded, gothic hot spot, where the pleasure's in the seeing as much as in the eating. In spite of its popularity, claustrophobia is unlikely due to the spacious interior. The staff, as beautiful as everyone else inside, doesn't let it go to its head. The Mediterranean-American food, by the way, isn't shabby either.
Gramercy, 225 Park Ave. South (bet. 18th and 19th Sts.), 533-2500, MC, V, AmEx, Entrées: $14-$20, ❶❻❹❺❻ *to 14th St.-Union Sq.* ♿ ⌐

Patria

Professionals give way to cover-girls as the sky darkens and the scene heats up in the multi-tiered dining area as lights

stream through the huge windows. The menu includes Latin American cuisine from countries ranging from Brazil to Mexico and comes out meticulously styled, like tamales cradled in corn husks; there's a prix fixe dinner every night for $54 a person.
Gramercy, 250 Park Avenue South (at 20th St.), 777-6211, MC, V, AmEx, Entrées: $19-$29, ❻ *to 23rd St.* ♿

Penang Malaysia

This lively, decked out Malaysian is usually packed on weekends and reasonably so; the food is innovative and tasty, the crowd generally young and hip, and there's live music and a lounge in the bar downstairs. Try eating down there to avoid the wait upstairs.
Upper West Side, 240 Columbus Ave. (at 71st St.), 769-3988, MC, V, AmEx, Diners, Entrées: $10-$19, ❶❸ *to 72nd St.* ⌐ ᪲

Perk's Fine Cuisine

"Every third person's a gangsta and the other two are buppies," said one Harlemite about this Harlem hangout. Savor succulent baby back ribs while vocalist Robert Fox serenades the ladies with his super-slick renditions of "Me and Mrs. Jones" and other R&B standards. Terrific bar menu; gracious waitstaff in the plush, expensive dining room downstairs.
Harlem, 553 Manhattan Ave. (at 123rd St.), 666-8500, MC, V, Entrées: $13-$22, ❶❸❻❶ *to 125th St.* ⌐

Peter Luger Steak House

Simply the superlative steak-house in New York City. Not for the faint of heart (and definitely not for vegetarians) the menu is limited to steak, salmon, and lamb chops, as well as an

amazing array of à la carte side-dishes. Informal, given the price of a meal, a reservation on a Friday or Saturday can be weeks in the waiting. Worth the wait, worth the cost, just plain worth it!
Williamsburg, Brooklyn, 178 Broadway (between Bedford Ave. and Driggs St.), (718) 387-7400, Cash Only, Entrées: $25-$35, ❹❶❷ *to Marcy Ave.* ♿

Petite Abeille

Scads of Tintin paraphernalia and tasty Belgian bites make this a popular feature of Little Belgium. Absolutely divine fries and *moules* (mussels)!
Greenwich Village, 400 W. 14th St. (bet. 9th and 10th Aves.), 727-1505, Cash Only, Entrées: $10-$12, ❶❸❹ *to 14th St.,* ❶ *to Eighth Ave.* ♿

Also at:
Greenwich Village, 466 Hudson St. (bet. Barrow and Grove Sts.), 741-6479, MC, V, Entrées: $10-$12, ❶❾ *to Christopher St.-Sheridan Sq.*
Chelsea, 107 West 18th St. (bet. Sixth and Seventh Aves.), 604-9350, Cash Only, Entrées: $10-$12, ❶❾ *to 18th St.*

Petite Crevette

Ignore the decor, which is in transition, and step inside this roomy Brooklyn Heights restaurant where a friendly and comfortable ambiance is promoted by the staff and patrons alike. For the best bites, ask waiter Lynn, who runs the dining room like "a big dinner party," for a suggestion from the fish, stews, or pastas and sit back to enjoy some of the freshest fish available. FYI, it's BYOB.
Brooklyn Heights, 127 Atlantic Ave. (at Henry St.), (718) 858-6660, Cash Only, Entrées $8-$13, ❷❸❹❺ *to Borough Hall* ♿ 🚲

Pietrasanta

A Hell's Kitchen neighborhood secret where the chef actually comes out of the kitchen to ask how customers are enjoying their meals. For an appetizer, try the succulent scallops in a rich pesto sauce, and order the pumpkin ravioli in sweet pepper sauce as an entrée. Delish!
Midtown, 683 Ninth Ave. (at 47th St.), 265-9471, MC,V, AmEx, Entrées: $8-$16, ❸❹ *to 50th St.* ♿

Pó

So popular that it is not uncommon to require reservations a month in advance, this charming little West Village Italian draws in customers with its warm atmosphere, reasonable prices, and generous portions. Whether the quality of the food lives up to the restaurant's reputation is debatable, it nonetheless makes for a trendy evening out.
Greenwich Village, 31 Cornelia St. (bet. Bleecker and W. 4th Sts.), 645-2189, AmEx, Entrées: $15, ❶❷❸❹❺❻❾ *to West 4th St.-Washington Sq.*

Popover Cafe

New England charm meets New York savvy at this convivial spot, one of the most popular brunch venues in the neighborhood. Feast upon gourmet omelets and excellent griddle specialties — and don't forget the popovers.
Upper West Side, 551 Amsterdam Ave. (bet. 86th and 87th Sts.), 595-8555, MC, V, AmEx, Entrées: $8-$17, ❶❾ *to 86th St.* ♿

Puglia

Like Pasta? Like Elvis? Then you're in luck — spend your time at large communal tables, chugging wine with your new friends as an Italian Elvis does his magic on a little Casio keyboard in the corner. By the time you leave, you'll be arm-in-arm with half the restaurant.

Little Italy, 189 Hester St. (bet. Mott and Mulberry Sts.), 226-8912, MC, V, AmEx, Diners, Entrées: $5-$10, ❹❺❻❼❷❻ *to Canal St.* ♿ 🚶

Qq

Quantum Leap

Handpicking the best in natural dishes that Mexico, Japan, and the Middle East have to offer, this healthy kitchen excels at weekend breakfasts which include whole grain, buckwheat, or blue-corn waffles and/or pancakes smothered with organic maple syrup. Not exactly the acetic way, but better than bacon.
Greenwich Village, 188 West 3rd St. (bet. Thompson and Sullivan Sts.), 677-8050, MC, V, AmEx, Entrées: $5-$10, ❶❷❸❹❺❻❼ *to West 4th St.-Washington Sq.* ♿

Queen Italian Restaurant

Downtown Brooklyn's pasta of choice for local suits and shoppers; try anything on the menu since it's difficult to go wrong, especially with the spicy, crisp pizza.
Downtown Brooklyn, 84 Court St. (bet. Livingston and Schermerhorn Sts.), (718) 596-5954, MC, V, AmEx, Entrées: $7- $25, ❹❺❻ *to Court St.,* ❷❸❹❺ *to Borough Hall* ♿ 🚲

Rr

Rialto

First-time visitors are consistently wowed; the understated SoHo ambiance and first-rate Continental food entice stunning neighborhood folks time and again. Feast on the Chef's Tasting Menu (a 3-, 5-, or 8-course meal), which includes a potato leek soup infused with roasted garlic, served in a demitasse cup. The staff shuffles back and forth to the magnificent garden out back. *SoHo, 265 Elizabeth St. (bet. Houston and Prince Sts.), 334-7900, MC, V, AmEx, Diners, Entrées: $8-$18,* **Q R** *to Prince St.* ⌐

Rib Shack

This venue's offerings of sweet potato pie, collard greens, and fried chicken will move the hearts of devoted soul food lovers. The employees are so friendly that they regularly garner tips, a wow considering that customers are only allowed to order take-out. *Jamaica, Queens, 157-06 Linden Blvd. (bet. Sutphin Blvd. and Guy Brewer Blvd.), (718) 659-7000, MC, V, AmEx, Entrées: $6-$8,* **E J Z** *to Sutphin Blvd.-Archer Ave.*

Richard's Place

Something about church just makes you hungry sometimes. Forget all you learned about gluttony and gorge yourself at Richard's scrumptious all-you-can-eat Sunday brunch. Prices leave enough for tithings. *Jamaica, Queens, 200-05 Linden Blvd. (bet. Francis Lewis and Farmers Blvds.), (718) 723-0041, MC, V, Entrées: $8-$12,* **E J Z** *to Jamaica Center-Parsons-Archer* &

Rikyu

The freedom to choose can be mind-boggling for early-bird diners taking advantage of the $9.95 prix fixe, with 17 dinner options. You can't go wrong with remarkably fresh sushi or any combination involving tempura, teriyaki, or cooked fish. *Upper West Side, 210 Columbus Ave. (bet. 69th and 70th Sts.), 799-7847, MC, V, AmEx, D, Entrées: $10-$17,* **1 2 3 9** *to 72nd St.* & ⌐ ♿

River Cafe

Whether the food is more seductive than the view of Lower Manhattan from this gem beneath the Brooklyn Bridge is a dilemma you probably won't have solved by the time you leave. The seafood is superior, the wine list is superior, the service is more than superior. Bring all of your superlatives along; you'll use them up by the time you head for home. *Fulton Ferry Landing, Brook-lyn, 1 Water St. (at Old Fulton St.), (718) 522-5200, MC, V, AmEx, Diners, D, Entrées: $25-$35,* **A C** *to High St.* & ⌐

Rocking Horse Cafe Mexicano

One of a string of Mexican restaurants along Eighth Ave. this is the most upscale, with fresh food, a perky waitstaff, and a popular brunch. Interesting twists on traditional fare include variations with crab and lobster, but the old standards are excellent as well — burritos, enchiladas, and margaritas. *Chelsea, 182 Eighth Ave. (bet. 19th and 20th Sts.), 463-9511, MC, V, AmEx, Entrées: $14-$20,* **C E** *to 23rd St.,* **1 9** *to 18th St.* ♿

Rosa Mexicano

A well-heeled clientele sips pomegranate margaritas at the crowded bar while waiting for a taste of well executed classics. Guacamole is prepared table-side and desserts like the tamal en cazuela dulce, a sweetish, warm cornmeal swirled with a chocolate sauce, make this a must. *Upper East Side, 1063 First Ave. (at 58th St.), 753-7407, MC, V, AmEx, Diners, D, Entrées: $17-$26,* **4 5 6** *to 59th St,* **N R** *to Lexington Ave.*

Ruby Foo's

Fun, cool, hip pan-Asian with everything from dim sum to sushi and a popular Sunday brunch. *Upper West Side, 2182 Broadway (at 77th St.), 724-6700, MC, V, AmEx, Entrées: $25,* **1 9** *to 79th St.* & ⌐

S ♨

Saigon Grill

One of the best and best-priced Vietnamese restaurants in the city, and a favorite of Upper West Siders. Not much elbow room, so go early to avoid the crowds. You'll be craving the fresh summer rolls for days afterward. *Upper West Side, 2381 Broadway (at 87th St.), 875-9072, MC, V, AmEx, D, Entrées: $7-$13,* **1 9** *to 86th St.* ♿

Sammy's Noodle Shop and Grill

Hurried urbanites took their time in warming up to this noodle shop's flavorful fare, though now it's an indispensable lunch fixture, with an annexed bakery serving fresh desserts. Try the roast meat soups and dumplings. *Greenwich Village, 453 Sixth Ave. (bet. 10th and 11th Sts.), 924-6688, MC, V, AmEx, D, Entrées: $7-$12* **F** *to 14th St.,* **L** *to Sixth Ave.* & ♿

Sammy's Roumanian

This bustling and lively restaurant hosts rich meals and a loud Yiddish band. Locals and other New Yorkers, none of whom are dieting, frequent the place. Red meat is a featured menu item. Chopped liver, and lots o' vodka are popular as well. *Lower East Side, 157 Chrystie St. (at Delancey St.), 673-0330, MC, V, AmEx, Entrées: $20-$25,* **F** *to Delancey St.,* **J M Z** *to Essex St.*

The Screening Room

Dinner and a movie is a classic date; find them both under one roof. Forgo popcorn for the house specialties like the pan-fried baby artichoke appetizer, cedar-planked salmon, and lemon icebox cake. The truly extravagant will splurge on one of the specialty cocktails. A less expensive lounge menu is available and the $30 prix fixe includes a three-course meal and movie admission.
TriBeCa, 54 Varick St. (at Canal St.), 334-2100, MC, V, AmEx, Diners, D, Entrées: $16-$23, ❶❾ *to Canal St.* ♿ 🚬

The Second Avenue Kosher Deli

Hit this legendary deli for the matzoh balls, blintzes, and other traditional dishes that beat your Grandma's. Recent renovations have dispelled some of the old-country flair which made the Deli a kosher home away from home, but completely unmanageable sandwiches and the miniature museum honoring stars of the Yiddish theater with a "walk of fame" still remain.
East Village, 156 Second Ave. (at 10th St.), 677-0606, AmEx, Entrées: $6-$16, ❻ *to Astor Pl.* ♿ 🚚

Second Street Cafe

This bastion of Park Slope café culture serves up light meals and an appealing array of desserts, including chocolate cookies that would put mom's to shame. The café is packed during lunch hours, seven days a week; on weekend evenings, however, seats are plentiful.
Park Slope, Brooklyn, 189 Seventh Ave. (at 2nd St.), (718) 369-6928, MC, V, AmEx, Entrées: $6-$12, ❼ *to Seventh Ave.-Park Slope* ♿

Shun Lee

Quite possibly New York's finest upscale Chinese, spitting distance from Lincoln Center; its glamour is defined by old-school, bejeweled Upper West Side matrons and their wizened escorts, complemented by excessive mirrors and a tiered dining floor. Exquisite dishes are served family-style in silver bowls; the chicken is tender and savory. Complemented a heated towelette proffered by the white-suited waitstaff.
Upper West Side, 43 West 65th St. (bet. Central Park West and Columbus Ave.), 595-8895, MC, V, AmEx, Diners, D, Entrées: $12-$20, ❶❾ *to 66th St.-Lincoln Center* 🚚

Siena

Though the decor may be minimalist, all-star chef Scott Bryan's cooking is anything but restrained. Leave your diet at the door and prepare for one of the wine-fueled, artery-clogging marathon meals that the Tuscan are famous for surviving.
Chelsea, 200 Ninth Ave. (bet. 22nd and 23rd Sts.), 633-8033, AmEx, Entrées: $13-$20, ❻❺ *to 23rd St.*

Sophia's Bistro

Downtown style has been creeping into the local neighborhood during the last year. This little bistro leads the onslaught, offering hip, romantic, dining. Pale yellow and red brick, flickering candlelight, and wine-colored drapery create a laid-back atmosphere.
Upper West Side, 998 Amsterdam Ave. (bet. 109th and 110th Sts.), 662-8822, MC, V, AmEx, Entreés: $6-$10, ❶❾ *to Cathedral Parkway (110th St.)* ♿ 🚬 🚚

Souen

Downtown New Yorkers may delight in their manufactured indulgences, but this unassuming, primarily macrobiotic restaurant has been helping them get in touch with their earthier side for twenty years. The Japanese-influenced menu specializes in dishes featuring tempeh, seitan, and organic vegetables, and the sugar-free futomaki and tempeh croquettes are noteworthy.
Greenwich Village, 28 East 13th St. (bet. University Pl. and Fifth Ave.), 627-7150, MC, V, AmEx, Dinners, D, Entrées: $8-$16, ❶❿❹❺❻ *to 14th St.-Union Sq.* 🚚

Soup Kitchen

While Seinfeld fanatics are bemoaning the end of an era, one remnant lives on: The lines at this pop-culture landmark are unreal at lunch time, but have you noticed how smoothly it moves along? Patrons have made up their minds what to order by the time they reach the counter of this famous take-out. Otherwise it's "No soup for you!"
Midtown, 259-A West 55th St. (bet. Eighth Ave. and Broadway), 757-7730, Cash Only, Entrées: $6-$8, ❼❿ *to 57th St.*

Sparks Steak House

One of the best steakhouses in New York City. Come with a full wallet and an empty stomach for incredible meat and seafood.
Midtown, 210 West 46th St. (bet. 2nd and 3rd Aves.), 687-4855, MC, V, AmEx, Diners, Entrées: $40, ❺❹❻❼ *to 42nd St.-Grand Central* ♿ 🚬

♿ = WHEELCHAIR ACCESS

🚬 = SMOKING SECTION

🚚 = DELIVERY AVAILABLE

Standard Notion

Bountiful cheap sides, like garlic mashed potatoes, save mediocre entrées, at this earnest Ludlow St. neophyte. Nightfall occasions the addition of votives to the back garden, and large picture windows flanking the front door lend the interior an airy, spacious feel. Service is charmingly eccentric, with none of the expected pretension, and everything comes at a price unusually low for such calculated ambiance.

Lower East Side, 161 Ludlow St. (at Stanton St.), 473-3535, MC, V, AmEx, Entrées: $6-$13, ❻ *to Second Ave.* ⌐ 🚲

Sud

The red bare brick, limited space, and French-speaking staff make you feel like you're in a real French bistro. A casual, unpretentious dining spot, Sud offers authentic, homemade French-Mediterranean cuisine that evokes Paris, though the service is quite an improvement: Don't be surprised if co-owner Danielle joins you for a brief chat at your table; her friendly personal service helps to give the tiny restaurant its charm.

Greenwich Village, 210 West. 10th St. (bet. Bleecker and 4th Sts.), 255-3805, MC, V, AmEx, Entrées: $15-$20, ❶❾ *to Chris-topher St.-Sheridan Sq.* ⌐ 🚲

Surya

This chic West Village Indian offers a unique array of tastes several notches above its counterparts in the East Village: fresh seafood glazed with a subtle date sauce, perfectly spiced basmati, and creamy deserts with a hint of cardamom. Wash it down with a "Tajamopolitan" or other unique specialty drinks.

Greenwich Village, 302 Bleecker St., (bet. 7th Ave. So. and Grove St.), 807-7770, MC, V, AmEx, D, Diners, Entrées: $16-$24, ❶❾ *to Christopher St.-Sheridan Sq.* 🚹 ⌐

*T*t

Tabla

One of the few restaurants where you can get American food infused with Indian spices. Be aware that your choices are prix fixe, à la carte, or a tasting menu; all are delicious.

Gramercy, 11 Madison Ave. (at 25th St.), 889-0667, MC, V, AmEx, Diners, D, Entrées: $52, ❻ *to 23rd St.* 🚹

Tartine

Situated at one of the West Village's most serene intersections, there's nothing more pleasant on a Sunday morning than brunch with the sun shining through the floor-to-ceiling windows and birds chirping. The menu is standard and portions are hardly generous, but the staff has orange juice on the table by the time patrons sit down. Alas, by noon the wait outside is 45 minutes, but here's a tip: They actually open at 9am for coffee, not the posted 10:30.

Greenwich Village, 253 West 11th St. (at West 4th St.), 229-2611, Cash Only, Entrées: $8-$12, ❶❷❸ *to West 14th St.,* ❶ *to Eighth Ave.* 🚹 🚲

Tavern on Jane

This tavern serves much more than pub food, but at pub food prices. While the fish and chips is a reliable delight, customers go crazy for the grilled leg-of-lamb with sour cherry sauce, potatoes au gratin and garlic spinach, and the Moroccan tuna, served with saffron, lemon and

garlic couscous, and wilted watercress get rave review. The atmosphere is cozy and inviting — regulars are bound to strike up a friendly conversation over a pint of beer. Simply put, you know a place is great when the staff hangs out there on their nights off.

Greenwich Village, 31 Eighth Ave. (at Jane St.), 675-2526, MC, V, AmEx, D, Entrées: $7-$15, ❶❷❸ *to 14th St.,* ❶ *to Eighth Ave.* 🚹 ⌐

Tavern on the Green

Only the well-connected score the best seats, but the crystal chandeliers and tranquil setting are impressive, if a tad garish, from any area of this legendary Central Park outpost. The oysters and steak, along with a mind-boggling wine list, help to solidify the Tavern's reputation as one of New York's most prestigious restaurants; in winter, twinkling lights on the surrounding trees make for quite a Yuletide scene.

Central Park, Central Park West (at 67th St.), 873-3200, MC, V, AmEx, Entrées: $13-$25, ❶❷ *to 72nd St.* 🚹 ⌐

Terrace

The exquisite view of upper Manhattan from this upscale dining room may finally convince your parents that living next to Harlem isn't so bad, or it may impress your date by revealing your uncanny ability to find romance in the most unexpected places. After trying the house risotto or grilled salmon, visit the rooftop garden. The open air and a much-needed cocktail will help you recuperate from the bill.

Morningside Heights, 400 West 119th St. (bet. Amsterdam Ave. and Morningside Dr.), 666-9490, MC, V, AmEx, Diners, D, Entrées: $25-$33, ❶❾ *to 116th St.* 🚹 ⌐

Time Cafe

Around mealtimes there are rarely many free tables in this vast, lofty space, and it's no wonder, since this is one of the better places filling the niche between greasy coffee shop and fancy restaurants. Health-conscious organic food and an extensive menu with selections like fancy tuna sandwiches and pan roasted penne are sure to satisfy nearly any craving.
East Village, 380 Lafayette (bet. Great Jones and 4th Sts.), 533-7000, MC, V, AmEx, Entrées: $12-$22, ❻ *to Bleecker St.* ♿ ❀

Also at:
Upper West Side, 2330 Broadway (at 85th St.), 579-5100, MC, V, AmEx, Entrées: $12-$22, ❶❾ *to 86th St.* ♿ 🛈 ❀

Toledo

The cherry wood, archways, and courtly dining hall of this midtown Spanish restaurant evoke the elegance of a bygone century. Ask, and the retinue of waiters will proudly point you to the best dishes. Or try the authentic paella prized for its fresh seafood and savory saffron rice. The sangria is almost too delicious for your own good, and after a few glasses you'll sing its praises like a troubadour.
Midtown, 6 East 36th St. (bet. Fifth and Madison Aves.), 696-5036, MC, V, AmEx, Diners, Entrées: $22-$26, ❻❾❶❿❻❼❿❻ *to 34th St.* ♿

Tom's Restaurant

"I came, I sat, I wrote" reads a note from Suzanne Vega on the wall of this venerable luncheonette, suggesting that it is this Prospect Heights favorite, not Tom's on 112th St. in Manhattan, immortalized in Vega's "Tom's Diner." Worthy of immortality,

Tom's is a charmer, founded in 1936 with prototypical Brooklyn fare, great egg creams, and terrific service. Closes at 4pm.
Prospect Heights, Brooklyn, 782 Washington Ave. (at Sterling Pl.), (718) 636-9738, Cash Only, Entrées: $3-$8, ❷❸ *to Eastern Pkwy.-Brooklyn Museum* ♿ ❀

Tom's Restaurant

Once you push through the occasional crowd from a Kramer's Reality tour (the southern façade serves as a cutaway shot in *Seinfeld*), you'll be surprised to see what the fuss is all about. Low prices, huge platters, late hours, and thick "Broadway" shakes keep kids comin' back to this greasy spoon.
Morningside Heights, 2880 Broadway (at 112th St), 864-6137, Cash Only, Entrées: $3-$10, ❶❾ *to Cathedral Parkway (110th St.)* ♿ ❀

Tonic

Natural light pours in through the skylights of this cavernous space, as patrons feast on cheap, eclectic café fare. A former Lower East Side kosher winery, Tonic has a performance space in back, encircled in red velvet; avant-garde and experimental films are played on Monday nights. Most endearing feature is the downstairs cocktail lounge with circular booths built within 2,500-gallon hard-wood wine casks.
Lower East Side, 107 Norfolk St. (bet. Delancy and Rivington Sts.), 358-7503, Cash Only, Entrées: $5, ❶❻❷ *to Essex St.,* ❻ *to Delancey St.* 🛈

Torch

This supper club is the first elegant eatery to have touched down on bar-laden Ludlow St.

Delight in the South American-infused French cuisine and nightly torch performances, or linger in the lounge area with a cocktail and smoke in hand.
Lower East Side, 137 Ludlow St. (bet. Rivington and Stanton Sts.), 228-5151, MC, V, AmEx, Diners, Entrées: $10-$20, ❻ *to Delancey St.,* ❻❶❷ *to Essex St.* ♿ 🛈

Trattoria Dell'Arte

Tons of well-heeled Manhattanites dine here on their way to a show, but the decor is the biggest celebrity at this huge modern Italian restaurant opposite Carnegie Hall: Busts of famous noses, enormous paintings of close-up body parts, and electric-colored walls make the space happening. This chic spot also boasts polished service and the tastiest bread in New York City.
Midtown, 900 Seventh Ave. (at 57th St.), 245-9800, MC, V, AmEx, D, Entrées: $17-$25, ❶❻ *to 57th St.* 🛈

Tribeca Grill

This flagship of the DeNiro mini restaurant empire is a haven for those who like to enjoy a little celebrity watching with their meal. Movie industry big shots from the nearby TriBeCa Film Center can be found sharing the spacious, dark wood and brick dining room with plenty of other notables and, of course, some commoners all there to enjoy New American cuisine delicious enough to distract you from your gape-eyed staring.
TriBeCa, 375 Greenwich St. (at Franklin St.), 941-3900, MC, V, AmEx, Entrées: $18-$28, ❶❾ *to Franklin St.* ♿ 🛈

Triple Eight Palace

After taking the escalator to the threshold of this Hong Kong extravaganza, you understand how they derived the "palace" part of the name. The multi-roomed restaurant assumes the air of a circus, what with the families chattering over fried and steamed noodles, shrieking toddlers playing chicken with rolling dim sum carts, and tables of heated woks threatening diners with third-degree burns. The dumplings, buns, and shellfish are excellent.

Lower East Side, 88 East Broadway (under the Manhattan Bridge), 941-8886, MC, V, AmEx, Diners, D, Entrées: $10, ❺ *to East Broadway.*

Turkish Kitchen

Turkish music brings to mind the minarets of Istanbul silhouetted across the Golden Horn, and shockingly red wallpaper coupled with a laundry list of kebabs strives to maintain exotic authenticity. Don't be afraid to experiment; just about anything with lamb is sure to be good.

Midtown, 386 Third Ave. (bet. 27th and 28th Sts.), 679-1810, MC, V, AmEx, Diners, D, Entrées: $10-$18, ❻ *to 28th St.*

Uncle Nick's Greek Cuisine

Serving enormous kebobs, salads brimming with stuffed grape leaves and olives, and huge wedges of flaming saganaki cheese, Uncle Nick's Greek Cuisine won't leave you hungry. The bustling atmosphere, attentive waitstaff, and speedy service make this restaurant great for pre-theater dining.

Midtown, 747 Ninth Ave. (bet. 50th and 51st Sts.), MC, V, AmEx, D, Entrées: $9-$15, ❹❻❼ *to 50th St.* ♿ 🚬 🚲

*U*u

Uncle Vanya

Delicious, inexpensive, authentic — what more could you possibly want? To top it off, the vodka flows freely, the food is hardy (the Russian dumplings are out of this world!), and there's often live music, a pleasant folk singer, although incomprehensible to non-russophones. In regard to that last feature, this is a good place to practice your budding language skills: The staff and virtually all the clientele are for real.

Midtown, 315 West 54th St. (bet. Eighth and Ninth Aves.), 262-0542, Cash Only, Entrées: $8-$12, ❸❹ *to 50th St.* 🚬

Under the Stairs

This bar/restaurant has been around for as long as anyone in the neighborhood can remember, and they still pack in for happy hour. Come for the lively crowd, the loud jazz on weekends, and Wednesday's bargain shrimp night.

Upper West Side, 688 Columbus Ave. (bet. 93rd and 94th Sts.), 663-3103, MC, V, AmEx, Entrées: $10-$13, ❽❾ *to 96th St.*

Union Square Cafe

One of New York's most popular restaurants, it's at a New York City landmark, and offers great food, a nice atmosphere, and friendly service.

Gramercy, 21 East 16th St. (bet Fifth Ave. and Union Sq. West), 243-4020, MC, V, AmEx, Diners, D, Entrées: $25-$35, ❹❺❻❼❽❾❿ *to 14th St.-Union Sq.* ♿

♿	= WHEELCHAIR ACCESS
🚬	= SMOKING SECTION
🚲	= DELIVERY AVAILABLE

*V*v

Viceroy

Come to this trendy spot for "see-food" — Chelsea's bold and beautiful are on display from the inside or out, with floor to ceiling windows providing a free peek. Viceroy features some great dishes (and the food's not half-bad either). Cool, comfortable, and art-deco make for a glam time. Plus, given who's biting, you never know what you'll catch.

Chelsea, 160 Eighth Ave. (at 18th St.), 633-8484, MC, V, AmEx, Diners, D, Entrées: $10-$20, ❶❾ *to 18th St.* ♿ 🚬 🚲

*W*w

Wave

Enjoy this Japanese restaurant's outdoor terrace. The stunning views of New York Harbor and the Statue of Liberty are the perfect backdrop for some of the finest sushi around. With the breeze off the water, and shade from the trees, there's no better place to chill on a hot summer day.

Lower Manhattan, 21 South End Ave. (at Battery Park), 240-9100, MC, V, AmEx, Diners, Entrées: $7-$18, ❶❾ *to Rector St.* ♿ 🚲

Well's

Since 1938, Harlemites have swooned over the homemade cornbread served with strawberry butter, as well as the waffles and fried chicken at this family-run legend. Monday nights feature a sixteen-piece big band.

Harlem, 2247 Adam Clayton Powell Powell, Jr. Blvd (at 132nd St.), 234-0700, MC, V, AmEx, Entrées: $11-$15, ❷❸ *to 135th St.* ♿ 🚬

Wok 'n Roll

They don't kick you out till 3am on weekends, and you'll never significantly alter the level of your water glass at this airy new dumpling house, where the polished wood decor and predictable noodle and dumpling fare feels like a friend's mom's dinner you can always count on. Fair prices keep it packed with NYU kids.
Greenwich Village, 169 Bleecker St. (at Sullivan St.), 260-6666, MC, V, AmEx, D, Entrées: $7-$13, ⒶⒷⒸⒹⒺⒻⓄ *to West 4th St.-Washington Sq.* 🚲

Ye Waverly Inn

One of the vestiges of 19th Century Village life, this former carriage house exudes a quaint, Colonial feel with wooden ceiling beams and old-fashioned offerings from both north and south, like Yankee pot roast and southern fried chicken, with excellent puddings and muffins. Occasionally, local celebs drop by.
Greenwich Village, 16 Bank St. (at Waverly Pl.), 929-4377, MC, V, AmEx, Entrées: $12-$17, ①②③⑨ *to 14th St.* 🚶 🚬 🚲

Zoë

About as good as SoHo gets, attentive waitstaff, elegant decor, and intricate yet subtle food all await at this SoHo hot spot. The crowd is a pleasing mixture of downtown denizens and suited professionals on their way home from work. The crowd does get funkier as the evening wears on. Perfect for a romantic date.
SoHo, 90 Prince St. (bet. Broadway and Mercer St.) 966-6722, MC, V, AmEx, Entrées: $18-28, ⓃⓇ *to Prince St.* 🚶

Zum Stammtisch

While German cuisine hardly qualifies as in vogue to chic Manhattan critics, its heartiness goes over well with the locals in the quiet neighborhood. Stained glass windows and dim lights bring to mind stodgy 19th-century German intellectuals debating Hegel over steins.
Glendale, Queens, 69-46 Myrtle Ave. (at Cooper Ave.), (718) 386-3014, MC, V, AmEx, Entrées: $7-$16 🚬

🚶 = WHEELCHAIR ACCESS

🚬 = SMOKING SECTION

🚲 = DELIVERY AVAILABLE

cafés c·a·f·é·s

In the early 1990s America gave birth to a coffee culture all its own. With Starbucks, New World Coffee & Bagels, and Timothy's World Coffee on every corner, it's easy to see this culture has taken root in New York, a city whose citizens are always looking for something to keep the pace top speed. Is Manhattan buzzing with energy? Or is everyone just addicted to the java? Witness people scurrying about with steaming paper cups in their hands, and don't be afraid to call them on their professed one-cup-a-day limit — depending on the size, one might mean 5.

While many New Yorkers could care less about lolling about in berets and rolling their own cigarettes, you will find a large quotient of European wannabes at **Cafe Lalo** (201 West 83rd St.), **Veniero's** (342 East 11th St.), **Caffé Dante** (79-81 MacDougal St.), and **French Roast** (458 Sixth Ave. and 2340 Broadway), to name a few. The nice thing about cafés like these is that it's just as acceptable to hang anonymously with your shades on as it is to strike up conversations with total strangers. In fact, many a New Yorker has been known to come away with a good story after spending a morning in the café with their noses in the paper and their ears pricked. So while we recommend the following joints for a caffeine jolt as alternatives to the big chains, be forewarned: If you've got a secret you want to keep, don't go blabbing it in places like **The Hungarian Pastry Shop** (1030 Amsterdam Ave.) or **Cupcake Cafe** (522 Ninth Ave.). If there's one thing you'll learn while hanging out in coffee houses, it's that New Yorkers really do care.

alt.coffee

Come for the comfy couches and friendly staff who will help with internet questions if needed. *East Village, 139 Ave. A (bet. St. Marks Pl. and 9th St.), 529-2233, Cash Only,* ⑥ to Astor Pl. ♿ ⌫

Basset Coffee and Tea Co.

Coffee and tea are a foregone conclusion; the secret attraction here is the eats. What the locals call "that dog place" dishes out gourmet comfort food like garlic mashed potatoes and homemade mac-and-cheese cafeteria-style, but without the hairnets. *TriBeCa, 123 West Broadway (at Duane St.), 349-1662, MC, V, AmEx, Diners,* ❶❷❸❾ to Chambers St.

Big Cup

Day-glo colors and paisley patterns might recall the '60s, but the very buff, short-coiffed gay male clientele is pure '90s. Lounge all day in comfy chairs, sip a mocha, and watch the cityscape tumble by. A major singles scene. *Chelsea, 228 Eighth Ave. (bet. 21st and 22nd Sts.), 206-0059, Cash Only,* ⒸⒺ to 23rd St. ♿

Bistro Jules

This cozy, authentic French café provides impoverished romantics with candles, trendy mood music, and wine affordable enough for the cash-poor to get sufficiently buzzed, leaving them enough change to pick up some roses on the way home. Spring through fall, the seating out front on the tiny sunken patio is ideal for leisurely afternoons of nursing lemonade and chain-smoking. Live jazz nightly. *East Village, 65 St. Marks Pl. (bet. First and Second Aves.), 477-5560, AmEx,* ⑥ to Astor Pl. ♿⌫

Bread & Butter

As out of place as it may seem, this place has the best fries you'll ever taste. Bread & Butter serves soups, salads, pastries, and sandwiches. People either take out or come in to sit on the benches lining the windows in this tiny yellow café and sip a cup of robust coffee. Owners Sam and Sean keep SoHo eating morning 'til night — they also own Rialto, a great dinner spot, and Cafe Habana, up the block. *SoHo, 229 Elizabeth St. (bet. Prince and Houston Sts.), 925-7600, MC, V, AmEx,* ⓃⓇ to Prince St., ❻❽❼❾ to Broadway-Lafayette St.

Bunnies' Feast

One of the neighborhood's newest and brightest lights when it comes to take out food, this bakery and pizza parlor has all the standard Italian selections, plus a whole caseful of wonderful desserts, including rum balls and brown sugar-glazed monkey bread. *Morningside Heights, 3141 Broadway (at La Salle St.), 666-4343, Cash Only,* ❶❾ to 125th St. ♿⌫

Café Con Leche

Cramped or cozy, depending on how tolerant you are of the neighboring conversation, this Cuban café pulses with upbeat salsa music and chatter. Standard dishes are perfectly prepared, from empanadas to "filete de pollo al limon." *Upper West Side, 424 Amsterdam Ave. (bet. 80th and 81st Sts.), 595-7000, MC, V, AmEx,* ❶❾ to 79th St. ♿

Also at:
Upper West Side, 726 Amsterdam Ave. (bet. 95th and 96th Sts.), 678-7000, MC, V, AmEx, ❶❷❸❾ to 96th St. ♿⌫

Café Gigi

Bring a good book or fine company to this underground haunt where locals lounge for hours, lost among pages of Joyce and Sartre while enjoying generously proportioned brunch dishes and infamous pizzas in oh-so-comfy antique cushioned chairs. *East Village, 417 East 9th St. (bet. First Ave. and Ave. A), 505-3341, MC, V, AmEx, D,* ⑥ to Astor Pl. ⌫

Cafe Kolonaki

The fun and cozy split-level coffee shop is fairly new to the Steinway shopping area. The decor is contemporary, and the staff is young and perky. *Astoria, Queens, 33-02 Broadway (at 33rd St.), (718) 932-8222, MC, V, AmEx, D,* Ⓝ to Broadway ⌫

Cafe Lalo

This bright and lively European café serves night owls until 2am Sunday through Thursday, and until 4am on weekends. Come for the vast menu of decadent drinks and desserts; Sunday brunch available. *Upper East Side, 201 West 83rd St. (bet. Broadway and Amsterdam Ave.), 496-6031, Cash Only,* ❶❾ to 86th St.

Café Milou

Named after Tintin's dog, this bistro is a breath of fresh air in the midst of trendy theme-oriented eateries on Seventh Ave. Opened by the Abraham Merchant, of Merchant's, with a menu created by an ex-Windows on the World chef; open til 2am. *Greenwich Village, 92 Seventh Ave. South (bet. Bleecker and Grove Sts.), 414-9824, MC, V, AmEx, Diners,* ❶❾ to Christopher St.-Sheridan Sq. ♿⌫

Cafe Mozart

A slice of Europe on the Upper West Side, perfect after a show or for late morning paper perusal.
Upper West Side, 154 West 70th St. (bet. Broadway and Columbus Ave.), 595-9797, MC, V, AmEx, ❶❷❸❾ *to 72nd St.*

Cafe Orlin

Blend in by ordering an espresso and whipping out some sort of portfolio. Leave it open on the table and enjoy a smoky omelet or a slice of chocolate cake. Most regulars are artsy East Village chain smokers cum aspiring directors. The low-angle view allows a glimpse of the shoes passing by on St. Marks Place.
East Village, 41 St. Marks Pl. (bet. First and Second Aves.), 777-1447, Cash Only, ❻ *to Astor Pl.*

Caffe Danté

Famous both for its Buffalo mozzarella and espresso, this space may be small but well arranged. If your stomach is craving a larger meal, check out the trattoria next door, which is under the same management.
Greenwich Village, 79-81 Macdougal St. (bet. Bleecker and Houston Sts.), 982-5275, Cash Only, ❶❾ *to Houston St.* ⟵

Caffé Roma

Tiny marble-topped tables and an ancient, snorting espresso machine seem to whisk you into the back alleys of Rome while you enjoy old-world cannoli like mama used to make, in portions bigger than mama ever imagined.
Little Italy, 385 Broome St. (at Mulberry St.), 226-8413, Cash Only, ❻ *to Spring St.*

Caffe Reggio

The standard by which Village cafés are measured, Caffe Reggio's charm makes it popular among students, hipsters, and aging Bohemians. The dark interior is suitable for curling up with a book or your significant other. Prices respect the starving artist's pocketbook.
Greenwich Village, 119 MacDougal St. (bet. Bleecker and 3rd Sts.), 475-9557, Cash Only, ❶❷❸❹❺❻❼ *to West 4th St.- Washington Sq.*

Caffé Sha Sha

The summertime patio is a refuge amidst the midday mayhem. Get your hands on some java and commit yourself to the entire Sunday Times.
Greenwich Village, 510 Hudson St. (bet. Christopher and 10th Sts.), 242-3021, Cash Only, ❶❾ *to Christopher St.*

Ceci-Cela

Homemade sorbet and café au lait evoke La Cote d'Azur at this charming patisserie perched on the edge of Little Italy. The chat room in back is oh-so-perfect for nibbling on petit-fours and playing post-structuralist salon.
SoHo, 55 Spring St. (bet. Mulberry and Lafayette Sts.), 274-9179, MC, V, ❻ *to Spring St.*

Chinatown Ice Cream Factory

If chocolate and vanilla make you groan with boredom, this tiny café will satiate even your jaded taste buds. Lick away at flavors such as red bean, green tea, taro, and lychee; the ginger is divine.
Chinatown, 65 Bayard St. (bet. Mott and Elizabeth Sts.), 608-4170, Cash Only, ❻❼❿ *to Grand St.*

Cupcake Cafe

A quaint bakery with pink walls and tin ceilings on the raunchiest stretch in Hell's Kitchen. Great donuts, waffles, and (duh!) cupcakes, with a few tables for immediate consumption. The location is unfashionable for a food pilgrimage, but come for old-fashioned sweets.
Midtown, 522 Ninth Ave. (at 39th St.), 465-1530, Cash Only, ❶❷❸ *to 42nd St.-Times Sq.*

Cybercafe

Spend serious quality time with computers. Options extend beyond basic net access to the latest games and sophisticated design and desktop publishing programs. To top it all of, the café makes a mean mocha.
SoHo, 273 Lafayette St. (bet. Spring and Prince Sts.), 334-5140, MC, V, AmEx, Diners, D, ❶❷ *to Prince St.*

Drip

This coffee bar also has its liquor license so you can speed on caffeine, then come down with a micro-brewed beer. Singles can leaf through binders chock full of bios while sipping lattes and nibbling on oversized Rice Krispies treats. Atmosphere is casual, friendly, and relaxed unless, of course, you do find a match!
Upper West Side, 489 Amsterdam Ave. (bet. 83rd & 84th Sts.), 875-1032, MC, V, ❶❾ *to 86th St.* ⟵

Duane Park Patisserie

Get an entire cake — those peddled by trendy TriBeCa restarants for $7 per slice — for less than $20. Perfect for impressing dinner guests or treating yourself, if gluttony is a favorite sin.
TriBeCa, 179 Duane St. (bet. Greenwich and Hudson Sts.), 274-8447, MC, V, AmEx, ❶❷❸❾ *to Chambers St.*

Fall Cafe

Settle into a cushy couch and finish a physics problem set or dig into your debut novel. Sustenance comes at starving student prices: $3 or less for soups, and a small coffee for less than $1.
Carroll Gardens, Brooklyn, 307 Smith St. (bet. President and Union Sts.), (718) 403-0230, Cash Only, **FG** *to Carroll St.* &

Ferrara Bakery and Café

America's oldest espresso bar, it's been around since 1892 and has been owned by the same family ever since. Everything is homemade!!!
Little Italy, 195 Grand St. (bet. Mulberry and Mott Sts.), 226-6150, MC, V, AmEx, Diners, D, **JMNRZ6** *to Canal St.*

Fort Tryon Cafe

With dark paneled wood walls and lead-framed windows, this airy café can't be beat for that countrified ambiance so hard to come by in the city. Cakes are tasty, and sandwiches and quiches make for an excellent mid-afternoon interlude while visiting The Cloisters.
Washington Heights, 1 Margaret Corbin Dr.(at Fort Tryon Park), 923-2233, MC, V, AmEx, **A** *to 190th St.*

French Roast

Art Nouveau dominates the decor at this airy, bustling café. Brunch and lunch available; try the consistently delicious soups. Open 24 hours.
Greenwich Village, 458 Sixth Ave. (at 11th St.), 533-2233, MC, V, AmEx, **ABCDEFO** *to West 4th St.-Washington Sq.* &
Also at:
Upper West Side, 2340 Broadway (at 85th St.), 799-1533, MC, V, AmEx, D, **19** *to 86th St.* &

Go Sushi

Pop culture's turning Japanese. This newcomer capitalizes on both the sushi trend and the still-burgeoning coffee-bar culture: sleek stools and tattered copies of *Paper* meet sushi samples of fatty tuna and salmon prepared fresh around-the-clock by an in-house chef. Wash it all down with Go's own freshly brewed ginger ale.
Greenwich Village, 3 Greenwich Ave. (bet. Sixth Ave. and 8th St.), 366-9272, Cash Only, **ABCDEFO** *to West 4th St.-Washington Sq.*

The Grey Dog's Coffee

Bring a novel, your laptop, or your friends to this warm rustic café where sunlight pours in through the open French windows and casts shadows on the pressed tin ceilings above. Order a big chunk of fresh-baked bread, a terrific cup of coffee, and amble back to one of the artsy tables with apples, fish, or chili peppers painted on top. At night the lights dim and the place becomes a casual wine bar.
Greenwich Village, 33 Carmine St. (bet. Bleeker and Bedford Sts.), 462-0041, Cash Only, **ABC DEFO** *to West 4th St., Washington Sq.* **19** *to Houston St.*

H&H Bagel

To certain New Yorkers, these bagels are good enough to qualify as a delicacy. The poppy and everything varieties go quickly, but the basic plain sourdough is something special, too. Call 1-800-NY-BAGEL to have mail orders delivered anywhere in the world.
Upper West Side, 2239 Broadway (at 80th St.), 595-8003, Cash Only, **19** *to 79th St.* &

The Hungarian Pastry Shop

The cafe's enduring reputation as Columbia University's intellectual hangout par excellence has suffered somewhat since the citywide smoking ban. Still the place of choice, however, to ostentatiously discuss Fellini or Godard, or write that dissertation on the hermeneutics of the Marquis de Sade while sipping chamomile tea and nibbling on a linzer torte.
Morningside Heights, 1030 Amsterdam Ave. (bet. 110th and 111th Sts.), 866-4230, Cash Only, **19** *to Cathedral Parkway*

Internet Cafe

New York's first cybercafé offers weekly classes for between $25 and $200. Or pay the $5 cover to listen to striving artists unleash their souls in the cozy pub. Gourmet beers, including a large Belgian selection, go well with live jazz, heard every night. .
East Village, 82 East 3rd St. (bet. First and Second Aves.), 614-0747, MC, V, **F** *to Second Ave.*

Krispy Kreme

While this was New York's original, now the Kreme is all over Manhattan. A southern import, they melt in your mouth so fast and taste so good that it's impossible to eat fewer than three.
Chelsea, 265 West 23rd St. (bet. Seventh and Eighth Aves.), 620-0111, Cash Only, **CE** *to 23rd St.* &

L Cafe

This dark, smoky café functions as a center of Williamsburg social life before 2pm, serving up sandwiches and bagels with a wide range of toppings for under $5. Add a bottomless cup of admittedly mediocre coffee and cruise on the caffeine/carbo speedball for the rest of the day.

Williamsburg, Brooklyn, 189 Bedford Avenue (bet. North 6th and North 7th Sts.), (718) 388-6792, Cash Only, ⓁＬ to Bedford Ave. ⌐

Masturbakers

The most popular item at this appropriately titled bakery, housed in the Old Devil Moon restaurant, is the penis cake. Their breast cake, bearing the words "Breast Wishes," runs a close second. With moist devil's food cake, rich frosting and naughty details, their bakery lives up to their motto: "tasty but tasteless."
East Village, 511 East 12th St. (bet. Aves. A and B), 475-0476, MC, V, Ⓛ to First Ave. ♿ ⌐

Nussbaum & Wu

Not your ordinary coffee stop — a Chinese pastry shop and deli collided to form this one. Well-lit with a great wrap-around counter, you just may decide to stay a while. Fresh sandwiches and yummy pastries, both Asian and non, are available here, not to mention bagels and, of course, coffee too.
Morningside Heights, 2897 Broadway (at 113th St.), 280-5344, MC, V, AmEx, Diners, D, ①⑨ to Cathedral Parkway (110th St.) ♿

On the Park Cafe

Filling the vacuum left behind by the sorely missed Harlem Cafe next door, this stylish little coffeehouse promises to be Harlem's answer to the Jackson Hole chain further downtown. Smack dab in the middle of fashionable Striver's Row, Harlem's most up-and-coming neighborhood. The park, St. Nick's is lovely and rustic.
Harlem, 301 West 135th St. (at Frederick Douglass Blvd.), 694-5469, Cash Only, ⒷⒸ to 135th St. ♿ ⚲

Once Upon A Tart

Delectable pastries, both savory and sweet, at lower prices than the standard coffeecakes served up by Manhattan's corporate chain espresso bars. Everything is made in their own bakery. Try a special that includes a tart and choice of salads.
SoHo, 135 Sullivan St. (bet. Houston and Prince Sts.), 387-8869, MC, V, AmEx, D, ⒸⒺ to Spring St. ⚲

Space Untitled

No doubt the $7 sandwiches finance the rent payments on this spacious café/gallery, but those on meal plans can take advantage of the space for the price of a cup of coffee. The crowd ranges from networking financiers to the ragged artists who need the former's money. The wine bar perks up at sundown with a handful of votives and a classier contingent.
SoHo, 133 Greene St. (bet. Houston and Prince Sts.), 260-8962, Cash Only, ⓃⓇ to Prince St. ⌐

Taylor's

One of the best things about culinary life in the West Village is this bakery, which has several other locations in downtown Manhattan. A fabulous selection of pastries, cakes, and other decadent desserts, as well as soups, sandwiches, and typical beverages. The scones can be amazing, but you should get there early or your choices will be limited.
Greenwich Village, 523 Hudson St. (bet. 10th and Charles Sts.), 378-2890, Cash Only, ①⑨ to Christopher St.-Sheridan Sq.

Veniero's

You can sit at the counter or at tables and treat yourself to scrumptious pastries and good drinks.

East Village, 342 East 11th St. (bet. First and Second Aves.), 674-7070, MC, V, AmEx, Diners, D, ⒺⓃⓇ④⑤⑥ to 14th St.-Union Sq. ♿

Yaffa Cafe

East Village funkadelic café with reasonably priced sandwiches, salads, pastas, omelets, and crepes, as well as a handsome selection of vegetarian items and unbelievable desserts. Enjoy the kitschy decor and sit out-doors when weather permits to observe the goings-on on St. Marks Pl. Open 24 hours.
East Village, 97 St. Marks Pl. (bet. 1st St. & Ave. A), 677-9001, MC, V, AmEx, ⑥ to Astor Pl. ♿

Yaffa Tea Room

Alice in Wonderland collides with New York eclecticism at this delightful salon. Burgundy velvet and antique crystal chandeliers make you feel like bohemian royalty as you sip your tea. Reservations required for high tea ($20), served Monday through Saturday 2pm-5pm. Remember to point your pinky like a lady.
TriBeCa, 19 Harrison St. (at Greenwich St.), 966-0577, MC, V, AmEx, Diners, D, ①②③⑨ to Chambers St. ⌐

nightlife

n·i·g·h·t·l·i·f·e
nightlife

New York's diverse after-dark scene caters to the tastes of martini-sipping, cigar-toking lounge enthusiasts, the local chapter of beer-chugging tavern lovers, and the elite underground network of dance clubbers alike. This night life mecca offers something for everyone from Tuesday night country line-dancing at X.I.T. (511 Lexington Ave., 371-1600) to cabaret shows at famous gay establishments in Greenwich Village, like The Duplex (61 Christopher St., 255-5438). Whether it's jazz in a basement dive, a crowded club throbbing with a trip-hop beat, or a spoken-word show in a smoky bar, New York is where it's at. Life for quite a few New Yorkers is nocturnal, though many drunken revels demand a glimpse of sunrise before they end in exhausted sleep — like no place else, this town accommodates!

As an amber hue settles on the skyscrapers of this city, and the workday recedes into distant memory, night life is launched in endless bars and clubs which offer happy-hour prices to giddy patrons. Note that while it's cost-effective to tank up on these cheap cocktails while you can, you might want to curb your appetite so that you avoid "bumbling-idiot" status before the wise ones even come out to play (around midnight), when the after-dark scene really gets going. Many New Yorkers not only consider 10pm an early start, they also have no concept of "the week night." On any given night of the week, after an extensive bar-hop, many a lively night-loving creature finds his/her way to live-music venues to catch a show of the latest local heroes, or hurries to hit the hottest dance clubs before they lose their cache and fall into the category of "weak" as most upscale party joints do when they start admitting everyone under the sun. When bars and clubs wind down around dawn, after-hours joints open up to pick up the slack until long after the more health-conscious early-rising joggers have finished their runs.

The writhing masses who frequent the night spots of this city are composed of two very distinct crowds: Manhattanites and bridge-and-tunnelers (aka commuters). The former consider themselves the true denizens of NYC's diverse night life universe, mostly because they can stick around the latest. (There's no reason not to stay out until sunrise when home is, at worst, a ten-dollar cab ride away.) Because distance is such a factor for bridge-and-tunnelers, they tend to inundate Manhattan's bars and clubs only on weekend nights. Many locals tend to steer clear of the massive weekend crowds, so they either take great pains in keeping their weekend favorites hush-hush for as long as they can, or they start their partying much earlier in the week.

Bar and club owners and party promoters pay very close attention to the social barometer of this city; they create a different theme party for every night of the week aimed at particular crowds, everything from ladies night to '80s night to gay night, and different styles of music from reggae to Latino to deep house or old-school groove, whether on the jukebox, on stage, or spun on a turntable courtesy of an in-house or a guest DJ. New York's hot night spots supply the space and the tunes, but the mixed bag of people can go a long way toward characterizing the night life scene.

With its close embrace, intricate footwork, and expressive freedom, Argentine Tango is as close to sex as you can get with your clothes on. While professional dancers may dislike the formula, for New York's tango addicts the connection is as clear as love and chocolate.

With three recent films devoted to tango (cryptically named *The Tango Lesson, Happy Together*, and *Tango*) and one by Robert Duvall rumored to be in the works, New York has become the central station for the international tango scene. Performers from Carnegie Hall and Broadway celebrate their birthdays at the local milongas; the dance schools — especially DanceSport (1845 Broadway, 307-1111), Dance Manhattan (39 West 19th St., 807-0802) and Sandra Cameron (20 Cooper Square, 674-0505) — compete aggressively to bring the most well-known Argentinean and Spanish instructors to teach special classes and private lessons. There is even a tango hotline (718-35-TANGO) to promote the latest venues.

"In the city where you can do anything you want seven nights a week, anyone can learn to tango," promised one tangoer. Indeed, you can dance every night into the early morning, and enthusiasts often can visit three places a night. Some of the best dance floors include Dance-Sport, Dance Manhattan, Sandra Cameron, Triangulo (675 Hudson St, 3N, 633-6445), and The 92nd Street Y (1395 Lexington Ave., 427-6000), the last of which attracts many dancers who first learned to tango the last time it was the rage. The dance schools, on the other hand, have a more urban professional clientele. Triangulo, which operates out of a loft renovated into a charming dance hall, attracts a far younger, far hipper crowd.

During the summer (loosely defined as anytime it isn't snowing), you can dance on the paving stones at the Bethesda Fountain in Central Park, right next to the gondola pond. Lincoln Center's Midsummer Night Swing dance festival heats up from June through July. Romantics will find the two restaurants devoted to tango: La Belle Epoque (827 Broadway, 254-6436) and Il Campanello (136 West 31st St, 695-6111), perfect places for dates, even without trying to dance.

t a n g o

Why is New York the city that never sleeps? The answer may well that bars are at the center of city life. Whether a place to unwind anonymously with a beer in a dark corner, a regular meeting-spot for friends, or just a pit-stop on the way to who-knows-where, these establishments are an integral part of the routine of many city-dwellers.

College and sports bars tend to attract a predominantly male clientele who want to drink, watch the game, and absorb the sweaty mascu-lin-ity that hovers around the pool table; these are (not surprisingly), located near colleges and frequently host fraternity events. Women can take advantage of the ladies' nights which these bars throw in an attempt to even the gender ratio. Amsterdam Ave. in the high 70s to mid-80s boasts a string of indistinguishable establishments which draw on the student populations of both Columbia University to the north and Fordham Law to the south; Hunter College and Marymount Manhattan College students fill the bars on the Second Ave. strip from the 60s to the 80s. The scene around New York University is somewhat shaped by the hip cachet of going to school in Greenwich Village, but even the bastion of BoHo harbors some frat hang-outs. As a result, beer is the drink of choice, pitcher after pitcher of it — and none of the sissy microbrew crap! Bud and other American beers dominate.

Bleecker St. is a popular path for college students and out-of-towners clad in jeans and jerseys. Up and down the strip folkie-rock-n-roll bands play in places like The Bitter End (147 Bleecker St., 673-7030). While much of Greenwich Village is saturated with typically horny, straight, beer guzzling boys and girls, it is also highly concentrated with established gay and lesbian bars. Over the past ten years Chelsea has emerged as the most aggressive man-to-man cruising scene in the city.

Twentysomethings eschewing the frat scene tend to congregate downtown at assorted holes-in-the-wall, usually in trendy neighborhoods like the Lower East Side and the East Village. The beautiful, well-groomed hipsters among the premarriage set may find themselves gravitating toward downtown's more upscale hideaways, where how your clothes hang starts to matter more as bouncers and their trusty velvet ropes begin to emerge like trolls beneath the bridge. If you have any aspirations of breaking into the elusive SoHo lounge scene, it's best to start by putting your self-image to the test in a friendlier environment.

Cabarets, piano bars, and hotel bars are part of a long tradition of metropolitan elegance where there are insiders and outsiders, and you know before entering into which category you fall. Such bars are often populated by the remaining New York blue bloods who gather uptown at The Oak Room (59 West 44th St., 840-6800), where the drinks are so expensive you'll be nursing one all night; the dress-up game is fun, though. Newer hotel bars like The SoHo Grand Bar (310 West Broadway,  965-3000), invite a more modern bunch of fashionable artists into its classic SoHo-styled cast-iron building. Cabarets tend to attract a large gay male clientele. For a real treat, check out the nightlife renaissance in Harlem by traveling to Lenox Lounge (288 Lenox Ave., 427-0253) or Showman's (375 West 125th St., 864-8941).

Would-be underage drinkers, beware! Despite rumors that you can get served anywhere in New York, this carte blanche has been threatened by the quality-of-life crusader, Mayor Rudy Giuliani. The crackdown has resulted in much stricter ID policies at the doors of bars, clubs, and music venues, especially on the weekends. If someone asks you for ID and the best you can do is your library card, save the drama for your mama and leave quietly.

The ultimate mixed bag descends upon neighborhood haunts and pubs, which are typically packed from Happy Hour (the time between 4pm and 7pm being the longest and happiest hour of the day) until closing. All across the city, with the possible exceptions of the business strongholds of Lower Manhattan and Midtown, students chat and jostle old men at the bar as they try to get the bartender's attention. Equal numbers of men and women flock to these low-key refuges but the pick up scene is nearly nil, since virtually no one is a stranger for long. These bars are easy to spot, since the people in them look genuinely happy to be there. Pubs are very similar in that they're friendly and populated mostly by regulars, and a fair share of them are Irish.

wacky bar themes

A small bunch of bizarre theme bars can be found in the unlikely neighborhoods of the East Village and the Lower East Side, roughly 50 blocks away from mega-commercial theme spots like Planet Hollywood and the Hard Rock Cafe. These curious little joints are born when someone expresses his/her quirky vision, a couple of friends choreograph his/her design, the walls get dolled up, furniture gets collected, and the glamorous staff dresses accordingly. Viola! A wacky, and more often than not unique brainchild is born.

A change from the standard stark-sofa-brick-wall-wood-floor places is down on East Houston at Idlewild (145 East Houston St., 477-5005), where the Den of Thieves used to be. This place is the pioneering concept of Eric Rasmussen and his partners Jim and Rob, who planned, researched, and, with the help of friends, undertook all the labor to create its innovative design. Since "Idlewild" was once the name of JFK Airport, the design of the bar mimics the interior of a 1969 commercial plane. The replica's precision is remarkably accurate, from the shiny silver-paneled ceilings and leather-upholstered borders to the blue, beige, and white fabric wallpaper and brushed silver bathroom doors. Seats line the "back" or the "front" of the imaginary plane where "passengers" sip Martinis, Metropolitans or Idlewilds

(Cosmopolitans with a splash of Chambord). The gorgeous bartenders, dressed in white shirts and ties, act as pilots; the bar-back wears a bright orange baggage-handler jumpsuit, but instead of bags he's schlepping racks of clean glasses and cases of beer. The bar even has a ventilation system that filters out cigarette smoke and recirculates

fresh air. The only thing that breaks the illusion is the lack of "vacant" and "occupied" switches on the bathroom doors. Idlewild, with its Lower East Side glam-makeover is worth jetting into, even if for only a cocktail.

Two other funky theme bars worth mentioning are Korova Milk Bar (200 Ave. A, 254-8838) and Galaxy (15 Irving Place, 777-3631). Korova Milk Bar is a requisite stop for film buffs and lovers of eye candy; the bar glorifies and imitates the cult classic, *A Clockwork Orange* (though its management claims otherwise!). Of course, there is always a showing of the strange and terrifying film noir on some eerie wall, as if the bar wasn't enough to remind patrons. Galaxy is adorned in the sophisticated colors of the night sky. Fiberoptic stars splatter the ceiling, illuminating the room with a galactic glow, and huge windows let in the refreshing evening air. Some notable Galaxy drinks served are "Bloody Mars" and "Cosmic-politans," and maybe they are trying to keep you in space with their dizzying array of hemp-based menu items. Spend a whirlwind night hopping from one of these theme bars to the next, and you'll have traveled 500 years into the past and straight to the stars. And, remember, when it comes time to hail a taxi to take you home, dodge the one in the middle — just because you're tipsy doesn't mean the city's slowing down for you!

Abbey Pub

Both the food and the atmosphere are comforting at this ideal neighborhood bar where older locals mingle easily with the collegiate crowd; the perfect spot to meet for beers and share a basket of fish 'n chips.
Upper West Side, 237 West 105th St. (bet. Broadway and Amsterdam Aves.), 222-8713, MC, V, AmEx, **①⑨** *to 103rd St.* ⬑

American Trash

Aaah, the great American melting pot. Bikers and bankers meet without colliding at this rare East Side dive; its subtitle — "professional drinking establishment" — suggests democracy among lushes.
Upper East Side, 1471 First Ave. (bet. 76th & 77th Sts.), 988-9008, MC, V, AmEx, **⑥** *to 77th St.* ♿ ⬑

Amsterdam Café

Although it looks like a European hotel bar, this local favorite is a great place to visit either alone, at the padded bar, or in large thirsty groups. Columbia students and locals alike come for pitchers, pub grub and sports TV in a relaxed restaurant atmosphere.
Morningside Heights, 1207 Amsterdam Ave. (bet. 119th and 120th Sts.), 662-6330, MC, V, D, AmEx, Diners, **①⑨** *to 116th St.* ⬑

Au Bar

Eurotrashy area natives romp through this lavishly decorated retro bar. Among the pitfalls are $7 drinks, a large cover fee, and highly selective doormen. As always, celebrities and beautiful women are quite welcome.
Midtown, 41 East 58th St. (bet. Park and Madison Aves.), 308-9455, MC, V, AmEx, Diners, **④⑤⑥** *to 59th St.,* **⓪⓿** *to Lexington Ave.* ⬑

Auction House

Mature customers populate this pricey, baroque lounge which serves as a bastion of the Upper East Side. Good-looking, fashionable women included.
Upper East Side, 300 East 89th St. (bet. First and Second Aves.), 427-4458, MC, V, AmEx, Diners, D, **④⑤⑥** *to 86th St.* ⬑

Automatic Slim's

Go way west to find this happening hangout for locals. When it gets late — very, very late — dancing on the bar is allowed; one might even say it's encouraged.
Greenwich Village (West Village), 733 Washington St. (at Bank St.), 645-8660, MC, V, **④⑥⑧** *to 14th St.,* **⓵** *to Eighth Ave.,* **①⑨** *to Chistopher St.-Sheridan Sq.* ⬑

B Bar

Models pose beneath the chic, globular lights of this NoHo social scene staple, though it's not the shi-shi mecca it once was. The spacious, enclosed outdoor seating is popular.
East Village, 40 East 4th St. (at Bowery), 475-2220, MC, V, AmEx, Diners, **⑥** *to Bleecker* ♿ ⬑

Bar 89

A fancy, stylish crowd and pricey drinks are nothing unusual in this neck of the woods; the main attraction is the fabulous unisex bathroom, whose glass doors must be latched ever so precisely to prevent exposing everyone in the room to things better kept private. While someone's inside, the glass becomes opaque.
SoHo, 89 Mercer St. (bet. Spring and Broome Sts.), 274-0989, MC, V, AmEx, **①⑨** *to Canal St.,* **⑥** *to Spring St.* ⬑

Bar d'O

Arguably the place that initiated the lounge craze Tuesdays, Saturdays, and Sundays feature Joey Arias and Raven-O hosting the all-night festivities.
Greenwich Village, 29 Bedford St. (bet. Sixth Ave. and Hudson St.), 627-1580, Cash Only, **①⑨** *to Christopher St.-Sheridan Sq.* ⬑

Barmacy

Owner Deb Parker (also of the Beauty Bar) welcomes private functions, film shoots, photo shoots, and "anything else you'd like to shoot except drugs" at her new East Village establishment. It's not reserved most nights, however, and Monday thru Friday, 5:30pm to 4am, a downtown crowd gathers to mingle and mellow out with the in-house DJ .
East Village, 538 E. 14th St. (bet. Aves. A and B), 228-2240, MC, V, **⓵** *to First Ave.* ♿ ⬑

Barracuda

Dark and cruisy in front, with a funky lounge complete with lava lamps, this recent offering attracts a young crowd of good-looking men and a smaller crowd of equally hip and attractive women more interested in chatting and having a good time than proving how beautiful they are.
Chelsea, 275 West 22nd St. (bet. Seventh and Eighth Aves.), 645-8613, Cash Only, **⑥⑧** *to 23rd St.,* **①⑨** *to 23rd St.* ♿ ⬑

Beauty Bar

Glitter-sparkled walls shimmer, reflecting off vintage hair dryers that act as lounge chairs at this 50's beauty salon turned bar. Owner Deb Parker's own collection of '40s hairpins and pomade ads add the final touches. Wednesday afternoon manicure/drink specials are a must.

East Village, 231 East 14th St. (bet. Second and Third Aves.), 539-1389, MC, V, **❶❷❸❹❺❻** to 14th St.-Union Sq. ♿

Big Sur
If the liveliness of the young working crowd enjoying rock music in comfortable seating doesn't please, attend the alternate social scene located by the unisex bathrooms. *Upper East Side, 1406 Third Ave. (at 80th St.), 472-5009, MC, V, AmEx, Diners,* **❻** to 77th St. ⬅

Blind Tiger Ale House
With 24 micro-brews on tap and bottled beers from 12 countries, this haunt satisfies just about anyone's palate for brew. The crowd's strictly white-collar, after-work, and non-Budweiser. *Greenwich Village, 518 Hudson St. (at 10th St.), 675-3848, MC, V, AmEx, D,* **❶❷** to Christopher St.-Sheridan Sq. ⬅

Blondies
Mounted televisions boasting an impressive range of sporting events play continuously above the blonde bartenders who helped, no doubt, give this boisterous sports bar its name. Try the "world-famous atomic wings." *Upper West Side, 212 West 79th St. (bet. Broadway and Amsterdam Ave.), 362-4360, MC, V, AmEx, Diners,* **❶❷** to 79th St. ⬅

The Boiler Room
More lounge than bar, the pool table is used only as seating, and classic disco mixed with current dance sets the stage for light cruising. Indulge after an expensive weekend with one-dollar beers and shots on Mondays. There's a mixed crowd in the early evening, but around nine, the boys take over.

East Village, 86 East 4th St. (bet. First and Second Aves.), 254-7536, Cash Only, **❻** to Second Ave. ⬅

Boomer's
For the true sports fanatic: know your stats and be ready to talk some serious trivia. The crowd of cheering, jeering, thirtysomething men largely ignores the standby pool table in favor of the twenty-three televisions. New York home of the Celtic's soccer supporter club, so know what you mean when asking about the "football" game. *Upper West Side, 349 Amsterdam Ave. (bet. 76th & 77th Sts.), 362-5400, MC, V, AmEx, Diners, D,* **❶❾** to 79th St. ⬅

Boots and Saddle
Urban and rural cowboys flock to this Western veteran, proving that denim is the friendlier gay male counterpoint to leather. Features happy hour M-F. 3-9pm and Saturday and Sunday Beer Blasts that boast $1.50 cans and draft and $2.50 bottles. *Greenwich Village, 76 Christopher St. (at Seventh Ave.) 929-9684, Cash Only,* **❶❾** to Christopher St. ⬅

Botanica
The former site of the old Knitting Factory, recently converted into a paradise for twentysomething drinkers — one of the few chic spots where room to sit and converse can be found without resorting to someone's lap. Try to get a bar seat to be in the middle of all the action — if not hang out near the bathrooms where everyone ends up eventually. *East Village, 47 Houston St. (bet. Mott and Mulberry Sts.), 343-7251, Cash Only,* **❻❶❻❻** to Broadway-Lafayette St. ⬅

The Break
Trendy club goers, gym boys, and Chelsea locals make this relatively low-key space the place to begin or end a night on the town. Recent renovations have made the small locale a little roomier, but be prepared to stand shoulder-to-shoulder with all sorts of attractive men. *Chelsea, 232 Eighth Ave. (bet. 21st and 22nd Sts.), 627-0072, Cash Only,* **❻❾** to 23rd St. ♿ ⬅

Brother Jimmy's
Anyone from south of the Mason-Dixon line will feel at home in this southern theme bar. Post-collegiates and pre-professionals come for the generous bartenders and Sunday special of $18.95 for unlimited beer and all the ribs you can stomach. *Upper East Side, 1461 First Ave. (at 76th St.), 288-0999, MC, V, AmEx,* **❻** to 77th St. ♿

Carnegie Bar and Books
This recently opened two-floor cigar kingdom attracts the same white-collar crowd as its city siblings. No smoking jackets but patrons do enjoy feeling literary among the bookshelves while nursing fabulous martinis. Live jazz rounds out the ambiance on weekends. *Midtown, 156 West 56th St. (bet. Sixth and Seventh Aves.), 957-9676, MC, V, AmEx, Diners,* **❶❷❸** to Seventh Ave. ♿

Carriage House
Home away from home for the cable-less of Park Slope who need their fix of the Knicks or the Rangers. Too much sports? Amuse yourself at the pool table or with the random karoke night. *Park Slope, Brooklyn, 312 Seventh Ave. (bet. Seventh and Eighth Sts.), (718) 788-7747, MC, V, AmEx, D,* **❻** to Seventh Ave.-Park Slope. ♿ ⬅

Cedar Tavern

Pay tribute to Willem de Kooning with a visit to this spacious tavern, which the famous abstract expressionist frequented. The patrons are no longer the counter-culture scenesters of the '60s, but the Tiffany lighting and the monumental 19thC. bar remains. *Greenwich Village, 82 University Pl. (bet. 11th & 12th Sts.), 929-9089 MC, V, AmEx, Diners, D,* ❶❷❸ ❹❺❻ *to 14th St.-Union Sq.* ♿ ⬅

Chumley's

Professionals and other scene-making twenty-somethings inhabit this atmospheric bar; tucked away behind an unmarked entrance that recalls its days as a former bootlegger's paradise. The term "86ed" as in being thrown out, derives from the speakeasy's address. Breathing room is impossible to come by after nine on weekends. *Greenwich Village, 86 Bedford St. (at Barrow St.), 675-4449, Cash Only,* ❶❷ *to Christopher St.-Sheridan Sq.* ♿ ⬅

Ciel Rouge

Gaze into a date's eyes while reveling in the anonymity and intimacy of this hip hideaway. Sexy and swanky, with all the illicit glamour of a Prohibition-era speakeasy, this retreat offers drinks for a sophisticated palate in the scarlet lounge complete with plush chairs and the ultimate in retro chic, a baby grand. *Chelsea, 176 Seventh Ave. (bet. 20th and 21st Sts.), 929-5542, Cash Only,* ❶❷ *to 23rd St.* ⬅

City Wine & Cigar Co.

Catering to celebrities, Wall Street suits and others who have "arrived," this Latin-style luxury lounge is firmly onboard the cigar bar bandwagon. Venture in only if you think you can, and want to, pull it off. *TriBeCa, 62 Laight St. (at Greenwich St.), 334-2274, MC, V, AmEx, Diners,* ❶❷ *to Canal St.* ♿ ⬅

Clarke's

"People don't drink like they used to anymore," laments owner Eugene. "In the '80s on drink-up nights they used to bring guys out of here on stretchers." The bar owes its spacious feel to extra-high ceilings, and a gallery of great athletes graces the walls. *Fordham, The Bronx, 2541 Webster Ave. (at Fordham Rd.), (718) 364-9503, Cash Only,* ❷❺ *to Grand Concourse* ♿ ⬅

Crazy Nanny's

Can you say Lesbian Central? Go on the weekends for a fun, racially-mixed crowd of trucker-types and femmes. *Greenwich Village, 21 Seventh Ave. South (at Leroy St.), 366-6312,* ❶❷ *to Christopher St.-Sherodan Sq.* ⬅

The Cub Room

"I've sworn off martinis, except at this place," remarks a patron of this lovely bar. Business attire is the unwritten dress code for the young and affluent who enjoy expensive cocktails and the serious pick-up scene, while lounging on the comfy furniture. *SoHo, 131 Sullivan St. (at Prince St.), 677-4100, MC, V, AmEx,* ❸❹ *to Spring St.* ♿ ⬅

Cubbyhole

Favored by friendly college aged women of various persuasions, this small, dark, dyke rendezvous spot lives up to the double or triple-entendre in its name. The bar has a $5 cover on Saturday nights from 8:30pm to 10pm. *Greenwich Village, 281 West 12th St. (at Fourth Ave.), 243-9041, Cash Only,* ❶❷❸❹❺❻ *to 14th St.-Union Square.* ⬅

Danny's Skylight Room at the Grand Sea Palace

While it claims to have one of the best sound and lighting systems in the city, most people go to this reasonably priced singing bar for — surprise, surprise — the skylight. *Midtown, 346 West 46th St. (bet. Eighth and Ninth Aves.), 265-8130, MC, V, AmEx, Diners, D,* ❶❷❸❹❺❻❼❽❾ *to 42nd St.* ⬅

Dive Bar

Sure, it's got dive written all over it, literally, but this clean haunt is pretty damn tame — even the resident pool sharks won't intimidate. Chug till 4am every day and don't overlook a menu strong enough to support a free delivery service. *Upper West Side, 732 Amsterdam Ave. (at 96th St.), 749-4358, MC, V, AmEx,* ❶❷❸❹ *to 96th St.,* ❺❻ *to 96th St.* ♿ ⬅

Doc Holiday's

"I'm trapped in here with the convicts who love me," moans bartender Tari — and she's just talking about the regulars. Weekends, this rollicking country-western joint in flooded with hell raisers who come from all over to admire the wild animal pelts on the walls and the even wilder staff who can often be found dancing on the bar. Try the home-style BBQ food. *East Village, 141 Ave. A (bet. 8th and 9th Sts.), 979-0312, Cash Only,* ❶ *to First Ave.* ♿ ⬅

Don Hill's

Don Hill's is consistently crowded with down town kids, especially on Wednesday nights for the Beauty party when kids come out to groove '70s and '80s style, and Hot Fudge Sundays, which features soul and hip hop music, and the Famous Squeeze

Box on Friday nights: a gay rock drag queen party. Live band or DJ nightly.
SoHo, 511 Greenwich St. (at Spring St.), 334-1390, MC, V, AmEx, D, ◯◯ to Spring St., ◯◯ to Houston St. ⚙

Drinkland

This hip downtown bar has three separate drinking areas, all decorated in Austin Powers-esque '60s kitsch. Most notable is the White Room, appropriately furnished in wall to wall white padded vinyl. Though the drinks are mediocre, Drinkland more than makes up for it in atmosphere and decor.
East Village, 339 East 10th Street (bet. Aves. A and B), 228-2453, Cash Only, ◯ to Astor ⬑

Ear Inn

A laid-back, homey atmosphere and reasonable prices on both food and liquor draws a crowd that's on the hip side of yuppie to this former brothel, located way west of the main drags. The sign once read BAR, but the burnt out 'B' gave way to its present 'E'. Ask about their seasonal poetry readings.
SoHo, 326 Spring St. (bet. Greenwich and Washington Sts.), 226-9060, MC, V, AmEx, ◯◯ to Spring St. ⚙ ⬑

11th Street Bar

Locals hungry for bar action untainted by Ave. A herds are breaking in this addition to Alphabet City nightlife. Narrow in front at the crowded bar, it opens up in the back with a handful of tables large enough to fit all your roommates, or your new friends.
East Village, 510 E. 11th St. (bet. Aves. A and B), 982-3929, MC, V, AmEx, ◯ to First Ave. ⚙ ⬑

Fez

A chic, artsy clientele hides out under Time Cafe at this Moroccan style bar whose decor is as lush as the menu offerings. Catch the legendary Mingus Big Band on Thursdays, arrive early to snag the comfiest seats.
East Village, 380 Lafayette St. (bet. 4th and Great Jones Sts.), 533-2680, MC, V, AmEx, ◯◯ to 8th St.-NYU, ◯ to Astor Pl. ⚙ ⬑

Flamingo East

Upstairs is chic and pretentious, full of film industry types, and usually reserved for private parties; the downstairs restaurant lounge is a bit more mellow. Wednesdays, observe them at their finest.
East Village, 219 Second Ave. (bet. 13th and 14th Sts.), 533-2860, MC, V, AmEx, Diners, ◯◯◯◯◯◯ to 14th St.-Union Sq., ◯ to Third Ave. ⬑

420 Bar and Lounge

This swank member of the Amsterdam scene, populated with the requisite clothes hangers and the men who finance their drinking, could teach those SoHo types a thing or two. Local scenesters, spared the cab ride downtown, don't seem to mind the pricey cocktails, but if you've come for the strip's notorious drink specials, you may be better served up the street.
Upper West Side, 420 Amsterdam Ave. (at 80th St.), 579-8450, MC, V, AmEx, Diners, D, ◯◯ to 79th St. ⬑

"g"

An alternative to the gym-obsessed Chelsea scene, this hotspot has arrived with quite a bang. Casual elegance is the key here. Subtly but well-lit, the bar is surrounded by lounges galore and, in an example of planning genius, a second bar in the back

features coffee and gourmet juice drinks. This place is so popular, the owners have recently ceased publishing their telephone number for fear of attracting Giuliani's goons on account of noise and overcrowding.
Chelsea, 223 West 19th St. (bet. Seventh and Eighth Aves.), Cash Only, ◯◯ to 18th St.

The Ginger Man

The suits turn out in jaunty little three-piece numbers to mix networking with cruising over cigars and rather anonymous-looking drinks in oh-so-stylish cocktail glasses.
Midtown, 11 East 36th St. (bet. Fifth and Madison Aves.), 532-3740, MC, V, AmEx, Diners, ◯◯◯◯◯◯ to 34th St. ⚙ ⬑

Heartland Brewery

Take the pulse of the after-work crowd at this hip Union Sq. bar; patrons move fast, talk fast, and drink fast, enjoying the award-winning house brews like Harvest Wheat while communing with cell phones, digital diaries, and sometimes even each other. For the more leisurely diner, plenty of seating is available, as well as a menu which ranges from basic meatloaf to falafel.
Chelsea, 35 Union Square West (at 17th St.) 645-3400, MC, V, AmEx, Diners, ◯◯◯◯◯◯ to Union Sq. ⚙ ⬑

Henrietta Hudson

Number one women's bar in NYC, internationally and nationally renowned. Although the scene is mostly women, the bar claims to be "male-friendly." There are DJs on the weekends and women's bands on Sundays.
Greenwich Village, 438 Hudson St. (at Morton St.), 924-3347, MC, V, AmEx, ◯◯ to Christopher St.-Sheridan Sq. ⬑

Her/She Bar

Popular Friday night party sponsored in part by the infamous and ubiquitous WOW promoters, where predominantly black and Latina women dance, cruise, and strut their stuff. Sports bras and bare midriffs abound below the hot lesbian porn shown on the televisions above the bar.
Chelsea, 301 W. 39th St. (at Eighth Ave.), 631-1093, Cash Only, 🅐🅒🅔 *to 42nd St.* 🚶

Hogs & Heifers

Appropriately named for the less-than-fragrant part of town in which it resides, this rowdy biker bar attracts the stars despite its meat-packing district address. Tim Roth was recently spotted exiting the dive, while Julia Roberts posed near the infamous bra-clad moosehead for People magazine.
Greenwich Village, 859 Washington St. (at 13th St.), 929-0655, Cash Only, 🅐🅒🅔 *to 14th St.,* 🅛 *to Eighth Ave.* ♿ 🚶

Idlewild

Its innovative design has people flocking from all over to check it out. The music is "consistently eclectic," the atmosphere is "loungy," and a DJ spins nightly. Dress code? Clean and casual.
Lower East Side, 145 East Houston St. (bet. First and Second Aves.), 477-5005, MC, V, 🅕 *to Second Ave.* ♿ 🚶

Irish Brigade Pub

Feisty female bartender serves a much, much older crowd interested in letting loose. Beers start at $1.50, pitchers at $6. Sometimes as a special treat, there's a DJ for dancing.
Washington Heights, 4716 Broadway (at Arden St.), 567-8714, Cash Only, 🅐 *to Dyckman St. (200th St.)* 🚶

Jimmy Armstrong's Saloon

According to the menu, "tasty vittles, good grog, and sweet music" draw the uptown music set to this jovial neighborhood pub which positively bursts with bonhomie. The top-rate jazz guitarists featured here six nights a week (Tues. through Sun.) are good enough to please the picky crowd of professional musicians, composers, and Juilliard students who frequent this friendly, lively place. Appease a hearty appetite with some of the scrumptious savories offered on the eclectic, moderately priced menu.
Midtown, 875 Tenth Ave. (at 57th St.), 581-0606, AmEx, 🅐🅑🅒🅓🅘🅙 *to 59th St.-Columbus Circle* ♿ 🚶

Jimmy's Corner

Escape the giddiness and rapacity of the Theater District at this easy-going local dive, the site of some scenes in Raging Bull. Owner Jimmy Glen subsidizes his career as a boxing trainer and manager with the revenues from his hopping bar business. An eclectic crowd of boxing fanatics, literati, grad students, and the occasional movie star gathers here.
Midtown, 140 West 44th St. (bet. Sixth and Seventh Aves.), 221-9510, MC, V, AmEx, 🅝🅡🅢 🅑🅓🅕🅖🅥 *to 42 St.-Times Sq.* 🚶

Julie's

Offering the mature elegance of The Townhouse Bar, but for women, the crowd is generally thirtysomething and professional, the proverbial lipstick lesbian. Wednesday nights sizzle with salsa and Sundays prove that the women are not to be outdone by the men by featuring a sexy tea dance at 4pm.
Midtown, 204 East 58th St. (bet. Second and Third Aves.), 688-1294, Cash Only, 🅐🅔🅖 *to 59th,* 🅝🅡 *to Lexington Ave.* 🚶

KGB

Old Soviet paraphernalia gives this small upstairs barroom an illicit feel, reinforced by the regular poetry readings and theater downstairs. Perfect for bringing out the inner subversive artist for a good stiff drink, preferably something with vodka.
East Village, 85 East 4th St. (bet. The Bowery and Second Ave.), 505-3360, Cash Only, 🅕 *to Second Ave.* 🚶

King

Libido at its most forthright rules this three-tiered yet cramped dance bar. Monday nights promise boys $1 drinks if they take off their shirts, which should give a clue as to what the clientele doesn't wear. A perfect venue for gym boys to flaunt their hard work. Cover varies from $5 to $10. Wednesdays offer an Amateur Strip Contest worth $200, the tamest of the contests.
Chelsea, 579 Sixth Ave. (bet. 16th and 17th Sts.), 366-5464, Cash Only, 🅛🅥 *to 18th St.* 🚶

Korova Milk Bar

Perhaps inspired by the milk bar in A Clockwork Orange, this night-spot is most definitely off-kilter, from the naked mannequins to endless video screens all showing something strange and terrifying. A mandatory stop for lovers of eye candy.
East Village, 200 Ave. A (bet. 12th and 13th Sts.), 254-8838, MC, V, AmEx, 🅛 *to First Ave.* ♿ 🚶

Lakeside Lounge

Come prepared to wait for your drinks since this hipster haunt deep in Alphabet City is packed even on nights the bartender calls "real slow." Lots of live bands; Open until 4am.
East Village, 162 Ave. B (at 10th St.), 529-8463, MC, V, AmEx, D, 🅛 *to First Ave.* ♿ 🚶

Lava

Lava is known for its sweet vodka drinks like the Lava Flow, Blue Lagoon and Purple Haze, all served in gigantic tiki bowls (good for six people), and if you'd like, the bartenders will set them on fire. Lava, of course, flows down the walls and trees litter the place. Live bands and DJs play under enormously high ceilings.

Chelsea, 28 West 20th St. (bet. Fifth and Sixth Aves.), 627-7867, MC, V, AmEx, ❻ to 23rd St. ♿ ⬑

Lenox Lounge

Variety is key to this venerable "hideaway" established in 1939. Hosts jazz performances on some nights, while Tuesdays cater to a gay crowd.

Harlem, 288 Lenox Ave. (bet. 124th & 125th Sts.) 427-0253, MC, V, AmEx, ❷❸ to 125th St. ♿ ⬑

Lexington Bar and Books

A pricey, high-class establishment with great ambiance and fantastic martinis make this cozy cigar bar a nice place to pretend you're all grown up along with the white-collar crowd. College students beware: "proper attire is required". Live jazz on Fridays and Saturdays.

Upper East Side, 1020 Lexington Ave. (at 73rd St.), 717-3902, MC, V, AmEx, Diners, ❻ to 77th St. ⬑

Liquor Store Bar

Huge front windows, an oak bar, and sidewalk seating render this bar utterly irresistible. The charming, slightly motley, group of local men welcome newcomers as a fresh audience for their stale jokes. Heaven for any true bar lover.

TriBeCa, 235 West Broadway (at White St.), 226-7121, Cash Only, ❶❾ to Franklin St. ⬑

Live Bait

Located right on Madison Square Park, curious passers-by and neighborhood locals find it hard to resist this oxymoronic urban rendition of the Louisiana bayou. Force your way past the boisterous happy hour crowd at the bar to the tables in back in order to sample the Cajun shrimp or the mesquite BBQ.

Gramercy, 14 East 23rd St. (bet. Broadway and Madison Ave.), 353-2400, MC, V, AmEx, Diners, ❻❻ to 23rd St. ♿ ⬑

Ludlow Bar

Dependably cool, and crowded on the weekends, this downstairs bar stakes all its seating on minimalist couches; the DJ changes night-to-night but the dancing never gets going until everyone's liquored up. Quite a pick-up scene, especially around the purple pool table.

Lower East Side, 165 Ludlow St. (bet. Houston and Stanton Sts.) 353-0536, MC, V, AmEx, ❻ to Second Ave. ⬑

Luna Lounge

No cover and no minimum draw a lively crowd of tattooed bohemians to this otherwise undistinguished bar. The dark, cavernous space hosts Alternative Comedy Nite, Mondays at 8pm.

Lower East Side, 171 Ludlow St. (bet. Houston and Stanton Sts.), 260-2323, Cash Only, ❻ to Second Ave. ⬑

Manitobas

Co-owners George Gilmore and "Handsome" Dick Manitobas, (lead singer of the Dictators) have recently opened this East Village bar. While only up and running since January, 1999, it has already made its mark on the neighborhood. The main room is decorated as a gin mill, while the downstairs resembles a Chinese brothel with red lanterns and large murals of lounging Asian women. Manitobas also features live music nightly, which, much like the scene, is eclectic and unexpected.

East Village, 99 Avenue B (bet. 6th and 7th Sts.), 982-2511, MC, V, AmEx, ❻ to Second Avenue ⬑

Mare Chiaro Tavern

Oooh and aaah at the huge photo of Frank Sinatra. Then go get yourself a drink at one of Little Italy's last genuine bars. Also known as "Tony's" in case you want to feel like a real local.

Little Italy, 176 1/2 Mulberry St. (bet. Grand and Broome Sts.), 226-9345, Cash Only, ❻❶❷ to Essex St., ❻ to Delancey ♿ ⬑

Max Fish

Hipsters live it up at this comparatively bright and lively Ludlow fave, once a hotspot, now just comfortably cool. Play pool with the regulars or spend a week's wages on pinball while enjoying local artist's work which is proudly hung on the walls.

Lower East Side, 178 Ludlow St. (bet. Houston and Stanton Sts.), 529-3959, Cash Only, ❻ to Second Ave. ♿ ⬑

Meow Mix

Bohemians of all persuasions are welcome at this campy but casual downtown dyke bar. The hub of the queer art scene, it hosts everything: comedy, poetry, performance art, theme parties, and both local and touring bands, usually of the post-punk girl variety. Pick up a calendar, and, if you're lucky, one of the cute, pierced, and well-tattooed chicks.

Lower East Side, 269 East Houston St. (at Suffolk St.), 254-0688, Cash Only, ❻ to Second Ave. ⬑

Metronome

Slightly more polished and pricey than the other Gramercy bars, Metronome draws an older professional crowd. There's dancing on Saturday nights, live jazz Wednesday through Saturday.
Gramercy, 915 Broadway (at 21st St.), 505-7400, MC, V, AmEx, Diners, ⓃⓇ *to 23rd St.* ♿ ⬑

Monkey Bar

"It's hip, it's hopping, and it's hot," said a fiftyish, dolled-up patron of this Art Deco masterpiece where a glamorous, older crowd sips cocktails and flaunts Chanel. The epitome of swank.
Midtown, Hotel Elysée, 60 East 54th St. (bet. Madison and Park Aves.), 838-2600, MC, V, AmEx, Diners, ⑥ *to 53rd St.* ♿ ⬑

Motor City Bar

"Professional creative types" too old to be carded flock to this unlikely Detroit theme bar, a harbinger of gentrification this far south of Houston. The vehicular bric-a-brac adorning the walls may strike some as a little corny. Slicker and a little less funky than other joints in these parts, locals like it "cuz there's elbow room."
Lower East Side, 127 Ludlow St. (bet. Rivington & Delancey Sts.), 358-1595, Cash Only, ⒿⓂⓏ *to Essex St.,* ⓕ *to Delancey St.* ♿ ⬑

Mugs Ale House

So many good beers on tap, most people never investigate the vast selection in bottles. Add to this the local contingent and a decent juke-box for a good reason why people come from Manhattan to drink here. Join 'em and fill in the blanks.
Williamsburg, Brooklyn, 125 Bedford Ave. (at North 10th St.), (718) 486-8232, MC ,V, AmEx, D, Ⓛ *to Bedford Ave.* ♿ ⬑

Meyer Lansky Lounge

Named after Jewish Mafia kingpin Meyer Lansky, this sophisticated new nightspot channels the spirit of the celebrated speakeasy whose site the club now occupies. Beautiful people proffer spirits and delectable kosher treats to the rhythms of classic jazz and lounge. Expect to run into Hasidim in the men's room, as the club shares its facilities with the deli out front. Humane door policy, but mixed groups of men and women have a better chance of making the cut. Closed on Shabbat.
Lower East Side, 104 Norfolk St. (at Delancey St.), 677-9489, MC, V, AmEx, ⒿⓂⓏ *to Essex St.,* ⓕ *to Delancey St.* ⬑

ñ

Savor pitchers of sangria while admiring the flamenco dancers who perform every Wednesday night. Don't even try to resist the tapas. It's tiny and little cramped, so stake out a space early and camp there all night.
SoHo, 33 Crosby St. (bet. Broome and Grand Sts.), 219-8856, Cash Only, ⒿⓂⓃⓇⓏⓆ *to Canal St.*

Nick's Pub

Definitely a place with a loyal clientele: if a regular is a no-show, the manager calls to see what's wrong. Renowned jazz musicians play to this low-key crowd, and allow local musicians to join in (that doesn't mean you can bring your recorder). No cover and no minimum.
Harlem, 773 St. Nicholas Ave. (at 149th St.), 283-9728, Cash Only, ⒶⒷⒸⒹ *to 145th St.* ⬑

Night Cafe

No pitchers, but plenty of pool at one of the neighborhood's most popular watering holes.

On alternate Wednesdays during the school year, Columbia's graduate writing students have an open mike. Locals good-naturedly tolerate the Columbians and their metaphors, and by 3am the jolly bartender's trivia games and a jukebox packed with billboard hits have loosened everyone up.
Upper West Side, 938 Amsterdam Ave. (bet. 106th and 107th Sts.), 864-8889, Cash Only, ①⓪ *to 103rd St.* ♿ ⬑

9C

Tiny space packs a down-to-earth crowd for the Sunday Blue Grass Jam and Alphabet City Opry on Monday nights. Formerly the Red Bar.
East Village, 700 East 9th St. (at Ave. C), 358-0048, Cash Only, Ⓛ *to First Ave.* ⬑

North Star Pub

For the true pub grub fan: this is where limeys go to dine. Great ales, a quiet but cheerful ambiance, and one of the largest collection of single-malt scotch in New York make this place worth a visit. Be sure to take the tasting tour of Scotland.
Lower Manhattan, 93 South St. (at Fulton St.), 509-6757, MC, V, AmEx, Diners, ⒿⓂ②③④⑤ *to Fulton St.* ♿ ⬑

Nowbar

Intimate without being cramped, the downstairs, which serves as a dance floor, is complemented by an upstairs that generally serves as a lounge. Creative indirect lighting renders the crowd, gay and straight, hip and festive, surprisingly visible.
Greenwich Village, 22 Seventh Ave. South (at Leroy St.), 293-0323, MC, V, AmEx, ①⑨ *to Houston St.* ⬑

The Oak Room

One of two lounges at the Algonquin Hotel where Dorothy Parker's mordant wit presided over a legen-dary circle of writers and critics in the 1920s. Dress up to fit in with the stylish crowd soaking up late-night cabaret performances in this stylized English tea room.
Midtown, 59 West 44th St. (bet. Fifth and Sixth Aves.), 840-6800, MC, V, AmEx, ❸❻❼❾ *to 42nd St.,* ❼ *to Fifth Ave.* ♿ ⌐

Oke Doke

Rumor has it that not even Jack Nicholson can always get past the octogenarian proprietor Elsie, the toughest doorwoman around, at this inti-mate, after-hours spot.
Upper East Side, 307 East 84th St. (bet. First and Second Aves.), 650-9424, Cash Only, ❹❺❻ *to 86th St.* ⌐

The Opium Den

Find shockingly clean downtown kids at this gothic lock-in. Saints and candles plastered around the room bring on a creepiness that prompts anyone to reach for another drink.
East Village, 29 East 3rd St. (bet. Bowery St. and Second Ave.), 505-7344, Cash Only, ❻ *to Second Ave.* ⌐

Orchard Bar

Enveloped in mellow music and dim blue lighting, low-key Ludlow types chat on the elongated sofas till dawn. Check it out to see what happens next.
Lower East Side, 200 Orchard St. (bet. Ludlow and Allen Sts.), 673-5350, MC, V, AmEx, ❻ *to Second Ave.* ♿ ⌐

Parnell's Pub

"It'll kill ya' or cure ya'," explains the red-headed waitress in her lilting brogue to customers inquiring about Guinness. Outfitted with a dark wood bar and plenty of Irish pride this bar and restaurant serves traditional dishes along with the infamous, coffee-colored brew.
Midtown, 350 East 53rd St. (at First Ave.), 753-1761, MC, V, AmEx, ❺❻ *to Lexington-3 Ave.* ❻ *to 51st St.* ♿ ⌐

Pete's Tavern

An honest-to-God neighborhood establishment, Pete's has been a gathering place in Gramercy for ages. Although known mostly as a bar, its mostly Italian menu is certainly adequate. Still, it's more a slice of 19th century London than a piece of pizza from Pisa.
Gramercy, 129 East 18th St. (at Irving Pl.), 473-7676, AmEx, V, DC, ❻❼❽❹❺❻ *to 14th St.-Union Sq.* ⌐

The Piper's Kilt

The best neighborhood bar in Washington Heights serves Irish-American food, like "Nachos à la Piper's Kilt," in a plush setting. Specials include a $10 weekend brunch with lots of food and bottomless drinks between noon and 3pm, a weekday lunch special between 11am and 3pm and dinner specials every night between 5pm and 10pm. The wide selection of beer starts at $2, pitchers at $6.50.
Washington Heights, 4944 Broadway (at 207th St.), 569-7071, MC, V, AmEx, Diners, D, ❹ *to 207th St.-Inwood* ⌐

Polly Esther's

Kitsch by the truckload here; psychedelia, beaded curtains and the requisite Brady Bunch and Sonny and Cher homages will satisfy every Gen-Xer's fantasy of Flower Power and free love. The prices aren't retro but at least they're reasonable.
Greenwich Village, 186 West 4th St. (bet. Sixth and Seventh Aves.), 924-5707, MC, V, AmEx, Diners, D, Cover: $8, ❶❷❸❹❺❻❼❾ *to West 4th St.-Washington Sq.* ♿ ⌐

Also at:
Upper East Side, 1487 First Ave. (bet. 77th and 78th Sts.), 628-4477, MC, V, AmEx, Diners, D, ❻ *to 77th St.* ♿ ⌐

Pravda

Go underground, literally. It's neither post-Soviet mayhem, nor is it a hard-core proletarian drinking establishment but the eighty flavors of vodka (includ-ing the decidedly bourgeois flavors: mango and raspberry), caviar, and rust-themed decor almost justify the name. High-class SoHoites eschew commu-nism for black market prices.
SoHo, 281 Lafayette (bet. Prince and Spring Sts.), 226-4696, MC, V, AmEx, ❻❷❺❻ *to Broadway-Lafayette St.,* ❹❿ *to Prince St.* ⌐

Revolution

Yuppies gather 'round the fireplace, smoke long cigarettes, and toss their heads back in mock laughter at this watering hole which is unusually hip and upscale for a Hell's Kitchen bar/restaurant.
Midtown, 611 9th Ave. (bet. 43rd and 44th Sts.), 489-8451, MC, V, AmEx, Diners, D, ❹❻❺ *to 42nd St.* ♿ ⌐

Rising Cafe

On any given night, this relaxed gathering place for Park Slope's sizable gay community hosts anything from readings to art openings. Equal parts coffee-

house and beer and wine bar, all are welcome; kids can amuse themselves in a play space.
Park Slope, Brooklyn, 186 Fifth Ave. (at Sackett St.), (718) 789-6340, Cash Only,
M N R to Union St. ♿ ⮐

Rodeo Bar & Grill
Don't expect cowboy hats and big belt buckles at this cozy wild west watering hole, but then again, don't let the giant stuffed buffalo above the bar surprise you. The menu is limited, but live free rockabilly bands keep the place swingin'.
Gramercy, 375 Third Ave. (at 27th St.), 683-6500, MC, V, AmEx, Diners, D, **6** to 28th St. ♿ ⮐

Saints
The gay community meets the Columbia community at this Morningside Heights Bar. Saints has it all: savvy bartenders, a crowd of professionals, students, and a few sinners. Also available for private parties.
Morningside Heights, 992 Amsterdam Ave. (at 109th St.), 222-2431, Cash Only,
1 9 to 110th St. ♿ ⮐

Shark Bar
A well-known hangout for upscale African-Americans. Low lighting and polished wood accents make this hideaway a romantic alternative to the other, more raucous, local bars. Bring a date to ward off post-collegiate singles hovering around the bar.
Upper West Side, 307 Amsterdam Ave. (bet. 74th and 75th Sts.), 874-8500, MC, V, AmEx,
1 2 3 9 to 72nd St. ♿ ⮐

Showman's
"Everything is copacetic" at this laid-back haunt, according to the Copasetics, Harlem's brotherhood of tap dancers, which makes this popular club its headquarters. Come for the

world famous jazz acts W-Sa.
Harlem, 375 W. 125th St. (bet. Morningside and St. Nicholas Aves.), 864-8941, MC, V, AmEx,
1 9 to 125th St. ⮐

The Slaughtered Lamb
One of the Village's best-known pubs, tourists flock to this horror-film theme bar to watch the shocker movies and consume slightly overpriced drinks.
182 West 4th St. (bet. Sixth and Seventh Aves.), 727-3350, MC, V, AmEx, Diners, D, **A B C D E F Q** to West 4th St.-Washington Sq. ♿ ⮐

SoHa
Stands for SOuth of HArlem and is a hip addition to Columbia's astonishingly limited bar scene. Vintage chandeliers, a purple pool table and plenty of couches make patrons forget they're in the square heart of the ivy league. The smart crowd, excellent music, and extensive beer and liquor selection help Morningside Heights dwellers forget that SoHo is "SoFa" away.
Morningside Heights, 998 Amsterdam Ave. (at 108th and 109th Sts.), 678-0098, V, MC, AmEx, **1 9** to 110th St. ⮐

The SoHo Grand Bar
This hotel bar is growing ever more popular. During the day guests and drop-ins meet for business over lunch martini's, at night sophisticated SoHoites spiral up the cast-iron, bottle cap staircase for a pre-dinner drink or night-cap.
SoHo, 310 West Broadway (bet. Canal and Grand Sts.), 965-3000, MC, V, AmEx, D,
A C E to Canal St. ⮐

Splash
This cavernous gay bar is packed with Chelsea gym types and boyish guppies. The real draw is the center stage: a shower stall,

with shows nightly. Straight women flock here to ogle the buff bartenders, who never, ever, wear shirts.
Gramercy, 50 West 17th St. (at Sixth Ave.), 691-0073, Cash Only, **1 9** to 18th St. ⮐

Spy Bar
Wear the trendiest outfit you can find and approach the bouncers with all the arrogance you can muster. Just remember: money and beauty aren't everything.
SoHo, 101 Greene St. (bet Prince and Spring Sts.), 343-9000, MC, V, AmEx, Diners, **C E** to Spring St., **N R** to Prince St. ⮐

Tatou
Rub shoulders with the young, chic and sartorially privileged at this swank little supper club. The setting is dark and romantic, with a decidedly glitzy demeanor.
Midtown,,151 East 50th St. (bet. Lexington and Third Aves.),753-1144, MC, V, AmEx, Diners, **E F Q** to 53rd St. ♿ ⮐

Teddy's Bar and Grill
The best bar food in Brooklyn, with plenty of beverages to wash it down with. Try a burger or go for dessert — sample the ice cream smothered in homemade hot fudge. One of the few places offering pitchers of really good beer.
Williamsburg, Brooklyn, 96 Berry St. (at North 8th St.), (718) 384-9787, MC, V,
L to Bedford Ave. ♿ ⮐

Temple Bar
The epitome of understated elegance: the dark wood interior is quietly beautiful, rather than forcibly chic. The perfect place to impress a date if money is no object.
East Village, 332 Lafayette St. (bet. Bleecker and Houston Sts.), 925-4242, MC, V, AmEx, Diners,

⑥ to Bleecker St., **⑧ⒹⒻⓆ** to Broadway-Lafayette St. ♿ ⬑

The Townhouse Bar

An extremely professional gay bar catering to well-dressed men with big bank accounts and the fellahs who love them. A piano bar in back exploits the somewhat pretentious ambiance. *Midtown, 236 East 58th St. (bet. Second and Third Aves.), 754-4649, Cash Only,* **❹❺❻** *to 59th St.,* **ⓃⓇ** *to Lexington Ave.* ⬑

Triad

Both floors of this lounge and restaurant stage acts of surprisingly high quality seven nights a week. Check out the upstairs theater for Off-Broadway productions and jazz, blues, and comedy acts; head downstairs to the relaxed Dark Star Lounge for open-mike on Mondays. *Upper West Side, 158 West 72nd St. (bet. Broadway and Columbus Ave.), 799-4599, MC, V, AmEx,* **❶❷❸❾** *to 72nd St.* ⬑

200 5th

An upscale crowd goes for dinner as well as drinks, at one of Park Slope's most popular night spots. Get there early on Friday nights for salsa dancing; other evenings are a bit more sedate. The cover varies and, more importantly, is negotiable. *Park Slope, Brooklyn, 200 Fifth Ave. (bet. Union and Berkeley Sts.), (718) 638-2925, MC, V, AmEx, Diners, D,* **ⓂⓃⓇ** *to Union St.* ⬑

Void

Video and a great free film series are the heart of this nightspot. Find out what the event is ahead of time and be prepared to appreciate it; there's no other social scene, just people lining the walls, mesmerized by the big screen. *SoHo, 16 Mercer St. (at Howard St.), 941-6492, MC, V, AmEx,* **❶❾** *to Canal St.* ♿ ⬑

The West End

This is Columbia students' favorite place to "Howl." All ages and majors dutifully carry on the legacy of beats Kerouac and Ginsberg at the writers' old hangout, though the ambiance is far from literary. Decent food and extensive beer selection draw a crowd that defies the frat boy stereotype. *Morningside Heights, 2911 Broadway (bet. 113th and 114th Sts.), 662-8830, MC, V, AmEx, Diners, D,* **❶❾** *to 116th St.* ♿ ⬑

The White Horse Tavern

A Village landmark, reputed to be the place where Dylan Thomas supposedly drank himself to death though the poets are long gone, supplanted by a decidedly pedestrian twenty-something crowd. Dinner essentials are served, including good burgers, and sidewalk dining, weather permitting. 1/2 price happy hour. *Greenwich Village, 567 Hudson St. (at West 11th St.), 243-9260, Cash Only,* **❶❾** *to Christopher St.-Sheridan Sq.* ⬑

Wonder Bar

Unwind after work at this mellow dive whose decor is a bit of a circus what with the R&B and funk DJ peeking through a hole in the wall while a blue polka-dot strobe lights up zebra-striped walls. *East Village, 505 East 6th St. (bet. Aves. A and B), 777-9105, Cash Only,* **❻** *to Second Ave.* ⬑

XVI

A hip-hop vibe moves the crowd in the downstairs lounge while upstairs the mood mellows. Sophisticates gather in the front hallway and goths congregate in the back. A friskier-than-usual, tourist-free, pick-up scene. *East Village, 16 First Ave. (bet. First and Second Sts.), 260-1549, AmEx,* **❻** *to Second Ave.* ⬑

WEBSTER HALL

PSYCHEDELIC THURSDAY
PRESENTS
GIRLS NITE OUT

clubs

While most of America heads to Disneyland to escape reality, New Yorkers look no further than the warehouses, caverns, and padded chambers of the city's nightclubs. Each of these spots provides a different array of diversions to help its cast of characters leave the real world behind.

New York's myriad dance clubs encompass every type of music, fashion, sexual preference, ego, and bank account. Mega-dance clubs, like **Life** (158 Bleecker St., 420-1999), seem to pump almost as much money in to their lands of make-believe as Disney — strobe lights and smoke

abound! These large venues care what you wear, the cursed velvet rope stands between you and what you want (a night of crazy gyrating and drink slamming). It cordons off the rabble from the celebrities and hard-core club kids. Towering bouncers will be eying the threads on the crowd, so if you want in, dress for the occasion.

Smaller clubs like The Sapphire Lounge (249 Eldridge St., 777-5153) are less trendy fashion-conscious venues and have a more intimate feel, with a local crowd. One club owner describes small clubs as "a living-room you don't have to clean up." And yet, it's so much more. Small club venues, with their low lighting, cushy couches, and close-dancing friendly clientele, are the wave of the '90s. Jahan Matin, manager of The Sapphire Lounge, says, "you don't have to be 'all that' to be at Sapphire, but if you are inside, you probably are!" Some of these smaller clubs haven't been granted cabaret licenses, which essentially means no dancing allowed, but a host of DJ's and live bands still play to the house, and there's plenty of undulating, grinding, or whatever you call that booty shankin' you do.

New York's dance scene is notoriously fickle, and this week's hottest club may get boarded up the next. Also, a place can host completely different crowds depending on the night of the week — drag ball on Tuesdays, punk "battle of the bands" on Wednesdays — or even shut its doors temporarily to throw a private party; many places are only open one or two (rotating) nights of the week.

To avoid unwanted surprises, use resources like *The Village Voice* and *TimeOut New York*. Space and site don't usually concern the club kids who follow parties as they travel from club to club; for the rest of us, keeping abreast of the oscillations of cutting-edge club trends is nearly a full-time job. These resources are useful in following certain DJ's or parties. Pick up any of the eye-catching fliers circulating the downtown area; many offer half-price entrance fees or list promoters' beeper numbers for getting on the invite guest list. Be prepared, the light on your answering machine will be blinking like mad once your name is out here.

lounges

Almost every year, a new trend dominates the downtown bar scene, one that dictates the style of newcomers and causes old favorites to adopt new gimmicks in order to avoid losing business. Recently, martini madness was the thing; the rise or fall of a hip establishment rested on its ability to serve up an extensive list of innovative, candy-coated versions of the classic cocktails that never failed to include the omnipresent Cosmopolitan.

But retro drinks alone could not sustain bar culture for long! Nowadays, the unwavering demand for something "new," coupled with a few dashes of inspiration from (and admiration of) the SoHo-model bar spectacle has led to the explosion of the lounge scene. Now the East Village, Greenwich Village, Gramercy, and the Lower East Side are teeming with new or newly renovated bars, replete with all the requisite lounge trappings: DJs, mood lighting, cushy lounge furniture, and a different party theme for every night of the week. Variations on the theme cater to nearly every whim by offering different styles of music and party scenes ranging from youthful hip-hop to more subdued classic jazz. The crowds and levels of formality follow suit: for beginners, try the long-running Salon Wednesday's party at Flamingo East (219 Second Ave., 533-2860), one of the original and best East Village lounges. Go to the trouble of finding the right spot and you'll be rewarded with the perfect home away from home at which to drink, meet cool people and, well, lounge.

The Bank

Black-caped and raven-garbed goth crowd into a dark, double-roomed realm where swaying and stomping approach a religious experience. Both Fridays and Saturdays boast the best selections of gothic, industrial, new wave, and eighties mope rock, with the occasional live band thrown in for variety. Thursday night is a "bound fetish party."
Lower East Side, 225 East Houston St. (at Essex St.), 505-5033, Cash Only, Cover: $3-15, ❻ to Second Ave. ♿ ⬑

Bowlmor Lanes

Mondays herald the Night Strike: How much do heavy house, drums-n-bass, and disco improve your bowling technique? With glow-in-the-dark pins and shoes, a strike or two is bound to happen.
Greenwich Village, 110 University Place (bet. 12th and 13th), 255-8188, MC, V, AmEx, Cover: $14 for "Night Strike", ❶❻❼❹❺❻ to 14th St.-Union Sq. ⬑

Coney Island High

Variety keeps both floors of this joint jumping throughout the week. Parties cover themes across the spectrum, drawing crowds to match. Recently they've been ex-huming some funky corpses of nightlife past, including Glamzoo and Beavher. What's next?
East Village, 15 St. Marks Pl. (bet. Second & Third), 674-7959, AmEx, Cover: $5-$15, ❻❼ to 8th-NYU, ❻ to Astor Pl. ⬑

Downtime

Part of the Recording and Rehearsal Arts building, this huge space, including a performance stage and a state-of-the-art sound system, is most-

ly populated by a large contingent of after-work professionals.
Midtown, 251 West 30th St. (bet. Seventh and Eighth Aves.), 695-2747, MC, V, AmEx, Cover: $5-$10, ❶❾ to 28th St., ❹❻❺ to 34th St.-Penn Station ♿ ⬑

El Flamingo

A glamorous aura of thirties art-deco attracts cosmopolitan crowds — no club kids here! The balcony lounge offers refuge from crowds and a view from which to scope out the dance floor.
Chelsea, 547 West 21st St. (bet. Tenth & Eleventh Aves.), 243-2121, MC, V, Cover: $10, ❸❺ to 23rd St. ♿ ⬑

Kit Kat Klub

Every Sunday from 10pm until dawn, draws lesbians, drag queens, and heteros with its seductive deep house, merengue, and salsa. A more mainstream crowd comes on Saturdays for a mix of hip-hop and reggae. The cover varies with the party.
Midtown, 124 West 43rd St. (bet. Sixth Ave. & Broadway), 819-0377, Cash Only, Cover: $20, ❶❷❸❻❼❷❸❼❾ to 42nd St.-Times Sq. ♿ ⬑

Hell

Once again, the meat-packing district offers elegance amidst its oftentimes squalid warehouses. The boys who brought Big Cup to Chelsea now bring this cozy yet really quite spacious lounge that mirrors the festive and not the infernal aspect of the mythical hotspot from which it takes its name. Organizers continue proving their flair for the unique with House in Hell on Thursdays featuring DJ Bert V.

Greenwich Village, 59 Gansevoort St. (bet. Greenwich and Washington Sts.), 727-1666, MC, V, AmEx, Cover: free, ❹❻❻ to 14th St., ❶ to Eighth Ave. ♿ ⬑

Krash

No doubt its parent club in San Juan would be proud of the Latin music this cavernous dance emporium serves up Mondays, Thursdays, Fridays, and Saturdays. Worth the tokens if you crave this beat.
Astoria, Queens, 34-48 Steinway St. (at Thirty-Fifth Ave.), (718) 937-2400, MC, V, Cover: $1-$10, ❻❼ to Steinway St.

Life

People throng in front of the massive doors as bouncers of the cooler-than-thou Spy variety let in a handful of poseur-types. Models and other self-involved people compose the clutter of heads found on the dance floor. Dancers in the know turn out for Sunday's gay party, without a doubt the home of the most grooveable music of the week.
Greenwich Village, 158 Bleecker St. (bet. Thompson and Sullivan Sts.), 420-1999, MC, V, AmEx, Cover: $20, ❹❶❸❻❻❶❻ to 6West 4th St.-Washington Sq.

The Lure

Leather-bound S&M boys manifest their darkest fantasies. Not exactly for the faint of heart.
Greenwich Village, 409 West 13th St. (bet. Ninth Ave. and Washington St.), 741-3919, Cash Only, Cover: free-$5, ❹❻❻ to 14th St., ❶ to Eighth Ave. ♿

Mother

Catering to a largely gay crowd, this meat-packing district venue comes across as dicier than the others on the block but cut-rate drinks reward the courageous. Once inside, the lure of the three rooms obviates the unpleasant exterior: a front-room lounge, a dance floor, and a dark, cozy downstairs retreat. Classic club memorabilia like "Jackie 60" t-shirts are available at the "souvenir shop."
Greenwich Village, 432 West 14th St. (at Washington St.), 366-5680, MC, V, AmEx, Cover: $10, **A****C****E** *to 14th St.,* **L** *Eighth Ave.* ⮐

Nell's

Three rooms on two floors offer an eclectic mix of music ranging from reggae, hip-hop, and jazz to Latin, funk, and disco. The elegance of the capacious upstairs room calls for a sophisticated drink from the well-stocked bar. Downstairs, relax in a more intimate lounge or move to house, R&B, or classics aimed at a stylish crowd described by the bouncer as a mix of "tourists, regulars, and DJs."
Chelsea, 246 West 14th St. (bet. Seventh & Eighth Aves.), 675-1567, MC, V, AmEx, Cover: $5-$10, **A****C****E** *to 14th St.,* **L** *to Eighth Ave.* ⮐

NV

Fashion types pout, air-kiss, and lounge as only they can inside this SoHo chicotorium. The DJs spin various genres, laced with Top Forty tunes. Leave the Airwalks at home: sneakers are prohibited.
SoHo, 289 Spring St. (at Varick St.), 929-6969, MC, V, AmEx, Cover: $20, **C****E** *to Spring St.* ⮐

Opera

With great martinis to help the swing, the dance floors pack in late-night crowds. Considered small by club standards, it still lures many a club kid.
Chelsea, 539 West 21st St. (bet. Tenth and Eleventh Aves.), 229-1618, MC, V, AmEx, Cover: $15-$20, **C****E** *to 23rd St.* ♿ ⮐

Rebar

Not the largest site in the area, but dubbed hip by the club kid crowd, which forms the lines snaking out onto Eighth Ave. Parties vary.
Chelsea 127 Eighth Ave. (at 16th St.), 627-1680, MC, V, AmEx, Cover: $5-$15, **A****C****E** *to 14th St.,* **L** *to Eighth Ave.* ♿ ⮐

Roxy

Almost always packed, the place plays host to track performers, AIDS benefits, and nonstop dancing. The crowd is different every night; Saturdays are gay.
Chelsea, 515 West 18th St. (bet. Tenth & Eleventh Aves.), 645-5156, Cash Only, Cover: $20, **C****E** *to 23rd St.* ♿ ⮐

The Sapphire Lounge

Drink before coming to this claustrophobic den of hip-hop. Sweaty fun awaits the aggressor who makes it to the middle of the floor. Deserted on weeknights. Happy Hour from 7pm to 10pm.
Lower East Side, 249 Eldridge St. (at Houston St.), 777-5153, Cash Only, Cover: $3-$5, **F** *to Second Ave.* ♿ ⮐

The Shadow

Different theme nights, live performances, and dance offerings attract huge crowds of older men and mostly women. The main floor sports several dance floors, bars, and a small room for the immobile. Take a break in the upstairs lounge. Women must be 23, men must be 25; bring ID. A strict dress code is enforced.
Chelsea, 229 West 28th St. (bet. Seventh and Eighth Aves.), 629-3331, Cash Only, Cover: $5-$10, **1****9** *to 28th St.*

Soca Paradise

Droves of Trinidadian and Guyanese natives come out every weekend as the sharp and calypso tunes blast until the wee hours, spun by various area DJs. Ladies get in free on Fridays and before 11pm on Saturdays. Delicious, traditional Caribbean cuisine is available.
Jamaica, Queens, 25-20 Jamaica Ave. (at Frances Lewis Blvd.), (718) 464-3600, Cash Only, Cover: $10-$12, **E****J****Z** *to Jamaica Cntr.-Parsons/Archer*

Vanity

Recent renovations have transformed this former neighborhood dive into a subterranean haven for house, drum and bass, and reggae lovers. All drinks are two-for-one during the 5pm-7pm Happy Hour.
Gramercy, 28 East 23rd St. (bet. Madison and Park Aves.), 254-6117, MC, V, AmEx, D, Cover: $10, **6** *to 23rd St.* ♿ ⮐

leisure

leisure
l•e•i•s•u•r•e

Think there's no escape from the city?
Hardly. There are plenty of places in and
around New York to unwind, de-stress, calm
down — or just get a tan. Central Park, for
instance, is filled with verdant slopes, rust-
ling trees, and tranquil, undisturbed pools.
Bring a picnic basket and watch the city
fauna at play. To keep the blood moving,
take a hike across the Brooklyn Bridge.
The views of Manhattan are unbelievable,
especially at sunrise. For a break from the
urban jungle, sample some of the natural
beauty of Long Island. Head for the beaches;
the beautiful white sand runs for miles.
If wilderness sounds better, then venture
upstate. Pitch a tent in one of the region's
thick forests, or go skiing in the Catskills.
For a different type of thrill, visit Coney
Island or Six Flags in New Jersey. We hear
that roller coasters are the quickest way
to forget landlord problems!

If you want to devote your leisure time
to the serious business of exercise, then
visit one of the top-notch gyms in the city
for an intense workout. Or stay outdoors
and join the hundreds of other people who
bike, blade, and jog in the various city parks.
Manhattan offers several other exercise
alternatives, like horseback riding, ice skating, and softball. Better yet, stay on the sidelines and take in a game at Yankee Stadium.
Whatever you choose, New York City has
an endless number of ways to keep the body
busy and the mind clear. Perhaps in
response to the daunting challenge of maintaining a human form while working a desk
job, New Yorkers pursue physical activity
with an almost pathological fervor; the gym
social set and company softball teams trying
to salvage their blood pressure are just the
most obvious examples of a serious subculture of exercise. The cult of the body, coupled with an almost burdensome desire to

have fun may drive yuppies to the racquet-
ball court and models to the Stairmaster, but
it is possible to utilize the city's manifold
resources as opportunities of true, uncom-
plicated relaxation time without letting the
muscled and Spandex-ed masses kill your
runner's high. Hit off-peak hours at the
gym: A mid-afternoon workout is a luxury,
as is late-night exercise. Venture into the
outer boroughs for expansive, serene parks,
and take advantage of any private spaces
to which you may have access through affiliation with a university or similar institution.
Like everything else, recreation in and
around New York is not only possible,
it's virtually limitless.

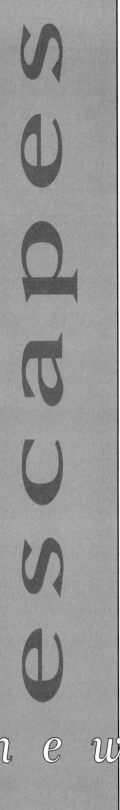

To the west of New York City lies New Jersey, accessible by the PATH (1-800-234-PATH) for only a dollar. For a quick sightseeing trip, make a beeline for Hoboken, Frank Sinatra's birthplace. Maxwell's Bar and Restaurant on Washington St. books acts rivaling those of New York's best rock clubs. Exploring the rest of the city can be a hit-or-miss affair, but some worthwhile shops, thrift stores, bars, and restaurants can be found along and just off of Washington St. Atlantic City is a hotbed of glitz and conspicuous consumption. All the major hotels, casinos, and shops line the famous boardwalk; straying from it might be dangerous at night. "Vegas on the Atlantic it is not," said a native New Yorker and long-time Atlantic City visitor, "but it's fun for a weekend." Call the Atlantic City Convention Authority and Bureau (609-449-7130) for travel information.

For outdoor fun, take a New Jersey Transit shuttle bus to the beautiful New Jersey shoreline. (Yes, we just used beautiful and Jersey in the same sentence!) Ocean Grove's wide, clean beach is complemented by the surrounding Victorian architecture, while Bayhead is reminiscent of New England, with fine sand, rough seas, and Cape Cod-style houses. Spring Lake boasts fine sandy beaches, tree-lined streets, mansions, cottages, and shops. Point Pleasant Beach is home to a boardwalk filled with cruising teens, while Belmar supports the majority of the shore's nightlife. For the ultimate in outdoor thrills, visit New Jersey's best amusement park, Six Flags Great Adventure. Don't pay the full cost of admission; look for special offers on Coke bottles and Burger King placemats. Meanwhile, for Bruce Springsteen fans, visit Asbury Park, The Boss' old stomping ground.

Sports fans should find happiness in New Jersey. The state leases space to football's New York Giants and hockey's New Jersey Devils, at the Meadowlands Sports Complex (201-935-8500) in East Rutherford, just twenty minutes from Manhattan's West Side. Meanwhile, the New Jersey Nets and new part-owner George Steinbrenner are taking their basketballing from the Meadowlands to Newark, where they hope the young, dynamic Stephon Marberry and Keith Van Horn will lead them out of their recent doldrums.

For a special retreat, visit Cape May, the nation's oldest seaside resort. The whole town was declared a historic landmark; there are over 600 gingerbread Victorian houses within the city limits. It's most appealing at the tail end of summer, just after Labor Day. Have tea at the Mainstay Inn and stroll down the beach promenade. Cape May Point State Park boasts one of the country's oldest lighthouses. Contact the Greater Cape May Chamber of Commerce (609-884-5508) for more information. Accessible from Cape May via ferry (1-800-64-FERRY) is Lewes, Delaware, a similar beachside town. Even if you're just along for the ride, the ocean air makes it worth the trip.

Long Island has long served as a playground for New Yorkers. The Island, as it is lovingly known, is easily accessible by the Long Island Railroad (LIRR) and offers a variety of recreational possibilities. In the summer, celebrities, society notables, and others head out to the Hamptons, a conglomeration of small towns on the island's eastern end. The well-endowed spend the warmer months in enormous private mansions on the shore (others may have to settle for renting a room in a house crowded with strangers and empty kegs) and their presence creates a flurry of business in the normally quiet towns. Tourists come as well, and not just for a glimpse of the rich and famous; the beaches in the Hamptons are beautiful, and some are relatively deserted. There are trendy shops and galleries to browse through in town, and for a real guilty pleasure, walk or drive through the residential blocks and stare at the mansions. When you're done checking out the lifestyles of the rich and famous, head out toward Montauk and sample some of the tastiest lobster you've ever had from one of the many roadside seafood restaurants. For more mansions and spectacular views outside of the Hamptons, head to Old Westbury Gardens (516-333-0048) and visit the replica of a Charles II style mansion on 150 landscaped acres. The grounds also offer excellent picnicking spots. The Sands Point Preserve (516-571-7900) is another area filled with beautiful mansions and exquisite gardens.

For a trek off the beaten path, take a day trip to Shelter Island, a secluded and peaceful place nestled between the north and south forks of Long Island's east end. Shelter Island is about 12 square miles and can only be reached by ferry, which ebbs the tide of tourism. Rent a sailboat and go fishing, or hike over the varied terrain and enjoy the peace and quiet. To get there, take the Sunrise Express Bus Service (516-477-1200) from Manhattan.

Stony Brook, a little town on Long Island 's North Shore, is an equally tranquil retreat. One of the Island's most historic enclaves, the town is filled with white Colonial homes and other remnants of early America. A peaceful harbor and an 18th Century grist mill top it all off. Nearby you will find Oyster Bay, another charming and rustic town, which is home to Sagamore Hill National Historic Site (516-922-4447), the former home of Theodore Roosevelt. This three-story, 22-room, Victorian house is an impressive sight (the guided tours frequently sell out on weekends, so get there early). Moving on to Upper Brookville you'll find the Planting Fields Arboretum (516-922-9200) which was recently named a State Historic Park. There is a 65-room Tudor mansion on the estate, as well as a rose garden and over 600 species of rhododendrons and azaleas. Visit during spring and enjoy the dazzling natural display.

Long Island has a number of beaches, but by

far the most popular is Jones Beach (516-785-1600), serviced by the ubiquitous LIRR. The beach is inundated with sunseekers on summer weekends, when people from all boroughs leave the city for some serious beach bumming. Long Island's most famous boardwalk is found here, and it offers such amenities as 1930s bath houses, outdoor eateries, miniature golf, and swimming pools. The sand is white and usually devoid of litter, so it's worth the train trip. Get there early and save a spot. The island has lovely parks, as well, and Eisenhower Park (516-572-0348) is surely the prettiest. There are facilities for everything from golf to cross-country jogging to cricket, as well as a boating lake and an a lakeside theater.

long island

W

hen people think of New York they undoubtedly picture Manhattan. The truth is, there are many attractions north of the city with a very different appeal. Beyond the City, beyond the staid suburbia of southern Westchester County, the Hudson Valley yields a wide variety of rustic towns, cultural institutions, and natural resources, all within ninety minutes of Midtown.

Arriving at and departing from the beautifully renovated Grand Central Station (Park Ave. at 42nd St., ❹❺❻❼), MTA Metro-North Railroad (532-4900) is the best way to head upstate, and at cheap prices. Just traveling the Hudson Line is a worthwhile experience. Its route is spectacular, hugging the eastern shore line of the eponymous river, passing through state parks and under majestic bridges. Worthwhile stops along the way include Peekskill, home of Washington Irving and Tootie, Blair and the rest of those girls from "The Facts of Life"; Cold Spring, an adorable village in Putnam County with numerous antique shops and darling eateries; Beacon, home of the minor league baseball team Hudson Valley Renegades (914-838-0094); and Poughkeepsie, the line's terminus, a small industrial city, home to beautiful Vassar College. Within a ten minute cab ride of Poughkeepsie's landmark station is Hyde Park, featuring The Roosevelt and Vanderbilt mansions (914-229-9115), as well as the internationally renowned Culinary Institute of America (914-452-9600). Commonly referred to as the CIA, the Institute houses several restaurants in which

upstate

students work, all of which are highly recommended, as are reservations.

More expensive but slightly faster, Amtrak (800-USA RAIL) also travels up the Hudson, departing from Penn Station (Seventh Ave. and 34th St., ❶❷❸❶❷❸❿). While you can take this line all the way to Montreal, manageable day or overnight trips are also options. Near the Rhinecliff station stop, the village of Rhinebeck has noteworthy inns and restaurants, the arty Upstate Films (914-876-2515), and a nearby fairgrounds that hosts the Dutchess County Fair and a very popular annual arts and crafts fair in the summer.

Further north on Amtrak is Saratoga Springs, a legendary resort town. Located just north of Albany, the town is famous for its healing mineral springs. It is also the site of America's oldest and most beautiful racetracks. The racing season attracts bluebloods and tourists alike, as does the summer entertainment. From June until August, the Saratoga Performing Arts Center (518-587-3330) has events almost every night. Saratoga State Park (518-584-2535) has two beautiful golf courses, four swimming pools, a dozen picnic areas, and several tennis courts. Reserve a spot at the Lincoln Mineral Baths (518-584-2011) well in advance and enjoy a fizzy dip and famous massages that made the town famous.

If your zest is for the western side of the Hudson, one stop with country charm is New Paltz, 90 minutes north of Manhattan by bus. Home to orchards, boutiques, and a branch of the state university, the town of approximately 6,000 permanent residents is located at the foot of the beautiful Shawangunk mountains. The nearby Mohonk Preserve (914-255-0919) and Minnewaska State Park Preserve (914-255-0752) are famous for their tarns, foliage, and rock climbing. Meanwhile, thirty miles to the north, quaint Woodstock is dramatically set in the Catskill Mountains. The town itself, famous for lending its name to a certain music festival in 1969, is a kooky collection of artisans, woodsmen, and ex-urbanites, with plenty nearby outdoor activities — among them skiing, fly fishing, rafting, and hiking. Both Woodstock and New Paltz are accessible via bus — Adirondack Trailways (967-2900) departs regularly from Port Authority Bus Terminal in Manhattan (Eighth Ave. and 42nd St., ❶❸❹).

hotels

Arlington Hotel

Anyone who loves antiques should consider this hotel — its stretch of 25th St. is given over to antique shops and on weekends an extensive antiques flea market springs up around the corner on Sixth Ave. between 25th and 26th Sts. Rooms are large and decorated with Asian art. The rate includes a complimentary continental breakfast, and there's a Chinese restaurant on the premises.
Gramercy, 18 West 25th St. (bet. Fifth and Sixth Aves.), 645-3990, Rooms: $114-$159, MC, V, AmEx, D, ❶❷ *to 23 St.* ⌐

Bed and Breakfast on the Park

By Prospect Park, a bigger version of the Baisley House, this B&B offers seven bedrooms and suites. Inside, the patrons get spoiled with elaborately carved moldings, stained glass windows, lush, ankle-skimming oriental carpets, and beds fit for kings and queens. The guilt-free decadence extends to the dining hall where guests eat sumptuously.
Park Slope, Brooklyn, 113 Prospect Park West (bet. 6th and 7th Sts.), (718) 499-6115, MC, V, AmEx, Rooms: $125-$275, ❼ *to Seventh Ave.-Park Slope* ♿

Deauville Hotel

Located in the quiet Kips Bay section of Manhattan, the Deauville has an old-fashioned feel. Rooms are large and sparsely decorated. Though the hotel itself may not have many facilities, the surrounding area is chock-a-block with cafés, movie theaters, and restaurants.
Gramercy, 103 East 29th St. (bet. Park & Lexington Aves.), 683-0990, MC, V, AmEx, Rooms: $110-$170, ❻ *to 28th St.* ⌐

East Side Inn

Everything from the sleek lobby to the hallways holds steadfastly to a Calvin Klein-esque palette of white, black, and beige. Though space is tight in the immaculate white rooms, the marblecl baths are larger than is standard. Continental breakfast is included in the price.
Gramercy, 201 East 24th St. (bet. 3rd and 2nd Aves.), 696-3800, MC, V, AmEx, D, Rooms: $145, ❻ *to 23rd St.* ⌐

Empire Hotel

By Lincoln Center, this budget-conscious hotel is a real find for visitors who want to explore the Upper West Side. The attractive rooms have a surprising number of amenities for the price, including CD players and VCRs. Columbia University relatives get a discount.
Upper West Side, 44 West 63rd St. (opposite Lincoln Sq.), 265-7400, MC, V, AmEx, D, Diners, Rooms: $160-$270, ❶❾ *to 66th St.-Lincoln Center.* ♿ ⌐

Four Seasons Hotel

Don't let the grand walk up from the lobby to the reception desk intimidate you, and forget all those models and celebrities milling around the lobby bar, too! If you've got the funds to sign on as a guest, the service is warm and welcoming without being obsequious. You could fit several typical New York apartments into the coolly elegant rooms, and here you get impressive cityscape views to boot!
Midtown, 57 East 57th St. (bet. Madison and Park Aves.), 758-5700, MC, V, AmEx, D, Rooms: $500-$10,000, ❻❼ *to Lexington Ave.,* ❹❺❻ *to 59th St.* ♿ ⌐

Foy House

Originally built in 1894, this B&B brownstone still holds most of its late 19th Century furnishings in pristine condition. An aura of authenticity and classicism permeate the three rooms and garden suite. The large wood silver holders in the dining hall and the love seat in the lower level are original pieces. For the real, homey bed and breakfast experience, come here.
Park Slope, Brooklyn, 819 Carroll Street (bet. Eighth Ave. and Prospect Park West), (718) 636-1492. Cash Only, Rooms: $95-$165, ❷❸ *to Grand Army Plaza,* ❻❼ *to Seventh Ave.*

The Gracie Inn

A quiet Upper East Side location and kitchenettes give the rooms the feel of private apartments. All were seemingly tended to by the heavy hand of Laura Ashley, what with the stenciled wallpaper, hardwood floors, floral patterned curtains and duvets, and down pillows. Complimentary continental breakfast is sent to each room.
Upper East Side, 502 East 81st St. (bet. York and East End Aves.), 628-1700, MC, V, Am Ex, D, Rooms: $199-$249, ❹❺❻ *to 86th St.* ⌐

Gramercy Park Hotel

Pre-war in more than simply architecture, this established outpost on Gramercy Park also attracts a largely pre-war clientele. Charm abounds here, and the neighborhood is an interesting one to explore, but more importantly, visitors here will be the secret envy of every New Yorker: The hotel holds a coveted key to private Gramercy Park, a privilege for which many local residents would kill.
Gramercy, 2 Lexington Ave. (at Gramercy Park), 475-4320, MC, V, AmEx, Diners, D, Rooms: $145-$200, ❻ *to 23rd St.* ♿ ⌐

Grand Union Hotel

Though it's just a short hop away from the Empire State Building, the Grand Union manages to stay pretty quiet. The elements of the decor — botanical prints, brass lamps, "antique" furniture — strive for elegance, but fall just short by being so obviously faux. The bathrooms, however, are gorgeous, marbled spectacles. *Midtown, 34 East 32nd St. (bet. Park and Madison Aves.), 683-5890, MC, V, AmEx, D, Rooms: $110-$150,* ❻ *to 33rd St.* ⌐

Larchmont Hotel

In a converted Beaux Arts brownstone on a prime block in the heart of Greenwich Village, the Larchmont is minutes away from New York University and Washington Square Park. Rooms are done in a tasteful safari theme, complete with animal prints and rattan furniture. The hotel calls its style European, a fitting label considering the shared bathrooms. But with two per six-room floor, availability is rarely a problem and all rooms have sinks. Breakfast is included in the room rate. *Greenwich Village, 27 West 11th St. (bet. Fifth and Sixth Aves.), 989-9333, MC, V, AmEx, Diners, D, Rooms: $70-$109,* ❶❷❸❾ *to 14th St.,* ❻ *to 14th St.* ⌐

Loews New York Hotel

With jacuzzis, personal trainers at your request, and a concierge on two levels to direct you to all the sights and stores in whose center the hotel rests, Loews has big city accommodations with a friendly staff ready to make you feel right at home. *Midtown, 569 Lexington Ave. (at 51st St.), 752-7000, MC, V, AmEx, Rooms: $189-$299,* ❻ *to 51st St.* ♿ ⌐

Madison Hotel

Near Chelsea and the boutiques of lower Fifth Ave., the Madison isn't much to look at on the outside, but inside the rooms are bright and spacious. Some have TVs, refrigerators, and newly renovated baths. *Gramercy, 21 East 27th St. (bet. Fifth and Madison Aves.), 532-7373, MC, V, AmEx, D, Rooms: $86-$105,* ❻ *to 28th St.,* ❻❼ *to 28th St.* ⌐

Park Savoy Hotel

Within close proximity of Central Park and Carnegie Hall, this hotel is a neighborhood bargain. Forgoing the creation of any public areas (there is no lobby to speak of), recent renovations went into improving rooms. Accommodations vary widely in size and are appointed with IKEA-like furniture; shamefully, despite the hotel's location, none have park views because the building is so short. *Midtown, 158 West 58th St. (bet. Sixth and Seventh Aves.), 245-5755, MC, V, AmEx, Rooms: $125-$145,* ❼❼ *to 57th St.* ♿ ⌐

Peninsula New York

A neophyte in the parade of luxury properties along the spine of upper Fifth Ave., the Peninsula was born with a silver spoon in its mouth — namely, a million-dollar location. Fantastic views abound from the renowned Pen-Top Bar & Terrace, and the outlook from the opulent day spa on the 21st floor is far from shabby. *Midtown, 700 Fifth Ave. (at 55th St.), 956-2888, MC, V, AmEx, D, Rooms: $535-$7,000,* ❻❼ *to Fifth Ave.* ♿ ⌐

Pickwick Arms

No frills, but it's often the best bet for savvy budget travelers who appreciate the warm lobby and the safe neighborhood and don't mind the forgettable rooms. The rooftop garden overlooking the skyscrapers makes this place an even bigger bargain. *Midtown, 230 East 51st St. (bet. Second and Third Aves.), 355-0300, MC, V, AmEx, Rooms: $65-$120,* ❻❼ *to Lexington Ave.,* ❻ *to 51st St.* ⌐

Plaza

The stuff of legends, the epitome of old New York, where every middle-American dreams of staying. Tons of movies, from *Home Alone II* to *Plaza Suite*, pay homage to the Edwardian romance of this classic. The parkside hotel seems dedicated to preserving this mystique, from its opulent lobby to the delicate splendor of the Palm Court restaurant. *Central Park, Central Park South (at Fifth Ave.), 759-3000, MC, V, Am Ex, Diners, D, Rooms: $290-$15,000,* ❻❼ *to Fifth Ave.* ♿ ⌐

Portland Square Hotel

The main attraction at the Portland Square is its proximity to Broadway. The hotel sells itself as a theater hotel and cites such famous former guests as James Cagney. Broadway mementos liven up the lobby. The basement gym, albeit tiny, is a plus. Shopping and the diamond district are nearby, as are Restaurant Row and, of course, virtually every show on the Great White Way. Try to snag a room on the eastern side of the hotel for a larger bathroom. *Midtown, 132 West 47th St. (bet. Sixth and Seventh Aves.), 382-0600, MC, V, Am Ex, Rooms: $60-$150,* ❼❼ *to 49th St.* ⌐

Riverview Hotel

Originally erected as the Seaman's Institute at the turn

of the century, the Riverview has been a neighborhood fixture for years; a small exhibit in the lobby houses a photo exhibit of the Titanic survivors who stayed here. Room sizes testify to the hotel's original naval hierarchy: They range from captain-worthy gargantuan to deck-swabber tiny. Near the Hudson, some of the hotel's rooms do indeed offer river views. The neighborhood is admittedly deserted at night, but many clubs and bars are nearby. *Greenwich Village, 113 Jane St. (at West St.), 929-0060, MC, V, AmEx, Rooms: $29,* **A****C****E** *to 14th St.,* **L** *to Eighth Ave.* ⌐

SoHo Grand Hotel

Currently the hottest hotel in New York, this newcomer made headlines as the first hotel in SoHo. Everything is in sync with the neighborhood: artsy, avant-garde types walk through the cutting-edge industrial lobby to their custom-designed digs. You can request a black goldfish to accompany you during your stay (and keep it if you want to when you check out!). In keeping with the cyber-sexy image, you can even make reservations on their website: http://www. SoHoGrand.com *SoHo, 310 West Broadway (bet. Canal and Grand Sts.), 965-3000, MC, V, AmEx, Diners, D, Rooms: $334-$354,* **A****C****E** *to Canal St.* ⌐

Stanford Hotel

Just blocks away are Madison Square Garden, Macy's, the Empire State Building, and Penn Station. The lobby is pure Las Vegas — lots of mirrors and glitz, and bordering on gaudy. Rooms are well-appointed and vary in size. Breakfast is included in the room rate, but a much wider gustatory variety lies just outside the hotel in the restaurants of 32nd St. (a.k.a. Little Korea). *Midtown, 43 West 32nd St. (bet. Fifth Ave. and Broadway), 563-1500, MC, V, D, Rooms: $110-$200,* **B****D****F****N****R** *to 34th St.* ⌐

Hotel Wales

An anomaly among the luxury properties of the Upper East Side, this homey, attractive hotel in venerable Carnegie Hill provides very nice rooms in an unexpectedly charming atmosphere. Its proximity to Museum Mile and Madison Ave. shopping is an added bonus. *Upper East Side, 1295 Madison Avenue (bet. 92nd & 93rd Sts.), 876-6000, MC, V, AmEx, Rooms: $229-$339,* **6** *to 96th St.* ⌐

Washington-Jefferson Hotel

In the newly-resurgent Hell's Kitchen neighborhood, near Times Sq., the Washington-Jefferson is a stone's throw from theaters, particularly Off-Broadway. The large, wood-paneled lobby is quiet and strewn with comfy sofas. Rooms are on the small side. *Midtown, 318 West 51st St. (bet. Eighth and Ninth Aves.), 246-7550, Rooms: $79-$109, MC, V, AmEx,* **C****E** *to 50th St.* & ⌐

Westpark Hotel

With Central Park and Lincoln Center just blocks to the north and the Theater District, Rockefeller Center, Carnegie Hall, and MoMA all within walking distance to the south, you can't beat the location. Though the public rooms are a bit worn around the edges, rooms are comfortable and pleasantly appointed with reproduction antiques and floral bedspreads. For a few dollars more, splurge on one of the suites, all of which have great views of Columbus Circle and Central Park. *Midtown, 308 West 58th St. (bet. Eighth and Ninth Aves.), 246-6440, MC, V, Am Ex, Diners, D, Rooms: $110-$240,* **1****9****A****B****C****D** *to 59th St.-Columbus Circle*

& While we have made every effort to maintain a high level of accuracy regarding wheelchair accessibility, this designation is based on information provided by each establishment.

ethnic enclaves

Picture yourself at a boardwalk café on the Black Sea, the clink of vodka glasses providing background music for a lazy afternoon of people-watching. Imagine walking down streets flanked by sari shops, each window display showcasing a kaleidoscope of shimmery fabrics in more colors, patterns and textures than you thought possible. Envision a gregarious party of Greeks shattering dishes in a restaurant crowded with compatriots.

A trip around the world to see these things in person may seem ambitious, but truth be known, you don't need to log airtime or hassle with cranky customs officials to get a little culture. For the cost of a subway token, you can journey to the distant shores of the Crimea, the motley malls of India, or the bustling streets of Greece, among dozens of other far-off lands — and be back in your New York digs by nightfall.

The city's vibrant ethnic neighborhoods — where sidewalk conversations in foreign languages are as ubiquitous as billboards festooned with foreign script — are convenient and affordable daytrip destinations, guaranteed to scratch your travel itch, or at least give it some temporary relief. The five boroughs are home to more than seven million people, over half of whom are immigrants or children of immigrants. In other words, a full third of the city was born outside of the U.S. That's the largest percentage of foreign-born New Yorkers since 1910, when two out of every five people in the Big Apple hailed from outside U.S. borders. Thanks to today's newcomers, and the neighborhoods they have cultivated, you can spend your weekend touring the world — it's a lot smaller than you think.

brighton BEACH

When the going got tough in the waning years of the Soviet Union, the Russians got going, en masse. A huge influx of émigrés — almost 9,000 in the early 1990s alone — has turned the Brighton Beach area of Brooklyn into a lively miniature of Odessa, the Black Sea port it evokes. Today, this faded stretch of the Brooklyn Riviera is home to

the largest Russian population in the U.S., boasting enough pierogi shops and lavish discotheques to make even the most Americanized transplant pine for home.

Ride the ❶ or ❷ line to its terminus and you'll emerge in a different continent — a place where signs advertise European fashions in fancy Cyrillic lettering and newspapers divulge the latest Moscow gossip with incredible accuracy. Along the wide beach boardwalk, Gucci-clad hostesses beckon passersby into cafés whose tables are filled with boisterous groups of locals. Typical of

most Russian social gatherings, the revelers feast on shashlik and pilmeni, toasting each other with such exaggerated gestures of jollity that you'll be tempted to join in. The sandy side of the boardwalk sees more sedate action — dozens of simultaneous chess matches are staged here all day long, reputations rising and falling with the tide.

Conclude your tour along Brighton Beach Ave., the community's main street, where you'll pass bakeries, restaurants, boutiques, nightclubs and grocery marts, predominantly owned, operated and frequented by native Russians. The walk is a voyage through another world; everywhere, emblems of the Russian culture underscore the community's collective nostalgia for a country changing faster than the ruble is falling. Forgo the Aeroflot for the subway, and see for yourself.

jackson HEIGHTS

If Queens is the Asia of New York City, Jackson Heights is the Indian Subcontinent. It's got curry houses. It's got sari shops. It's got bookstores stocked with Sanskrit dictionaries and deluxe editions of the Kama Sutra — by God (or should we say Vishnu?), it's even got a movie theater showing epic family sagas. Throw in a few million more people, turn up the heat, and hey, you've got three countries — India, Pakistan, and

Bangladesh — transported across the world and miniaturized into one very conveniently located Queens enclave.

The nucleus of the community is 74th St. A collection of colorful stores — Sagar Sari Palace, Shri Krishna Jewelers, Ayurvedic Herbal Centre — draw their clientele from the surrounding neighborhood of South Asians. It's the kind of place where women swathed in silk saris push baby carriages, where the sound of spoken Hindi and Urdu set the street abuzz, and a piece of Bengali milk fudge is never too difficult to find.

Outside the Patel Brothers supermarket on 74th St., sidewalk vendors sell "I ♥ Allah" key chains and thick, grass-green editions of the Qur'an. Venture inside and you'll find an inventory of curry pastes, chutneys and spices that reads like the index to *The Classic 1,000 India Recipes*.

But that's not all. Across the way, at the local branch of Indo-US Books, the selection of Indian memorabilia includes: veda, gitas, tantras, mantras, dabbas, deities, jeweled pillows, bronze idols, tea vessels, and much, much more. Almost too much — arrive with only the money you care to spend. In Jackson Heights, most things are stamped with "Made in India" or "Product of Pakistan" stickers. But the prices, they're all-American.

flushing

You won't need a passport to hang out in Flushing, but you may need an interpreter. This Queens neighborhood sees Indian restaurants open next to Asian apothecaries, Colombian bakeries share the block with Korean churches, and Jewish synagogues compete with Buddhist temples for the biggest crowd. But if you had to pick the culture with the largest presence, it would be Chinese. Immigrants from Hong Kong, Taiwan and the Chinese mainland form the bulk of this predominantly Asian community, giving it the feel of Chinatown among the suburbs.

Near the intersection of Main St. and Roosevelt Ave., the Hong Kong Mall includes a video store, selling flicks imported from the Orient, and a gigantic supermarket with the ultimate selection of herbal teas and noodles. The market, located on the top floor of the indoor mall, is a place to get lost, between aisles of seasoned pork knuckles, past caches of durian fruit amid stacks of sweet kum quat packets. Cruise through the market unnoticed, inspecting hundreds of exotic and eccentric foods, listening to Chinese-style elevator music and taking in the scent of burning joss sticks. As for the rest of the neighborhood, you'll find tea stores, dumpling houses, herb pharmacies and temples galore. Not bad for an easy ride on the Queens-bound ❼ train, not surprisingly dubbed the "Orient Express."

Greenpoint

The next time you crave your grandmother's kielbasa, don't fret. You can get all the Polish smoked sausage you want in Greenpoint, a quaint Brooklyn neighborhood that could easily be Warsaw's westernmost suburb. The "restauracjas" near the corner of Manhattan and Greenpoint Aves. serve up Poland on a platter with their buckwheat, stuffed cabbage and pierogi specials — and the short-order cooks, taxi drivers and market clerks deliver it, accent and all. Venture here on the Queens-bound ❻ train, and you'll be slavisitized by simple osmosis.

The Polish presence in New York isn't new — exiled Poles have been coming to the city since the 1830s. But among the post-WWII and post-Communism refugees, more and more began flocking to Greenpoint. The effect was a profusion of aptekas, not pharmacies, and "Produkts Polski" everywhere. Ads in the neighborhood began stringing more and more consonants together. Words like zloty, serdeczna, and pravda started swishing through the streets. The immigrants even imported some of their own architecture — an onion-domed church rises behind a schoolyard along Bedford Ave. Its spiky spires are an apt reminder that you don't have to trek to another hemisphere for your grandmother's home cooking.

washington HEIGHTS

The Dominican Republic has been New York City's number one source of new faces since the 1970s, when large numbers of Dominicans fled their Caribbean home for the less-than-tropical barrios of the Northeastern United States. By the early '90s, almost a quarter of the immigrant flow had settled in Manhattan's Washington Heights district, where the flavor of Dominican culture is for sale at the scores of tiny eateries located up and down Broadway and St. Nicholas Ave. Menus at local luncheonettes boast bistec encebollado, octopus salad, guanabara shakes and cold Presidente beer, served to the beat of merengue music bumping from every available speaker. The food fiesta continues at neighborhood grocery stores like the Mi Pais Supermarket on St. Nicholas Ave. and 183rd St., where the Dominican flag flys above island staples, including coconut soda, starchy, green plantains and all manner of yuca — undoubtedly the same yuca the vendors across the street use for their deep-fried empanadas.

Another tip-off that the area is the Dominican Republic's uptown annex is the proliferation of travel agencies offering ticket specials to Santo Domingo and the beach resort of Puerto Plata (only $318!). The community keeps one collective foot in the DR and one in New York City, shuttling back and forth with such regularity that the lines between old world and new seem purely geographical. This group of people, who know each other from another incarnation, gives the enclave its tight-knit, DR-by-proxy feel. And even though Washington Heights has a strong Russian, Jewish, and Greek presence, it's the slang from the streets of Santo Domingo (and Santiago and Higuey) that rises above the international fugue.

astoria

Souvlaki-on-a-stick and other Greek treats may strike you as things to be picked up in Athens, say, at a stand around the corner from the Parthenon. But think again. The Astoria district of Queens is home to one of the world's largest Greek populations outside of Greece, and even though the East River is a poor substitute for the Mediterranean, the neighborhood's Greek nightclubs, all-night Greek taverns, and Greek gift shops (where the selection of music CDs includes

a whole lot more than Yanni) should be enough to satisfy your jones for all things Hellenistic.

In the 1980s, Greeks were the largest immigrant group arriving in Astoria. Migration has dwindled considerably, but the Greek community that's found its niche at the end of the ⓝ line, near the intersection of 31st St. and Ditmars Blvd., is already well-entrenched. Neighborhood mainstays like the Corfu Center and the Titan grocery market draw busloads of Greeks in search of a hometown newspaper or the perfect batch of olives. Until recently, even the services at St. Irene Chrysovalantou Orthodox Church were conducted in Greek.

Just south of Little Greece, on the tree-lined streets around Steinway, another community of Mediterranean expats, including Moroccans, Egyptians, and Turks, is flourishing, allowing you a peek into the exotic cultures of North Africa and the Middle East: Old men suck hooka pipes at the Egyptian Coffee shop, cars affixed with the crescent moon and star sticker roll down the street, and Mecca magnets sell beside cases of fresh spinach pies at the convenience store. The skyscrapers of Manhattan rise in the distance, but in Astoria, you won't really notice.

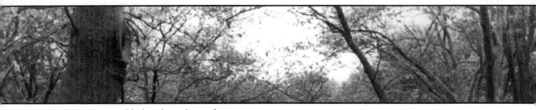

Manhattan is speckled with pockets of green that accommodate Frisbee or sun-bathing, though for large-scale undertakings — a long run, softball — more defined parks are usually in order. Each urban borough maintains at least one major park: Manhattan's Central Park, immortalized in paeans and crime stories alike; Brooklyn's Prospect Park, hub of outdoor activity in King's

cer games lending a residential feel.

Van Cortlandt Park, bordered by Riverdale to the west and Kingsbridge to the south, is accessible by the ①⑨ to 242nd St.-Van Cortlandt Park. Though a bit more dilapidated then Central and Prospect Parks, "Vannie" succeeds by being modern and utilitarian. Iit further redeems itself with authentic golf greens, renovated tennis courts, several rea-

County; sprawling Van Cortlandt Park in the Bronx; and Flushing Meadows Corona Park in Queens, offering respite from urban anxiety.

Central Park, designed by Frederick Law Olmsted and opened in 1859, runs from 59th to 110th Sts., bordered by Central Park West and Fifth Ave. Another major Manhattan park is Olmstead's three-tiered Riverside Park on

sonably well-kept softball diamonds, and a 3.6 mile trail for joggers and bikers.

Flushing Meadows Corona Park, New York City's largest, and the site of the 1939 and 1964 World's Fairs, is bordered by its name-sakes: Corona to the east and Flushing to the west. The ⑤⑦⓪②⑦ subway lines all stop nearby. Among the parks numerous resources

the Upper West Side, a slim strip of green along the Hudson River on the upper half of the island.

Prospect Park, yet another Olmsted design, is bordered by Park Slope to the west, Prospect Heights to the north, and Flatbush to the east. In keeping with the Brooklyn mien, Prospect Park is mellow even on week-ends, with family barbecues and pick-up soc-

are the enormous World's Fair Ice Skating Rink, the nearby USTA National Tennis Center, and Shea Stadium. In summer, head over to Meadow Lake for sailing lessons or ride the carousel located on 111th St. and 54th Ave.

Finally, Floyd Bennett Field in Queens is the ideal spot for model airplane builders to test-fly their toys.

parks

running

The opportunities afforded by the city are accompanied by precautions unique to the area that even the most seasoned athlete should note. Some of the most scenic jogging paths, like those in Riverside Park on the Upper West Side, provide very poor support for knees and ankles, so if you plan on running regularly, invest in high-quality shoes which will absorb the impact of concrete. Always be aware of your surroundings, including other runners, bikers, rollerbladers, cars, kids, strollers, and pedestrians.

The reservoir at Central Park, located roughly in the middle of the park from about 86th to 96th Sts., is circumscribed by a scenic, if somewhat narrow, 1.57 mile soft-surface path ideal for jogging. Beware the onslaught of shuffling and huffing "runners" on weekends, and women should be forewarned that in the late evening hours, the path is notoriously dangerous. More ambitious types should try the Outer Loop (6.1 miles) along the circular drive, or the Lower Loop (1.7 miles), which begins at 72nd St. and follows the drive around the southern periphery. Runners seeking camaraderie should contact the New York Road Runner's Club, Inc. (860-4455), headquartered near the newly-christened Jackie O. Reservoir at the eastern entrance to the park on 90th St. The club's activities include group runs and running classes, a weekend jog at 10am, a marathon prep, a New Year's Eve run, and a Central Park Safety Patrol. During summer evenings, the traffic is closed off in the Park.

Riverside Park is a beautiful place to run for those who don't mind the pavement, since the infrequent strips of dirt are ill-maintained and subject to ruts and mud. Avoid the relatively steep hill at the junction of the Upper West Side and Morningside Heights by staying on the lower level at 96th St. The best place to veer down towards the riverside path, where a small houseboat community docks and optimistic fishermen occasionally cast their lines, is around 86th St. since the West Side Highway is too close for comfort further north. A quarter of a mile track is maintained at 72nd St. Further north, at Riverbank State Park, there's a quality track, though on hot, windless days, a nose plug for heavy breathing may be in order.

Also in Manhattan, a jogging path follows the East River from Sutton Pl. all the way up to Gracie Mansion, though don't expect to catch Rudy, flanked by bodyguards à la Bill, running alongside you. Downtown, the West Side Highway Path is a newly refurbished strip for downtown joggers, bladers, and bikers that can seem as circus-like as the boardwalk on Coney Island on busy days.

When traffic is cut off on Saturdays and Sundays in Prospect Park, the roughly two-and-a-half-mile route looping around the park makes a good jog. For post-jog relaxation, the interior path offers shady groves and gaggles of swans.

New York Road Runners Club, Inc.
(see Running article)
860-4455

Achilles Track Club
An international club for athletes with disabilities.
354-0300

Front Runners
A gay and lesbian running group.
724-9700

Millrose A.A.
Ideal for the amatuer looking to get serious. $20 membership fee.
663-5641

Moving Comfort New York
Ladies only, but you've got to be able to do 10K in forty minutes.
222-7216

Warren Street Social and Athletic Club
Training and competition.
807-7422

Riding a bike in Manhattan is an excellent and inexpensive means of transportation and exercise, but it can get a bit wild so observing the following precautions can help you avoid falling prey to cabs and bus drivers:

· Claim space in a lane so as to avoid pedestrians and opening car doors; many major avenues have bike paths as well.

· Always ride on the right with traffic; drivers don't always watch out for obstacles to their left side, which is where you'll be when riding against traffic.

· Wear a helmet without fail.

· When on a Central Park path or other bike paths, don't hang a U-turn.

· It's perfectly permissible to take your bike on the subway (you'll get buzzed through the door after depositing a token or swiping your MetroCard), though the commuter trains require a pass for bikes.

cycling

Century Road Club Association
Members race in Central Park 20 times annually between March and November. In addition, there are two open races a year. *222-8062*

Five Boroughs Club
For the safest, most scenic routes around all around the city, including a five borough marathon of sorts, advertised as "forty-two miles of traffic-free biking." *www.bikenewyork.org*

Sundance Outdoor Adventure Society
An athletic group organized for gays and lesbians. *598-4726*

S P O R T S   A N D

Two city pools are particularly clean and accessible, though invariably crowded on weekends, especially during the sweltering summer months: Carmine Street Pool (1 Clarkson St., 242-5228, ❶❾ to Houston St.) and John Jay Park (East 77th St. and Cherokee Pl., 794-6566, ❻ to 77th St.). New York City's other indoor and outdoor pools vary in popularity and cleanliness and are too numerous to list.

City beaches are open from Memorial Day through Labor Day weekends from 10am to 6pm. The main ones are all found in the outer boroughs:

swimming

Orchard Beach
The Bronx, (718) 885-2275, ❻ to Pelham Bay Pk.

Manhattan Beach
Brooklyn, (718) 946-1373, ❷❻ to Sheepshead Bay

Coney Island and Brighton Beach
Brooklyn, (718) 946-1350, ❷❻ to Brighton Beach, ❸❹❻ to Stillwell Ave.-Coney Island

Rockaway Beach
Queens, (718) 318-4000, ❹❺ to Rockaway Park Beach-116th St.

South Beach
Staten Island, (718) 816-6804

New York has numerous ice skating possibilities, and even more for in-line skating. Both are favored pastimes of the active urbanite.

Some words of wisdom: Central Park, in particular on weekends in the spring and summer, is packed with people who have not yet perfected maneuvering on blades, so don't assume they'll honor the right-of-way or even be able to brake. Other parks, where it's not such a social scene, are a little less like a circus.

In-line skaters can attempt the advanced slalom courses in Central Park by the Bandstand and west of the Great Lawn by the restaurant Tavern on the Green, where on weekends experienced skaters do informal exhibitions for a large crowds of spectators. Watch and learn, especially on Dead Road, from about 66th to 69th Sts. in the middle of the park, where dance skaters go to strut their stuff.

skating

Wollman Rink
Central Park, Sixth Ave. & 59th St., 396-1010, Admission: $3-$4, Rental: $6, ● *to 57th St.*

Lasker Rink
Central Park, East Dr., 396-0388, ●● *to 110th St.*

World's Fair Rink in Flushing Meadows Corona Park
Flushing, Queens, (718) 271-1996, ● *to Willets Point-Shea Stadium*

Abe Stark Rink at Coney Island
Coney Island, Brooklyn, On Boardwalk (at West 19th St.), (718) 946-3135, ●●● *to Stillwell Ave.-Coney Island*

Kate Wollman Rink
Prospect Park, Brooklyn, (bet. Ocean and Parkside Aves.), (718) 282-7789, Admission: $4, Rental: $3.50, ● *to Prospect Park*

RECREATION

Regulation-sized softball and baseball diamonds are located around 100th St. on the eastern side of the park; the Heckscher Ballfields at West 65th St. are well-maintained but often claimed by amateur, fiercely territorial, leagues known more for mild spectator value than for open field policies. There are huge, under-utilized Astroturf fields atop the 145th St. incinerator in Riverside Park that are a good alternative to the Central Park melee.

Five softball diamonds and two baseball diamonds, accessible from the 9th St. and Park West entrance, are well-maintained at Prospect Park and a bit friendlier than their Manhattan counterparts.

softball

Batting Cages at Chelsea Piers
Ten balls for $1, or reserve a cage. *Chelsea, Pier 62 (23rd St. at Hudson River), 336-6500, MC, V, AmEx, Open: weekdays 9am-10pm, weekends 9am-9pm,* ●●● *to 23rd St.*

To reserve a field in a city park:
Manhattan
408-0226
Bronx
(718) 430-1800
Queens
(718) 520-5933
Brooklyn
(718) 965-8919
Staten Island
(718) 816-6529

With a university affiliation, you will most likely have access to courts. If you need to search out city courts, Central Park's mid-area facilities around 96th St. (360-8133) are among the most happening, though only those with season permits can reserve a court in advance. However if you don't mind the wait, queue up with the others waiting to plunk down $5 to play on an unreserved court for an hour; bring a deck of cards and join in a game of bridge or poker. Riverside Park's clay courts near 96th St. are well-maintained by neighborhood volunteers. If you don't mind the trek to Queens, tennis courts abound at the prestigious USTA National Center (718-592-8000), the site of the US Open.

tennis

Other Courts Include:
New York Health and Racket Club
Piers 13 and 14 (at Wall St.), 422-9300, MC, V, AmEx, ❹❺ *to Wall St.*

NYHRC Tennis Courts
110 University Pl. (bet 12th and 13th Sts.), 989-2300, MC, V, AmEx, ❶❶❻❹❺❻ *to 14th St.-Union Sq.*

Central Park Tennis Center
West 96rd St. and Central Park West, 280-0205, MC, V, ❸❻ *to 96th St.*

Tower Tennis
1725 York Ave. (at 89th St.), 860-2464, AmEx, ❹❺❻ *to 86th St.*

Columbus Tennis Club
795 Columbus Ave. (at 99th St.), 622-8367, MC, V, ❸❻ *to 96th St.*

Stadium Racket Club in Mullaly Park
11 East 162nd St., (718) 588-0077, MC, V, AmEx, ❸❻❹ *to 161st St.-Yankee Stadium*

QUEENS
Long Island City Indoor Tennis
(718) 784-9677

The fitness craze culminated in the '90s with a saturation of sleek, comfortable weight lifting and fitness facilities all over the city. They attract all walks of life: Dancers tone up on dance machines; grade-school teachers work on their deltoids; and stockbrokers take on the Stairmasters. The social underpinnings of the city gym experience might merit a separate write-up in this book's nightlife section, but suffice it to say that the following conversation was overheard on Broadway near Reebok Sports Club: "Haven't I seen you at the gym? My name's Rick." "Oh yeah, you're the ab guy, right?"

Location is the biggest determinant of atmosphere: Midtown clubs attract a more corporate mix, while gyms in the Village cater to an artier crowd. All the spandex and muscle at these places can be intimidating but don't give up. Many gyms, including the ubiquitous Crunch, pride themselves on a "non-judgmental," laid-back policy. Shop around since most facilities cheerfully allow trial-periods on a no-strings-attached basis.

Bally Total Fitness
14 locations in Manhattan, (800) 230-0606, MC, V, AmEx, 1 year membership: $600-$700

Crunch
7 locations in Manhattan, 758-3434, MC, V, AmEx, D, 1 year membership: $750-$850

New York Health and Racquet Club
7 locations in Manhattan, 269-9800, MC, V, AmEx, 1 year membership: $700-$1500

New York Sports Club
70 locations in Manhattan, 868-0820, MC, V, AmEx, 1 month membership: $73-$79

Reebok Sports Club
Upper West Side, 160 Columbus Ave. (at 67th St.), 362-6800, MC, V, AmEx, Membership: $1075 to join, $170/month, ❶ ❾ *to 66th St.-Lincoln-Center.*

gyms

Watching others expend their energies in athletic pursuits can be just as satisfying as exercising yourself. New York boasts several notable arenas hosting our beloved home teams.

Although the house that Ruth built has an alleged date with a wrecking ball scheduled for sometime in the early 21st Century, Yankee Stadium remains, after nearly 75 years of witnessing baseball history, the most scenic and historic venue the city offers for viewing **professional sports**.

Shea Stadium, home of the Mets, has served as baseball's other venue in the city since its 1964 opening brought National League baseball back after the Dodgers ignominious departure in 1957. While Shea and the Mets lack the tradition and lore of the Yankees, its accessible location and the revitalization of the team, spearheaded by the long-term signing of Gen X idol Mike Piazza, help keep Shea packed with higher attendance.

Located above Pennsylvania Station, Madison Square Garden, New York City's celebrated indoor arena, has been an exciting place to be lately, with both the Knicks and the Rangers enjoying strong teams and exciting playoff runs through the '90s. Although the undermanned Knicks failed to get Patrick Ewing his ring in last June's finals, optimism remains high the squad in 1999-2000, led by swing men Allen Houston and Latrell Spreewell. At the spacious Garden, fans can see the floor even from the worst seats, and the crowd is often raucous enough to qualify as a secondary attraction. Other events at the Garden include Rangers games, the NIT college basketball tournament, ice shows, dog shows, tennis tournaments, and concerts.

Yankee Stadium
(718) 293-6000, Tickets: $8-$50,
B**D****4** to 161st St.-Yankee Stadium

Shea Stadium
123-01 Roosevelt Ave. (at 126th St.),
(718) 507-8499, MC, V, AmEx, D, Tickets:
$10-$30, **7** to Willets Point-Shea Stadium

Madison Square Garden
For the Knicks: 465-5867, Tickets: $22-$250,
For the Rangers: 465-6741, Tickets: $22.50-$140,
MC, V, AmEx, D, **A****C****E****1****2****3****9** to 34th St.-Penn Sta.

Ballet Academy East
Itching to test those dancing shoes? Drop in here and for $12 you can sample one of the jazz, ballet, or tap classes.
Upper East Side, 1651 Third Ave. (bet. 92nd and 93rd Sts.), 410-9140, **6** to 96th St.

Bicycle Habitat
If the quality of a bike store can be determined by counting the number of customers' bikes that are chained outside, then this is one of the best in the city. Customers here are serious about their bikes and the same people can be found day after day checking out new models, picking up parts or just discussing their obsession.
Greenwich Village, 244 Lafayette St. (bet. Prince and Spring Sts.), 431-3315, MC, V, AmEx, **N****R** to Prince St. ♿

Big City Kites Co.
Kites in all shapes and sizes, from the standard diamond to more elaborate types.
Upper East Side, 210 Lexington Ave. (at 82nd St), 472-2623, MC, V, AmEx, D, **4****5****6** to 86th St.

Blades Boards & Skates
The helpful staff would readily join their patrons on Astor Pl. at one of the wheels-only lunch break congregations. Slick new styles of in-line skates, roller skates, and skater gear also available at the standard, not-so-unconventionally prices.
Greenwich Village, 659 Broadway (bet. Bleecker and Bond Sts.), 477-7350, MC, V, AmEx, D, **B****D****F****Q** to Broadway-Lafayette St., **6** to Bleecker St.

Body Strength Fitness
Want a hard body and a calm mind? BSF offers free weights, personal training, aerobic classes, as well as massage, body sculpting, kick boxing, Pilates, and energy healing. Customize a workout plan to suit your needs.
Upper West Side, 250 West 106th St. (at Broadway), 316-3338, MC, V, AmEx, Diners, D, **1****9** to 103rd St.

Capitol Fishing Tackle Co.
Rounding out an eclectic mix of stores on this block, this emporium specializes in everything an angler would ever want or need: rods, hook, tackle, etc. No chance of blending in with the loyal clientele of piscine nimrods unless you're one of them.
Chelsea, 23rd St. (bet. Seventh and Eighth Aves.), 929-6132, MC, V, AmEx, D, **1****9** to 23rd St.

recreation listings

Deep-Sea Fishing on the Pastime Princess
Party-fishing boat offers excursions to troll for bluefish, flounder, and mackerel.
Brighton Beach, Brooklyn, Emmons Ave., Pier 5 (bet. Mansfield Pl. and Bedford Ave.), (718) 252-4398, **B****D****F** *to Stillwell Ave./ Coney Island*

Gotham Bikes
A good place to buy or rent a bike without being intimidated by a staff of gearheads trying to push an Italian racing model when you just want to ride through the park like Mary Poppins.
TriBeCa, 112 West Broadway (bet. Duane and Reade Sts.), 732-2453, MC, V, AmEx, **1****2****3****9** *to Chambers St.* ♿

Hamilton Fish Recreation Center/Pool
Just $25 per year buys membership to this and many other municipally run pools and fitness centers around the city. Don't expect state-of-the-art equipment or classes; just a workout without an attitude.
Lower East Side, 128 Pitt St. (at East Houston St.), 387-7687, Cash Only, **F** *to Second Ave.* ♿

H.T. Dance Company
"Dance is not only doing your own good work," says director H.T. Chen, "it should have a social value as well." Since 1980, the company's small black-box theater has hosted the Arts Gate Center, which teaches dance, piano, and martial arts to children and adults year round.
Chinatown, 70 Mulberry St. (at Bayard St.), 349-0126, Cash Only, **J****M****N****R****Z****6** *to Canal St.*

♿ = *wheelchair accessible*

Paragon
Whether the game is badminton, snowboarding, or basketball, this sports superstore is sure to have the right gear. The shoe department often has better deals than the chains.
Chelsea, 867 Broadway (at 18th St.), 255-8036, MC, V, AmEx, **L****N** *to 18th St.*

tribeca bodyworks
The largest Pilates center in New York City also has a physical therapy office and offers both private and group classes. Set in a renovated loft, this place has got style: go on and make an appointment while you still can!
Tribeca, 177 Duane St. (bet. Hudson and Greenwich Sts.), 625-0777, **1****2****3****9** *to Chambers St.*

Village Chess Shop
Play chess from noon to midnight with fellow experts, or indulge by purchasing sets made from materials ranging from nuts and bolts of ivory (is that legal?) and onyx.
Greenwich Village, 230 Thompson St. (bet. Bleecker and 3rd Sts.), 475-9580, MC, V, AmEx, **A****B****C****D****E****F****Q** *to 4th St.-Washington Sq.* ♿

Central Park
Bike Rentals
The cost is $8 - $14 per hour, depending on the bike; ID required. Open from the end of March to the end of October.
East Dr. (at 74th St.), 861-4137, MC, V, AmEx, Diners, D, **6** *to 77th St.*

Bird-Watching at the Charles A. Dana Discovery Center
Over 270 different species of birds have been sighted in the park; expect to see about 150 species in the course of a year.

The Central Park Conservancy and the Audubon Society (691-7483) organize bird-watching walks in May.
(see Central Park Sites & Parks)

Board Games
Chess players are welcome at the Chess and Checkers House at 64th St., west of the Dairy.
East Side of Park, **6** *to 68th St.-Hunter College*

Claremont Riding Academy
Horses are $35 per hour for experienced riders only. A half-hour private lesson is $42. Stables are on Central Park West (bet. 89th and 90th Sts.). For the more sedentary, horse-drawn carriages leave from 59th St. on the east side.
175 West 89th St. (at Amsterdam Ave.), 724-5100, MC, V, **B****C** *to 86th St.,* **1****9** *to 86th St.*

Fishing
The Harlem Meer stocks wide-mouthed bass for fishing on a strictly catch-and-return basis. Bamboo rods and other equipment are available free of charge at the Charles A. Dana Discovery Center.
(see Central Park Sites & Parks)

Organized Tours
The Central Park Conservancy (360-2726), Columbia University's Big Onion Walking Tours (439-1090), and The New York Historical Society (873-3400) all give historical tours of the park.
Call (718) 291-6825 for info

Park View at the Boathouse
The Boathouse rents boats at $10 per hour plus a $30 deposit; model boat regattas and races are held on weekends on Conservatory Water. Open March-October
Fifth Ave. at (72nd St.), 517-2233, MC, V, **6** *to 68th St.-Hunter Coll.*